ORDER AND HISTORY

VOLUMES IN THE SERIES

Volume Three — Plato and Aristotle

ERIC VOEGELIN

ORDER AND HISTORY

VOLUME THREE

Plato and Aristotle

LOUISIANA STATE UNIVERSITY PRESS

Coniugi Dilectissimae

In consideratione creaturarum non est vana et peritura curiositas exercenda; sed gradus ad immortalia et semper manentia faciendus.

(In the study of creature one should not exercise a vain and perishing curiosity, but ascend toward what is immortal and everlasting.)

ST. AUGUSTINE, *De Vera Religione*

Preface

Order and History is a philosophical inquiry concerning the principal types of order of human existence in society and history as well as the corresponding symbolic forms.

The oldest civilizational societies were the empires of the ancient Near East in the form of the cosmological myth. And from this oldest stratum of order emerged, through the Mosaic and Sinaitic revelations, the Chosen People with its historical form in the present under God. The two types of order, together with their symbolic forms, were the subject matter of Volume I, *Israel and Revelation*.

In the Aegean area emerged, from the stratum of order in cosmological form, the Hellenic polis with the symbolic form of philosophy. The study of Polis and Philosophy matches, in the organization of *Order and History*, the earlier one on Israel and Revelation. Because of its size this second study had to be divided into the present Volumes II, *The World of the Polis*, and III, *Plato and Aristotle*. The two volumes, though each stands for itself in the treatment of its respective subject matter, form a unit of study.

Brief sections of the two volumes have been previously published as "The World of Homer" (*The Review of Politics*, Vol. 15, 1953, 491–523), "The Philosophy of Existence: Plato's *Gorgias*" (*The Review of Politics*, Vol. 11, 477–98), and "Plato's Egyptian Myth" (*The Journal of Politics*, Vol. 9, 307–24).

As in the earlier volume I want to say my thanks for the material aid, which facilitates the final work on this study, to the institution that wishes to remain unnamed.

ERIC VOEGELIN

1957

Table of Contents

Analytical Table of Contents

PART ONE

Plato

CHAPTER 1

Plato and Socrates

Aristocles the son of Ariston was born 428/27 B.C. from a noble
Athenian family. On his mother's side he could trace his lineage to
Solon. The name Plato he received, according to the various traditions,
either from his wrestling-master because of his robust figure, or from
his friends because of the breadth of his forehead; inevitably there were
also less friendly suggestions which connected the name with the
breadth of his style, and puns were made on Plato and platitudes. His
youth fell in the period of the Peloponnesian War (431–404); he was
in his twenties when he witnessed the regime of the Thirty Tyrants
and their overthrow by the democratic party. The years of his manhood were filled with the internecine wars of the Hellenic poleis and
their leagues; and in his last years he still could observe the rise of Macedonia under Philip II. He died at the age of eighty-one, in 347. In the
year after his death the Third Sacred War was concluded with the
Peace of Philocrates, and Philip II became the chairman of the Amphic-
tyonic League. In 338 the battle of Chaeronea was followed by the
congress of Corinth and the foundation of an Hellenic League embracing all poleis except Sparta under the military command of Macedonia.
In 337, ten years after Plato's death, the League declared the war on
Persia. The age of Alexander and Empire had begun.

The motives which induced the young man of a well-connected
family not to pursue his natural career in the politics of Athens but instead to become a philosopher, the founder of a school, and a man of letters, are revealed by Plato himself through an autobiographical passage
of the *Seventh Letter* (324b–326b), written about 353, when he was in
his seventies:

"When I was young I felt like so many others: as soon as I should
become my own master, I thought, I would immediately enter public
life. But my way was crossed by certain events in the affairs of the
polis." The first opportunity seemed to have come with the revolution

that led to the government of the Thirty. Some of the autocratic rulers were Plato's relatives, and they invited him to participate in the administration. In view of his inexperienced youth it was not surprising that he expected the new rulers to lead the polis from an unjust life to a just one; and he gave his mind diligently to them, to see what they would do. (Whether this phrase means actual participation in the regime, perhaps in a minor function, does not become clear.) Disillusion came soon. The former government looked like a golden age compared with the present one. And in particular he was shocked by the policy of the Tyrants, well-known in our own time, to consolidate their regime by involving citizens, among them Socrates, in criminal actions which would make them reliable supporters because a change of the regime would expose them to the vengeance of the victims. Socrates, "whom I would not hesitate to call the justest man at the time," resisted such involvement at the risk of unpleasant consequences; and Plato withdrew in disgust from the oligarchic regime. When the democratic revolution had abolished the Tyrants, Plato, though somewhat sobered about Athenian politics, again would have been willing to participate. The returned democrats, while marring their victory by many a personal revenge, were on the whole remarkably moderate. Still, they charged Socrates, of all people, with impiety (*asebeia*), prosecuted him, found him guilty, and slew him, the very man who had resisted criminal action against a democratic partisan at the time of the Tyrants.

As Plato considered all this, and observed the men who were active in politics, with their laws and customs, and as he advanced in age, it appeared to him ever more difficult to manage public affairs properly. For without friends and trusty companions one could not do anything at all; and they could not be found among old acquaintances because the polis was no longer managed according to the principles and customs of the forefathers. To acquire new friends, however, was impossible without great difficulties. Though at first he had felt the urgent desire to take part in politics, he became dazed by the spectacle of a general breakdown. He did not cease to contemplate means for improving the situation, but as regards action he continued to wait for the right moment. Finally, he arrived at the conclusion that only a deliberate effort of an almost miraculous kind could repair the bad state in which all poleis of the time found themselves, and then only under favorable circumstances. Thus, praising right philosophy, he was compelled to declare that it alone enabled one to discern what is right in the polis, as well as in the life of the individual. And the races of man would have no cessation from evils until either the race of the right and truly philosophizing gained political rule, or the race of rulers in the poleis, by some divine dispensation, began to philosophize truly. "With this conviction I came to Italy and Sicily, when I went there for the first time."

The autobiographical passage reports an evolution in the life of Plato that began when he was about twenty-three years old and reached its climax when he was about thirty-eight. Something like a crisis must have occurred around 390 B.C., for into this time falls the violent outburst of the *Gorgias*, perhaps in response to the attack of Polycrates on Socrates, with its transfer of authority from the statesmen of Athens to the new statesman Plato. Then followed the extended voyage to Italy and Sicily of 389/8 and, soon after the return, perhaps around 385, the foundation of the Academy. He had understood that participation in the politics of Athens was senseless if the purpose of politics was the establishment of just order; he had, furthermore, seen that the situation in the other Hellenic poleis was just as bad as in Athens, if not worse; and above all he had understood (what modern political reformers and revolutionaries seem to be unable to understand) that a reform cannot be achieved by a well-intentioned leader who recruits his followers from the very people whose moral confusion is the source of disorder. When he had gained those insights in the course of fifteen years, he did not fall, however, into despair or sullen resignation, but resolved on that "effort of an almost miraculous kind" to renew the order of Hellenic civilization out of the resources of his own love of wisdom, fortified by the paradigmatic life and death of the most just man, Socrates.

The autobiographical declaration will be our guide in the study of the "almost miraculous effort." We are not concerned with a "Platonic philosophy" or "doctrine" but with Plato's resistance to the disorder of the surrounding society and his effort to restore the order of Hellenic civilization through love of wisdom. His effort was a failure in so far as his dream of an Hellenic empire, in the form of a federation under an hegemonic polis, infused by the spirit of the Academy, could not be realized. The unification of Hellas came through the power of Macedonia. Nevertheless, it was a success, probably beyond any expectations entertained by Plato at the time when he founded the Academy, in as much as in his dialogues he created the symbols of the new order of wisdom, not for Hellas only, but for all mankind. In the following chapters we shall trace this effort from the *Gorgias,* in which Plato transferred the authority of Athenian order to himself, to its climax in the *Laws,* in which the order of wisdom became the analogue of cosmic order.

The present chapter has the nature of a preface to the study of the effort proper. Its first section will deal with the origin of the Platonic effort in the paradigmatic life and death of Socrates. Its second section will deal with Plato's participation in the politics of his time, as far as its character can be discerned in the *Letters*.[1]

§ 1. SOCRATES

Socrates the son of Sophroniscus was born in 469 B.C. and died from the hemlock in 399 B.C. Concerning his life the only primary source extant seems to be the affidavit sworn by his accuser Meletus, as reported by Diogenes Laertius II, 40: "Socrates is guilty, not to recognize the gods recognized by the polis, and to introduce other new divinities [*daimona*]; he is also guilty, to corrupt the youth. Penalty death." The reconstruction of an "historical" Socrates seems to be an impossible task,

---

[1] Of the vast literature on Plato I shall list only the works that I feel have substantially affected my own interpretation: Richard S. H. Bluck, *Plato's Life and Thought* (London, 1949). Francis M. Cornford, *Plato's Cosmology. The Timaeus of Plato translated with a Running Commentary* (London-New York, 1937); *Plato and Parmenides* (London, 1939); *Principium Sapientiae* (Cambridge, 1952). Paul Friedlaender, *Platon* I (Berlin and Leipzig, 1928); II (1930). Victor Goldschmidt, *Les Dialogues de Platon. Structure et Methode Dialectique* (Paris, 1947); *Le Paradigme dans la Dialectique Platonicienne* (Paris, 1947); David Grene, *Man in His Pride. A Study in the Political Philosophy of Thucydides and Plato* (Chicago, 1950); Kurt Hildebrandt, *Platon. Der Kampf des Geistes um die Macht* (Berlin, 1933). Werner Jaeger, *Paideia. The Ideals of Greek Culture,* II (New York, 1943); III (New York, 1944). Gerhard Krueger, *Einsicht und Leidenschaft. Das Wesen des Platonischen Denkens* (2d ed., Frankfurt, 1948). Paul Shorey, *What Plato Said* (Chicago, 1933). A. E. Taylor, *Plato. The Man and His Work* (6th ed., London, 1949); *A Commentary on Plato's Timaeus* (Oxford, 1928). Important for the understanding of details was Harold F. Cherniss, *Aristotle's Criticism of Plato and the Academy* (Baltimore, 1944); *The Riddle of the Early Academy* (Berkeley, 1945); and Simone Pétrement, *Le Dualisme chez Platon, les Gnostiques et les Manichéens* (Paris, 1947). For the older treatment of Platonic politics cf. Sir Ernest Barker, *Greek Political Theory. Plato and His Predecessors* (London, 1918); furthermore, the sections on Plato in such standard histories of political ideas as George H. Sabine, *A History of Political Theory* (revised ed., New York, 1950); and Alfred Verdross-Drossberg, *Grundlinien der Antiken Rechts—und Staatsphilosophie* (2d ed., Vienna, 1948). The crisis of our time has thrown up a considerable amount of anti-Platonic literature, reflecting various ideological positions. For a survey and criticism of this class of literature see the recent works by Ronald B. Levinson, *In Defense of Plato* (Cambridge, Mass., 1953) and John Wild, *Plato's Modern Enemies and the Theory of Natural Law* (Chicago, 1953).

considering the lack of sources. The Socrates who formed Plato was the Socrates as seen by Plato.[2]

We shall, first, circumscribe the central issue of the Socratic trial, as seen by Plato in the *Apology*; and, second, characterize the myth of the Socratic soul that unfolds in the work of Plato.

1. *The* Apology

The divine, regenerative force of order, transmitted by Socrates to Plato, had come to Socrates from the omphalos of Hellas, from Delphi.

A friend of Socrates, Chaerephon, had put to the oracle the question whether any man was wiser than Socrates, and the Pythia had answered that none was wiser than he. The answer was puzzling to Socrates who knew that he had no wisdom. And yet the god could not lie, for that was against his nature. Hence, Socrates began to test the answer by involving men renowned for their wisdom into conversation, in order to find one wiser than himself. Then he would go to the god, with the refutation in his hand. The first victim of Socratic examination into his wisdom was a well-known politician. He turned out to be not too wise, though he was thought of as wise by many and even more so by himself, and Socrates tried to impress on him that he was in error when he thought himself wise. Understandably he aroused the hatred of the politician as well as of several among those present. Still, he discovered on the occasion that he was wiser indeed than his victim, for while neither of them knew "anything really beautiful and good" he at least was aware of his ignorance and, thus, had a slight edge over the reputedly wise man. Further examinations of a similar nature had the same result, and increased the number of enemies.

The issue is joined between the pride of human wisdom that leads to disorder in the life of the individual, as well as of society, and the existence in obedience to the god. For "in truth, the god alone is wise, and by his answer he intended to show that human wisdom is worth little or nothing." Socrates goes about his task in obedience to the god. He tries to shake up the Athenians individually, and the most conceited

---

[2] The best introduction to the Socratic problem is Werner Jaeger's chapter "The Memory of Socrates" in *Paideia* II. The reader will find a splendid picture of the historical Socrates in A. E. Taylor, *Socrates* (New York, 1932). The reasons why a picture of the historical Socrates cannot be reconstructed have been set forth in Olof Gigon, *Sokrates. Sein Bild in Dichtung und Geschichte* (Bern, 1947). An important recent study on Socrates as seen by Plato is Romano Guardini, *Der Tod des Sokrates* (1947); (4th ed., Dusseldorf and Munich, 1952).

among them first, to lead them back to true order. He is the gift of the god to Athens, given as a gadfly to the polis to stir it back into life. Recalling an Heraclitian phrase he admonishes his judges not to be out of temper, like a man suddenly awakened from sleep; they must spare him, for not easily will they find a successor to him to arouse and persuade and reproach them. The man who stands before them accused of *asebeia* is the true servant of divine order, sent by the Delphian god to save the impious accusers.

In the speeches of the defense three actions are going on at the same time: the trial of Socrates ending in his condemnation; the trial of Athens ending in the rejection of the savior; and the separation of Socrates from the polis ending in the solitude of his death.

The first speech is the defense speech proper. Socrates proves the accusation of *asebeia* unfounded, for he cannot be impious who tries to reform the polis under the order of the god of Delphi. Moreover, he refers to his Daimonion, well-known to everybody, that divine voice which made itself heard every time it wished to hold him back from an action. He assures the judges that the Daimonion had never counselled him to desist from his inquiry concerning the wisdom of other men. Somebody might argue that the proper way for him to save the community would have been to seek office and to use its power for the good of the polis. That way, however, he had to reject as futile, because the officeholders were so corrupt that they would not permit anybody to refrain from participating in their crimes. He would have found his death long ago if he had held an office of importance and tried to be honest. And again he was confirmed in his attitude by the Daimonion, as it raised its warning voice distinctly every time he considered this possibility.

The rottenness of the polis, described by Thucydides, had become the ultimate obstacle to a reform within constitutional forms; the direct appeal to the individual citizen had become necessary; and the pathos of the Periclean Funeral Oration had become the reforming will of the devoted citizen. Power and spirit had separated in the polis so far that a reunion through ordinary means of political action had become impossible. Socrates speaks as the representative of the divine power of Hellas; and he stresses the irony that he, the only Athenian who believes in the gods to such a degree that he follows their orders and risks his life, is accused of impiety by the very men whose disbelief in things divine is the reason for decay.

The atmosphere must have been tense. More than once Socrates had to admonish the large court not to break out in noisy demonstrations that would disturb his defense. One can imagine how incensed a considerable number among the Five Hundred must have been by the conduct of Socrates and his assurance that he would go on with his god-ordained task, even if they let him off lightly. Still, there were others who must have sensed the fatal hour, for the court divided almost evenly: only 281 of the 500 found him guilty.

The first speech had been technically the defense, in due legal form, against the accusation. After the verdict the trial of Athens overshadowed the trial of Socrates. The manifestation of the Delphian god in Socrates had been revealed, as well as his mission for the polis. Now the people had judged Socrates, and the gods had condemned the people.

With the second speech begins the separation of Socrates from the polis. According to procedural law the plaintiff had to propose a punishment, and the defendant, when found guilty, had to make a counter-proposal. The accuser had demanded the death penalty. On the level of the spiritual drama, however, the savior had been rejected and the man Socrates was now free. Hence, the second speech is a play of the free soul in the moment of suspense between the decision of fate and its fulfillment. He reconsiders his service to the city. What would be the proper reward for the man who is the benefactor of the polis and needs all his time to pursue his god-willed mission? It would seem most appropriate that he should be compensated with the highest honor granted to an Athenian citizen, a place at the public table in the Prytaneion. That honor would be much more fitting for him than for the victors at Olympia. His language is almost to the word that of Xenophanes a century earlier. Nevertheless, the situation has changed from the first insight into the order of wisdom and a reproach by the mystic-philosopher, to the inexorable call to duty by the savior who, facing death, acts as the instrument of God. The demand, however, is not blunt. The charm of Socrates, as always, lies in his superiority to the situation. His soul is quiet; and in his reflections he is the ironic onlooker while forces divine and human have chosen his earthly person as the field for their clash. His demand for a place in the Prytaneion is serious, for he should receive

it as the man of the highest rank in the spiritual order of the polis; and
it is not serious, for he knows that he will not receive it in the actual
order of Athens. It serves as an ironical starting point for a reflection on
practical alternatives. Socrates refuses to make a serious counterproposal,
for that would be an admission of guilt. Fear of death would not induce
him to make it, for death is not an evil while the other course would
be an evil. And what should he suggest? Jail? But what should he do
in jail? Or exile? That would only continue his troubles, for how could
strangers be expected to tolerate him when even his fellow citizens could
not stand his action? Hence, in obedience to the law, which requires
him to make a proposition, he proposes an insignificant fine. After this
proposal the court sentenced him to death.

The third speech is addressed to the judges, those who condemned
him and those who acquitted him. First he reminds the judges who had
voted for his death of the sad fame that is now theirs, to be the men
who have killed Socrates. And he warns them that they will not escape
the fate which they tried to avert by putting him to death, for others
will arise and demand the account of their lives which they refused to
him. Then he addresses himself to the judges who found him not guilty
and reveals to them the secret order that had governed the proceedings
of the day: At no point of the whole procedure had his Daimonion
warned him; hence, the course taken by him was approved by the gods.

The *Apology* concludes with the great theme that will run through
the work of Plato: "And now it is time for us to go, I to die, and you to
live." The philosopher's life toward death and the judgment in eternity
separates from the life of the dead souls. And then the pathos of the
moment is relieved by the last irony of Socratic ignorance: "Who of us
takes the better way, is hidden to all, except to the God."

2. Drama and Myth of the Socratic Soul

The drama of Socrates is a symbolic form created by Plato as the
means for communicating, and expanding, the order of wisdom founded
by its hero. We have to touch, therefore, the thorny question why the
dialogue should have become the symbolic form of the new order. No
final answer, however, can be intended with regard to a question of such
infinite complexity. We shall do no more than modestly list a number of
points which under all circumstances must be taken into consideration.[3]

[3] The most penetrating study of the question is the chapter "Dialog" in Friedlaender's *Platon* I.

Plato was strongly influenced by Aeschylus. We are familiar with the Aeschylean problem of Peitho, the persuasive imposition of right order on unruly passion. In the *Prometheus* the personified forces of the soul were engaged in the struggle for the order of Dike, with the solution, suggested towards the end, of redemption through the representative suffering of Heracles. The drama of the soul proved, furthermore, to be the substance of the process of history in the *Oresteia,* as well as of constitutional procedure in the *Suppliants.* Tragedy in the Aeschylean sense was a liturgy of Dike, and in particular it was a cult of the political Dike. Tragedy as a political cult, however, will lose its meaning when the people for whom it is written and performed are no longer able to experience the drama of Dike as paradigmatic for the order in their own souls. The tension of order and passion that had been mastered by the cult of tragedy had broken into the open conflict between Socrates and Athens. The cult had become senseless because from now on tragedy had only one subject matter, the fate of Socrates. In so far as the Platonic dialogue was animated by the tension between Socrates and Athens, it was in the history of Hellenic symbolic forms the successor to Aeschylean tragedy under the new political conditions.

But why should there be tragedy at all, and in its succession the Platonic dialogue? The answer must be sought in the Aeschylean and Platonic understanding of society as an order of the soul, as well as in the understanding of the soul as a social order of forces. The order of the soul as the source of order in society and the parallel construction of the two orders will occupy us at greater length in the analysis of the *Republic.* For the present we shall only stress the conception of order as an Agon of forces that will not give way to a nondramatic conception until the victory for wisdom and justice is achieved. Only when the tension of conflict has subsided and the new order is established can its expression assume the form of a static dogma or a metaphysical proposition. Tendencies in this direction are to be observed in the late work of Plato; and the nondramatic form breaks through in the esoteric work of Aristotle. This victory of the new order has, however, the unsatisfactory consequence that the "bad man" of the dramatic play gets lost. We shall have to deal with that question again in the analysis of the *Republic* with its agonal pairs of concepts.

If the dialogue is understood as the successor to the public cult of tragedy, the question will arise to whom the new symbolic form is addressed, if the decisive public, the people of Athens, does not want to listen. One answer to this question is given by Plato in the Digression of the *Theaetetus*. Even the most stubborn politician or sophist, who in public will not listen to the philosopher, still is man and can be stirred up in private. The hard shell of his corruption can be pierced and the anxiety of existence can be touched. The dialogue is an exoteric literary work, accessible to everybody individually who wants to read it. The personal conversation between Socrates and the individual Athenian citizen is continued through the instrument of the dialogue.

The dialogue, however, can be conducted only if it does not degenerate into an exchange of rhetorical harangues without existential communication among the speakers. Decisive for this point are the scenes in *Protagoras* and *Gorgias* where Socrates threatens a walkout unless the sophistic partner stops his speechmaking and enters into the argument. The dialogue is the symbolic form of the order of wisdom, in opposition to the oration as the symbolic form of the disordered society. It restores the common order of the spirit that has been destroyed through the privatization of rhetoric.

In the concrete situation, among the living, however, the law of the dialogue cannot be enforced. The opponent will not listen at all, or he will respond with rhetoric and thereby break the possibility of communication, or he will enter the argument but not be moved existentially even when he is beaten intellectually. The order of Athens was not regenerated either by Socrates or Plato. Socrates had to die in the attempt. And Dike achieved no victory. Is the dialogue a futile gesture after all?

In answer to this question Plato lets stream into the dialogue the force of Thanatos, of the Socratic death. In the *Phaedo* Thanatos becomes the cathartic power that cures the soul of the sickness of the earth. Life is comparable to a submarine existence with only a glimmer of the world above. Death is the liberating force. It enables the soul to live free of the denseness of the lower atmosphere; and when the end has come, it brings the reconvalescence from the illness of life. The last word of the dying Socrates to his friend is: "Crito, I owe a cock to Asclepios." Thanatos is the force that orders the soul of the living, for it makes them desirous of stripping themselves of everything that is not noble and just. The soul is immortal; and death is the incision in its existence which permits the readjustment of station after the earthly period has given the soul its chance for development. Hence, the situation of the dialogue does not end with life. It continues into the beyond; and the speaker of the dialogue in the beyond is an eternal judge who has sanctions at his disposal. The inconclusive situation among the living is made conclusive by the Myth of Judgment in the *Gorgias* and the *Republic*. Moreover, the myth of the judgment developed as a content of the dialogue affects the substance of the dialogue itself. In the *Apology* we have seen the multiple levels of action. On the political level Socrates is condemned by Athens; on the mythical level, Athens has been condemned by the gods. The dialogue is itself a mythical judgment. The Socrates of the *Apology* leaves his judges in no doubt that others will ask them the questions which they tried to escape by sentencing him to death. The "others" have come. And the dialogue is the continuation of the trial.

The situation is quite different when the dialogue is conducted with success in the circle of Socrates, Plato, and their friends. Then the positive force of the Socratic soul, its Eros, comes into play. To create existential community through developing the other man's true humanity in the image of his own—that is the work of the Socratic Eros. It is a force closely related to Thanatos. To the desire for Death and its catharsis corresponds the erotic *enthousiasmos*. Thanatos orients the soul toward the Good by relieving it from the sickness of appearance; Eros is the positive desire for the Good. Man has to die, and in his desire to make the best in himself a perpetually living force, he tries to rejuvenate himself through procreation. He has received life once through his birth and he wishes to continue it through rebirth in his children. Those in whom the desire is only bodily have physical children. Those in whom it is spiritual rejuvenate themselves through procreation in the souls of young men, that is, through loving, tending, and developing the best in them. That is the force which animates the world of the Platonic dialogue. The older man, Socrates, speaks to the younger man and, through the power of his soul, awakens in him the echoing desire for the Good. The Idea of the Good, evoked in the communion of the dialogue, fills the souls of those who participate in the evocative act. And thus it becomes the sacramental bond between them and creates the nucleus of the new society.

Death and Love are intimately related as orienting forces in the soul of Socrates. In the *Phaedo* philosophy is the practice of dying; in the *Symposion* and *Phaedrus* it is the eroticism of the soul for the Idea which creates the procreative community among men. Eros dominates his life because it is a life towards death; and his Eros is powerful because existence in the expectation of catharsis through death gives the proper distance to the incidents of earthly life. The nobility of the soul, which manifests itself in the pursuit of the good and the avoidance of the ignoble in personal conduct, endows him with the power over other men who are willing to open their souls to the influence of the noble. Eros, thus, becomes an ordering force in social relations. Only the noble souls are attracted to the erotic, evocative communion; the lesser souls remain indifferent or resist. The erotic attraction and indifference, the power and response in the erotic relation, create the ranks of the spiritual hierarchy. The force of Eros shades off into the force of Dike, as did the force of Thanatos.

§ 2. Eros and the World

We have spoken of the crisis in Plato's life that occurred about 390 B.C. If the *Gorgias* be taken as the expression of his mood at the time, the situation in Athens must indeed have seemed unbearable to him. In 389 he embarked on the extended travel that led him to Italy and Sicily. In Syracuse he formed the friendship with Dion, the brother-in-law of Dionysius I. After the death of the tyrant, in 367, Dion thought the time propitious to use his influence with his nephew, Dionysius II, for a reform of government. He appealed to Plato to come to Syracuse and to support the attempt with his presence. Plato, who at the time was sixty years of age, followed the request with many hesitations. This was the beginning of his involvement in Sicilian affairs which outlasted the murder of Dion in 354.[4]

1. *Plato and Sicily*

While in the nineteenth century it has been the habit among scholars to underrate the importance of Plato's intervention in Sicilian politics, and even to doubt the authenticity of Plato's letters, we are faced more recently with the danger of exaggeration in the opposite direction. The mere numbering of the Sicilian travels as the first (389/8), the second (366/5), and the third (361/60), is apt to create the im-

---

[4] The most important ancient sources on the Sicilian affairs in which Plato was involved are the essays by Plutarch on *Dion* and *Timoleon*. The best modern treatment is Renate von Scheliha, *Dion. Die Platonische Staatsgruendung in Sizilien* (Leipzig, 1934).

pression of a continuity of political effort, running through a period of perhaps forty years. As a matter of fact, after the first journey nothing happened at all for more than twenty years. Plato's efforts went into the foundation and management of the Academy, and for all practical purposes he considered it the final field of action in his life. The revival of an active interest in Sicily was induced from the outside, and the necessity was accepted with reluctance. This revival came, furthermore, after the *Republic* had been finished, at a time when, in the literary field, Plato was occupied with the great trilogy of *Theaetetus-Sophist-Statesman*. Hence the problems of Sicily have no immediate bearing on the formation of Plato's ideas before the *Laws*. And even with regard to the *Laws* we have to use some caution in weighing the influence of the Sicilian situation. It is tempting, of course, to see in the *Laws* a code for the Sicilian reform, and the *Seventh Letter* leaves no doubt about the close connection of the *Laws* with the task of drafting a model code for the reform intended by the party of Dion. Nevertheless, we shall see that the *Laws* is definitely more than a political *livre de circonstance,* even if the Sicilian problems furnished the momentum of an occasion.

When all these reservations are made there remains, however, the fact that the participation in Sicilian politics left deep traces in the formation of Plato's ideas. The *Seventh Letter* which assesses, on occasion of the Sicilian problems, the relation between Plato's ideas and the reality of his age, ranks equal in importance with the *Republic* and the *Laws* for the understanding of Platonic politics. It is not a piece of private correspondence; it has the character of an open letter. Its occasion was the request of Dion's friends for advice in constitutional matters and it is, indeed, addressed to the "companions and friends of Dion." The advice itself, however, fills only a comparatively small part of the document (330c–337e); the larger part consists of an account of Plato's relations with the rulers of Syracuse. This larger part has the character of an apology for Dion and for Plato himself. Intrinsically it is addressed to the general public and its connection with the advice is rather loose. Moreover, it is quite possible that the apologetic part was written in the years preceding the publication of the *Letter* itself. The need for the publication of the various parts in the form of the *Letter* arose through the unfortunate end of Dion's attempt to reform the constitution of Syracuse. Dion was murdered by the opposition and in the actual killing were involved two men who, while not belonging to the Academy, were sufficiently close to the Platonic circle that for the general public the Academy was connected in an unsavory manner with the murderous plot. To dispel somewhat the shadow that had fallen on the Academy was probably the principal reason for the publication of the *Letter* in its ultimate form in 353.

In Syracuse, at the court of Dionysius I, Plato met Dion. At the time Plato was forty Dion was probably twenty years of age. Of the relationship between Plato and Dion we know little beyond an occasional hint. The realm of Eros is not open to the public. The *Seventh Letter* reveals only that Dion responded to the discourse of Plato more keenly and more enthusiastically than any other young man whom Plato had ever met (327a–b). Nevertheless, this meeting was "the beginning of everything" (327a). Under the influence of Plato, Dion embarked on the new life, "preferring Arete to pleasure and luxury"; and he persisted in it, much to the disapproval of the court. After the death of the tyrant in 367, it seemed possible that the group of Dion's friends in Syracuse could win over the young successor to the Platonic way of life. Dion requested the presence of Plato because now if ever seemed to arise the hope of having the ruler of a great polis become a philosopher (328a). Plato finally accepted the invitation, though with great misgivings, for a young man like the tyrant might have an impulse one day and a contradictory one the next—an apprehension that was amply justified by the events (328b). The relation with Dionysius II, however, we shall discuss later.

From the *Letters* we can conclude that the bond which united Plato with Dion was a most intimate union of heart and mind. In the opening paragraph of the *Seventh Letter*, Plato reminds the recipients of their assurance that their convictions (*dianoia*) are the same as Dion's; only if this is true will Plato assist them with advice. And what were Dion's convictions? No conjecture is necessary because they were the convictions that had been formed through the discourse with Plato. Dion's policy was Plato's; the latter can speak in the name of the dead friend because the union between them was so close that it left no room for differences (323e–324b). In the formula which precedes the advice of the *Eighth Letter*, Plato expressly designates what he has to say as his and Dion's "joint counsel." "I shall interpret" this counsel as Dion himself would pronounce it if he were alive (355a).

In the *Seventh Letter* Plato elaborates in a more general manner the conditions which the patient has to fulfill if he is desirous of Platonic advice (330d–331d). If a physician has to advise a sick man who lives in a way injurious to his health, he first will demand of him "to turn his life around." If the patient consents, then the advice may extend to other points; if he does not consent, then a self-respecting physician will not continue his treatment. The same principle is valid for political counsel. If a polis does not want advice, or if quite obviously it would not take it, Plato will not approach it self-invited; and certainly he will not use constraint. With regard to Athens, in particular, he clarifies his attitude by stating that he would consider it sinful to use constraint against "father or mother." Neither would he estrange them by useless admonitions, nor would he play the flatterer and counsel them to satisfy desires which he himself "would rather die than be addicted to." If a man considers the constitution of his country imperfect he ought to speak, provided the admonition is not obviously useless or would lead to his own death as in the case of Socrates. Under no circumstances, however, must he ferment violence and revolution in his fatherland. All he can do is pray for the best for himself and his polis.

The condition for advice is an existential community on the terms of Plato. Under this condition he is willing to advise the companions of Dion, as he has advised Dion himself and later Dionysius II; and perhaps the God will grant that the third time salvation will result from the counsel (334d). No doubt, however, should exist about the meaning of the terms. Plato reminds the recipients of the *Letter* that the same advice is valid for them that had been formerly extended by Dion and Plato to the tyrant. They had counselled him to lead a life of daily discipline that would result in self-control. A personality, thus, would be built that would attract loyal friends and companions (331d–e). The formation of a group would be the next step; the bond of this group would have to consist in *philia* and harmony with regard to *arete* (332d). But no such group could be formed for further action unless he had first produced in himself an intelligent and temperate character (*emphron, sophron*) (332e). If we translate these conditions into a modern terminology, we might say that Plato demanded, as the condition of his advice, a conversion to Platonism and the formation of something like an order. This order would be the nucleus for the regeneration of the polis.

The admonitions to the recipients of the *Seventh Letter* reveal in part the nature of the union between Plato and Dion—though no more of it than can enter into a general formulation. Quite possibly, however, we find a clearer reflection of it in the description of the erotic experience in the *Phaedrus* (particularly 252–256). In pre-existence the souls of the lovers follow in the train of a god. When they have fallen to earth each is in search of the beloved companion who carries in his soul the nature of the god whom they had formerly followed. The followers of Zeus desire that the soul of the beloved have the nature of Zeus; and they inquire, therefore, whether he has the nature of a philosopher and ruler. When they have found him and fallen in love with him they do what they can to strengthen this nature in him. They search their own souls; and they find their own divine nature in their fascinated gaze at the nature of the god in the beloved. Thus they become possessed of him and form their own character, as far as that is possible for man, into participation in the god. And since they believe the beloved to be the cause of this transformation, they love him all the more; and what they receive from Zeus, like the Bacchae, that they stream back into him to make him as like to their god as possible.

The erotic union has sacramental character, for the nature of the god becomes incarnate in the community of the erotic souls as in its mystical body. Not all souls, however, have followed the same god in their pre-existence. And only those who have followed Zeus are the chosen instruments for actualizing the god of political order in society. The symbol of the "Sons of Zeus" has its experiential basis in the eroticism of the philosopher-rulers. One can go perhaps even a step further, as Hildebrandt does in his *Platon,* where he suggests that the passage in *Phaedrus* seems deliberately to avoid the nominative *Zeus;* the name of the god appears always in the genitive *Dios.* In particular the construction *Dios dion* in 252e, however, makes it probable that these stylistic peculiarities are meant as a hint that Dion is the partner of the relationship which Plato celebrates in the dithyramb of the *Phaedrus.* The suggestion gains in probability if we consider the epitaph which Plato wrote for his friend, with the closing line: "Dion, thou, who made rage with Eros my heart."

The intimacy of the erotic relationship, though not beyond words, is beyond the written word. The wisdom of the soul which is engendered through Eros cannot and must not be put down on paper as a teachable doctrine. In the *Phaedrus* Socrates-Plato says that it would be simplicity to leave or receive an art (*techne*) in writing, under the belief that the written word would be reliable and clear. Writing is like painting; the creation of the painter has the likeness of life, but when you would ask it a question it would remain silent. Words, when they are written down, will fall into the hands of those who cannot understand them; and when they are abused they cannot defend themselves (275c–e). There is another word, however, the word graven with understanding into the soul of the learner, that can defend itself and knows when to speak and when to be silent. And Phaedrus answers: "It is the idea-word that you mean, living and with a soul, of which the written word justly is called no more than an image" (276a). The idea-word (*tou eidotos logos*) is the medium in which the tenderness and strength of the erotic mania express themselves; it is the vehicle of communication by means of which the erotic souls attune one another to the harmony of the cosmos; and it is the fragile vessel in which the god becomes incarnate in community.

The attempt to formulate the intimacy of the erotic community as a doctrine is worse than futile: it is the desecration of a mystery. That is the personal insult which Plato had to suffer at the hands of Dionysius II. We have seen that Plato had his misgivings about the seriousness of the tyrant's desire to become a convert to philosophy. As soon as he arrived in Syracuse and saw that his apprehensions were justified, he submitted therefore the seriousness of the tyrant to the infallible test (*peira*). He mapped out for him the course of study which a man, if he is truly desirous, will follow with zeal in spite of its hardships; while the man who is only tempted by some vanity will soon find the course impossible because it entails a change in his way of life. Dionysius did not pass this test. He was vain enough, however, to consider himself a philosopher and to put down in writing, and to circulate, what he had learned from the discourse with Plato and from secondary sources. That breach of confidence gave Plato the occasion to express himself, in the *Seventh Letter*, more distinctly on the problem of written publication of his doctrine.

Those who publish what they have learned, whether from direct instruction, or through other information, or through their own discovery, certainly have understood nothing. He himself has never written directly on the core of his philosophy, and never will, for it cannot be put into words like other knowledge. Understanding can come only after the long preparatory period of studies and discipline. And then it will be generated in the soul like a blaze by a leaping spark; and once this fire of understanding is lighted it will never burn down. Besides, if he thought that the doctrine could be written down, he would do it himself. But even if it were possible, it would hardly be advisable. For those who are able to understand, the very few, will surmise the truth anyway and discover it at the merest hint. The others who cannot understand it would despise the revelation and expose it to contempt; while still others, because nothing is touched in them existentially, would be filled with vanity and high hopes as if now they were in the possession of some sacred knowledge (341b–342). Hence no serious man will write of the really serious things for the many. Therefore, "when there comes anything before your eyes, for instance of a legislator on laws, it cannot have been the most serious matter to him, if he is a serious person himself, but that will still lie in the most beautiful and noble place of his mind" (344c). To these explanations should be added the warnings to Dionysius himself, in the *Second Letter,* written perhaps ten years earlier than the *Seventh.* The best safeguard against misunderstandings is to learn by heart and not to write at all. "Therefore I have never written anything on it [*i.e.*, on the essence of philosophy], and that is the reason why there is not and never will be any writings by Plato himself, but those which go by his name, are by Socrates who has become beautiful and young." The warning is followed by the request to read the letter repeatedly and then to burn it (314c). Publication is the unforgivable insult to the "leader and lord" (*hegemon kai kyrios*) in these matters (345c).

The endeavors of the Platonists were no more than a brief episode in the disastrous Sicilian history. The spirit of the Platonic reform was revived in the reorganization of the island by Timoleon, beginning in 344, but the civil war flared up again, in 323, and this formerly most promising area of Hellenic colonization fell in the end to the Carthaginians and to their successors, the Romans.

2. *The Letter to Hermias of Atarneus*

Of a quite different historical importance was the expansion of Platonism in the East. By the Peace of Antalcidas in 387/6 the Greek cities in Anatolia had passed under Persian administration. Within this administration, however, it was possible for a skilful leader to attain a status of semi-autonomy for his territory. One Hermias, a man of lowly origin, was able to achieve control over some mountain places in the Troad. He could extend his domain over the coastal cities, at least down to Assos; he received public recognition from the Persian satrap and was allowed the title of prince. The capital of his realm was Atarneus.

In the expansion of Hermias, two Platonists, Erastus and Coriscus of Scepsis, were of decisive influence. Having completed their course in the Academy, they had returned to Scepsis. They seem to have advised Hermias to temper somewhat the form of his tyranny, with the result that the coastal cities joined voluntarily the dominion of Hermias. What Plato had planned for Sicily, that is, a reform of the government in Syracuse that would induce the other cities to enter into a hegemonic federation, succeeded on a smaller scale in Anatolia. The organization of the government under Hermias and the Platonists is not known in detail. We only know that Hermias allotted to Erastus and Coriscus the city of Assos as their special domain and that a treaty with the city of Erythrae was concluded in the name of "Hermias and the companions." Around Erastus and Coriscus there existed quite probably a Platonic circle, for in 347, when Aristotle and Xenocrates left the Academy, they went to Assos; during the next few years something like a daughter Academy developed in the city. Among the pupils of Aristotle at this time was Callisthenes, his nephew, the later campaign historiographer in the suite of Alexander. For the close relationship among the members of the ruling group of Platonists there is further evidence in the fact that Aristotle married the niece of Hermias.

The rule of Hermias came to an unfortunate end as a consequence of his Hellenic policy. He considered his realm a bridgehead for the impending war of Macedonia against Persia. His negotiations with Philip were betrayed to the Persians; and the satrap who conducted the subsequent campaign against Atarneus got hold of the person of Hermias. Under torture he did not betray the plans of Philip and, finally, he was crucified. When he was asked for the last grace that he requested, he answered: "Tell my friends and companions that I have done nothing unworthy of philosophy or weak." The message was delivered to Aristotle and the friends at Assos. In his commemorative hymn to the dead friend, Aristotle praised Arete for whom to die is an envied fate in Hellas: Hermias went to Hades for her sake like Achilles.

The motif of Achilles, the protagonist of the Hellenes against Asia, is more than a poetic ornament. Hermias died in 341. The military alliance with Philip in preparation for the Persian war has to be dated probably in 342. This is the year in which Aristotle went to Pella to become the educator of Alexander. The romantic picture of the King of Macedonia searching Hellas for the greatest philosopher (who at that time was not the distinguished public figure) for his great son (who at that time was not the Great), must be somewhat tempered by the reality of the political link between Atarneus and Macedonia and the probability that Aristotle's mission in Pella was in part diplomatic. The tutor of Alexander was not only the great philosopher, he was also the son-in-law of Hermias, engaged in political negotiations that would lead to the Hellenic conquest of Asia. This was the atmosphere in which Alexander grew up and was formed. And we see, indeed, the motif of Achilles reappear in the early years of Alexander's campaigns, which were conducted in the *imitatio Achillis*.[5]

The chain of human relations, which ends with the second Achilles setting out for the conquest of Asia, begins with Plato's *Sixth Letter*, the founding document of the union between the three men who organized the realm of Atarneus. It has to be dated somewhere in the last years of Plato's life, that is, between 350 and 347. The *Letter* is addressed to the three men in common, that is, to "Hermias and Erastus and Coriscus." It has the character of a sacred constitution. A god seemed to have good fortune in store for them when he brought them together; for their company will be to each other of mutual benefit. Nothing could add more to the strength of Hermias than the acquisition of loyal and uncorrupt friends; and nothing is more necessary for Erastus and Coriscus than to add the worldly wisdom of an experienced ruler to their wisdom of the Idea. "What then have I to say?" To Hermias, that he can assure him of the trustworthiness of the two Platonists, and advise him to cling to their friendship by all means. To Coriscus and Erastus, that they should cling to Hermias and be bound with him in the one bond of *philia*. Such a bond, however well knit, may become strained. In this case they should submit their diffi-

---

[5] For a more circumstantial account and for the sources cf. Werner Jaeger, *Aristotle*, trans. by Richard Robinson (2d ed., Oxford, 1948) Chap. 5, "Aristotle in Assos and Macedonia."

culty to Plato; his counsel, rendered with justice and reverent restraint, will heal the friendship and community surer than any charm. Having thus recommended the friends to each other, and having made himself the partner in their community as its guardian and arbiter, Plato reflects on the Letter itself: "This Letter all three of you must read; the best would be all three together, otherwise at least two; as much in communion [*koinê*] as possible, and as often as possible. You must recognize it as a contract and binding law, as it is just. And you must swear to it with a not a-music seriousness as well as with the playfulness that is the brother of earnestness. You must swear to it by the God who is the guide in all things, present and future; and by the lordly father of the guide and author; whom we shall see in his clearness, if we are truly philosophers, as far as it is possible to men who are blessed."

The document is so clear that it hardly requires interpretation. The philosophers and the king have, indeed, entered into the existential communion of *philia*. Their bond is the faith that was kindled by Plato. In his name they should cling to each other; and to his healing power they should refer any strains on their bond. We see emerging in outline the conception of an Hellenic theocratic empire of federated communities of Platonists with its center in the Academy. The sacred symbol of the union between the companions is the Letter, to be read and re-read in communion. The rite of reading it and swearing to it should be celebrated in that mood of suspense between seriousness and play which is the appropriate mood toward a myth. And they should swear by the guiding god as well as by the father of the guide and author—a theological symbolism which at this period of Plato's life probably signifies the divine forces of the *Timaeus*, that is, nous-in-psyche and the Demiurge.

CHAPTER 2

The Gorgias

"War and battle" are the opening words of the *Gorgias*, and the declaration of war against the corrupt society is its content. Gorgias, the famous teacher of rhetoric, is in Athens as the guest of Callicles, an enlightened politician. It is a day of audience. Gorgias receives visitors and is ready to answer all questions addressed to him. Socrates, accompanied by his pupil Chaerephon, calls at Callicles' house in order to see the great man. The ultimate motif of the battle is not stated explicitly but indicated, as so frequently with Plato, through the form of the dialogue. Gorgias is somewhat exhausted by the stream of visitors and the hours of conversation, and he lets his follower Polus open the discussion; Socrates leaves the opening game to Chaerephon. The battle is engaged in as a struggle for the soul of the younger generation. Who will form the future leaders of the polity: the rhetor who teaches the tricks of political success, or the philosopher who creates the substance in soul and society?

1. *The Existential Issue*

The substance of man is at stake, not a philosophical problem in the modern sense. Socrates suggests to Chaerephon the first question: Ask him "Who he is" (447d). That is for all times the decisive question, cutting through the network of opinions, social ideas, and ideologies. It is the question that appeals to the nobility of the soul; and it is the one question which the ignoble intellectual cannot face. From this initial question unfold the topics of the dialogue: the function of rhetoric, the problem of justice, the question whether it is better to do injustice or to suffer injustice, and the fate of the unjust soul.

Through their attitudes toward the enumerated topics Plato characterizes his contemporaries. Gorgias is let off comparatively lightly. Socrates involves him in the problem whether the teacher of rhetoric should also instill the knowledge of justice in his pupils so that they will not misuse their art. Gorgias, in the best advertising style, praises his art and admits that the rhetor has to teach justice; he condemns the misuse of rhetoric but he declines responsibility for pupils who misuse his teaching. At this point the situation of the dialogue enters into the argument. Socrates, too, declines responsibility for the misdeeds of a young man who has listened to his teaching, but his condemnation would take the tangible form of banishing the young man from his presence and washing his hands of him; the breach of comity could not be healed. Gorgias has to lapse into an embarrassed silence because his fine advertising speech is given the lie by the presence of the unscrupulous and vulgar Polus, his follower and partisan in the dialogue, a glaring object lesson of the evil consequences of his corrupting activity. And his embarrassment does not become less when young Polus rushes to the support of his master and starts to berate Socrates.

The following scene with Polus is a masterpiece of the Platonic art of comedy. The undertone of grimness, however, as well as our contemporary experiences, remind us constantly that in a decadent society the ridiculous intellectual is the enemy of the spirit and that he is powerful enough to murder its representatives physically. Polus is indignant. Since he cannot grasp the difference between existential honesty and intellectual argument, he has not understood that he is the cause of embarrassment for his master; he believes it to be Socrates with his quibbling about definitions. Socrates should not have raised the question whether the rhetorician could and should teach justice. Since nobody will ever deny that he knows what justice is and that he can teach it, the question is unfair and should not be asked. To involve a man in a contradiction by forcing from him an admission on a point which he is ashamed to deny, betrays gross boorishness (*agroikia*) on the part of Socrates (461b–c).

This is the cue for Socrates to turn on the unfortunate master of etiquette with his "My most distinguished Polus!"

First he subtly suggests the existential issue. He thanks Polus for coming to the rescue of the debate. For men provide themselves with friends and sons so that, as they grow old and stumble, the younger generation will help them up again in words and actions (461c). After this slap at the product of Gorgian education, he formulates the condition under which he will enter into discussion with him. The condition elaborates the existential issue: Polus will have to restrain the prolixity of speech (*makrologia*) in which he indulged earlier, because the interminable suave flow of clichés in his speech makes discussion impossible. The condition of Socrates touches upon a problem, familiar to all of us who have had experiences with rightist or leftist intellectuals. Discussion is indeed impossible with a man who is intellectually dishonest, who misuses the rules of the game, who by irrelevant profuseness seeks to avoid being nailed down on a point, and who gains the semblance of victory by exhausting the time which sets an inevitable limit to a discussion. The only defense possible against such practices is the refusal to continue the discussion; and this refusal is socially difficult because it seems to violate the rules of comity and the freedom of speech. Polus immediately jumps at this argument and indignantly objects that he is not permitted to talk at such length as he pleases. But the war is on. Socrates is horrified at the idea that in Athens, the most free-spoken city of Hellas, Polus of all men should be prevented from talking at his pleasure—and then reminds him that his freedom to be prolix would destroy the freedom of his interlocutor, if the latter were not permitted simply to go away when he was sick of the oration. After this threat of a walkout, Polus submits to the Socratic condition.

The critical revelation of Polus' character comes when Socrates has exacted the admission that a man who does evil does not what he truly wills. For a man can truly will only what is good; if he commits acts which are unjust he acts against his true interest. If he indulges in evil acts in the mistaken belief that they serve his interest, he reveals thereby that he is powerless to do what he truly wills. Hence the tyrant is powerless. When this absurdity is reached, Polus can no longer restrain himself. He breaks away from the argument and starts sneering: As if you, Socrates, would not like to have power to do in the polis what seems good to you; as if you were not jealous when you see anyone killing or plundering or jailing people at his pleasure! (468e). By this sneer, Polus declares his own level of existence. He is the type of man who will piously praise the rule of law and condemn the tyrant— and who fervently envies the tyrant and would love nothing better than to be one himself. In a decadent society he is the representative of the great reservoir of common men who paralyze every effort at order and supply mass-connivance in the rise of the tyrant. Moreover, Polus furnishes the subtle reason for political paralysis in the advanced stage of social decomposition. His sneer at Socrates implies that his personal vileness is the measure of humanity. He is firm in the conviction that every man will indulge in vile acts if he has a chance to get away with it. His outburst against Socrates is motivated by honest indignation against a man who breaks the camaraderie of the canaille and pretends to be superior. And he cannot be brushed off; he insists. He gives a thumbnail sketch of Archelaus, an unsavory individual who recently had gained the rulership of Macedonia by an impressive series of crimes. According to Socrates the successful tyrant would have to be unhappy. The absurdity is glaring. Polus taunts Socrates, saying that he is not going to tell him he would rather be any other Macedonian than Archelaus (471a–d). And he can be persistent because he knows that all the best people are on his side. He still breaks away from the argument because he sincerely disbelieves that anybody can in good faith maintain propositions as absurd as the Socratic. With something like despair he charges that Socrates maliciously does not want to agree with him, "for surely you must think as I do" (471e). The battle lines are now drawn more clearly. Socrates assures Polus that he will, indeed, find the majority siding with him, and offers a list of names from the best Athenian families, including that of Pericles, who will all agree with Polus. Socrates will stand alone; but he will refuse to be deprived by false witnesses of his patrimony, which is the truth (472a–b).

Nevertheless, we have not yet reached the point of murder. This is a discussion, and Polus has accepted the conditions of Socrates. His attempt to break out and to beat Socrates down by the appeal to what everybody thinks has failed. The two great clubs used by vulgarity for silencing the spirit, the "Holier Than Thou" argument and the "That's What You Think," have proved ineffective. Now Socrates forces Polus on to the admission that doing injustice is worse than suffering injustice, and that doing injustice without suffering punishment is the worst of all, and hence that the notorious Archelaus is more miserable than his victims and still more miserable because he escapes the due punishment for his misdeeds (479d–e). Once this is admitted the value of rhetoric has become doubtful. What purpose can it serve to defend oneself against a justified accusation and to be acquitted, if what the guilty should do is to accuse himself and to seek his punishment. If rhetoric were used for this purpose, and only then, it would be of value (480b–d). As a matter of fact, however, it is used for the purpose of defending the criminal and to secure the gains of injustice. For such purposes it may be useful, but not for the man who does not intend to commit injustice (480e–481b).

Polus is forced into admission, but the admission is sulky. He cannot deny that the conclusions follow from the premises, but the results are absurd (*atopa*) (480e). He is embarrassed, like Gorgias, but with a difference. For Gorgias still has some sense of decency; he is aware of the existential conflict underlying the intellectual clash, and his conscience worries him. Polus is too hardened to be worried by a conscience; he is intellectually beaten, but his defeat cannot touch off a spark of decency in him. Still, he is bound by the rules of the game.

The violent reaction comes from the activist, from Callicles, the enlightened politician. He has followed the course of the debate with increasing astonishment and wrath and now he asks Chaerephon whether Socrates is in earnest about these things or whether he is joking. Being assured that he is in earnest, he turns on Socrates: if that were true, would not the whole of human life be turned upside down; and would we not do in everything the very opposite of what we ought to be doing? (481c). Callicles has rightly sensed the revolution in the words of Socrates. This is not a mere intellectual game. If Socrates is right, then the society as represented by the politician Callicles is wrong. And since the wrong goes to the spiritual core of human existence, the society would be corrupt to the point that it can no longer have a claim to the loyalty of man. The existence of the society in history is at stake. The battle has now reached the real enemy, the public representative of the corrupt order. And Callicles does not hesitate to join battle.

2. *Pathos and Communication*

The scene with Callicles is opened by Socrates again with a determination of the existential issue. He knows what he has to expect; he warns Callicles that truth is still the guiding star of the debate and that no pressure of opinion will be of the least avail. The existential differences between the speakers are now more precisely defined by the variants of Eros. Socrates is in love with philosophy, Callicles with the demos of Athens.[1] When Callicles speaks he does not dare to contradict his love; he is a politician of the type "Them are my sentiments, and if you don't like them I can change them" (481d–e). In a few sentences, rich in implications, Plato has predetermined the inevitable course of the debate. In the two Erotes of Socrates and Callicles is implied the later development of the *Republic* with its distinction of the good and the evil Eros. Here, in the *Gorgias,* the situation is revealed in which the conception of a metamorphosis of Eros originates. The issue at stake is that of communication and intelligibility in a decadent society. Are the existential differences between Socrates and Callicles so profound that the bridge of a common humanity between them has broken down? In the *Theaetetus,* where Plato comes close to characterizing the enemies as beasts, he nevertheless restores community by observing that in private conversation it is possible at least to scratch the thick crust of the vulgarian and to touch in him a spark of his renounced humanity. The bridge, thus, is not broken; but where are its points of support on both sides? They cannot be found on the level of principles of conduct, for this is precisely the level on which the protagonists meet in "war and battle." On the level of politics no compromise is possible; the political form of the *città corrotta* is the civil war. The case of Polus has shown that intellectual agreement is not followed of necessity by existential understanding. The level of communication, if there is one to be found at all, lies deeper. And to this deeper level Plato must now appeal, for otherwise the debate with Callicles would be only a repetition of the existentially inconclusive bout with Polus. This deeper level Plato designates by the term *pathos* (481c).

Pathos is what men have in common, however variable it may be in its aspects and intensities. Pathos designates a passive experience, not an action; it is what happens to man, what he suffers, what befalls him fatefully and what touches him in his existential core—as for instance the experiences of Eros (481c–d). In their exposure to pathos all men are equal, though they may differ widely in the manner in which they come to grips with it and build the experience into their lives. There is the Aeschylean touch even in this early work of Plato, with its hint that the *pathema* experienced by all may result in a *mathema* different for each man. The community of pathos is the basis of communication.

---

[1] A more detailed account of this scene would have to go into the homo-erotic implications; Socrates refers to *philosophia* as *ta ema paidika* (482a).

Behind the hardened, intellectually supported attitudes which separate men, lie the *pathemata* which bind them together. However false and grotesque the intellectual position may be, the pathos at the core has the truth of an immediate experience. If one can penetrate to this core and reawaken in a man the awareness of his *conditio humana,* communication in the existential sense becomes possible.

The possibility of communication on the level of pathos is the condition under which the debate in the *Gorgias* makes sense. The reminder is necessary at this juncture, as we have said, because otherwise the following argument with Callicles would be senseless. The possibility, at least, of breaking through to the pathos must be open. This does not mean, however, that the operation will actually be successful. Callicles no more than Polus will be won over. On the level of politics the tragedy will run its course to the murder of Socrates. But when the appeal remains ineffective, what meaning can the potential community of the pathos have? We have to realize the seriousness of the impasse, if we want to understand the conclusion of the *Gorgias.* The impasse means that historically and politically the bond of humanity is broken; the Polus and Callicles are outside the pale of human comity. Does it mean, as the inevitable consequence seems to be, that they should be killed on sight as dangerous animals? The answer of the *Gorgias* is a definite No. In the *Apology* Socrates had warned his judges that others would come after him and with renewed insistence ask the questions for which he had to die. The prediction is fulfilled; now it is Plato who asks the questions and who is in danger, as we shall see, of suffering the fate of Socrates. But the repetition would be a senseless sacrifice; and is there an alternative to the organization of a revolt with the purpose of exterminating the Athenian rabble? The conclusion of the *Gorgias* formulates the conditions under which the community of mankind can be maintained even when on the level of concrete society it has broken down. The condition is the faith in the transcendental community of man. The incrustation of the evildoer that remains impenetrable to the human appeal will fall off in death and leave the soul naked before the eternal judge. The order that has been broken in life will be restored in afterlife. In the *logique du coeur* the Judgment of the Dead is the answer to the failure of communication in life. We shall come back to this point later. For the moment we have to be aware that Plato reminds us of the community of pathos at the beginning of the Callicles scene in order to prepare the Judgment of the Dead as the transcendental continuation of a dialogue which does not achieve existential communication among the living.

3. *The Inverted Philosophy of Existence*

The Eros of Socrates is the ruler of the scene. Callicles will have to refute not Socrates but his love, the truth of philosophy; and if he does not refute Eros, then a discord will sound through his whole life and Callicles will never be in agreement with himself (482b). Callicles scorns the appeal to come into agreement with the pathos of Eros. The opening sentence of his lengthy answer (482c–486d) settles the existential issue as far as his own person is concerned. Callicles rejects the appeal of Socrates by inverting it; and he inverts it by transposing it to the vulgarian level. Plato achieves a brilliant dramatic effect by revealing the double meaning which an argument has when the partners are not in existential communication. Socrates has restrained the rhetorical prolixity of Polus and he has sharpened the issue by warning Callicles that no appeal to mass opinion will avail against the law of harmony with the Eros of truth. Now Callicles inverts these warnings and calls Socrates a regular *demegoros*, a popular speaker who gains his success by catering to the prejudices of the masses. Moreover, he ridicules the Socratic theme of *pathos* when he accuses Socrates of ranting in a demegoric manner because he has managed to have Polus suffer (*pathein*) the same mishap (*pathos*) which Gorgias has suffered (*pathein*) before him when Socrates goaded him into the admission that the rhetorician has to teach justice (482c). Socrates gained this advantage by the trick of playing on the conflict between nature (*physis*) and convention (*nomos*). Conventionally one says that doing evil is worse than suffering evil; by nature, suffering evil is the worse. Gorgias and Polus were afraid of violating the convention and that involved them in their contradictions (482c–483a).

Obviously, Callicles is no mean adversary. He is not going to be trapped like his predecessors in the contradictions of a half-hearted position. He matches the Socratic existential appeal by a philosophy of existence of his own. The *pathos*, which Socrates had understood as the exposure of man to experiences which touch the core of his existence, has become in the hands of Callicles a mishap in the discussion. This change of meaning to a setback in the competitive race indicates the direction of Callicles' interpretation of existence. Existence must not be interpreted in terms of the Eros towards the Agathon, but in terms of the stronger or weaker *physis*. Nature is the fundamental reality, and the victorious assertion of the *physis* is the meaning of life. The order of the soul, which for Socrates originates in the eroticism of the mystic, is brushed aside as a convention invented by the weaker natures to restrain the stronger ones. Nobody prefers the suffering of injustice really to its doing; those who say so are of a slavish nature; no man of a lordly nature would agree (483a–c). This is not the attitude of a second-rate rascal like Polus who is conscious of being canaille; this is the deliberate transvaluation of values from an existential counterposition. Callicles knows that he can maintain it only if he can invalidate the Socratic position. With his distinction of *physis* and *nomos* he strikes at the heart of Socratic eroticism: "You pretend only that you are searching for truth! As a matter of fact, you are propagating what holds a vulgar appeal for the masses!" (482e). Polus was still in despair: how could a man entertain such fantastic propositions as Socrates? Callicles knows the motive: Socrates is in the game like everybody else; he is a demagogue who seeks favor by a pretense of respectability. Callicles is in the know of ideologies; he gets behind the other man and reveals the dubious motive behind the façade of ideas. The theoretical attack on the Socratic existential position becomes a political attack on the demagogue.

But why should Callicles, the politician, be so excited about the preacher of a morality that will keep the slavish subjects content while not hampering the superior man who sees through the swindle? The situation is complicated. The Socratic appeal is fraught, indeed, with a real danger for the politician. The characterization of convention as an invention implies that the inventor himself is aware, at some level of his consciousness, of the artificial character of moral principles. Polus was outspoken enough on the point that *nobody* would side with Socrates, that *everybody* envies the tyrant. The restraint of convention, thus, is tempered by the connivance of the victims of tyranny. When a society has reached this degree of corruption, which from the point of view of Callicles is quite desirable, the harmonious connivance in criminality may, indeed, be gravely disturbed by a man who tries to persuade the people that conventions are not conventions, that their truth can be confirmed through recourse to the existential experiences in which they have originated, and that they must be taken seriously. If an appreciable sector of the people should fall for the Socratic preaching, the situation might become unpleasant for Callicles and his type.

There is more, however, to the resistance of Callicles than the fear of a Socratic popular success. The situation of the dialogue is not that of an assembly of the people. Members of the ruling class are among themselves. In such company the propositions of Socrates are in bad taste. It is the same complaint as that of Polus. But while Polus was indignant because Socrates did not conduct himself *en canaille*, Callicles protests that Socrates does not conduct himself as a gentleman of the superior type. The subsequent remarks of Callicles have, therefore, in spite of their threatening undertone, the character of a not altogether unfriendly admonition to Socrates to mend his ways. They are of special interest in as much as they are somewhat improbable as the remarks of a younger man to the historical Socrates, as well as because they contain some details which do not quite fit the circumstances of Socrates' life. These admonitions have an autobiographical touch. Callicles holds forth in a manner in which a friend of the family might have on occasion given Plato a piece of his mind.

Callicles opens his admonitions with a clarification of the terms justice and injustice. The conventional lawmakers define justice in such a manner that they will terrify the stronger man who otherwise would get the better of them, while they declare it shameful and unjust if a man desires to have more than the others (*pleonektein*) (483c). Justice and injustice in the conventional sense are distinguished as desire for equality and pleonexy. By nature, however, pleonexy is just; and just order, in the animal realm as well as among humans, among cities as well as among peoples, is the rule of the stronger over the weaker one (483c–d).[2] The men who make history follow this law of nature; for on what other grounds could Xerxes' invasion of Hellas be justified? Certainly not by the conventions which we teach our best and strongest men from their youth in order to tame them like young lions. If a man had sufficient strength, he would break all these charms; the slave would rise in rebellion and become our master; and the light of jus-

[2] The problem of pleonexy is intimately connected with the "inverted" philosophy of existence. When the new philosophy of existence recurs, in the seventeenth century A.D., the problem of pleonexy also reappears. Locke makes the curious attempt to propagate pleonexy as conventional justice; he institutionalizes the "desire to have more than the other man" by transforming government into a protective agency for the gains of pleonexy.

tice would shine forth. Socrates would understand all this, if only he would drop philosophy and turn to more important things. Philosophy is an elegant accomplishment, if pursued with moderation in younger years, but if a man indulges in it and carries it on in later life, he will be ignorant of the things which a gentleman ought to know. He will be inexperienced in politics; he will not be able to hold his own in a debate; he will be ignorant of human character and of its motivations through pleasures and passions.[3] When such men get involved in business or politics they will cut a ridiculous figure, just as a man of affairs would make himself ridiculous in a philosophical debate.[4] One has to combine the two accomplishments and to balance them properly. Thus, it is not a disgrace for a young man to be interested in philosophy; on the contrary, its study is becoming to a freeman and who neglects it will never be a superior man with noble aspirations. But indulgence makes the man effeminate; he will be shy of public gatherings where men distinguish themselves; he will hang around in corners with three or four admiring youths but never speak out like a freeman. Callicles assures Socrates of his goodwill and affection; he asks him whether he is not ashamed of being in the notoriously defenseless position of a philosopher. For what would he do if someone had him arrested for a wrong which he has not committed? He would be confused and would not know what to say; and before a court he might not even be able to defend himself against the death penalty. And what is the value of a man who cannot defend himself against his enemies, of a man whom, so to speak, one may hit with impunity?[5]

The position of Callicles hinges on the identification of good and just with the self-assertive expression of the stronger nature. The debate between Callicles and Socrates which follows the admonition proves the position untenable. We need not follow this long debate in detail (486d–522), but we must single out the principal arguments of Socrates because they have remained to this day the classical catalogue of arguments against the "inverted" philosophy of existence which characterizes the age of enlightenment and positivism of a civilization. We shall

[3] Cf. Bentham's attack on the "ascetic" type.

[4] In this part of the admonition we probably have to see the origin of the Diversion of the *Theaetetus*.

[5] This section of the Callicles speech is distinctly autobiographic. One has to realize the situation of Plato in Athens and the effect which advice of this kind must have had on a proud man who was conscious of his qualities.

find the same theoretical situation recurring in the eighteenth and nineteenth centuries A.D.

The position of Callicles has a fundamental weakness, characteristic of this type of existentialism. Callicles does not seriously deny the relative rank of virtues. He is not prepared to deny that courage ranks higher than cowardice, or wisdom higher than folly. When he identifies the good with the strong, he acts on the inarticulate premise that there exists a pre-established harmony between the lustiness represented by himself and the social success of virtues which he does not discern too clearly but to which he gives conventional assent. Socrates, in his argument, uses the technique of pointing to facts which disprove the pre-established harmony and involves Callicles in contradictions between his valuations and the consequences of his existentialism.

The first and most obvious attack is directed against the harmony between strength and goodness. Callicles had maintained that the rule of the strongest is justice. Now Socrates raises the question whether inferior people, if they are numerous enough, cannot be stronger than the better ones. And if so, would then the more numerous weak who impose the despised conventions not be the stronger ones; and would, as a consequence, the argument for justice by nature against justice by convention not break down? Callicles is incensed at the idea that a rabble of slaves should lay down the law for him because they happen to be physically stronger. He withdraws immediately and insists that when he said "the stronger" he had meant of course "the more excellent." Thus the first defense of the principle that the survival of the fittest entails the survival of the best has broken down.

The "excellent" are finally defined by Callicles as the men who are most wise and courageous in affairs of state. They ought to be the rulers, and it would be fair if they had more than their subjects (491d–e). Socrates counters with the question: Should they have more than themselves? This question brings a new outburst from Callicles. A man should not rule himself. On the contrary, goodness and justice consist in the satisfaction of desires. "Luxury, license and freedom" (*tryphe, akolasia, eleutheria*), if provided with means, are virtue and happiness (*arete, eudaimonia*); whatever is said to the contrary is the ornamental talk of worthless men (492c). It is not difficult for Socrates to suggest desires of such baseness that even Callicles squirms. But he has become stubborn and insists on the identification of happiness with the satisfaction of desires; and he refuses to distinguish between good and bad pleasures (495b).

The resistance of Callicles gives Socrates the opportunity to introduce the question whether men who are admitted by Callicles to be good (such as the wise and courageous) feel more pleasure than those who are admitted to be inferior (such as the cowards). The result of the inquiry is the conclusion that a coward can experience, quite possibly, more pleasure than a wise and courageous man. By the reasoning of Callicles, therefore, the cowards would have to be considered the better men because they experience more happiness in the hedonistic sense. This contradiction, finally, compels Callicles to admit the distinction of good and bad pleasures (499c).

With this admission the case of Callicles is lost. Socrates can, step by step, force his adversary's unwilling assent to the positive philosophy of existence, from which the later position of the *Republic* is derived. In the present context we have to concentrate on the existential enmity between Callicles and Socrates-Plato and on the critical analysis of political corruption. Above all, Socrates now resumes the issue of communication in a more radical manner. Only if the soul is well-ordered can it be called lawful (*nomimos*) (504d); and only if it has the right order (*nomos*) is it capable of entering into communion (*koinonia*) (507e). The pathos is no more than a precondition for community; in order to actualize it, the Eros must be oriented towards the Good (*agathon*) and the disturbing passions must be restrained by Sophrosyne. If the lusts are unrestrained, man will lead the life of a robber (*lestes*). Such a man cannot be the friend (*prosphiles*) of God or other men, for he is incapable of communion, and who is incapable of communion is incapable of friendship (*philia*) (507e). Friendship, *philia*, is Plato's term for the state of existential community. *Philia* is the existential bond among men; and it is the bond as well between Heaven and Earth, man and God. Because *philia* and order pervade everything, the universe is called *kosmos* (order) and not disorder or license (*akosmia, akolasia*) (508a).

4. The Transfer of Authority

The meaning of order in existence is re-established. The existential issue between Socrates and Callicles can now be taken up in earnest. Socrates restates the order of evils: (1) It is bad to suffer injustice; (2)

it is worse to commit injustice; (3) it is worst to remain in the dis-order of the soul which is created by doing injustice and not to ex-perience the restoration of order through punishment. The sneer of Callicles—that the philosopher is exposed to ignominious treatment—can now be met on the level of the philosophy of order. Callicles had taken the stand that it was of supreme importance to protect onself effectively against suffering injustice. Socrates maintains that the price of safety against injustice may be too high. The suffering of injustice can be averted most effectively if a man acquires a position of power, or if he is the companion of the powers that be. The tyrant is in the ideal position of safety against injustice. About the nature of the tyrant there are no doubts, and the companion of the tyrant will be acceptable to him only if he is of a similar nature, that is, if he connives in the injustice of the ruling power. The companion of tyranny may escape the suffering of injustice but his corruption will inevitably in-volve him in the doing of injustice. Callicles agrees enthusiastically and again reminds Socrates that the companion of the tyrant will plunder and kill the man who does not imitate the tyrant. The argu-ment is nearing its climax. The sneers of Callicles can be effective only against men of his own ilk. They fall flat before a man who is ready to die. Do you think, is the answer of Socrates, that all cares should be directed towards the prolongation of life? (511b–c). The "true man" is not so fond of life, and there may be situations in which he no longer cares to live (512e). The argument is not yet directed per-sonally against Callicles, but we feel the tension increasing towards the point where Callicles is co-responsible, through his conniving con-duct, for the murder of Socrates and perhaps of Plato himself. The social conventions, which Callicles despises, are wearing thin; and the advocate of nature is brought to realize that he is a murderer face to face with his victim. The situation is fascinating for those among us who find ourselves in the Platonic position and who recognize in the men with whom we associate today the intellectual pimps for power who will connive in our murder tomorrow.

It would be too much of an honor, however, to burden Callicles personally with the guilt of murder. The whole society is corrupt, and the process of corruption did not start yesterday. Callicles is no more than one of a kind; and he may even get caught himself in the morass which he deepens. Socrates raises the question of the good statesman on principle. Goodness and badness are now defined in terms of advancing or decomposing the order of existence. A statesman is good if under his rule the citizens become better; he is bad if under his rule the citizens become worse, in terms of existential order. Socrates reviews the men who are the pride of Athenian history: Themistocles, Pericles, Cimon, Miltiades; and applying his criterion he finds that they were bad statesmen. They have bloated the city with docks and harbors and walls and revenues, and they have left no room for justice and temperance. The conclusive proof for the evil character of their rule is the ferocious injustice committed against them by the very citizens whom it would have been their task to improve. The present generation is the heir to the evil that has accumulated through the successive rules of such "great" statesmen. And men like Callicles and Alcibiades who cater to the evil passions of the masses might well become their victims. So, what does Callicles want with his admonitions to conform to the habits of politics and to become a flatterer of the demos? Does Callicles seriously suggest that Socrates should join the ranks of those who corrupt society still further? Is it not, rather, his task to pronounce the truth which would restore some order? But Callicles cannot break out of the circle of his evil. He can only repeat that the consequences for Socrates will be unpleasant.

The Socratic answer fixes the position of Plato: No doubt, the consequences may be unpleasant; who does not know that in Athens any man may suffer anything; nor would it be a surprise if he were put to death; on the contrary, he rather expects a fate of this kind. And why does he anticipate his death? Because he is one of the few Athenians who cares about the true art of politics and the only one in his time who acts like a statesman (521d).

This last formulation, by which Plato claims for himself the true statesmanship of his time, is important in several respects. In the construction of the *Gorgias*, this claim destroys the authority of Callicles to give advice to anybody with regard to public conduct. The man who stands convicted as the accomplice of tyrannical murderers and as the corruptor of his country, does not represent spiritual order, and nobody is obliged to show respect to his word. The authority of public order lies with Socrates. With regard to the relation of Plato to Athens the claim stigmatizes the politicians who are obsessed by the "love of the people" (*demou Eros,* 513c) as the "adversaries" (*antistasiotes,*

513c) of the existential order represented by Socrates-Plato; the authoritative order is transferred from the people of Athens and its leaders to the one man Plato. Surprising as this move may seem to many, Plato's claim has proved historically quite sound. The order represented by Callicles has gone down in ignominy; the order represented by Plato has survived Athens and is still one of the most important ingredients in the order of the soul of those men who have not renounced the traditions of Western civilization.

5. *The Judgment of the Dead*

The transfer of authority from Athens to Plato is the climax of the *Gorgias*. The meaning of the transfer and the source of the new authority, however, still need some clarification. Let us recall what is at stake. The transfer of authority means that the authority of Athens, as the public organization of a people in history, is invalidated and superseded by a new public authority manifest in the person of Plato. That is revolution. And it is even more than an ordinary revolution in which new political forces enter the struggle for power in competition with the older ones. Plato's revolution is a radical call for spiritual regeneration. The people of Athens has lost its soul. The representative of Athenian democracy, Callicles, is existentially disordered; the great men of Athenian history are the corruptors of their country; the law courts of Athens can kill a man physically but their sentence has no moral authority of punishment. The fundamental *raison d'être* of a people, that it goes its way through history in partnership with God, has disappeared; there is no reason why Athens should exist, considering what she is. The *Gorgias* is the death sentence over Athens.

But what is the nature of the authority that renders judgment? Plato reveals it through the myth of the Judgment of the Dead, at the end of the *Gorgias*. Callicles has reminded Socrates repeatedly of the fate that awaits him at the hands of an Athenian court. In a final answer Socrates says that he would rather die with a just soul, than go into the beyond with a soul full of injustice. For this would be the last and worst of all evils (522e). The reason for his resolution he sets forth in the myth.

From the Age of Cronos there stems a law concerning the destiny of man, which still is in force among the gods: that men who have led just and holy lives will go, after death, to the Islands of the Blessed, while those who have led unjust and impious lives will go to Tartarus for punishment. In the Age of Cronos, and even until quite recently in the Age of Zeus, the judgments were rendered on the day on which the men were to die; the men as well as the judges were alive. As a result, frequent miscarriages of justice occurred. For the men "had their clothes on," and the apparel of the body covered the true character of the souls; and the judges themselves were hampered "by their clothes" in perceiving correctly the state of the soul before them. The complaints about misjudgments came to Zeus and he changed the procedure. Now the judgments are passed on the souls after death; and in judgment are sitting Minos, Rhadamanthys, and Aeacus, the dead sons of Zeus (523–524a). Stripped of their bodies, the souls reveal their beauty or deformity; the judges can inspect them impartially because nothing indicates their earthly rank, and they can send them correctly to the Islands of the Blessed or to Tartarus. The purpose of punishment is twofold. By temporary suffering the souls will be chastised unless they are too bad; some of them, however, are incurable and their eternal suffering will fill the improvable souls with fear and thus contribute to their chastisement. The utterly bad souls who suffer eternal punishment seem to be always (if we can trust the authority of Homer) the souls of men who in their bodily existence were rulers and potentates; for the greatest crimes are always committed by those who have power. If, however, a good soul appears before the judges, it is most likely to be the soul of a man who has been a philosopher and who has refrained in his lifetime from interfering with the affairs of other men (526c).

The myth of the *Gorgias* is the earliest of the Platonic poems that concern a philosophy of order and history. It is very simple in its construction. Nevertheless, it contains in a rudimentary form the meanings expressed, by a more differentiated symbolism, in the later poems of the *Republic,* the *Statesman,* and the *Timaeus.* The present myth owes its value to its elemental terseness and its closeness to the experiences expressed in it.

Socrates opens his story with the warning that he is, indeed, telling the "truth," even though Callicles may consider the myth no more than a pretty tale (523a). In an abbreviated form Plato raises the issue of the truth of the myth which becomes the object of elaborate discussion in the *Timaeus.* Hence we shall follow the same procedure as in the analysis of the other myths, that is, we shall not search for the "truth" on the level of the "pretty story" but translate the symbols into the experiences of the soul which they articulate. The first symbols which offer themselves for such translation are the ages of Cronos and Zeus. They signify the historical sequence of the age of the myth and of the age of the differentiated, autonomous personality. Plato introduces them in the *Gorgias* for the purpose of dating the change in procedure for the judgment of the dead. In the Age of Cronos, and "until quite recently in the Age of Zeus," the souls were judged while they were still "alive"; that is, the judgment was biased by regard for the worldly station of the soul. Now the souls are judged when they are "dead," that is, in their nakedness, without regard to worldly rank. This change in the mode of judgment is quite "recent"; that is, in historical time, Plato is speaking of the new order of the soul inaugurated by Socrates. Under the new dispensation, the naked souls are judged by the "Sons of Zeus." The Sons of Zeus are the men of the new age, the philosophers in general, and primarily Plato himself. These Sons of Zeus are "dead." We have to ascertain, therefore, the meaning of the symbols "life" and "death" in the myth.

The meaning of death in the myth has been carefully prepared by incidental remarks in the dialogue itself. When Callicles praised the life of hedonistic happiness, Socrates suggested that in this case life would be something awful (*deinos*). Euripides might even be right in saying that life is death, and death is life. Most likely, at this moment we would have to be considered dead; for it would be true what a sage has said: that our body (*soma*) is our tomb (*sema*) (493a).[6] The true life of the soul, thus, would be its existence free of the prison of the body, in a life preceding or following its earthly entombment. Concerning the meaning of pre-existence and postexistence Plato has expressed himself at length in other dialogues. The great symbolization of pre-existence is given in the myth of the *Phaedrus*. Let us recall only one passage which clarifies the meaning of the "Sons of Zeus." In *Phaedrus* (250b) Plato speaks of the happy existence "when we [*sc.* the philosophers] followed in the train of Zeus," seeing the forms of eternal being which now can be recalled through anamnesis. Concerning the idea of postexistence, in particular with regard to the purification of the

---

[6] The image of life as an entombment of the soul in the body recurs in other contexts. In *Phaedrus* 250c, for instance, Plato speaks of the souls in the state when they were still "pure and untombed" by the body.

soul in afterlife, there is an important passage in the *Cratylus* (403–404b). In this passage Plato rejects as unfounded the fear which men have of the ruler of the underworld. His names, Pluto and Hades, indicate that he is rich and consequently does not want anything of us, and that he has the knowledge of all noble things. If the souls who dwell in his presence had really reason to fear him, at least now and then one would escape from him. But, as a matter of fact, they like to dwell with him; they are bound to him by their active desire; for he has the knowledge of virtue and he points to the souls the path to their perfection. In life, however, the souls have not fully developed this desire for perfection. That is the reason Pluto wants them only after they are freed from the passions of the body. Only after death will they be free to follow undisturbed their desire for virtue (*peri areten epithymia*). By this desire Pluto binds the souls to himself, for in the relation with him they will at last achieve a purification of which they were incapable as long as they were obsessed by "the fear and frenzy of the body." No compulsion, thus, is necessary to make the souls undergo their cathartic suffering in the underworld; on the contrary, here at last the soul is free to pass through the desired catharsis that was prevented in earthly existence by the obstacle of the body.

The various passages cast some light on the mythical play with the symbols of life and death in the *Gorgias*. Death can mean either the entombment of the soul in its earthly body, or the shedding of the body. Life can mean either earthly existence, or freedom of the soul from the frenzy of the body. The shifting between these several meanings is the source of the richness of the *Gorgias*.

Let us begin with the meaning of the symbols on the level of history. In the historico-political process those who live lustfully like Callicles are the "dead," entombed in the passion and frenzy of their body; they are judged by the "living," that is, by the philosophers who let their souls be penetrated by the experience of death and, thus, have achieved life *sub specie mortis* in freedom from somatic passion. The transfer of authority means the victory of the life of the soul over the deadliness of earthly passions. This tension between the life of the soul and the tomb of the body, however, has only "recently" developed in history. Formerly, in the age of the myth, the distinction between life and death had not been so clear; at that time earthly existence could easily be mistaken for the life of the soul. The soul had first to be separated from the body through the experience of death. Only when Thanatos had entered the soul could it be distinguished clearly from the *sema* of the body; only then could its nonsomatic nature, the co-eternity of its existence with the cosmos and the autonomy of its order, become intelligible. The life and death of Socrates were the decisive events in the discovery and liberation of the soul. The soul of Socrates was oriented towards the Agathon through its eroticism; and the Agathon invaded the soul with its eternal substance, thereby creating the autonomous order of the soul beyond the passions of the body. Through this catharsis, the soul in its earthly existence received the stigmata of its eternal postexistence. The life of Socrates was the great model of the liberation of the soul through the invasion of death into earthly existence; and the *imitatio Socratis* had become the order of life for his followers, and above all for Plato. Only now, when the Sons of Zeus have died, when death embraces them in life, is the catharsis of the soul revealed as the true meaning of life; and only the souls who have died have the clearness of view which enables them to judge the "living." The authority of the judges, thus, is the authority of death over life.

But what is the status of those who do not have the experience of death in existence and through this experience gain the life of the soul? On this question hinges the problem of history as a meaningful order, *i.e.*, as the process of revelation. The revelation of divinity in history is ontologically real. The myth of the people and the poets is *really* superseded by the myth of the soul. The old myth is in full decadence; it is corroded by pleonexy and reason, as evidenced by Gorgias, Polus, and Callicles. The order of the soul as revealed through Socrates has, indeed, become the new order of relations between God and man. And the authority of this new order is inescapable. To bury oneself in the tomb of bodily existence (the escape of Callicles) is of no avail; the way from the old myth leads, not to the darkness of nature, but to the life of the soul; and the soul must die and, divested of its body, stand before its judge. The new order is understood secretly even by those who meet it with sulkiness and recalcitrance, for this secret understanding binds the partners of the dialogue together at least for its duration. We remember the passage of the *Cratylus*. The "desire for virtue" is present even if it is obscured by the *mania* of the body; and it will reign freely when the obstacle of the body is removed. In so far as the dialogue is an attempt at existential communication, it is an attempt to liberate the soul from its passions, to denude it of its body. Socrates speaks to his interlocutors as if they were "dead" souls, or at least, as if they were souls who are capable of death. On the part of Socrates, the dialogue is an attempt to submit the others, at least tentatively, to the catharsis of death. The judgment of the dead thus is enacted in part in the dialogue itself, concretely, in the attempt of Socrates to pierce through the "body" of his interlocutors to their naked souls. He tries to make die, and thereby to make live, those who threaten him with death. Hence Socrates, after he has finished the tale of the myth, turns to Callicles for the last time and offers him an exhortation of his own in exchange for his former friendly admonitions. He assures Callicles that he is persuaded of the truth of the judgment and that he wishes to present his soul undefiled before the judge; and that, to the utmost of his powers, he exhorts all men to be equally persuaded. He now exhorts Callicles, therefore, to take part in this combat (*agon*), which is the agon of life and greater than any other. Otherwise he will suffer before his eternal judges the fate which he predicted for Socrates before the earthly judges. "Follow my persuasion"—and he will lead Callicles to *eudaimonia* in this life and after death (527c). The existential appeal is now supported by the ultimate authority of the demand to submit freely to the inevitable judgment right here and now: to enter the community of those whose souls have been liberated by death and who live in the presence of the judgment.

The barriers between the earthly existence of the soul and its post-existence have broken down. Catharsis is the meaning of existence for the soul on both sides of the dividing line of disembodiment. The catharsis which the soul has not achieved in earthly existence will have to be achieved in postexistence. Hence the punishment, the *timoria*, which the soul will have to undergo in afterlife does not differ from the punishment which it has to undergo in this life for the purpose of purification. This purifying *timoria* is a social process; it can be applied by gods or by men. Those who are touchable by it are those whose misdeeds (*hamartemata*) are curable; they are able to undergo the purification by pain and suffering. And there is no other way for the soul to be delivered from evil (*adikia*) "in this world or the next" (525c). In this idea of the catharsis through suffering "in this world or the next," there can again be felt the Aeschylean touch of the wisdom through suffering as the great law of the psyche for gods and men.

The curable soul, thus, is permanently in the state of judgment; to experience itself permanently in the presence of the judgment, we might say, is the criterion of the curable soul; "only the good souls are in hell," as Berdiaev, on occasion, has formulated the problem. This conception, however, would have an unexpected consequence if it were understood not existentially but dogmatically. If the symbol of punishment in afterlife were misunderstood as a dogmatic hypothesis, the not-so-good souls might arrive at the conclusion that they will wait for afterlife and see what is going to happen then; if suffering is the lot of the soul under all circumstances, they can wait for their share of suffering (which is no more than a dogmatic assertion) in postexistence and meanwhile enjoy some pleasurable criminality. It is a problem in the psychology of dogmatic derailment similar to that which has arisen in some instances in Calvinism: if the fate of the soul is predestined, some may arrive at the conclusion that it does not matter what they do. This psychological derailment, through the dogmatic misunderstanding of the existential truth of the myth, Plato forestalls by the threat of eternal condemnation for the incurable souls. In the symbolism of the myth eternal condemnation is the correlate to the refusal of communication on the level of the myth of the soul; eternal condemnation means, in existential terms, self-excommunication. The revelation of the divinity in history moves on; the authority rests with the men who live in friendship with God; the criminal can achieve nothing but the perdition of his soul.

CHAPTER 3

The Republic

§ 1. The Organization of the Republic

The *Republic* is a dialogue of considerable length, articulated by dramatic scenes, as well as by the main topics of discussion. That organization, to which the analysis must constantly refer, is not marked, however, by external subdivisions. One can refer to passages of the *Republic* only by the Books, Chapters, and Stephanus pages of the manuscript and printing tradition. It is necessary, therefore, to supply the reader with the following schema:

Organization of the Republic

Prologue
(1) I.1   327a—328b. Descent to the Piraeus
(2) I.2—I.5.   328b—331d. Cephalus. Justice of the Older Generation
(3) I.6—I.9.   331e—336a. Polemarchus. Justice of the Middle Generation
(4) I.10—I.24.   336b—354c. Thrasymachus. Justice of the Sophist
Introduction
(1) II.1—II.10.   357a—369b. The Question: Is Justice Better than Injustice?
Part I: Genesis and Order of the Polis
(1) II.11—II.16. 369b—376e. Genesis of the Polis
(2) II.17—III.18. 376e—412b. Education of the Guardians
(3) III.19—IV.5. 412b—427c. Constitution of the Polis
(4) IV.6—IV.19.   427c—445e. Justice in the Polis
Part II: Embodiment of the Idea
(1) V.1—V.16.   449a—471c. Somatic Unit of the Polis and the Hellenes
(2) V.17—VI.14.   471c—502c. Rule of the Philosophers
(3) VI.15—VII.5. 502c—521c. The Idea of the Agathon
(4) VII.6—VII.18. 521c—541b. Education of the Philosophers
Part III: Decline of the Polis
(1) VIII.1—VIII.5.   543a—550c. Timocracy
(2) VIII.6—VIII.9.   550c—555b. Oligarchy
(3) VIII.10—VIII.13. 555b—562a. Democracy
(4) VIII.14—IX.3.   562a—576b. Tyranny

Conclusion
(1) IX.4—IX.13.   576b—592b. The Answer: Justice is Better than Injustice
Epilogue
(1) X.1—X.8.   595a—608b. Rejection of Mimetic Art
(2) X.9—X.11.   608c—612a. Immortality of the Soul
(3) X.12   612a—613e. Rewards of Justice in Life
(4) X.13—X.16.   613e—631d. Judgment of the Dead

The reader will find his way through the schema best if he starts, not from the beginning, but from the middle:

(1) The right order of man and society is for Plato an embodiment in historical reality of the idea of the Good, of the Agathon. The embodiment must be undertaken by the man who has seen the Agathon and let his soul be ordered through the vision, by the philosopher. Hence, at the center of the *Republic*, Part II, 2–3, Plato deals with the rule of the philosopher and the vision of the Agathon.

(2) That center piece is preceded and followed by the discussion of the means that will secure the adequate physiological and spiritual substance for a well-ordered polis. Part II, 1 deals with marriage, the community of women and children, and the restraints on warfare among the kindred Hellenes. Part II, 4 deals with the philosophical education of the rulers who will preserve the order in existence.

(3) The central Part II, the Embodiment of the Idea, is preceded by the genetic construction of the right order for a polis in Part I; and it is followed by an analysis in Part III, of the phases of decline through which the right order, once established, will have to pass. The three parts together form the main body of the dialogue, with their discussion of the right order, its embodiment, its genesis, and its decline.

(4) That main body, then, is framed by an Introduction and a Conclusion. The discussion of right order was occasioned by a debate about the question whether justice is better than injustice, or whether the unjust man will not fare better than the just man. The introductory raising of the question is balanced, after the long discussion of right order, by the concluding answer that justice is preferable to injustice.

(5) The main body of the dialogue, together with its Introduction and Conclusion, finally, is framed by the Prologue of Book I and the Epilogue of Book X.

A confrontation of the brief summary with the schema shows that the organization contains elements of meaning beyond the symmetrical

arrangement of subdivisions from a center. The three parts of the main
body are interlocked, indeed, on more than one level of meaning. Parts
I and III, for instance, not only balance but also complement each other,
in that Part I describes the polis of the idea with its aristocratic form
of government, while Part III describes the four declining forms of
government. Both parts together give a complete theory of five forms
of government. And that, indeed, is Plato's intention, for at the end of
Part I Socrates embarks on the description of the four declining forms,
but is interrupted by his friends who want to hear him speak first on the
possibility of realizing the polis of the idea. Part II, the center piece of
the *Republic*, thus, is introduced as a digression, and when it has run its
course, the topic adumbrated at the end of Part I is resumed. Nevertheless, I and III on the forms of government are not separated by II in
order to provide symmetry and balance, but they really balance each
other by subject matter, in so far as Part I deals with justice and right
order, while Part III deals with injustice and disorder. The central Part II,
furthermore, though introduced as a digression, is interlocked by subject
matter with both I and III. For, in as much as it contains a theory of the
substance in which a just order can be embodied, it belongs with Part I
which describes the structure of the just order; and in as much as Part
II deals with the embodiment of the idea, it belongs with Part III which
deals with its disembodiment. Parts I and II, on the form and substance of
just order, are set off against Part III, on the decline of just order in both
form and substance. Parts II and III, on the embodiment and disembodiment of the idea, are set off against Part I, on the structure of right order.

Moreover, the schema has articulated only the main parts of the
organization and the main divisions immediately under them. It has not
gone into the rich substructure which quite frequently also has a bearing
on the organization of the whole work:

(1) The subdivision of Part I, 1, the section on the genesis of the
Polis will serve as an example. The section develops first the idea of a
plain peasant community as the model of right order (Bk. II, 11–12).
When Glaukon is not satisfied with the simple life, Socrates is willing to
enrich the idea, and lets the first, "healthy" community (II, 11–12) be
followed by a luxurious, "feverish" community (II, 13–16). At that
point matters, of course, cannot rest. The larger scale of the community,
with a more differentiated civilization, including equipment for warfare, requires a saving remedy in form of properly educated guardians.

The dialectics of the debate in Part I, 1 drives on to the analysis of Part I, 2, so that the whole structure of Part I ultimately arises from the conflict in the first section of the part.

(2) The construction is of special interest, because Plato repeats it in Part II. Again Part II, 1 is subdivided by the famous "waves" of opposition which Socrates expects against his proposals. The first wave he fears when he suggests equal treatment for men and women in the well-ordered polis, including common gymnastic exercises in the nude; the second, greater wave, when he suggests community of women and children. The construction is continued into the following section 2, when he expects the third, the greatest wave to swallow him because of his proposal that philosophers should rule. The sequence of the waves is not as intimately connected with either the persons of the drama or the subject of their discussion as the division of Part I, 1 into the healthy and the feverish polis. But precisely because in Part II the device is artificial, it reveals the deliberateness of the construction. Plato wanted it to be clear beyond a doubt that the marriage institutions and the rule of the philosopher-kings belonged together as the means for providing a social substance in which the idea could find its body in history.

(3) And, finally, we find the construction repeated in Part III, 1. For the first section of the part titled Decline of the Polis deals not only with timocracy, but first with aristocracy, that is, the right order of the polis, and explains why the order of the idea, once embodied in suitable substance, will inevitably start on the decline. The causes of the decline from aristocracy to timocracy, once they have begun to operate, cannot be halted. The transition from the first to the second form in Part III, 1 draws after it the further transitions to the forms treated in the remaining sections of Part III.

The construction of the first section in each of the main parts has a bearing not only on the internal organization of the respective part, but the parallelism proves, in our opinion, that the three parts distinguished in our schema were actually intended as such by Plato.

The examples given in the two preceding paragraphs are sufficient to show the complexity of the organization. Moreover the list must not even be continued. For the examples also show that a schema of the *Republic* is not merely a table of contents, but a construction whose validity depends on a correct interpretation of Plato's intentions. While the schema had to be given as a basis for further analysis, it now turns out to be the first step of the analysis itself. That point will become clear as soon as we compare our schema with others. Professor Cornford, for instance, treats our Part II, 1, the Somatic Unity of the Polis, as an appendix to the preceding Part I, and lets the central part begin with the Rule of Philosophers. The procedure can be justified, if one interprets the section on marriage and women as an elaboration of a previous hint (424a) concerning the subject, and discounts Plato's construction of the three "waves" as an irrelevant formality.[1] But in order to adopt the interpretation, one must disregard more than a formality: one must disregard Plato's conception of a social substance that is receptive for the embodiment of the idea by virtue of its qualities of *both* the hereditary endowment and the psyche. We are, beyond questions of literary organization, in the middle of Plato's philosophy of order. Understandably we prefer to follow Plato's hint of the three "waves" in our interpretation, rather than Professor Cornford's assumption that Plato was a clumsy artist.[2]

Our own schema has the closest affinity with that of Kurt Hildebrandt.[3] Nevertheless, there are one or two slight differences which reveal the difficulties of interpretation even at the level of literary organization. Hildebrandt finds in the Epilogue not four, but only three sections. They are: (1) Rejection of Mimetic Poetry; (2) Eternal and Earthly Justice; (3) The New Poetry of the Eternal Cosmos. His section (2) pools into one our sections Immortality of the Soul and Rewards of Justice in Life. The procedure is puzzling because the two sections just mentioned contain nothing on Eternal Justice. The problem of Eternal Justice appears only in the last section, in the myth of the Judgment of the Dead. Since Hildebrandt does not explain the point, we can only suspect that he compressed the four clear sections into three, with a little violence of title, because he could find only three sections in the Prologue, and wanted to have in Prologue and Epilogue the same number of subdivisions of three. The section he left inarticulate in the Prologue was our (1), the Descent to the Piraeus. The full weight of the brief opening chapter of the *Republic*, deliberately balancing the de-

---

[1] Francis M. Cornford, *The Republic of Plato* (New York, 1945). The schema, xi–xiii; the justification of the point in question, 144.

[2] There are other differences between Professor Cornford's schema and ours. The most important one is Cornford's treatment of Epilogue 1, on the Rejection of Mimetic Art, as another "appendix," which does not fit into the context of Book X.

[3] Kurt Hildebrant, *Platon*. The schema is on p. 397.

scent into the underworld at the end of the Epilogue, apparently escaped Hildebrandt. Well chosen, however, is his title "The New Poetry of the Eternal Cosmos" for the Judgmnt of the Dead, because it stresses the "Rejection of Mimetic Poetry" (which proved a stumbling block to Cornford) as an essential section of the Epilogue.

The construction of the schema, thus, is itself part of the interpretation. Nevertheless, it organizes the problems which Plato treats in the *Republic* only in a rough approximation. One cannot use the schema as a table of contents and let the analysis relate what Plato has to say on each of the topics in the main parts, in Introduction and Conclusion, in Prologue and Epilogue. The last reflections on Hildebrandt's well-chosen title for the Judgment of the Dead indicate the nature of the difficulty. The title is apt because it connects Plato's myth with his rejection of mimetic poetry. The myth of the Judgment of the Dead will be appropriately treated, therefore, in a discussion of poetic forms, of the connection between experiences and their form of expression in art, and of the necessity of abandoning old forms, and creating new ones, when the experiences to be expressed have changed. At the same time, however, the Judgment of the Dead is a descent into the underworld balancing the descent into the Piraeus; and the analysis must explore the symbolism of the descent. Under still another aspect the Judgment of the Dead contains a mythical description of Necessity throning at the center of the cosmos. The myth of cosmic order completes the study of right order in the individual psyche of the philosopher, as well as in the polis of the idea. The order of man and society is part of the embracing cosmic order. The great problems of Plato, thus, are not blocks of meaning locked up in the subdivisions of the schema, but are lines of meaning winding their intricate way through the whole work. Moreover, in some cases the schema is just articulate enough to point to a problem which does not appear in the organization of the work at all. The Prologue, for instance, has sections on the justice of the "Older" and the "Middle Generation," followed by a section called the "Justice of the Sophist." One wonders what has become of the younger generation. As a matter of fact, the younger generation is not lost, but, represented by Glaukon and Adeimantus, carries the dialogue in community with Socrates. The *Republic* gains its specific meaning in the historical situation of Athens from the fact that there is a younger generation in search for the right order which it cannot find in the surrounding society.

In the following analysis we shall, therefore, not relate the contents of the dialogue in the order of the schema but rather trace the dominant problems through the work, following the order of their appearance in the chain of motivating experiences. We shall begin at the beginning, with the descent of Socrates to the Piraeus.

§ 2. The Way Up and the Way Down

The *Republic* is cast in the form of an account, given by Socrates to a group of friends, of a discussion which he had had the day before in the house of Polemarchus in the Piraeus. Socrates begins his account with a description of the occasion:

> I went down, yesterday, to the Piraeus, with Glaukon the son of Ariston, to offer my prayers to the goddess, and also wanting to see the festival, in what manner they would arrange it, since it was conducted for the first time.
> The procession of the citizens, I thought, was splendid; but no less worthy appeared the one arranged by the Thracians.
> Prayed we had and watched; and then we turned back to the town.

When turning back, however, they are seen by Polemarchus and his friends who also have been at the procession. Socrates gives way to Polemarchus' urgent invitation. They all proceed to the house, there to have dinner; and, afterwards, they will watch the torch race of the Thracian horsemen and the night festival. At the house there are assembled, besides Socrates and Polemarchus, the two brothers of the host, the orator Lysias, and Euthydemus; the Chalcedonian sophist Thrasymachus; two minor figures, Charmantides and Cleitophon; Glaukon and Adeimantus, the two elder brothers of Plato; and, finally, the host's father Cephalus. The opening conversation between Socrates and the old Cephalus leads toward questions of a just life, and the dialogue proper is on its way.

The first chapter of the *Republic* sets the dialogue into motion. Its opening passage, just quoted, assembles symbols that recur in its course. And the first word, *kateben* (I went down), sounds the great theme that runs through it to its end.

Socrates walked down the five miles from the town to the harbor. Down went the way from Athens to the sea in space; and down went her way from Marathon to the disaster of the sea power in time. Socrates was a man of his people and participated in its fate. With the people, streaming down on the festive occasion, he went to the Piraeus with its mixed population of citizens and foreigners. For, with the unfolding of Athenian sea power under Pericles, the Piraeus had grown through the influx of foreign traders and workers. The Thracian businessmen, seamen, and harbor workers had brought with them their cult of Bendis. It had been recognized by Athens as a public cult, at least since 429/8, and found adherents among the citizens. Cult fraternities of Thracians and citizens had formed and now they had organized a great public festival in honor of Bendis with rival processions.[4] Socrates went along to watch the spectacle; and, while he found the effort of his co-citizens excellent, the foreigners proved their equals in putting up a dignified public appearance. Athens and Thrace had found their common level in the Piraeus. As a citizen, with due respect for recognized cults, he offered his prayers to the foreign goddess who had come to the polis over the sea—but then he wanted to go back to Athens. At that point, however, he was detained. He had gone down, and now the depth held him as one of them, friendly, to be sure, but with a playful threat of force by superior numbers, and a refusal to listen to his persuasion to let him go (327c). In the depth that held him he embarked on his inquiry; and he used his persuasive powers on his friends, not to let him free to go back to Athens, but to make them follow him to the polis of the Idea. From the depth of the Piraeus the way went, not back to the Athens of Marathon, but forward and upward to the polis built by Socrates with his friends in their souls.

The *kateben* opens the vista into the symbolism of depth and descent. It recalls the Heraclitian depth of the soul that cannot be measured by any wandering, as well as the Aeschylean dramatic descent that brings up the decision for Dike. But above all it recalls the Homer who lets his Odysseus tell Penelope of the day when "I went down [*kateben*] to Hades to inquire about the return of myself and my friends" (*Od.* 23. 252–3), and there learned of the measureless toil that still was in store for him and had to be fulfilled to the end (23.249–50).

All of the associations have their function in the *Republic*, as we shall

---

[4] On the cult of Bendis, as well as its introduction to Athens and the lavish state support in the fourth century, see Martin P. Nilsson, *Geschichte der Griechischen Religion*, I (Munich, 1941), 784f.; also the article "Bendis" in Pauly-Wissowa. A probable date for the inauguration of the public festival which the Socrates of the dialogue attended is *c.*411 B.C.

see, but the Homeric *kateben* is the one more immediately intended in the construction of the Prologue. For the Piraeus, to which Socrates descends, is a symbol of Hades. The goddess whom he approaches with prayer is the Artemis-Bendis, understood by the Athenians as the chthonian Hecate who attends to the souls on their way to the underworld.[5] And the immediately following scene confirms and clarifies the meaning of the symbol in so far as the old Cephalus is moved to his reflections on justice by his impending descent to Hades. For "there," as the tales (*mythoi*) go, men must pay what is right in compensation for the wrong they have done "here" (330d–e). To be sure, the interest of Cephalus in justice, while sincere, is not less shallow than his motivation by tales about punishment in Hades; and the old man, when the debate becomes more strenuous, retires to sacrifice and sleep. Nevertheless the little scene illuminates the profounder concern of Socrates, as well as the function of the Piraeus as the Hades that motivates his inquiry into the nature of justice and right order.

The descent of Socrates to Hades-Piraeus in the opening scene of the Prologue balances the descent of Er, the son of Armenius the Pamphylian, to the underworld in the closing scene of the Epilogue. Moreover, Plato underlines the parallel between the underworlds of Socrates and Er by a play with symbols. For the festival of the Piraeus in honor of Bendis is characterized by the equality of the participants. Socrates can find no difference in the quality of the processions; a common level of humanity has been reached by the society of which Socrates is a member. In Hades, in death, again all men are equal before their judge, and Er, the teller of the tale, is a Pamphylian, a man "of all tribes," an Everyman. In the organization of the dialogue the symbolic byplay on the pamphylism of both the Piraeus and Hades, thus, confirms and strengthens the parallel. At the same time, however, it leads back to the great issue that sets the dialogue moving. For it is the pamphylism of the Piraeus that makes it Hades. The equality of the harbor is the death of Athens; and at least an attempt must be made to find the way up to life.

The Descent formulates a problem and the Judgment provides a resolution. In the Descent the human condition appears as existence in Hades, and the question arises: Must man remain in the underworld, or has he the power to ascend from death to life? In the Judgment Plato

---

[5] K. Kerenyi in C. G. Jung and K. Kerenyi, *Einfuehrung in das Wesen der Mythologie* (Zurich, 1951), 164, and *passim* in the study on "Das Goettliche Maedchen."

expresses his conviction of the reality of the power and describes its
modus operandi.[6] The Pamphylian myth tells of the dead souls who in
afterlife receive reward or punishment according to their conduct in
life. The bad souls will go to their suffering below the earth, the good
souls to their blessed existence in heaven. After a thousand years they
come up, or down, from their abode to the seat of Lachesis at the center
of the cosmos, there to draw their lot and to choose their fate for the
next period of life. When they are assembled, the Herald of Lachesis
steps up to a platform and announces to them the rules governing the
proceedings (617d–e):

> Ananke's daughter, the maiden Lachesis, her word:
> Souls of a day! Beginning of a new cycle, for the mortal race, to end
> in death!
> The daemon will not be allotted to you; but you shall select the
> daemon.
> The first by the lot, shall the first select the life to which he will
> be bound by necessity [Ananke].
> Arete has no master; and as a man honors or dishonors her, he will
> have her increased or diminished.
> The guilt [*aitia*] is the chooser's; God is guiltless [*anaitios*].

The cosmic law is terse, but its meaning is clear. Plato restates the
problem of freedom and guilt, with slight variations of Homeric and
Heraclitian symbols. With Homer he shares the aetiological concern.
More radically than the poet he declares God, the one God, to be guiltless (*anaitios*). Divine substance has found its symbol, in the *Republic*,
in the idea of the Agathon. And the Good can cause only good, not evil.
The position is an impoverishment of the problem of theodicy, compared with Homer and Aeschylus who both recognized evil that was
caused neither by the gods of right order nor by man. And, let us hasten
to say, it is not Plato's last word in the matter either, as we shall see in
the analysis of the *Statesman* and the *Laws*. Still, in the *Republic* he
insists uncompromisingly that the souls lead the lives they have chosen
for themselves. Recalling the Heraclitian B 119: "Character—to man—
daemon," Plato declares the daemon, to whom man is bound in life by
necessity, the result of his free choice. For the Arete of the soul has no
master; and when man bewails the consequences of his contempt for
Arete, he has nobody to blame but himself.

---

[6] In the present context we are dealing with only one of the several problems of the
Pamphylian myth.

The choice is free. And man has to bear the responsibility for the daemonic necessity of his life. But the choice cannot be wiser or better than the character which makes it. The aetiological speculation on the sources of good and evil has radically eliminated the gods, but the dialectics of freedom and necessity falls now with its full weight on man and his character. Man's choice of his daemon in the other world is guided by the character he has acquired during his preceding life in this world. And the souls in Hades make odd choices. Those who formerly have led a dubious life, and as a consequence not only have suffered punishment themselves but also seen the suffering of others, generally are cautious. Those who previously have lived a good life in a well-ordered polis, and participated in Arete from habit rather than from love of wisdom (*philosophia*), are apt to make foolish choices. They will jump, for instance, at a glittering tyranny and discover too late the evil of the soul in it (619b–620d). This is the great danger in the terrible hour of choice. And in order to reduce, if not to avert, the danger, man in this life should concentrate all his effort on one thing: To find the man who will enable him to distinguish between a worthy and an unworthy life, so that he can make a reasonable choice, with his eyes fixed on the nature of the soul, not diverted by the circumstances and events, pleasant or unpleasant, of a life. He will be able to make the right choice when he can recognize as bad, a manner of life that pulls the soul down and makes it more unjust, and as good, a manner of life that leads the soul upward toward a higher state of justice. When a man goes down to Hades, he must carry with him an adamantine conviction (*doxa*) that the quality of a life must be judged by its suitability to develop the Arete of justice in the soul (618b–619a).

The souls of the dead choose a life, and with the life the daemon that of necessity goes with it. Into their choice they can put no more wisdom than they have acquired. And on that occasion is revealed, as we have seen, the value of certain types of life. Those who have suffered punishment for the evil they have done, and have gained wisdom through suffering (in the Aeschylean sense), are likely to make a better choice than others who have led a righteous life and were rewarded with heavenly bliss. The relation between Arete and the course of a life is complicated. In the dialogue Socrates must face certain blameless characters who will arouse sympathy. There is old Cephalus who furnishes an instance of the man who leads a reasonably righteous life and is willing to compensate for the minor offenses he committed by means of his wealth. He represents the "older generation" in a time of crisis, the men who still impress by their character and conduct that has been formed in a better age. The force of tradition and habit keeps them on the narrow path, but they are not righteous by "love of wisdom," and in a crisis they have nothing to offer to the younger generation which is already exposed to more corruptive influences. The venerable elder who arouses our sympathy will not lose it on closer inspection, but the sympathy will be tempered by a touch of condescension, if not contempt, for his weakness. For the men of his type are the cause of the sudden vacuum that appears in a critical period with the break of generations. All of a sudden it appears that the older generation has neglected to build the substance of order in the younger men, and an amiable lukewarmness and confusion shifts within a few years into the horrors of social catastrophe. In the next generation, with Polemarchus, the understanding of justice is already reduced to a businessman's honesty. And it comes almost as a relief when in the sophist Thrasymachus there appears a real man who pleads the cause of injustice with luciferic passion. He at least is articulate, he argues and one can argue with him, and Socrates can come to grips with a problem that remains evasive when represented by respectability and venerable tradition without substance. A pattern, a paradigm of life, thus, is not easy to choose, for the conventional standards of desirability do not apply to the divine substance of order in the soul, to the daemon. Hence, Plato does not offer recipes for moral conduct; and with regard to a right paradigm of life he does not go beyond a hint that in such matters the mean (*to meson*) is preferable (619a). The point must receive some emphasis because it will recur in the interpretation of Plato's construction of a right order for the polis, which all too frequently is misunderstood as a recipe for a good constitution.

The souls choose their daemon in Hades, at the point of death, between a past life that has slipped from them and a future life on which they have yet to decide. In the language of the myth Plato has expressed the existential situation of every man at the dead point of decision between his past and his future, that is, the situation of his present in which mysteriously wells up the freedom of Arete. And Plato himself explains the meaning of the mythical imagery when he interrupts the tale of the choice in order to point the lesson (618b–619a). The freedom of the present is not of much use unless the Arete of wisdom has been honored so that a right decision can be made, honoring it still more in the future. And such wisdom has not much chance to grow without lively concern about it. In the loneliness of its death between the past and the future, a soul is apt to discover that its previous life has not equipped it with the wisdom to choose rightly the paradigm of the next one. When the choice is made the soul will bewail it and will put the blame for its woes "on fortune, the daemons, and everything else, except itself" (619b). And from such misery in the depth of a freedom empty of substance will grow the insight that the first step on the way up must be the search for a helper. From the Hades of the myth we are transposed back to the Hades of the Piraeus with its equality of the lonely souls and their freedom without substance. Socrates is the man who can help the others, who will enable them to diagnose the right and wrong paradigms of life, who will build up in them wisdom and, thus, add substance to the Arete of which they have only the freedom.

When the helper is recognized, the freedom of existence without substantive order is overcome through the free community with Socrates. But at the same time the equality of the dead souls in Hades is abolished. The new community has substance because it has its hierarchical center in Socrates. The order of Socrates supersedes the egalitarian order of the Piraeus. Socrates wanted to go back to Athens but he gave way to the friendly urging of the majority of equals. It was agreed that they should have dinner at the house of Polemarchus and then join the crowd for the sights. But the community that has drawn Socrates in its midst is never to see the torch race of the Thracians or the night festival. Once the "snake charmer" (357b) has drawn them into the ban of his discourse, they have risen from the realm of the dead and live in the presence of his charm. At the end of the Prologue, the Bendideia are still mentioned, by Thrasymachus, who concludes his debate with Socrates formally by complimenting him on his entertainment, now completed, at the festival of Bendis (354a). But the others will not give up, and the discussion continues with Thrasymachus present to the end. It is a long and difficult discussion, reminding one of the Odyssean "measureless toil." When the polis of the Idea has been built (at the end of Book IV) Socrates wants to bring it to a conclusion by passing on to the bad forms of government. But again the friends will not let off. They insist that he explain his hints about the position of women and the institution of marriage, and even Thrasymachus (here speaking for the last time) energetically pleads for continuation. To Socrates' admonition that listen-ing to discourse should have a measure, Glaukon gives the final answer: "The measure of listening to discourses of this kind is the whole life for wise men" (450b). The charm of Socratic discourse is the resurrection of the soul from death to life with the savior.

The theme is elaborated by Socrates in the concluding passage of the *Republic* (621b–d). When the myth of the Pamphylian, who brought it up from Hades, is told, Socrates reflects that the myth was saved and not forgotten. "And it will save us, if we let ourselves be persuaded by it." And then Plato gently changes the Socrates who told the myth of Er, into the Er who could tell it because he went down to Hades, by substituting Socrates for the "it" in the just quoted sentence. "If we let ourselves be persuaded by me," we shall believe the soul to be immortal and capable to endure whatever befalls by the way of evil or good. For-ever holding to the "upward way," we shall pursue justice (*dikaiosyne*) and wisdom (*phronesis*), that we may be friends to ourselves and the gods in this world and the next. And thus both here and in that journey of a thousand years "we shall fare well" (*eu prattomen*).

Socrates is the savior because he is the philosopher who has travelled the way up from the night of Hades to the light of Truth. This Parmeni-dean component in Plato's work dominates the center of the *Republic* in the Parable of the Cave with its ascent to the vision of the Agathon. We shall deal with it in the later course of this chapter. In the present context, we must only mention the symbolism that links the ascent to the Idea with the descent to Hades in Prologue and Epilogue. When Plato, by means of the Parable, has clarified the nature of the philoso-pher, of his truth and his ordering function in a community, the practical question arises how such men can be produced: "How can they be led upward to the light, as some men are fabled to have ascended from Hades to the gods?" (521c). Having established the symbolic relation with the Hades to which the philosopher must descend before he can ascend to the light, Plato speaks of the *epanodos,* the ascent of the soul from the day that is night (*nykterine*) to the true (*alethine*) day, and uses the term almost technically as a definition of "true philosophy" (521c). And then, when the technical meaning of *epanodos* is established, he leads it back to the myth of the Cave and speaks of the "*epanodos* from the subterranean cavern [*katageios*] to the sun" (532b). The play of the symbols illuminates the relations between the episodes and problems of the *Republic:* The Piraeus of the Prologue becomes the Hades of the Epilogue, and they both blend into the subterranean Cave of the parable. The empty freedom of the Piraeus, with its celebration of the chthonian divinity, becomes the empty freedom of Arete in Hades, and they both blend into the play of the shadows in the Cave. The night festival (*pannychis*) blends into the night of Hades, and both into the nightly (*nykterine*) day of human existence in the central part of the *Republic.* And the Socrates, finally, who engages his friends in the discourse on justice, blends into the Er, who is sent back by the Judges from Hades as the "messenger [*angelos*] to mankind" (614d), and both blend into the philosopher, who must return from the vision of the Agathon to help his fellow prisoners.

When we follow the play of the symbols, as we have just done, we become aware of a problem that arises from the construction of the *Republic,* but is not elaborated in the dialogue itself. The construction clearly places the *epanodos* to the light in the center of the work, and balances it symmetrically by the descents to the Piraeus and Hades. That in itself would reveal no more than the skill of Plato the artist. It is disquieting, however, that the truth of human existence can be found *both* by descent and by ascent. The truth brought up from the Piraeus by Socrates in his discourse, and the truth brought up from Hades by the messenger Er, are the same truth that is brought down by the philosopher who has seen the Agathon. We are reminded of the Heraclitian paradox (B 60): "The way up and the way down is one and the same." Moreover, the sameness of the up and the down is stressed by Plato through his use of the word *ekei* (there). Beyond its basic meaning as an adverb of space, it could be used euphemistically when referring to the underworld and the dead. In that sense Cephalus uses it, when he reflects that "there" one has to pay for what one has done "here" (330d); the messenger Er, furthermore, was sent from "there" to tell mankind what he had seen (614d); and in the context of the Cave, finally, Plato speaks of the "dwellers there" (520c), using the same phrase as in 427b when he refers to the dwellers in Hades. But then he speaks of the divine paradigm of order which the philosopher has seen "there" and is now supposed to stamp on society (500d–e). The identification of the upper with the nether There as the source of Truth raises formidable questions with regard to the ontological status of a pattern that is laid up in heaven, but also can be found through descent to the depth. In the *Republic,* as previously said, such questions are neither articulated nor answered. But they become the central problem for Plato in the *Timaeus*.

While the problem does not become topical, the experience from which it arises is present in the *Republic*. From the symbols that organize the dialogue as a work of art we must now descend to the experience that motivates the symbols:

(1) The subject of the experience is not any of the dramatis personae, but Plato himself. The myth told by Er is retold by Socrates in a dialogue written by Plato. The messenger from Hades is absorbed by Socrates the savior, and the savior Socrates by the philosopher-poet who created the dialogue. The message from Hades to mankind is transformed into the concrete Socratic discourse with the friends, and the discourse with its contracted audience is transformed, and expanded again, into the message for mankind through the *Republic*.

(2) The Platonic experience itself is circumscribed by the symbols and their transformations. Plato descends to the Piraeus with Socrates as everybody does, to the Hades with Er as every man, and he is chained in the Cave as are his fellow prisoners. But not everybody is held by the depth. The Socrates of the Prologue subtly breaks the friendly bonds, and those who wanted to hold him are drawn into the charmed life of his discourse. One of the prisoners in the Cave is forced to turn around and is dragged up to the light. And the Er of the Epilogue is sent back by the Judges as the messenger to mankind.

(3) Hence, there is the Plato who resists the spirtual death and disorder of Athens, symbolized by the Piraeus, and brings to life the new order of the soul—and we may ask: From where comes that new life and its strength of resistance to death? Then there is the Plato who is forced and dragged up to the light—and we may ask: What power forces and drags him? And, finally, there is the Plato who is sent by the Judges as the messenger to mankind—and we may ask: Who are the Judges who send him?

The multiplicity of symbols, casting their light now on this, now on that facet of the experience, suggests a richness not exhausted by the dialogue, as well as a dimension in depth that cannot be measured at all. The Platonic are intimately related with Heraclitian and Aeschylean symbols, because they express the same experience of the soul, of its depth and its forces, of its life and resistance to death, with an intensity and clarity that is Plato's own. And this experience of the psyche motivates the directional ambivalence of the symbols. From the depth of the psyche wells up life and order when historically, in the surrounding society, the souls have sunk into the depth of death and disorder. From the depth comes the force that drags the philosopher's soul up to the light, so that it is difficult to say whether the upper There is the source of his truth, or the nether There that forced him up. And the philosopher descending from the mouth of the Cave brings the same message as Er ascending from Hades: The apparently hopeless situation of the soul at the point of its death—that it has the freedom of Arete but not the wisdom to use it— is not hopeless; forces of life are there to help. But the source of the help is hidden; we can only say it is There.

There is more to be said about the Platonic experience of the psyche. But that much will be sufficient at the present stage of the analysis. And it will be sufficient, in particular, to warn us to read into Plato neither a mystical union with God, nor any other neo-Platonic or Christian developments. Plato's philosophizing remains bound by the compactness of the Dionysiac soul.

§ 3. The Resistance to Corrupt Society

In the depth the soul experiences its death; from the depth it will rise to life again, with the help of God and his messenger. The depth of existence, the anxiety of the fall from being, is the Hades where the soul must turn toward life or death. It is a terrible hour of decision, for in the night where life and death are confronted they are difficult to distinguish. Arete is free, but wisdom is weak. In its freedom the soul resists death. But the forces of existence, past and present, are strong as well as deceptive; persuasively they pull the soul to accept their death as life. In its freedom the soul is willing to follow the helper. But in order to follow his guidance, it must recognize him as the guide toward life; and life looks strangely like death when it drags the soul up to die to the depth in which it lives. Nevertheless, the struggle itself becomes a source of knowledge. In suffering and resisting the soul discerns the directions from which the pulls come. The darkness engenders the light in which it can distinguish between life and death, between the helper and the enemy. And the growing light of wisdom illuminates the way for the soul to travel.

Plato was supremely conscious of the struggle and its polarity. Philosophy is not a doctrine of right order, but the light of wisdom that falls on the struggle; and help is not a piece of information about truth, but the arduous effort to locate the forces of evil and identify their nature. For half the battle is won when the soul can recognize the shape of the enemy and, consequently, knows that the way it must follow leads in the opposite direction. Plato operates in the *Republic*, therefore, with pairs of concepts which point the way by casting their light on both good and evil. His philosopher does not exist in a social vacuum, but in opposition to the sophist. Justice is not defined in the abstract but in opposition to the concrete forms which injustice assumes. The right order of the polis is not presented as an "ideal state," but the elements of right order are developed in concrete opposition to the elements of disorder in the surrounding society. And the shape, the Eidos, of Arete in the soul grows in opposition to the many *eide* of disorder in the soul.

In developing such pairs of concepts, which illuminate truth by opposing it to untruth, Plato continues the tradition of the mystic-philosophers, as well as the poets back to Hesiod, who experienced truth in their resistance to the conventions of society. His continuation, however, must be to a certain extent a restoration under the new aggravated conditions. For between the age of Xenophanes, Parmenides, and Heraclitus and the age of Plato lies the century of sophistic destruction. His pairs of concepts carry, therefore, the burden of a complicated historical situation. In Plato's immediate environment the sophist is the enemy and the philosopher rises in opposition to him; in the wider range of Hellenic history, the philosopher comes first and the sophist follows him as the destroyer of his work through immanentization of the symbols of transcendence. The Platonic pairs of concepts, therefore, hearken back to the mystic-philosophers, and at the same have a new weight and precision in order to match the weight and precision that untruth has gained through the sophists. The component of resistance in Plato's work, as well as its expression by the pairs of concepts, thus, is somewhat complex. In order to present its various aspects adequately, we shall analyze first the principal pairs, with due regard to their historical affinities; then, Plato's description of the sophistic idea of justice, that is, of the enemy from which the further dialogue must move away.

1. *The Pairs of Concepts*

A first pair of concepts is concerned with the nature of justice and injustice.

Justice and injustice are in the soul what health and disease are in the body (444c). Health is defined as the establishment of an order by nature among the parts of the body; disease as a disturbance of the natural order of rule and subordination among the parts (444d). The establishment of an order by nature in the soul in such a manner that, of the various parts of the soul, each fulfills its own function and does not interfere with the function of the other parts, is called justice (*dikaiosyne*) (444d). And more generally: "Arete is health, beauty, and well-being of the soul; vice [*kakia*] its disease, ugliness, and infirmity" (444d–e).

Since the concept of justice is developed for the purpose of criticizing the sophistic disorder, its meaning must be understood in relation to its opposite. For the designation of sophistic disorder Plato uses the term *polypragmosyne,* the readiness to engage in multifarious activities which are not a man's proper business; and on occasion he uses the terms *metabole* (change or shift of occupation) and *allotriopragmosyne* (meddlesomeness, officious interference) (434b–c; 444b). "One man cannot practice with success many arts" (374a)—that is the principle on which the participants of the dialogue have agreed. *Polypragmosyne* covers the various violations of the principle, such as the attempts to practice more than the one craft for which a man is specifically gifted, as well as the desire of the unskilled to rule the polis to its detriment. When applied to the soul it refers to the inclination of appetites and desires to direct the course of human action and to claim the rulership of the soul which properly belongs to wisdom. *Dikaiosyne,* on the other hand, covers right order on all levels in opposition to *polypragmosyne*—with the qualification, however, that Plato is inclined to narrow the meaning of justice to the right order of the soul and the polis, while the division of labor on the level of crafts is only a figuration of justice proper, a "shadow of justice" (*eidolon tes dikaiosynes*) (443c–d).

If we survey the range of meaning of the two concepts, as well as their experiential motivation, we can recognize their affinity to the Heraclitian opposition of *polymathie* and true understanding. The "much-knowing" of Heraclitus has become the "much-doing" of Plato. The disorder that manifested itself in the generation of Heraclitus in the obfuscation of wisdom through far-flung superficial knowledge has now reached the level of action through dilettantic meddlesomeness. Moreover, we can now catch the full flavor of the previously discussed Hippias anecdote as the symbolization of the sophist who both knows and does too much, whose polypragmatic omniversality expresses the sink-

ing of a society into disorder and injustice. And, finally, in this context
we must mention the Democritus Fragment B 80: "Shameful it is to
meddle [*polypragmoneonta*] with others' business, and not to know
one's own [*oikeia*]." The *oikeopragia* (minding one's own affairs) of
434c, as well as other passages of the *Republic*, especially 433e, strongly
recall the Democritian dictum.

The analysis of the first pair of concepts reveals a peculiar obstacle
to the adequate interpretation of Plato's intention in English, or in any
other modern language. The difficulty will not only recur in the analysis
of further pairs, but is of general interest for the history of philosophical
language in Western civilization. Plato created his pairs in his resistance
to the corrupt society that surrounded him. Both members of the pair
acquired technical meaning in the course of the dialogue. From the concrete struggle against the surrounding corruption, however, Plato
emerged as the victor with world-historic effectiveness. As a consequence,
the positive half of his pairs has become the "philosophical language" of
Western civilization, while the negative half has lost its status as technical vocabulary. We can translate Plato's *dikaiosyne* as justice, but we
have no technical term to translate his *polypragmosyne* as the opposite
of justice. The loss of the negative half of the pair has deprived the
positive half of its flavor of resistance and opposition, and left it with
a quality of abstractness which is utterly alien to the concreteness of
Plato's thought. We cannot recapture that militant concreteness of
dikaiosyne which made it possible for Plato to use *oikeopragia* (another
untranslatable term) as a synonym. The negative members of the pairs
generally are lost; the only one that has survived is the term "sophist"
itself.

The loss makes itself felt in the most embarrassing manner in the
second pair that we now have to consider, *philosophos* and *philodoxos*.
We have philosophers in English, but no philodoxers. The loss is in this
instance peculiarly embarrassing, because we have an abundance of philodoxers in reality; and since the Platonic term for their designation is lost,
we refer to them as philosophers. In modern usage, thus, we call philosophers precisely the persons to whom Plato as a philosopher was in
opposition. And an understanding of Plato's positive half of the pair
is today practically impossible, except by a few experts, because we think
of philodoxers when we speak of philosophers. The Platonic conception

of a philosopher-king, furthermore, is so utterly strange to us because our imagination substitutes a philodoxer for the philosopher intended by Plato. We must remain aware of this predicament as we now approach the second pair (480).

Socrates demands that in a healthy society the philosophers should be rulers. The demand makes it necessary to explain what a philosopher is, for obviously he does not mean some of the persons who even in the Athens of his time were referred to by the term. Socrates hastens to assure his partners in the dialogue that he means the true (*alethinos*) philosopher; and the true philosopher is the man who loves to look with admiration (*philotheamones*) at the truth. The truth of things, however, is that which they are in themselves (*auto*). Some men can see beauty only as it appears in the many beautiful things, but are unable to see beauty "in itself." Those who are able to see the "one" in the "many" things are the true philosophers, to be distinguished as such from the connoisseurs, the art lovers, and practical men. And what has been said for the case of "beauty" is also valid for the "just" and the "unjust," the "good" and the "evil" (475e–476b).

After the initial clarifications Socrates introduces the technical terms. Only the knowledge of being "in itself" can truly lay claim to the title of knowledge (*episteme*); the knowledge of being in the manifold of things is opinion (*doxa*). The object of knowledge (*episteme*), thus, is identified by the Parmenidean term being (*to on*). What, however, is the object of opining? It cannot be not-being (*to me on*), for of not-being (still following Parmenides) we have no knowledge at all. Hence, Doxa is a faculty (*dynamis*) of the soul in between knowledge and ignorance, while its object correspondingly must be a realm between (*metaxy*) being and not-being. For this intermediate realm Plato coins the term *to planeton*, that which is wandering or erring between being and not-being [7] (479d).

Plato's *modus procedendi* is fascinating for the philosopher because here he can observe the continuity in which the Parmenidean symbol Being is made to absorb all being "in itself" at which we arrive by advancing from the "many" things to the "one" reality that appears in a whole class (*genos*). In so far as Plato uses for the being "in itself" the

---

[7] I suspect that Plato in forming the series *on, me on, planeton* was punning. Following this intention one would have to interpret the *planeton* as a "being" that is in wandering or erring motion between true being and not-being.

term "idea," the Parmenidean Being is made to embrace the realm of
ideas, while his world of illusion (*doxa*) becomes the realm of the many
things in which the ideas are incarnate. Moreover, Plato does not neglect
the opportunity to draw other symbols of the mystic-philosophers into
his exposition. The Heraclitian sleepwalkers, for instance, appear in the
question whether men who have no sense of being "in itself" be not like
"dreamers, waking or sleeping" in so far as they put images in place of
reality (476c). And, finally, when he speaks of the *philodoxos* as the
man who cannot bear the idea that "the beautiful, or the just, or any
other thing, is one" (479a), we remember the Xenophantic "the One
is the God." "The one" (*hen*) now becomes the subject of which not
only "god" can be predicated but also the "just" and the "beautiful."
Step by step we can follow the process in which the Ionian "one," the
Parmenidean "being" and the Xenophantic "god" merge into the Platonic being of the ideas.

A third pair of concepts moves in the tradition of Xenophanes. It
is the pair of *aletheia* (truth) and *pseudos* (falsehood or lie). The pair
refers to true and false, or proper and improper, presentation of the
gods. We can be brief on the problem because the essentials of the Platonic position have been discussed already on the occasion of Xenophanes' notion of "seemliness." [8]

The pair of concepts has a long history. It was developed for the
first time by Hesiod when he opposed his true history of the gods to
current false stories. Xenophanes, then, sharpened the issue to the criteria of "seemliness" in the symbolization of gods, and rejected anthropomorphic symbols. Moreover, the motivating experience became clear,
that is, the discovery of a universal humanity which can be recognized
as such only in relation to a universal transcendental realissimum. The
one, unseen, greatest god, who is the same for all men, is correlative with
a sameness of men that is now found in the sameness of their transcendental experiences. Plato, finally, introduced the "types of theology" as the conceptual instrument for clarifying the issue.

True humanity requires true theology; the man with false theology is
an untrue man. "To be deceived or uninformed in the soul about true
being [*peri ta onta*]" means that "the lie itself" [*hos alethos pseudos*]
has taken possession of "the highest part of himself" and steeped it into

[8] *Order and History* II, Ch. 6, 2, 1.

"ignorance of the soul" (382a–b). With regard to the content of "true" theology Plato singles out two rules as the most important ones: (1) God is not the author of all things but only of the good ones (380c), and (2) the gods do not deceive men in word or deed (383a). The rules of the true type are critically pointed against a complex of falsehood that is promulgated not only by Homer and Hesiod (the targets of Xenophanes), but also by the tragic poets and the sophists. We remember that in the *Protagoras* Plato made the great sophist insist on the poets, hierophants, and prophets as the precursors of his art. The poets are pooled with the sophists as the source of disorder in the soul and society. If order is to be restored, the restoration must begin at the strategic point of the "ignorance of the soul" by setting aright the relation between man and God. This is the problem which dominates the *Republic* as a whole, and it dominates in particular the social critique. The attack on the corrupt society is not directed against this or that political abuse but against a disease of the soul. In so far as the presentation of the gods by the poets disturbs the right order of the soul, the poets must be condemned along with the sophists. The restoration requires a turning-around (*periagoge*) of "the whole soul" (518d–e): from ignorance to the truth of God, from opinion about uncertainly wavering things to knowledge of being, and from multifarious activity to the justice of tending to one's proper sphere of action.

We have arranged the pairs of concepts on a line that leads from the praxeological periphery of minding one's business, through the philosopher's ability to discern being "itself" in the manifold of appearance, to the center of the soul where its truth originates in the truth of God. The pairs must be understood in their aggregate as the expression of a man's resistance to a social corruption which goes so deep that it affects the truth of existence under God. Philosophy, thus, has its origin in the resistance of the soul to its destruction by society. Philosophy in this sense, as an act of resistance illuminated by conceptual understanding, has two functions for Plato. It is first, and most importantly, an act of salvation for himself and others, in that the evocation of right order and its reconstitution in his own soul becomes the substantive center of a new community which, by its existence, relieves the pressure of the surrounding corrupt society. Under this aspect Plato is the founder of the community of philosophers that lives through the ages. Philosophy is, second, an act of judgment—we remember the messenger to mankind sent from Hades by the Judges. Since the order of the soul is recaptured through resistance to the surrounding disorder, the pairs of concepts which illuminate the act of resistance develop into the criteria (in the pregnant sense of instruments or standards of judgment) of social order and disorder. Under this second aspect Plato is the founder of political science.

The various functions, as well as the problems which they imply, are held together by Plato at the point of their origin in the experience of resistance through a comprehensive pair of concepts, the pair of "philosopher" and "sophist." The philosopher is compactly the man who resists the sophist; the man who attempts to develop right order in his soul through resistance to the diseased soul of the sophist; the man who can evoke a paradigm of right social order in the image of his well-ordered soul, in opposition to the disorder of society which reflects the disorder of the sophist's soul; the man who develops the conceptual instruments for the diagnosis of health and disease in the soul; the man who develops the criteria of right order, relying on the divine measure to which his soul is attuned; the man who, as a consequence, becomes the philosopher in the narrower sense of the thinker who advances propositions concerning right order in the soul and society, claiming for them the objectivity of *episteme*, of science—a claim that is bitterly disputed by the sophist whose soul is attuned to the opinion of society.

The meaning of the term "philosopher" in its compact sense, at the point of its emergence from the act of resistance, must be well understood if one wants to understand Plato's science of order. For in the resistance of the philosopher to a society which destroys his soul originates the insight that the substance of society is psyche. Society can destroy a man's soul because the disorder of society is a disease in the psyche of its members. The troubles which the philosopher experiences in his own soul are the troubles in the psyche of the surrounding society which press on him. And the diagnosis of health and disease in the soul is, therefore, at the same time a diagnosis of order and disorder in society. On the level of conceptual symbols, Plato expresses his insight through the principle that society is man written in larger letters (368d–e). Justice is sometimes spoken of as the virtue of a single man, sometimes of a polis (368e). The *Republic,* though it begins as a dialogue on the just life of the individual, can become an inquiry into order and disorder in society, because the state of the individual psyche, in health or disease, expresses itself in the corresponding state of society. A polis is in order when it is ruled by men with well-ordered souls; it is in disorder when the souls of the rulers are disordered. "Must we not agree that in each of us there are the same forms [*eide*] and habits [*ethe*] as in the polis? And from nowhere else do they pass there?" (435e). Plato answers the questions in the affirmative: "The forms [or dispositions, *eide*] of men have as many varieties as the forms of government [*politeia*] . . . for the forms of government stem from the human habits [*ethe*] that are in them" (544d–e). Not only the good polis is man written large, but every polis writes large the type of man that is socially dominant in it.

We have traced the Platonic insight to the point where it results in a general proposition that can be detached from its motivating experience. The validity of the principle in its general form will occupy us in subsequent sections of this chapter. For the present we must return to the motivating experience, that is, to the opposition to the sophist. Two types of man and society, the philosophic and the sophistic, are opposed to each other. Plato's good polis is the philosopher written large, while the surrounding, corrupt society is "the greatest of all sophists" (492b). The implications of the insight, at the point where resistance is first illuminated by concepts, are all but lost in our modern interpretations of Plato's work. Today Plato has become a philosopher among others; and our modern term even includes the philodoxers to whom he was opposed. For Plato the philosopher is literally the man who loves wisdom, because wisdom puts substance into the freedom of his Arete and enables the soul to travel the road toward salvation. In the philosopher who resists the sophist lives a soul which resists the destruction of Arete. The philosopher is man in the anxiety of his fall from being; and philosophy is the ascent toward salvation for Everyman, as the pamphylic components of the myth suggest. Plato's philosophy, therefore, is not *a* philosophy but *the* symbolic form in which a Dionysiac soul expresses its ascent to God. If Plato's evocation of a paradigm of right order is interpreted as a philosopher's opinion about politics, the result will be hopeless nonsense, not worth a word of debate.

2. *The Sophistic Doxa of Justice*

The resistance depends for its success on a precise understanding of the enemy, and Plato indeed analyses the various aspects of sophistic corruption with care. Since the *Republic*, however, is the drama of resistance, the presentation of sophistic evil is interwoven in a subtle counterpoint with the Socratic act of resistance that culminates in the evocation of the paradigm of right order. The Prologue has its climax in the scene with Thrasymachus where a truculent sophist professes in no uncertain terms his conception of justice. The brashness of his manner, his indulgence in discourtesy, and even demands for money, are calculated to set off the gentle persuasiveness of the philosopher, his *peitho*. At the end of the scene he is tamed and becomes a well-mannered companion for the rest of the dialogue. The dramatic victory of persuasion over violence prefigures the reflections on the philosopher's *peitho* in *Republic* VI. Thrasymachus himself is preceded in the Prologue by Cephalus and Polemarchus, the older and middle generation of the corrupt society. We have previously suggested their function in the drama. They represent the generations which are still respectable in their form of life but cause by their emptiness of substance the vacuum in which dangerous figures like Thrasymachus can exert their influence unchallenged. The sequence of Cephalus, Polemarchus, and Thrasymachus dramatizes the aetiology of decline to the point where the crisis becomes articulate in the sophist who proclaims his disease as the measure of human and social order.

The views of Thrasymachus on justice can be summarized briefly. They are concentrated in the proposition that "the just is the interest of the stronger" (338c). The meaning of the proposition is illustrated by the various types of government which make laws according to the interest of the politically strongest group. The democracies make democratic laws, the tyrannies tyrannical laws, and so forth. Such laws, made in the interest of the ruler, are imposed on the subjects as "just," and whosoever transgresses them is considered "unjust" (338a–339a). Moreover, "the just and his justice are another man's good," whether it be in a partnership from which the unjust man will have the greater profit, or in the payment of income tax where the evader will profit at the expense of the honest taxpayer, or in the use of public office for private

profit. That the unjust is the happiest and the just the most miserable
man becomes especially obvious, however, in the case of tyranny, when
injustice is committed on a grand scale. For society finds terms of repro-
bation only when criminality is committed on a small scale. The great
political criminal is admired by everybody. Men dislike injustice only
because they are afraid of becoming its victims, not because they hesitate to commit it. Once more, therefore, "justice serves the interest of
the stronger, while injustice is a man's own profit and interest" (343b–
344c). As a consequence, the language of virtue and vice must be
abandoned as unsuitable to the problem. Neither is justice a virtue,
nor injustice a vice. The phenomena that go under these names would
be better characterized as "noble simplicity" and "well-counselled
shrewdness" respectively (348c–d).

The Thrasymachus scene concludes the Prologue, but the lines of
construction run on into the Introduction and Part I (of the schema).
The older and middle generations, who have caused the disaster by
their emptiness and weakness, are now followed by the younger generation, Glaukon and Adeimantus, the victims of the corrupt society. In
their role as the victims they draw a general picture of the pressure
which the surrounding society through its various agencies brings to
bear on their souls with such intensity that they can barely resist. In
the Thrasymachus scene the soul of the individual sophist becomes
articulate; the following scene with Glaukon and Adeimantus introduces the sophistic society in the massive impact of its existence. The
Introduction, thus, is carefully linked to the Prologue, in so far as the
sequence of the scenes dramatizes the principle that society is man
written large. The sophistic man is followed by his enlargement in the
sophistic society. Glaukon and Adeimantus, however, because they feel
themselves victims, are not accomplices. They are the young men who
feel the pressure of Thrasymachus and his ilk as destructive and, therefore, now turn to Socrates for enlightenment and help. They are healthy
enough not to believe what is hammered into them every day concerning justice. They are willing to resist. The discomfiture and silencing
of Thrasymachus has not satisfied them. Now they will spread before
Socrates for his inspection and refutation the whole body of opinion on
the topic of justice held by the multitude and dinned into their ears.
They are the men who in the depth recognize in Socrates the savior.

And it is not too venturesome to suggest that in the persons of his two brothers Plato represented himself as the young man who found the much-needed help of Socrates. By virtue of their role as the victims who resist the pressure of evil, the scene of the two young men furnishes the dramatic link between the old society of Cephalus, Polemarchus, and Thrasymachus, which the younger men are willing to leave, and the new order, evoked by Socrates in Part I of the *Republic*, which they are willing to enter with their helper. Moreover, the opinions, the *doxai* about justice, which the young men are going to present, will be followed by the Socratic *episteme* of justice. The dramatic sequence of doxa and episteme in the act of resistance, thus, prepares the later technical discussion of the "philosophical terms."

The opinions, the *doxai*, concerning justice and injustice can be classified either according to their content or according to their source. In the presentation of *doxai* by Glaukon and Adeimantus the two principles of classification interpenetrate, but they must be distinguished because in the construction of the dialogue as a drama they have different functions:

(1) According to their content three principal opinions can be distinguished, which Glaukon proposes to present: (a) The common view concerning nature and origin of justice; (b) the opinion that men who practice justice do so reluctantly, and by necessity, not because justice is a good; and (c) the opinion that the life of the unjust is happier than the life of the just man (358c). The three opinions are understood as *doxai* in the later developed technical sense, in so far as they do not penetrate to the essence of justice as the greatest good and of injustice as the greatest evil (366c). That the *doxa* leaves them in the dark about the essence of justice is the grievance of the young men; they implore Socrates to show them why justice is a good in itself and not only a good in relation to reputation, honors, and other worldly advantages (367e). In the construction of the drama the exposition of the *doxa* by content, thus, prepares the exposition of the Socratic *episteme*. For Socrates, the savior of the souls, must respond to the appeal of the young souls in danger and confusion.

(2) The sources of *doxa* can be distinguished as: (a) Panegyrists of injustice in general, and sophists in particular; (b) parents; (c) poets and prose writers; and (d) mendicants, prophets of Orphic, and other mysteries. The question is, What shall a youth believe and do

when all authorities of the society in which he lives conspire to confuse him and to prevent his true knowledge of justice through daily insinuation of Doxa? (366b–367a). In the construction of the dialogue this object lesson of the victims of a corrupt society points to the reflections on the concrete society as "the greatest of all sophists" in *Republic VI*.

Glaukon opens his survey, as he has proposed, with the first doxa, the common view concerning the question "what is and whence comes justice" (358e).

"Originally" (*pephykenai*), men say, to do injustice was good, while to suffer injustice was bad. Then it turned out that the evil was greater than the good; when men had tasted of both and found themselves unable to flee the one and do the other, they were ready to agree on laws and mutual covenants; and they called just and lawful what was ordained by the laws. This is the origin and nature (*ousia*) of justice, as a mean between the best (to do injustice without punishment) and the worst (to suffer injustice without power of retaliation). Justice, therefore, is not loved as a good in itself, but honored because of a man's infirmity to act unjustly. The strong, the real man would never enter into such an agreement; he would be demented if he did. This is the commonly received view of origin and nature (*physis*) of justice (358–359b).

The passage requires a word of commentary because it is exposed to misinterpretation in more than one respect. In the doxa justice is explained genetically as the result of weighing the advantages and disadvantages of unregulated action; after due consideration justice will be pragmatically honored as the more profitable course. In order to indulge in the utilitarian calculus, however, one must already "know" what justice is, in the sense that the word "justice" occurs in the environment of the calculating opiner and is accepted by him in a conventional sense. The explanation of a calculated decision for just conduct is not an inquiry into the nature of justice. Hence, one cannot find in the passage a theory of either the nature of law or the law of nature. In particular, one must beware to render the word *pephykenai* as "by nature," as is sometimes done, for it means in the context no more than "originally," in the sense of "genetically first." The term *physis* (nature) occurs in the whole passage only once, with the meaning of "essence" or "true character," as a synonym for *ousia*. Moreover, the words *physis* and *ousia* occur in the presentation of a sophistic doxa concerning justice. Hence, they can mean at best that the conception of justice developed in the doxa is what a sophist believes to be the nature of justice. If we disregard the context and accept the doxa concerning justice as a theory concerning the nature of justice, we have accepted the sophist and rejected the Plato who develops in the *Republic* his *episteme* concerning the nature of justice in opposition to the sophistic *doxa*. That would be the misunderstanding on which we had to reflect previously, on occasion of the concepts of *philosophos* and *philodoxos*. If we use the term philosopher in the modern sense, which includes the philodoxer, we have made nonsense of the work of Plato. In the same manner, if we use the term "theory" so that it includes the "opinion" to which Plato opposed his *episteme*, we have made nonsense of the whole problem of Doxa and the sophistic corruption of society.

The same considerations apply to the interpretation of the passage as an early, if not the first, instance of a "contract theory." The word "contract" (*syntheke*), it is true, occurs in the passage; and within our doxographic conventions it is legitimate to classify Glaukon's report of the doxa in this manner. It is doubtful, however, whether our historiographic conventions are theoretically tenable in this point. As far as Plato is concerned the contractual explanation of law and justice is an instance of *doxa*. The doxic state of the soul is the subject matter under discussion—not justice and its nature. Hence, again, we must make up our mind whether we want to follow the intention of Plato or the moderns who tear this particular doxa out of context, dignify it with the name of a theory, and speak of a history of the "contract theory." If we follow Plato, the "contract theory" has no history but is a type of Doxa that is apt to appear and to reappear without continuity with earlier appearances whenever the doxic state of the soul appears in history—as for instance in the sixteenth and seventeenth centuries A.D. If we follow the moderns we would, as historians, misrepresent the intention of Plato; and we would, as political scientists, undo the achievement of Plato in classifying the phenomena of social disintegration. The classification of the contractual explanation of law as a *doxa* in the technical sense, as opposed to *episteme* (science, theory), certainly is a most valuable insight. We must not let ourselves be overawed by the fact that famous figures in the modern history of political thought, as Hobbes or Locke, entertained a "contract theory." For a doxa does not become a theory through the fact that it has a great vogue among modern thinkers of renown. If, on the other hand, we follow Plato, then we have in his classification an important instrument that will enable us to diagnose the doxic state of soul and society when its symptom, the "contract theory," appears.

The validity of the doxa concerning the origin of law rests on the assumption that men would commit injustice if they were free to do so, and that only enlightened self-interest induces them to agree on the laws. This assumption is the second doxa held by the multitude.

Glaukon clarifies the meaning of the second doxa through the myth of Gyges and his ring. First he tells the myth as a paradigm of conduct, and then he proposes a mental experiment. Let us assume there exist two such rings which make their bearers invisible at their will, the one possessed by a just man, the other one possessed by an unjust man. And then let us ask the question: Could anyone imagine the just man of such adamantine nature that he would stand fast in justice, keep his hands off other people's property and women, not kill at his will, and generally act "like a god among men"? (360b–c). The answer is an energetic No. If the fear of punishment were removed the actions of the just man would be like those of the unjust man. He would follow his desires (*epithymia*), for everybody believes that injustice is more profitable than justice. And if a man had the opportunity to take another man's goods and did not use it, he would be considered a demented wretch—though everybody would praise him from fear that he himself might become a victim of injustice (360c–d).

The second doxa not only supplies proof for a presupposition of the first one, but also elucidates the nature of Doxa in general. The mental experiment applies the paradigmatic myth of Gyges and his ring to human conduct at large. The myth is the dream of invisibility that will free a man from normal social sanctions so that he can indulge his desires. Hence, the mental experiment, with its result to which "everybody" would give his assent, operates with a dream-anthropology: What would a man do if social sanctions were removed and if there were no problems of spiritual and moral order? The hypothesis formulates a real problem because there are, indeed, phases in history, the periods of crisis, where internal and external controls break down to such an extent that an appreciable number of persons in a society can live, in various degrees of realization, as it were in the dream of their desires. The fall into the dream is a potentiality of man. The temptation is permanently present and the struggle for order requires an equally unceasing effort. In *Republic* IX the subject is pursued further in the interpretation of tyranny as the realization of dream desires. The doxa now comes more clearly into view as the type of rational construction—the term "theory" should be avoided—that will appear when order is interpreted from the position of dream existence. The experience of participation in a universal order (in the *xynon* in the Heraclitian sense) is lost; reality is reduced to the life of passions in the individual human being; hence the universality of order must be reconstructed out of the only elements that are experienced as real. If passion is the only reality, the order —which after a fashion exists even in a corrupt society—must be construed as the result of an agreement between the passionate individuals.

The artificial construction of a common world out of the "private worlds" in the Heraclitian sense was most elaborately carried out in the seventeenth century A.D., in a similar situation, by Hobbes. In the Hobbesian case it became especially clear that the contractual agreement was motivated by a passion of the same class as the passions which had caused the isolation of the individual. For Hobbes made "fear of death" the overriding passion that will induce men to renounce full satisfaction of their other passions. This *summum malum* of the individual motivated the creation of artificial order, when the universal *summum bonum* was no longer experienced as a binding and ordering reality. The disappearance of the *summum bonum* (in Hobbes's Christian world of thought the equivalent of the Heraclitian *xynon*), that is, the loss of the universal realissimum left the dreamworlds of the individuals as the only reality.

The resulting reconstruction of a common world out of the dreamworlds, finally, is an odd repetition of the Hesiodian theogonic speculation on the narrower theater of the individual soul. The victory of Jovian Dike over the chthonian forces is repeated in the victory of the agreement concerning law over the uncontrolled passions. With Hesiod the life of man is still part of the life of the cosmos, and the advent of Dike, as a consequence, will be a cosmic event. The way of the growing soul leads from theogonic speculation in the medium of the old myth to the experiences of transcendence of the mystic-philosophers and of Plato. The way of the disintegrating soul leads from theogonic speculation to the doxic caricature of the sophists. We are touching here on the more subtle reasons for Plato's ambivalent attitude toward the poets: the old myth of the poets can become diaphanous and dissolve into the myth of the soul of Socrates-Plato, but it also can become opaque and degenerate into the individualistic caricature.

The third doxa maintains that the life of the unjust man is happier than the life of the just man. Glaukon again uses the method of the mental experiment. In order to arrive at a proper understanding of the issue the two types, the unjust and the just man, must be assumed in their extreme purity. The unjust man is assumed to be a master of his craft, a man who will commit his unjust acts so cleverly that he will not get caught but, on the contrary, gain the reputation (*doxa*) of justice; and if he should get into a tight spot he is assumed to be equipped with the necessary ruthlessness and connections to extricate himself from it, again with the appearance (*doxa*) of perfect justice. The just man, on the other hand, is assumed to be pursued by the reputation of injustice because, if he were socially successful as the result of his justice, we would not know whether he is happy because of his justice or because of the honors and rewards; to his death, therefore, he shall be assumed to be truly just while appearing unjust (360e–361d). The fate of the two types is inevitable. The just man will undergo persecutions and ultimately be put to death under tortures; the unjust man will lead a happy and successful life, rich in honors, and his wealth will enable him to dedicate gifts to the gods and make him dear to them (361d–362c). When such a fate befalls the just man, then, according to the opinion of the multitude, he will understand at last that he should appear, not be, just. In the actions of the unjust man, on the other hand, one may find genuine truth (*aletheia*), for the unjust man does not suffer from a split between appearance and reality; he does not live for appearance (*doxa*), he does not want to appear, but really to be, unjust (362a).

The preceding reflections are perhaps Plato's masterpiece in his attempt to penetrate the nature of social corruption. Its terseness is almost impossible to unravel. Nevertheless, let us try to articulate the main levels of the involved thought:

(1) The stratum of traditions. The doxic man accepts the historically grown standards of justice and injustice; he does not pretend that the one is the other.

(2) The split between appearance and reality as a general possibility. Dike and Nomos may be in conflict in the sense that just action is in conflict with the external standards of law, customs, and mores of a society—the problem of the tragic poets.

(3) The split between appearance and reality as a historical tension. The standards of just conduct in a society do not evolve at the same pace as the differentiating consciousness of justice; the just conduct by social standards becomes "appearance" in relation to the "true" justice of the differentiated consciousness of the mystic-philosopher.

(4) The power of society over the individual. Whether the individual conduct be "truly" just or unjust, the fate of the individual will on the whole depend on his conformity with the standards that are socially recognized.

(5) The split of consciousness in the corrupt society. The split between "appearance" and "reality" of justice is recognized by the members of the corrupt society, but the power of society is on the side of "appearance." Hence, the pursuit of "reality" is unprofitable to the point of being deadly.

(6) The absorption of reality by *doxa*. While the consciousness of the split does not disappear, the accent of reality shifts from truth to the socially overpowering appearance—the dream tends to become reality.

(7) *Doxa* becomes *aletheia*. The accent of reality has shifted so far that "truth," in the sense of conformity of a man with himself, is achieved by the will to be unjust in order to harmonize with society.

Plato's penetration of the problem is, indeed, masterful in so far as he recognizes the crucial point of moral crisis in society. The primary source of the crisis is not an error about justice but the shift of what we called the "accent of reality" under social pressure. Man is essentially social; to live in truth against appearance when the power of society is thrown on the side of appearance is a burden on the soul that is impossible to bear for the many, and hard to bear for the few. The pressure for external conformity penetrates the soul and compels it to endow the *doxa* experientially with *aletheia*. The last step would be the complete blinding of the soul by cutting off—through organized psychological management—the restorative recourse to the experience of transcendence as we find it in the modern political mass movements.

Glaukon's account of the three principal doxai is followed by Adeimantus' account of variegated doxai from various sources. They all have in common the fact that they opine about justice under its pragmatic aspect. Parents admonish their sons to be just, not because justice is a virtue in itself, but for the sake of reputation and social success that will be gained by just conduct (362e–363a). The parents go even farther than the sophists in their pragmatic zeal; for they not only dangle social rewards before the just boy, but they also draw on Homer, Hesiod, and Musaeus for promising the favor of the gods in this world and the next (363b–e). And then there is the host of various speakers, mystery-prophets, and soothsayers who insist that justice is honorable but burdensome, while injustice and dishonesty are more pleasant and profitable; that the successful wicked are happier than the honest poor; that the gods send calamities to good men and happiness to the wicked ones; and that the rich men can atone for their sins by sacrifices (363e–365a).

The net result of such concerted pressure of authorities is the demoralization of youth. If the sages prove that "appearance [*to dokein*] is stronger than reality [*aletheia*] and the lord of happiness," then the young men will follow the path of injustice and take the appropriate measures to avoid unpleasant consequences. In order to conceal their injustice they will join political brotherhoods and clubs; in order to ward off the consequences in courts and assemblies they will use the sophistic art of rhetoric; and as far as afterlife is concerned all problems are answered by the previously discussed sequence—that probably there are no gods, that they do not care about the affairs of men if they should exist, and that they can be pacified by prayers and sacrifices if they should happen to care (365a–366b).[9]

Under such conditions a man has little chance to develop unwarped his full human, *i.e.*, his philosophical stature; and his chances will even decrease in proportion to the greatness of his gifts. For the nature (*physis*) of the true philosopher (491e) is distinguished by the virtues of justice, temperance, courage, love of wisdom, unrelenting zeal in

[9] *Order and History* II, Ch. 11, 1.

the search for true being, greatmindedness (*megaloprepeia*), ability
to learn (*eumatheia*), and good memory. Such natures are rare, and
like other rare plants they will degenerate more thoroughly when put
in the wrong soil than the more common ones. Great crimes and accomplished misdeeds are committed not by ordinary men, but spring
from great natures ruined by evil influences of their environment
(491d–e). The general social environment in courts, assemblies, and
theaters is the principal formative influence on young men, not the
teaching of this or that individual sophist. The many who exert the
continuous pressure are "the great sophist" (492a–b). The individual
sophists who teach for money have no doctrine of their own, but echo
the opinion (*dogmata*) of the multitude; and that is what they call
their wisdom. The professional sophist is rather comparable to a man
in charge of a "great beast"; he will study the habits of the animal
and find out how to manage it. Good will be what the beast likes, and
bad will be what arouses its temper (493a–c).

The critique of Plato has at last reached its real aim, the corrupt
society, the great beast itself. The doxic state of mind in single individuals is not of decisive importance. Only when the society in its
broad mass is corrupt will the situation be truly critical because the
doxic state has become self-perpetuating through social pressure on the
younger generation and, in particular, on the most gifted men. Human
Arete is of little avail under such circumstances; when in such a state
of society (*katastasis politeion*) a man does not suffer damage, whatever he saves is saved by dispensation of a god (*theou moira*) (492e–
493a).

§ 4. The Creation of Order

The survey of sophistic doxai by Glaukon and Adeimantus ends
with a cry *de profundis* to Socrates the helper. The social authorities offer
them nothing but opinions about just and unjust conduct, as well as
about the attendant rewards and punishments. The young men, however, want to know what justice and injustice are "in themselves, by
their own inherent force," and why the one is the "greatest good," the
other the "greatest evil" a man can have in his soul (366e). If a man
knew that, he would be his own "best guardian," for he would be
afraid to enter "into communion with the greatest of evils" through

unjust deeds (367a). They do not want to hear further stories about the superiority of the one to the other under the aspect of their external consequences; they want to know what they do to a man's soul (367b). Socrates has admitted that justice is one of those "greatest goods," "whose goodness springs from their nature, not from opinion," like sight, hearing, intelligence, and health (367d). If that is true, they want to hear it praised for that reason.

That is the appeal to which Socrates cannot turn a deaf ear. He must "come to the rescue," though he doubts his ability, for it would be "impious" not to come to the defense of justice (368b–c). And thus the inquiry (*to zetema*) begins (368c).

1. *The Zetema*

From the formulation of both the program and its purpose it should be clear that the inquiry is concerned with the reality of order in soul and society, not with "ideals." Nevertheless, the point needs emphasis because it is a firmly established convention in our time to speak of Plato's "ideal state" and "ideal justice." We are facing the difficulty, previously discussed, that the negative members of Plato's pairs of concepts have dropped from the philosophical vocabulary and that, as a consequence, the sensitive understanding for Plato's resistance to Doxa is lost. To be sure, one can exert critical caution and define "ideal state" as a synonym for Plato's "good polis." Still, the synonym is at best misleading. For the polis, whose nature Plato explores, is a species of the genus "state" and not the genus itself—if we allow the term "state" at all as a suitable generic term for political organizations. And to translate the Platonic language of "good," "best," "right," or "by nature" with "ideal" is superfluous. Moreover, critical caution is frequently not exerted, so that the term "ideal state" carries the connotation of a "political ideal" to which other ideals can be opposed. An "ideal" in this sense, however, is precisely what Plato calls a doxa. And once that connotation creeps in, Plato is liable to be treated, not as a philosopher, but as one of the many philodoxers, as indeed he is, in our time, in the considerable literature which deals with Plato's philosophy as if it were a political ideology whose sinister motives must be brought to light. Within a few generations the Plato of the "ideal state" has been transformed into a "political ideologue." This astonishing transformation will become intelligible if we see it in the light of Plato's own analysis of social corruption. The generation which attributed to Plato the creation of an "ideal state" had no evil intentions. Ideals were quite respectable at the time, and to ascribe them to Plato was praise. But even at that time the evil was lurking, for in common parlance an idealist was an impractical person who indulged his subjective valuations in opposition to reality; and the connotation of subjectivity in "ideal" undermined the objectivity of Plato's inquiry into the nature of reality. The way from the well-intentioned, but philosophically no longer sensitive generation, which translated the "good polis" as an "ideal state," to the generation which attacks Plato as an "ideologue," is the way from Cephalus to Thrasymachus.

The inquiry, the *zetema,* is the conceptual illumination of the way up from the depth of existence. The initial materials for the inquiry are furnished by the motivating experiences of depth and direction; the initial tools by the meanings of words in common parlance, as well as in pre-Platonic technical usage. From the initial situation the inquiry proceeds through an analysis of experiences, which gradually brings new experiential materials into view and, at the same time, refines the initial meanings into the technical meanings of concepts. In both respects the inquiry, undertaken in the *Republic* for the first time in history, was an enormous effort since the phenomenology of experiences was handicapped by the shortcomings of the available terminology, and the development of terminology by the difficulties in the analysis of experiences. In spite of the inevitable handicaps the zetetic effort was so successful, with regard both to the classification of experiences and the development of concepts, that the first philosophy of order is still the classic work of its kind to which we must always return for information on material detail, as well as on methods.

In the motivating experience of the inquiry we can distinguish two components: (1) the experience of the depth itself and (2) the experience of a direction from the depth upward. In the experience of the depth we can, further, distinguish two strands:

(1a) In the Pamphylian Myth, at the end of the *Republic,* the dead souls are forced to choose a pattern, a paradigm of life. With the pattern they choose the daemon, the divine substance of the soul. And on the quality of the daemon depends the quality of the soul on the scale of justice and injustice.

(1b) In the Prologue and Introduction, society is experienced as a psychic aggregate, exerting a pressure on the individual psyche, which man finds difficult to resist. The substance of society is experienced as psyche. That experience of the depth, with its two strands, would leave us in the empty freedom of choice, exposed to the misery of social pressure. It is anxiety without hope. No inquiry concerning order could originate in the depth. The inquiry is a possibility because there is also present the experience of a direction.

(2) The soul feels itself in supreme danger (618b), because it might enter into community with evil (367a). It is in fear (367a) of such a fate; therefore it becomes a seeker (*zetetes*) and disciple (*mathetes*) of the man who can help it to develop the power (*dynamis*) and knowledge (*episteme*) that will enable it to make the right choice (618c), so that in the end it will become the best guardian (*aristos phylax*) of its own Arete.

The depth of experience is not unrelieved night; a light shines in the darkness. For the depth can be sensed as misery, danger, and evil only because there is also present, however stifled and obscured, the sense of an alternative. The illuminating inquiry, the *zetema*, is not carried from the outside to the initial experience, as if it were a dead subject matter, but the element of seeking (*zetesis*) is present in the experience and blossoms out into the inquiry. The light that falls on the way does not come from an external source, but is the growing and expanding luminosity of the depth. On the one hand, therefore, the concepts of the inquiry do not refer to an external object, but are symbols evolved by the soul when it engages in the exegesis of its depth. The exegesis has no object that precedes the inquiry as a datum, but only levels of consciousness, rising higher as the Logos of the experience becomes victorious over its darkness. The inquiry continues, on rising levels of logical penetration, the substantive struggle between good and evil that rages in the depth. On the other hand, therefore, the concepts and propositions do not primarily tender information about an object, but are the very building blocks of the substantive stature into which the soul grows through its inquiry.

Such problems of philosophizing may appear extraordinary to the conventions, less philosophic than philodoxic, of our time, but they were not extraordinary at the time of Plato. His situation as a philosopher, it is true, had become complicated through the sophistic development which he resisted, but it was essentially still the situation of the Heraclitian *zetesis*. The well elaborated sophistic position required a correspondingly elaborate attention to minutiae of the problems which made impossible the grandiose simplicity of expression that characterized the earlier thinker. But we still can hear behind Plato the Heraclitus who could simply say: "I explored [*edizesamen*] myself" (B 101); and who could compress the result of his inquiry, the growth of the soul into its own stature, into the sentence: "To the soul is peculiar a Logos that augments itself" (B 115). A comparable simplicity was recaptured only in early Christianity in the magnificent opening of the Gospel of St. John, where the Logos of God is the light of man that shines in the darkness and is not submerged by it.

While the resistance to the sophists complicates the Platonic inquiry, it does not change its nature as a self-illumination of the soul through augmentation of its Logos. The concepts developed in its course must be treated with constant awareness of their place and function in the *zetema*. For zetetic symbols, as we shall call them, have variegated structures, corresponding to the stage of clarification reached by the inquiry. Sometimes they approach the nature of concepts which refer to objects of the external world. For the most part, however, they draw their meaning from the experience whose logical luminosity they are. Torn out of context they lose the luminosity intended by the inquirer; they become opaque and will puzzle by their apparent senselessness and inconsistency. The interpretation must, therefore, under no circumstances try to extract a Platonic "doctrine" of order from the *Republic,* but must fix the levels of clarification and explore the symbols developed on each of the levels.

We shall start with the symbols on the lowest level, at the point where the inquiry emerges from the despair of the depth.

On that lowest level we find a rudimentary philosophical anthropology, as well as something like a theory concerning the relation between the order of man and the order of society. Man is equipped with a pattern of life, the paradigm of his choice in Hades, and associated with it is a daemon of a more or less virtuous complexion. The same structure of paradigm and daemon is to be found in the polis. It has a pattern of institutional order, its *politeia*; and it has a daemon, represented by its ruling part. The pattern allows Plato to speak of a sophistic or philosophic polis, according to the nature of the ruler whose psyche determines the complexion of its Arete. Man and polis, furthermore, have parallel structures, not by accident, but by virtue of a principle of which Plato speaks only metaphorically or discursively, without giving it a technical name: The polis is man written in larger letters. In order to facilitate the analysis, we shall call it the "anthropological principle." In the aggregate we find, thus, a group of interrelated concepts, which can be arranged in the following parallel columns:

Man	Polis
Daemon	Ruler
Paradigm of Life	Politeia

These are indeed the basic symbols that run through the course of the inquiry and determine the organization of the *Republic*.

The orderly simplicity of the concepts is deceptive. When Plato uses them in the course of the inquiry they reveal an amplitude of imprecision that allows them to represent variegated components of the motivating experience. First of all, it turns out that there is no one–one relation between a daemon and his paradigm. Justice is not the privilege of a particular walk of life, but for everyman the virtue of minding the business for which he is gifted. An infinitude of paradigms, therefore, is compatible with Arete; and in limiting the spectrum Plato does not go beyond the hint that the "mean" is preferable to extremes. Moreover, the same observations apply to the paradigm of order in a polis. To be sure, Arete is one, but there is more than one type of politeia in which she can live. In this connection we do not even have to recall that Plato developed a "second best polis" in the *Laws;* for in the *Republic* itself, in the course of his inquiry, Socrates develops three different paradigms of a good polis—leaving it to the modern critics to debate which of the "ideal states" is more ideal than the others.

Arete and paradigm in the polis, thus, are movable against each other within certain limits. On the one hand, it is a matter of indifference whether the polis of the philosophers has the institutional paradigm of a monarchy or an aristocracy. On the other hand, in the transition from philosophic aristocracy to timocracy, the institutional paradigm does not change when the Arete in the soul of the rulers declines. From the language of the preceding sentences it appears, furthermore, that the term "politeia," used by Plato in preference to paradigm when speaking of a polis, is not strictly synonymous with the latter term. For the politeia is a paradigm seen under the aspect of the soul which animates it. Plato is not interested in forms of government without regard to the animating psyche; and the paradigm in the strict sense, therefore, makes its presence felt mainly when a particular paradigmatic feature is stressed as a matter of indifference compared with the all-important embodiment of a well-ordered soul.

Since Plato, while concerned with designing the "paradigm of a good polis" (472a), is interested in paradigmatic elements only in so far as they have an intelligible bearing on health or disease of the soul, his drafting, even of a desirable paradigm, will stop when a point of diminishing returns is reached. Socrates, who is tireless as long as he elaborates the *paideia,* the education that will form the souls of the guardians in his good polis, roundly refuses to go into details, not only of customs and mores, but even of civil, commercial, and criminal law, because such legislative matters will take care of themselves if only the souls of the legislating rulers are in good order (425a–d). Moreover, he restrains himself deliberately at this point in order not to give the false impression that good order in a polis can be created through institutional devices. He considers it, on the contrary, a symptom of disease in a polis when the citizens are feverishly active with patching up this or that gap in the law, but do not dare to touch the well-known source of the multitude of minor evils. They act like patients, permanently in search of a panacea, but unwilling to mend the way of life that causes the disease. In such a polis the general constitution (*katastasis*) of society must remain untouched, and any attempt at essential reform will be considered treason and threatened with death (426b–c). The goodness of a polis has its source not in the paradigm of institutions, but in the psyche of the founder or ruler who will stamp the pattern of his soul on the institutions. It is not the excellence of body that makes the soul good, as Socrates insists in opposition to a much quoted piece of athletic wisdom, but the good soul will by its virtue make the body the best possible (403d).

The paradigm now appears in the role of an institutional body without an ordering virtue of its own. From its skeletal deadness we are referred back to the life of the soul. The essential character of a politeia does not stem from its paradigm, but from the politeia in the soul of its rulers. "Politeia" is, indeed, Plato's favorite term when he speaks of the right order in the soul of the philosophers. The term, thus, moves from the side of the polis, in our columns of symbols, to the side of man; and within the column it moves up from the external pattern of a life, its paradigm, into the order of the soul.

With that evolution of the term politeia we reach, however, a point at which the whole group of concepts, together with their zetetic intention, becomes questionable. There arises, first of all, the practical question why a paradigm for the right order of a polis should be developed at all, if the good politeia can be realized in the soul of the philosopher without his engaging in the hopeless task of reforming the corrupt society. There arises, second, a theoretical question with regard to the validity of the anthropological principle. Under its assumption Plato plays back and forth, in the *Republic*, between the order of the polis and the order of the soul, illuminating the one by the other. Now, however, it appears that the principle is at least not reversible, if valid in other respects. We may accept the thesis that the relevant features of a political order stem from the psyche of its rulers, but we cannot ignore the fact that in a polis there live numbers of people who do not conform to the pattern set by the rulers. Right in the middle of Plato's corrupt society there exist the philosophers, engaged in a Socratic inquiry, holding up to the society the paradigm of right order as they find it in the politeia of their souls. By his concrete existence as a politically ineffectual philosopher in the Athens of the fourth century B.C., Plato proves that the order of the psyche is not absorbed in its entirety by the order of the polis. A part of human order, perhaps its most important part, finds its institutional paradigm, not in the polis but in communities of a different kind, in Plato's case in the foundation of the Academy. The historical fact of an order of the psyche outside the order of the polis, finally, leads to the third, the ontological question whether all of the order of the psyche can enter into political order at all. The possibility must not be overlooked that Plato, with his search for an adequate expression of the psyche in the order of a best politeia, has manoeuvred himself into an ontological impasse. The questions of this kind, far from being raised as criticisms, are the very questions which agitated Plato profoundly. But they do not become topical at the lower level of inquiry; they emerge from the main course to which we shall now turn.

2. *The Foundation Play*

The inquiry concerning the "paradigm of a good polis" (472e) is organized as a play within the play. Plato casts the Socrates of the dialogue in the role of an *oikistes* (378e–379a), of the founder of a polis who drafts a constitution, as so frequently in the history of Hellas her statesmen had drafted constitutions for a new colony to be established or for their own polis to be reformed. Such drafts, however, were not undertaken unless a concrete political situation required them; they were meant to be realized. Since the inquiry concerning the paradigm could be conducted quite well without the play of foundation, the pretense deliberately introduces a problem of realization that is not inherent to the establishment of criteria for the quality of a political order. To be sure, when a philosopher establishes criteria of good order, he will have an eye on the political environment and see whether it lives up to the criteria or not. But his observation, as in the case of Aristotle, need not go beyond an occasional contemptuous remark that none of the Hellenic poleis could reform its politeia in such a manner that it would be good by his standards. Plato's pretense, which introduces an apparently unnecessary problem, affects the course of the dialogue as a whole, as well as the treatment of details in the inquiry. Its motivations must be well understood, especially since the device of a founding play is repeated in the *Laws*.

An exploration of Plato's motives must beware of wild speculations, in which interpreters frequently indulge, concerning his intentions to play a political role as the reforming statesman of Athens. Whether he had such intentions we do not know, because no sources exist; at best one could argue *ex silentio* that he had none. The motive must be found within the realm of meaning circumscribed by the dialogues. And within that realm we recall the *Gorgias* where Plato let his Socrates claim the true statesmanship of Athens in opposition to the famous figures of the fifth century who by their policies had engineered the ruin of the polis. Hence, there can be no doubt that Plato was seriously in competition with the statesmen. And in view of the paradigmatic importance which he ascribed to Solon on various occasions,[10] we are justified in speaking of a Solonic component in his personality. He was in competition, however, not with regard to political action, but with regard to the spiritual authority, which during the Peloponnesian war and its aftermath, with its obvious breakdown of ethos, the polis and its leaders had lost. The authoritative guidance for the order of existence had, as a matter of historical fact, devolved from the Nomos of the polis to men like Socrates and Plato, as well as to the

[10] *Republic* 599e; *Phaedrus* 258b–c; *Timaeus* 20e.

founders of the schools of the fourth century; and it had devolved so completely that the language of competition is perhaps inapposite, since the polis held its rank as competitor by historical momentum rather than by its living substance. The element of political competition entered, rather, from the side of Plato in so far as he conceived his spiritual authority as a statesman's authority to restore the order of the polis. Human existence meant political existence; and restoration of order in the soul implied the creation of a political order in which the restored soul could exist as an active citizen. As a consequence, he had to burden his inquiry concerning the paradigm of good order with the problem of its realization in a polis. We have no means to go back of this motive. That Plato conceived his spiritual authority as political must be accepted as the impenetrable mystery of the way in which his personality responded to the situation. In the history of symbols the fact of his response has burdened the philosophy of order with the "mortgage" of the polis that we discussed in an earlier context.[11]

While Plato is profoundly serious in his competitive position as the philosophical statesman, he has no illusions with regard to the possibilities of political success. The paradigm should be realized concretely in a polis, but he has no hope of finding a political followership that will undertake the task under his guidance. In a famous page of the *Republic* he lets Socrates elaborate the position of the philosopher-statesman in his time with care: "The worthy disciples of philosophy will be only a very few. . . . One who belongs to that small company and has tasted of the sweet and blessed possession of philosophy; who has watched the frenzy of the multitude and has seen that there is no soundness in the conduct of politics, and nowhere an ally at whose side a champion of justice might escape destruction; but that he would be like a man who has fallen among wild beasts; and that he would be destined to perish if he should refuse to join in their misdeeds; that singly he cannot hold out against the fury of all; that he would perish without helping thereby his polis, or his friends, or himself—one who has weighed all this will hold his peace, and go his own way, like a traveller in a storm of dust and sleet who seeks shelter under a wall. And as he sees lawlessness spreading on all sides, he is content if he can keep himself clear of the iniquity of impious deeds while his life lasts and, when the end comes, depart, with good hopes, in security and peace" (496). Adeimantus

---

[11] *Order and History* II, Ch. 6, 1.

agrees that indeed that would be a great achievement, to be corrected
by Socrates: "Yes; but not the greatest, since fortune has denied him
the politeia to which he belongs; in that politeia he would grow to his
fullness, and save not only his private but also the public weal" (497e).
The passage leaves no doubt about the philosopher's withdrawal from
politics and its reasons. The justice of the soul is more precious than
participation in politics; and it must be purchased, if the circumstances
are unfortunate, at the price of a diminution of human stature. The
withdrawal from politics is heavy with resignation, for the fullness of
growth, the maximal augmentation (497a) of man, can be achieved
only through participation in the public life of the polis.

The posture of the statesman-philosopher has led to the paradox that
the human stature will decrease when the justice of the soul increases.
Plato was keenly aware of it; and toward the end of the inquiry he
returned to the problems of statesmanship and realization of the
paradigm in order to relieve, and perhaps even to dissolve, the paradox.
For that purpose he resumed the initial request of Glaukon and Adeimantus to receive the help from Socrates that will enable them to become the "best guardians" of their Arete. The request is now recognized
as the correct formula for the right order of the soul. Children should
be educated in such a manner that there "will be established within
them, as in a polis, a politeia" in which the best element will be the
guardian and ruler (590e–591a). The establishment of the "politeia
within oneself" is the aim of education in general, as well as of the
inquiry that now is drawing to its end in particular. A man thus formed,
"a wise man" (591c), will keep his eye fixed on that politeia within
himself (591e), and do what he can to preserve its order intact by
steering a middle course between extremes of wealth and poverty, public
honors and insignificance (591e–592a). At this point of the dialogue
the phrase of the "politeia within oneself," which hitherto appeared as no
more than a metaphor, is suddenly given a new existential meaning.
For to Glaukon's suggestion that such a man would not willingly take
part in politics Socrates surprisingly answers: "By the dog, indeed he
will; in his own polis he certainly will, though not in the city of his
birth, unless a divine fortune lets that come to pass" (592a). Glaukon
understands: "You mean in the polis that we have now gone through
as founders, and set up in our discourse [en logois], for I think that it
exists nowhere on earth" (592a–b). And Socrates concludes: "Well,

there is perhaps a paradigm of it set up in heaven [*en ourano*] for him who desires to behold and beholding to settle in it. It makes no difference whether it exists concretely [*pou*] now or ever; that polis and none other is the one with which he is concerned" (592b). The brief exchange is an artistic miracle. Without change of terminology, through a slight switch from metaphor to reality, the inquiry into the paradigm of a good polis is revealed as an inquiry into man's existence in a community that lies, not only beyond the polis, but beyond any political order in history. The leap in being, toward the transcendent source of order, is real in Plato; and later ages have recognized rightly in the passage a prefiguration of St. Augustine's conception of the *civitas Dei*.

Nevertheless, a prefiguration is not the figuration itself. Plato is not a Christian; and the surprising development occurs at the end of an inquiry that started from the luminous depth of the Dionysiac soul. We must now consider the implications of the answer to the earlier paradox.

To be sure, the paradox is dissolved. The statesman in the philosopher, who feels his stature diminished when the proper field of action is denied to him, has disappeared. Sliding through the metaphor to reality, participation in politics now means concern with the transpolitical politeia that is set up in heaven and will be realized in the soul of the beholder. The soul is a one-man polis and man is the "statesman" who watches over its constitution. The dissolution through the ultimate shift to the soul and its transcendent order, however, does not cancel the validity of the whole preceding inquiry into the paradigm of the good polis. For Plato was an artist and when he wrote the earlier parts of the inquiry he knew, of course, where he would end. The dissolution of the paradox must, therefore, not be understood as an intellectual solution of a puzzle, but as the spiritual "augmentation" of existence produced through the process of the *zetema*. The paradox remains intact at its own stage of the inquiry. To live in an age of social corruption and to be denied one's proper field of action in public is really a misfortune; and the honoring of Arete is no substitute for the inevitable diminution of stature. Yet, the price must be paid, because in the hierarchy of goods political life ranks lower than eternal life. The *techne metretike*, the art of measurement under the aspect of death, leaves no doubt on the point. The paradox, thus, remains as unsolved intellectually as it was, but the bitterness of renunciation is spiritually overcome through the growth of the soul into the transcendent politeia. And that growth was achieved by passing through the stages of the inquiry. We remember Glaukon's quick understanding that Socrates was speaking of the politeia which they had just been building, as "founders," *en logois*. The *en logois* has the double meaning of "in words [or discourse]" and "in thought," inseparable in the Hellenic culture of the spoken, not written, thought. But one cannot think, to the point of articulation in discourse, thoughts of this kind without affecting one's psyche. Though the plural *en logois* does not denote the Heraclitian Logos that augments itself, the "setting up" of a polis *en logois* definitely connotes the Logos of the soul that is transformed into the polis which it thinks. The polis that is beheld *en logois* becomes through beholding the polis of the soul. There can be hardly a doubt that the inquiry contains a good deal of Plato's spiritual autobiography.

3. *The Cognitive Inquiry*

In order to achieve their goal of founding a good polis the founders must know what it is and they must have a method to find it. Hence, within the play of foundation there is conducted an inquiry into the nature of the good polis. An understanding of that secondary inquiry in the cognitive sense, however, presents certain difficulties to the analysis. Both the methods and the conceptual tools of philosophical inquiry were yet in formation; and Plato was not discursive on either his epistemology or his methodology. Hence, the nature of the object, as well as the methods of its exploration, must be inferred from the actual procedure. Moreover, the issues are obscured by a richness of vocabulary that owes its wealth less to artistic reasons than to its state of imperfection.

We shall begin the analysis of this area of the *Republic* with Plato's formulations of the goal. The object to which Socrates and his friends devote their cognitive attention is designated variously as a "good polis," the "paradigm of a good polis," a "best politeia," a "schema of the politeia." As qualifying attributes to polis and politeia appear the following phrases: "good" (434e; 449a; 472e; 543c), "good in the full sense of the word" (427e), "the best" (497c), "the best we can make" (434e), "the best governed" (462d), "right" (449a), "eudaimonic" (420b), "well ordered" (462e). The essential features of the paradigm are assembled by Plato himself at the end of the inquiry in the cognitive sense: The best governed polis will have community of wives and children; all will have the same education; the pursuits of men and women must be the same in peace and war; rulers will be those among them who have proved themselves best in philosophy and war. The rulers will provide plain, camp-like settlements for their soldier-citizens, so that there will be nothing private for anybody; and they will have no private property. Since they are athletes of war and philosophical guardians of the polis, they shall receive annual payments for their sustenance from the worker-citizens, and devote their entire attention to keeping themselves and the polis fit (543a–c).

With regard to the methods employed in the exploration, Plato's use of the terms *eidos* and *physis* suggests the medical literature in the background. The constitution of a polis, as well as the character of a man, has an *eidos*, a typical form; and there are as many *eide* of constitutions as of human characters (544d–e). There is no reason to assume that the meaning of the term in Plato's usage differs from the meaning it has in the Hippocratic treatises, or in Thucydides, or quite probably in Athenian conversation of the time in general.[12] The *eidos*, or *idea*, is the combination of symptoms that characterizes a disease, the combination that later (Galenus, Aretus) came to be called the syndrome, the clinical picture. The terminology was originally developed by the Ionian physicians of the fifth century B.C. who raised medicine to the level of a critical craft, an *episteme*. The terminology, then, proved equally useful in describing the disease of a society and was used in this sense, as we have seen, by Thucydides in the study of the great Kinesis. And since the penetration to the essential picture, to the "nature" of a thing, to the "thing in itself," [13] has the same structure when it concerns, not a disease of man or society, but a "normal" state of order, it is not surprising that, finally, Plato adopted the useful vocabulary. Hence, Plato's use of the terms *eidos*, *idea*, and *physis* suggests an empirical search for characteristics, as well as combinations of characteristics, which derive their quality of essentials from the constancy of their occurrence in things of a common sense class under observation.

The meaning intended by Plato becomes a bit more explicit when he speaks of the good polis as a "polis founded according to nature [*kata*

---

[12] Friedlaender, *Platon* I, 16ff. Cf. the section on Thucydides in *Order and History* II, Ch. 12, 3, 2.

[13] Cf. the passages from *Ancient Medicine* and *Nature of Man* quoted in *Order and History* II, Ch. 12, 3, 2.

physin]" (428e). The occasion for using the phrase is given by the observation that a polis will be "well counselled" and "wise" as a whole when it is ruled by the smallest group among its citizens that possesses a special knowledge (*episteme*), that is, the *episteme* of "guarding" or "ruling." Since the persons who partake of that knowledge "which of all crafts [*ton allon epistemon*] alone deserves the name of wisdom," are "by nature [*physei*] the fewest," a polis governed by them will be established "according to nature" (428e–429a). The phrase that the rulers or guardians are the smallest class "by nature" thus implies no more than the empirical observation that the class of men distinguished by wisdom, in the Platonic sense, is consistently smaller than the class of competent agricultural workers, or retail traders, or any other class of craftsmen. Only in so far as that quantitative relation is to be observed with a regularity that suffers no exception, can it be dignified as a "natural" trait in the constitution of being.

In the passage 428e–429a the term *physis* is used twice. It occurs, first, in the observation that the philosophical guardians are the smallest of all classes of craftsmen; and second, in the proposition that a polis will be established according to nature when the smallest class actually rules. In the first instance the empirical intention of the observation is clear, even if somebody should be able to classify crafts in such a manner that one even smaller than the craft of guardians in the Platonic sense should emerge. In the second instance the case is not so clear. Even if we admit that a polis should be wisely ruled we rightly wonder what such a postulate has to do with nature and empirical observations. For our common sense experience shows that a polis, or any political organization, is rarely ruled with wisdom. The answer to such doubts and questions is to be found through the recognition that the order of human existence in society is not an object of the external world that could be discovered at all through the classification of data given to sense experience. Plato, as we have seen, was only mildly interested in the paradigms as dead skeletons of order; he shifted to the term politeia because the essential element of order in a paradigm is the animating psyche. And the discovery of the order of the psyche is the task of the philosopher's *zetema*, resulting in the augmentation of the Logos in his soul. There is no knowledge of order in the soul except through the *zetema* in which the soul discovers it by growing into it. Hence, Plato does not go beyond empirical observation when he introduces the order of the philosopher's soul as the cri-

terion for the "nature" of order in the polis. On the contrary, he uses
the only empirical knowledge that we have. The polis will be in a
eudaimonic state only if its order is traced "by painters who use the
divine paradigm [*theion paradeigma*]" (500e). And that "painter"
is the lover of wisdom (*philosophos*) who through his association with
divine order (*theios kosmios*) has himself become orderly and divine
(*kosmios te kai theios*) in the measure allowed to man (500c–d).

While the introduction of the divine paradigm, as it lives in the
philosopher's soul, does not transcend the limits of empirical observation,
it introduces a formidable further problem in so far as it makes the existence of an order by nature depend on the philosopher's historical existence. There was an order of society, expressed through the symbolic
form of the myth, before there were philosophers. The discovery of the
psyche, in its turn, with its *zetesis* and *epanodos*, its erotic reaching out
toward the *kalon* and its vision of the *agathon*, its understanding of
death and immortality, supersedes with its new authority the older authority of the myth. And the philosopher's authority, in its turn, will
be superseded by the revelation of spiritual order through Christ. The
order "by nature," thus, is a stage in the history of order; and a theory
of order in the Platonic sense requires for its systematic completion a
philosophy of history. That problem was present, as we have seen, even
in the *Gorgias;* and it will occupy Plato with growing intensity in the
later dialogues, the *Statesman,* the *Timaeus,* and the *Laws.*

4. The Poleogony

The cognitive inquiry itself is not conducted in direct attention to
its object but by means of a further symbolic form, closely resembling
the Hesiodian theogony. Since no term exists to designate such a form
when the polis, not the gods, is its subject, we shall coin the term "poleogony." The series of forms within forms, thus, is continued—we
never reach the resting point of direct speech—and since all of them have
a bearing on the construction of the *eidos,* we shall recapitulate them:

(1) There is first the dialogue of the *Republic* as the comprehensive
symbolic form;

(2) within the dialogue is conducted the *zetema,* the inquiry that
leads from the darkness of the depth to height and light;

(3) within the *zetema* is enacted the play of founding the good
polis, with Socrates in the role of the *oikistes;*

(4) within the foundation play is conducted the cognitive inquiry into the nature of the good polis.

And now we find that

(5) the inquiry passes through "ages" of the polis, comparable to the Hesiodian generations of the gods, until the ultimate and complete order is reached. Since, however, the form of the dialogue is not abandoned, the poleogony does not become an epic but retains dramatic form.

(6) Moreover, the dramatic form is not only retained within the "ages" of the poleogony, but the "ages" themselves represent the characters of the dramatis personae. Hence, the poleogonic form, far from being a whim, is intimately connected with the form of the dialogue itself. The polis has a genesis because the participants of the dialogue let the substance of their personality successively enter into its nature. The elements of the complete *eidos,* thus, are not introduced as so many objects of inquiry, but enter through dramatic action. The series of forms leads back to its beginning. The analysis will presently show that the problem of the poleogony in action is less complicated than it sounds. As a matter of fact, the symbolism is clearly developed and easy to understand once it is recognized. But it must be recognized if one wishes to avoid the bad mistakes of interpretation that all too frequently are made.

A theogonic speculation is, among other things, an attempt to make the relations between forces of the psyche intelligible through a story of their "genesis." From the lowest to the highest they follow one another as generations of gods; and since the forces are experienced as conflicting their sequence in the tale will be a sequence of struggles and victories, until the highest ordering force of the soul emerges victoriously. That is the element of theogonic speculation that can be transferred from the organization of the polytheistic myth to nonmythical speculations on order. Within the *Republic* itself we have noted the sophistic doxa concerning the origin of order through contract; and on that occasion we reflected on the close relation between the sophistic speculation and the Hesiodian theogony. Now, in the poleogony, Plato uses the form himself and arranges the constellation of experienced forces as a sequence of orders with increasing complexity.

The four orders of the poleogony are the following:

(1) The primitive polis (369b–372c). The order of the polis rests on the mutual supply of necessities through division of labor. It is

characterized by the attributes true (*alethine*) and healthy (*hygies*) (372e).

(2) The luxurious polis (372c–376e). To the primitive basis are added, roughly, the civilizational accoutrements of contemporary Athens. It is characterized by the attributes luxurious (*tryphosa*) and feverish (*phlegmainousa*) (372e).

(3) The purified polis (376e–445e). The luxurious polis is unsatisfactory. It must be purified through reduction of the extremes of poverty and wealth, as well as through a proper education for the ruling class, the guardians. To the polis thus purified (399e) apply the attributes good (*agathe*) and right (*orthe*) (449a).

(4) The philosophers' polis (449a–541b). That is the polis in which the rulers have gone through their education as philosophers. It is referred to as the *kallipolis* (527c), the fine or beautiful polis. There may be the touch of irony in the reference, that has been on occasion observed. But the designation is certainly not quite ironical, for in a later context (543d–544a), without any touch of irony, the last polis is called better (*kallion*) than the previous "good" polis. The term *kallipolis* seems to be intended as a characterization of the polis that has reached the height of government (543a) in the same manner as the previous types of order had their corresponding attributes.

The poleogonic construction begins in best theogonic style from the beginning (*ex arches*), with a constellation of elemental forces to be harmonized by order. The various propositions involved in the construction have appeared on and off in our analysis, and we shall now assemble them in a coherent picture. Man, that is the first proposition, is not self-sufficient (*ouk autarkes*), but has many needs that can be satisfied adequately only by the services of others. Moreover, men are differently gifted by nature so that one man is more skilled for a specific task than other men. By developing the respective gifts into skills a group of men can achieve a more satisfactory equipment with the necessities (*anankaia*) of life. All the gifts and skills that enter into the satisfactory compound, however, are human gifts, so that society as a whole is man written in larger letters. The principle conducive to order, present from the beginning and later developed into the virtue of justice, is attention to the business for which a man is specifically gifted. Neglect of one's own business and meddling in things that are by nature another man's specific chore will reduce the effectiveness of the order and ultimately upset it.

The result of the construction is a plain community of free peasants, craftsmen, and small traders, neither rich nor poor, exerting birth control so that no increase of population will face them with the dilemma of poverty or expansion through war. That is the community which Socrates calls true and healthy. We have the feeling that Plato looks with a certain nostalgia on this idyll of the healthy, active, peaceful, and pious freemen whose necessities of life are satisfied; and we may even suspect that a preference on occasion expressed by Socrates himself moves in the background of the lovingly drawn primitive order. But in such matters nothing can be proven.

While the primitive polis is an order by nature, and an healthy and true one at that, it does not give room to all the forces of human nature. It would be the good polis if all men were satisfied with the necessities of life and simple pleasures. But by far not all men are; and one of them is present in the person of Glaukon who is more disgusted than attracted by the healthy and true order. To be sure, he is in search of Arete; but he also is the scion of an aristocratic family. He does not want to have his life cooped up in the existence of a peasant-householder who sits at dinnertime on a hard chair, beaming on his frugal meal and the family, who on festive occasions joins in the singing of pious hymns, and the next morning happily goes back to tilling the soil. He wants, among other things, to spend an occasional night in the more elegantly and comfortably appointed house of a Piraeus merchant, in the company of Socrates, engaged in philosophical discourse. Contemptuously he dismisses the healthy order as a "polis for pigs" (372d). What Glaukon and Adeimantus want is a polis with the amenities of civilization to which they are accustomed, and in which they can play a social role comparable to their present one.

Socrates is quick to recognize the new force; the young men shall have the polis in which they can find their place. It is the luxurious polis, complete with luxury crafts, actors, dancers, nurses, chambermaids, and cooks. It will have a much larger territory to accomodate the swollen population, it will have conflicts with neighboring poleis of a similar complexion and expansion, it will be involved in wars, and it will need, therefore, an army. A group of citizens, however, who by virtue of their specialization in the art of warfare are the guardians (*phylakes*) of their polis, are a potential source of danger. Unless they are properly selected, trained, and educated, they will be the masters of their fellow citizens rather than their helpers and guardians. Mutual suspicion will breed hatred and the internal tensions are bound to destroy the polis. The inherent instability of the luxurious polis drives on to the consideration of further forces which are apt to restore stability to the order under investigation.

The transition from the primitive to the luxurious polis was motivated by the human type in the person of Glaukon, whose endowments are too rich to find their fulfilment in the simple life. The force was recognized as legitimate by Socrates, but the consequent enlargement of the order led to an impasse. For the noble youth has the gifts, the high-spirited character (*thymoeides*), and the nature of a lover of wisdom (*philosophos physis*) that would suit him for the career as a guardian in the larger polis, but he does not have the accomplishments of a ruler. If the Glaukon type were let loose without further polish the result would be unfortunate. In order to avoid a disaster, the prospective guardians must undergo a rigorous training and education. And in its course it will turn out that not all of them can be developed to the full stature of a ruler. The guardians will, therefore, subdivide in two groups: a larger group of inferior status, the helpers (*epikuroi*), and a smaller group of men who can be educated to the point where they become guardians (*phylakes*) in the pregnant sense. And the principles of this education cannot be provided by the hopefuls who have the gifts but not the accomplishment; they can be furnished only by a helper of a superior order, by Socrates himself. Hence, with the third stage of the poleogony the force of Socrates enters into the nature of the polis as the physician who will cure the luxurious but feverish polis and restore it to health, while preserving its civilizational scale.[14]

Since with Adeimantus and his luxurious polis Socrates also accepts the traditional education (*paideia*) of the body through gymnastics, of the soul through music (376e), his therapy assumes the form of a critical expurgation of traditions. In this section of the *Republic* the great conflict between the order of philosophy and the order of the myth comes to its head. The culture of the myth is disintegrating, and its

---

[14] Since the work of Plato is exposed in our time to generous misunderstanding and downright vilification, it is worth noting that the transition from the second to the third stage of the poleogony explains, as elaborately as any political scientist may wish, why government by a high-spirited, idealistic elite as an alternative to democracy in an age of crisis is not only undesirable, but disastrous. Plato explicitly rejects the alternative of a philosophically unkempt elite.

disintegration bifurcates in the manner to which we have referred on
previous occasions. On the one hand, the language of the myth becomes
unseemly (Xenophanes) when the order of existence can be expressed
more truly in the language of the philosopher's soul and its experience
of transcendent divinity. On the other hand, the language of the myth
becomes opaque when it passes through the minds of enlightened fundamentalists. When the myth is no longer experienced as the imaginative
symbolization of divine forces, but as a realistic collection of dirty stories
about the gods, the educational influence even of Homer can become
disastrous. In his relation of the myth of Gyges and his ring the young
Glaukon glibly assumes that his invisible man, when he indulges his
passions, acts "like a god among men." And we remember the examples
of enlightened destruction in the Herodotean treatment of Homer or in
Thucydides' Melian Dialogue. Hence, the war between Plato and the
great poets is conducted on two fronts. On the one hand, the art forms
of "mimetic" poetry are unsuitable to the experiences which Plato is
seeking to express artistically. That part of the conflict becomes articulate
in Book X of the *Republic*. On the other hand, the attack is directed
against the influence which the great poets exert when they are read with
a flatness of understanding which is not Plato's. That part of the conflict becomes articulate in the Socratic expurgation of the poets *ad usum
Delphini*. What is at stake in the conflict is neither the excellence of
Homer as a poet, nor even the language of the myth, so brilliantly used
by Plato himself, but the order of the soul.

In order to expurgate the media of *paideia*, Socrates develops "types"
of symbols and symbolic actions, classified as injurious or helpful to the
building of right order in the souls of the guardians. He begins with the
previously analyzed types of theology and continues with types of tales
concerning afterlife in Hades, as well as forms of conduct that could
be considered as models by the readers of the tales. From the contents
of tales he proceeds to types of poetic representation (purely narrative
dithyrambs, purely imitative drama, the mixed narrative and drama of
the epic); further, to the symbolic gestures and actions of songs, har-
monies, and rhythms; and, finally, to the types of gymnastics and their
effects on the formation of the soul.[15] Such an expurgated system of
paideia is the true politeia; and in order to preserve it in existence, insti-

---

[15] I do not go into the details of the educational program because they are set forth admirably
by Werner Jaeger in his *Paideia*, II.

tutions of enforcement and supervision are needed, briefly designated by Socrates as the *epistates,* the overseer (412a). As the passage suggests, Paideia and Politeia cannot be separated. Hence, the expurgation of types that has begun with types of theology and gone through the types of musical and gymnastic gestures, continues into the institutions and manner of life of the guardians. For there is nothing in the order of a life which does not affect the order of the soul. Since the Socratic guardianship is not defined by the external position of a man, but as an "indwelling conviction that at any time he must do what according to his conviction is the best for the polis" (413c), the soul of the guardian must not be exposed to temptations of personal interest that would falsify the convictions. Wives and children should be in common among the guardians, so that no family interest will tempt them (423e–424a); they should have no private property beyond the necessities, no habitations that are not accessible to the public at any time, especially no treasure and ornaments of gold and silver; they should have common settlements and common meals; and derive their sustenance from annual payments by the worker citizens.

If the *eidos* of the good polis were no more than an object of cognition, the poleogony could be considered completed with its third stage. There are three social strata now in the polis: the working population (*georgoi, demiourgoi*), the guards (*phylakes*), and the rulers (*archontes*). The workers were introduced by the agreement about necessities that led to the healthy or true polis; the guards by the protest of Glaukon and the recognition of a civilizational scale that gives room to men of his type; and the rulers by the Socratic purification and education, which differentiated from the guardians those among them who could be maximally formed by a Socratic Paideia. All three of the poleogonic stages, thus, are preserved in the final *eidos* of the good polis. Socrates indeed pretends completion and wants to go on to the *eide* of the bad constitutions (449a–b).

The impeccably realistic construction of the *eidos* out of the human forces present in the drama has resulted, however, in a nonexistent Politeia. We are thrown back to the situation of resistance to the corrupt society, in which the inquiry originated. Realism requires the incorporation of the Socratic Paideia in the good Politeia because the criteria of right order of human existence can be found nowhere but in the soul of the philosopher. But adherence to realism leads into conflict with the reality of the surrounding society. The great conflict between the spiritual authority of the philosopher and the factual authority of society is expressed but not solved by the construction of the *eidos*. And the unsettled state of the issue drives on to the fourth stage of the poleogony with the question whether social circumstances are at least imaginable under which the order recognized as good could become the order of a concrete polis. The element of foundation comes into play again in that the *eidos*, which as an object of the cognitive inquiry has incorporated the order of the Socratic soul, is at the same time a draft for a constitution originating in the founding authority of the philosopher's soul.

Before giving way to the pressure of the younger men to reveal the condition under which the good polis can become reality, Socrates once more stresses the cognitive character of the inquiry. "A paradigm was what we wanted" when we were looking for the nature of justice and injustice; when "looking at such a paradigm" we can apply it to ourselves and recognize our share of likeness; we are not obliged to prove that justice can be transplanted into reality; we have created a "paradigm of the good polis" in our discourse; and its validity is not impaired if we cannot offer a recipe for its realization (472c–e). The paradigm, thus, is a standard by which things can be measured; and the reliability of the measure is not diminished, if things fall short of it, or if we have no means to bring them closer to it.[16]

Having thus safeguarded the nature of the paradigm as a true standard independent of its realization, Socrates announces the famous condition: "Unless either the philosophers become kings in the poleis, or those who now are called kings and rulers become philosophers, genuinely and adequately, so that political power and philosophy meet in one, and the common natures who now pursue the two separately are forcefully excluded, there will be no rest from evil for the poleis, nor, I believe, for the human race either. And not until that happens, will this politeia of ours have a measure of growth and see the light of the sun" (473c–d). Coming, as it does, at the last stage of the poleogony, the postulate should not be surprising. The true order that is real in the philosopher's soul can expand into social order only when somebody with a philosopher's soul imposes it on the polis. The Socratic Paideia of the third poleogonic

[16] It is perhaps not unnecessary to stress again that a paradigm, in the sense of standard, is not an "ideal." The standard is true because it expresses the reality of order in the philosopher's soul. And the existence of Plato, as well as of the order in his soul, is not an "ideal" but an historical fact.

stage will remain the soul of the Politeia only in discourse unless a ruler with a Socratic soul undertakes the work of education. While the condition for the realization of the good politeia, thus, is clear and simple, the chances that philosophers will become kings are slim. In the Parable of the Pilot (488a–489d) Plato lets Socrates explain that the people at large, in the democracy of his time, are not in a position to recognize a philosopher and his usefulness by their own initiative. Moreover, the power-seeking politicians take care to prevent such recognition and to secure rulership for themselves. And the philosopher cannot help them because he cannot impose himself on them. For in the true order of things those in need of a ruler must come to the door of the man who knows how to rule. The ruler, if he is really good, will not implore his natural sujects to let themselves be ruled by him (489b–c).

5. The Phoenician Tale

The poleogony is a symbolic form closed within itself. Nevertheless, embedded in it are numerous subsections by which it is linked to the dialogue of which it is itself an enclosure. The first of these subsections to be considered is the Phoenician Tale, toward the end of Book III (414b–415d). It has its place in the third stage of the poleogony, at the point where the construction of the polis with its three strata of workers, helpers, and guardians is completed. At this point Socrates suggests the following procedure:

The founders of the polis will tell its citizens "a sort of Phoenician tale." They will try to persuade, first the rulers and soldiers, and then the rest of the polis, that their training and education were things they had imagined as in a dream. In truth, during that time, they had been under the earth where they themselves, as well as their weapons and other equipment, were moulded and prepared. When they were finished, the earth as their mother delivered them, so that now they had to take care of the country and defend it as their mother that had brought them forth. Moreover, they had to regard the other citizens as their brothers and the offspring of the same mother earth. While they were all brothers, the tale will go on, the god when he fashioned them meant some of them to be rulers and therefore mixed gold into their race. Into the helpers he mixed silver; and iron and brass into the farmers and craftsmen. Still, they were all close kinsmen; and while the races usually would breed true, it might also happen that golden fathers would beget sons

with silver or brass, and in like manner different offspring would come
forth from the other races. Hence, it was the first and most important
command of the god to the rulers that they must sort out the children
and direct them to the social function in keeping with their metal composition. For an oracle says: The polis will perish when iron or brass is
its guardian.

The circumstantial setting of the tale affects and clarifies its meaning.
The "founders" had agreed that falsehoods are reprehensible in their
polis, and only the rulers are permitted to use it on occasion, as a sort of
medicine, for the welfare of the polis (389b–c). Socrates now refers to
the former agreement; he wants to contrive such a lie, presumably of a
beneficial nature, though the purpose is nowhere stated (414b). Its
contents, the Phoenician tale, is not new. Such things have happened
before in many parts of the world, according to the poets who were believed; but they have not happened recently, and it would be hard to
make people believe today that they could happen again. (414c). Socrates
obviously procrastinates with his introduction, especially since the lie is
so comprehensive and big (*gennaion*).[17] When from the introductory
hedgings and warnings we now turn to the contents of the "lie," the
satirical intention of the Tale becomes clear. For what is that event that
happened in many places in the past but did not happen recently, that
story that once could be told and believed but would be difficult to believe if somebody told it today; what is that "Big Lie"? It is the simple
truth that all men are brothers. The good order of the polis requires
everybody to mind his own business according to his natural gifts. Now
that the natures of the rulers, guardians, and workers are distinguished,
and the Paideia for the rulers has been elaborated, Socrates must stress
that in spite of their differences they still are all equal as brothers. Within
the poleogony it is the same sequence of issues as in Romans and I Corin-
thians, where St. Paul first distinguishes the charismata and their function
in the community, and then sternly reminds his Christians that, in spite
of their different endowments, they still are all members of the one body
of Christ and that the most devoted service is worthless unless formed
by love. To Socrates the physician the differences are as it were dream
images (*oneirata*), while the reality (*aletheia*) is the equality of brother-

---

[17] The translation as a "noble lie," frequently to be found, is a mistake. *Gennaios*, when
applied to things, means "good of their kind, excellent" (Liddell-Scott). Applied to a lie it
would mean a big lie, a "whopper." Jowett's translation as "audacious" is correct but a bit
stuffy.

hood (414d). The introduction of the supreme truth as an unbelievable Big Lie is one of the bitterest pages in a work that heaps so much bitter scorn on Athens.

The word translated as lie, the Greek *pseudos*, has more than one meaning. The agreement among the founders that only the rulers are permitted to use an occasional *pseudos* for the benefit of the polis, was embedded in the discussion of tales (*mythoi*, or *logoi*) as an instrument of education. Such tales may be true (*alethes*) or false (*pseudos*) (376e); and Plato enjoys the paradox that the education of children begins with untrue stories, that is, with fables and myths. For such a *mythos* told to children is untrue (*pseudos*) as a whole, but nevertheless is also true (*alethes*) (377a). The myth that has its truth is a *pseudos* in the sense developed by Hesiod; it is the myth of the old style to be superseded by the truth of the soul and its new modes of expression. The meaning of the Phoenician tale is not exhausted by its function as a satire on the unbrotherly Athens torn by political factions; the *pseudos* must be weighed as a myth in its own right and its meaning, or rather the multiplicity of its meanings, must be ascertained:

(1) The myth deliberately recalls Hesiod and his metal ages through the story of the metals mixed into the races of the citizens. In its context, at the stage where the paradigm of the good polis is completed, it is an explicit warning not to misunderstand the stages of the poleogony as phases of political growth in historical time. The elements of the *eidos*, distended in the time of the poleogony, must be understood as co-existent in the structure of the politeia. The successive metal ages of the speculative form are simultaneous in the *eidos*. Under this aspect the Phoenician tale prepares the systematic discussion of the unity of man in the diversification of types, both in the individual man and in the man written large, in the immediately following section of the *Republic*.

(2) The insistence on introducing the problem of equality by means of the myth draws attention to the methodological question whether the truth conveyed by the *pseudos* could be conveyed by any other means at all. To be sure, in part, the use of the myth supports the satirical intention in so far as the Athenians had an almost identical myth of their origin from mother earth, and prided themselves on being all of equally noble descent because of this *isogonia* (*Menex.* 237b ff.). The heavy accent on the incredibility of brotherhood underlines the unbrotherliness

of the Athenian brothers. Nevertheless, we must not overlook the primary philosophical motive for the introduction of the myth, that is, the ineffability of the equality of men. The understanding of a universal humanity originates in the experience of transcendence; and the ineffable kinship of men under God revealed in the experience can immanently be expressed only through a myth of descent from a common mother or father. The myth, thus, is with methodological correctness introduced at the point where the sense of a common humanity, overriding the differences of gifts and social positions, had to be evoked.

(3) The myth, finally, is explicit on its own function, as well as on its relation to the preceding construction of the paradigm. The whole elaborate training for their position should be understood by the rulers and guardians, and secondarily by the rest of the citizens, as a dream (*oneirata*). The truth and reality (*aletheia*) is their brotherhood. The distinction of dream and reality is pointed against the evil of pride that may take possession of the rulers in the politeia. And that pride will not be easily checked even by a myth of brotherhood. Hence, the tale raises the differences themselves, of which men might pride themselves, into the realm of the myth by attributing them, not to personal gifts and education, but to the metal mixed by the god into the race. As a consequence, the construction of the politeia as a whole acquires the characteristic of an *oneiron*, a dream, while the true reality is the inexplicable mystery of human existence in community, with its equality and inequality, impenetrable to rational analysis and communicable only through the truth of the myth. The *pseudos* that begins as a Big Lie is subtly transformed into the Great Truth.

(4) Behind this play of dream and truth there again looms unmistakably the shadow of Heraclitus. We recall the sleepwalkers who live in their private worlds, having abandoned the common world of those who are awake in the Nous. The social differentiation of the good polis is in danger of becoming a war between the private worlds unless the pride of gifts and position, as well as the indulgence of securing position for unworthy offspring, are recognized as the fall from the truth. When the rulers promote their children to rulership even though they are not of the metal of their fathers, and disregard the gold rising from the lower ranks, the polis will perish, because it ceases to be the cosmos of waking life where wisdom rules and becomes the chaos of private worlds in which

men indulge the dreams of their passions. The good polis will become a nightmare when men forget that their existence has reality only as long as it enacts the dream-play of God.

6. *The Models of Soul and Society*

The Phoenician Tale contracts the succession of the poleogonic stages into the simultaneity of the three social strata in the good polis, and lets the membership in a stratum be determined by a definite human character. Human nature is diversified into several types, frequently referred to by Plato as "natures," and the problem of order is the harmonization of the types in social super- and sub-ordination. The problem, implied in the poleogony and contracted in the Tale, is then elaborated in an extensive classification of forces in the soul, types of characters and virtues, and the corresponding classification of social strata, their characters and virtues, in Book IV of the *Republic*. The schema developed is briefly the following.

In the soul there can be distinguished three forces: the appetitive, the spirited, and the rational element. The three forces stand to one another in an hierarchical relation in so far as the rational element is the highest organizing element of the soul, while the appetitive element stands lowest in rank. The stratification of the forces in the soul is used by Plato in the construction of a characterology when he distinguishes three types of characters according to the predominance of one or the other element in the individual soul. The anthropology is rounded out by a classification of ordering powers in the soul, of virtues (*aretai*), which bring order into the field of the forces. The ordering powers are wisdom (*sophia*), courage (*andreia*), temperance (*sophrosyne*), and justice (*dikaiosyne*). Wisdom is the ordering power that is nourished from the rational element in the soul; courage the power that is nourished from the spirited element, that is, from an affect of indignation that rushes to the defense of rational insight. Temperance, however, is not strictly co-ordinated with the appetitive element in the soul; it is rather conceived as an agreement, or consent, of the elemental forces to the claim of the highest force to rule the soul. Justice, the keystone of the system of ordering powers, is that disposition of the well-ordered soul by virtue of which each part fulfills its proper function. The following table will best show the construction of the model of the soul:

Stratum	Character	Ordering Powers		
Logistikon	Philomathes and Philosophon	Sophia		
Thymoeides	Philonikon and Philotimon	Andreia	Sophrosyne	Dikaiosyne
Epithymetikon	Philochrematon and Philokerdes			

The model of the soul is then used in the construction of the corresponding model of the polis:

Stratum	Character	Ordering Powers		
Archontes	Bouleutikon	Sophia		
Phylakes	Epikourikon	Andreia	Sophrosyne	Dikaiosyne
Georgoi	Chrematistikon			

The model is, finally, used in a psychology of ethnic characters. The
Hellenes are characterized by their love of knowledge (*philomathes*),
the Thracians and Scythians by their high-spiritedness (*thymoeides*),
the Phoenicians and Egyptians by their love of money (*philochrematon*)
(435e–436a).[18]

The models with their parallel construction of the soul, society, and
ethnic types carry to its extreme the anthropological principle that society
is man written in larger letters. One must beware, however, to treat
them as a final "doctrine," for they are rigid and defective in more than
one respect. The classification of character types according to the three
metals was abandoned by Plato in the *Laws* and replaced by the more
supple symbolism of the metal chords which in every soul exert their
pull, in varying strength, in various directions. And in the more immediate context Plato cautions the reader that his problem has aspects
which do not become topical at the present level of discussion (435d).
The formal polish of the models, far from being a sign of final solution,

[18] The arrangement of the models in tables from Ueberweg-Heinze, *Grundriss*, I (Praechter),
(13th ed., Basel, 1953), 275.

reflects the enormous effort that has gone into the construction of problems recognized for the first time by Plato as the fundamentals of a philosophy of order. The recognition of the problems is the great achievement that compels again and again the return to the Platonic models even if their solutions can no longer be accepted. One or two of these problems must be briefly noted.

First of all, Plato recognized it as a trait in the constitution of being that men are both equal and unequal. By means of his characterology he tried, therefore, to construe the differences among human "natures" as variants of the dynamic relations between the component parts, equal to all men, of the soul. Human nature is conceived as dispersed in variants over a multitude of human beings, so that only a group as a whole will embody the fullness of the nature. Order in society then would mean the harmonization of the variant types in correct super- and sub-ordination. Clearly, the conception will burst the limits of the "good polis" when its implications are thought through, for there is no guaranty that any concrete society will ever contain the various types in such mixtures that a "good polis" can result at all. We remember Plato's own experience with his Athens and his awareness that the soul has problems of order beyond the order of the polis. Moreover, once the problem of diversification of human nature is recognized, it cannot be artificially restricted to the limits of a polis. Plato himself uses the model of the soul beyond the interpretation of the polis that is man written large, when he applies it to the classification of ethnic characters. Mankind as a whole, beyond the limits of a concrete society, is the field over which the types are distributed; and perhaps only mankind as a whole, with its constellation of the main civilizations, will reveal the fullness of human nature, so that any concrete society will achieve only a relative "goodness" within its historical limitations. Once he recognizes the problem, the best a philosopher can do for his own civilization is to ascribe to it a higher "goodness" than to any other group known to him—as Plato does when he ascribes to the Hellenes the variant of preponderant wisdom. Plato's procedure remained a model for the construction of civilizational history through the ages and was still alive in Bodin's philosophy of history.

The various human natures can be construed as variants of the one human nature only if the soul is recognized as a field of forces which can enter into various configurations, the *eide,* or characters. That is

the second problem, or rather complex of problems, recognized by
Plato. Though the understanding of the psyche had massively advanced
since Homer through the mystic-philosophers and the tragedians, a
theoretization of its problems had hardly begun. What through the
work of Plato and Aristotle became the faculties, forces, and dispositions of the psyche were in the prevalent conception still separate
faculties and organs of man, just as in the time of Homer. The formulation of the anthropological principle itself (435e) is, therefore, followed in the *Republic* by an inquiry into the unity of the soul that holds
the various forces together, beginning with the revealing reflection
that matters begin to get difficult "when you ask whether we do all
these things with the same thing or whether there are three things and
we do one thing with one and one with another—learn with one part
of ourselves, feel anger with another" and so forth (436b). The achievement of Plato's models will perhaps be understood best if we realize
that he started practically from the Homeric state of the problem. In
his early years Plato was still close to the Socratic conception that virtue
is knowledge, which in its turn was still close to the Homeric notion
of right action through "seeing." And now, in the models, we find a
sophia that is nourished from the rational part of the soul, the *logistikon*,
present in all men at all times, but still of no avail unless a virtue higher
than wisdom sees to it that wisdom will indeed prevail in the soul over
the passions. That higher virtue is Dikaiosyne. When we consider that
in the ethics of Aristotle justice as an ethical virtue is outranked by
the dianoetic virtues, and especially by *phronesis;* that in the system of
the Roman jurists of the classical period it is outranked by *jurisprudentia;*
and that in Christian ethics it is outranked (as one of the four cardinal
virtues) by the theological virtues of faith, hope, and love, we understand that Plato by means of his Dikaiosyne is grappling with the
transcendental constitution of order in the soul. The soul of the Platonic
model is no longer an open field of forces whose action can be attributed
by man to the gods, but a closed entity with an ordering power that
does not draw its strength from any of the three forces located by the
model within the soul. The Dikaiosyne which imposes right order on
the forces within the soul has its origin outside the soul. The place of
Dikaiosyne in the model points toward transcendent reality as the source
of order.

7. *The Agathon*

The models of good order in soul and society point toward a constitution of the soul beyond the three forces and the four virtues.
Moreover, the deliberate realism in building the paradigm of the good
polis leaves us with the question why the paradigm developed should
be dignified with the attribute "good" at all. Is not the *eidos* of the
models perhaps the form of a very bad polis? Plato is quite aware of
such questions. The Socrates of the dialogue cautiously avoids the issue
of goodness while developing the paradigm that supposedly is good,
and hints at the ulterior problem only by the warning that the matter
at hand will never be apprehended accurately (*akribos*) by the methods
used. There is a "longer and harder way" that leads to the goal (435d).

The longer and harder way is finally undertaken in Books VI and
VII of the *Republic*. Socrates reminds his friends of the former warning (504a–b). There is a thing greater than justice and the other
virtues (504d), and that greater thing is the measure of the less perfect
ones (504c). The earlier development of the models is now reduced
to the rank of an outline or sketch (*hypographe*) to be superseded by
the more exact elaboration (504d). The men who will be the rulers of
the good polis must go through the course of the "greatest studies"
(*mathemata megista*) in order to possess the true measure of right order
(504a). The politeia will be perfectly organized only when its guardian
has the knowledge of such matters (506a–b). That knowledge is concerned with the idea of the good (*tou agathou idea*) in relation to which
"just things and all the rest that belongs here" become useful and
beneficial (505a). When they have fixed the "gaze of their soul" on
the good itself (*to agathon auto*), they shall use it as a paradigm for the
right ordering (*kosmein*) of the polis, the citizens, and themselves for
the rest of their lives (540a–b).

What is the Idea of the Agathon? The briefest answer to the question will best bring out the decisive point: Concerning the content of
the Agathon nothing can be said at all. That is the fundamental insight
of Platonic ethics. The transcendence of the Agathon makes immanent
propositions concerning its content impossible.

The vision of the Agathon does not render a material rule of conduct, but forms the soul through an experience of transcendence. The
nature of this experience and the place of the Agathon in it is described

by Socrates indirectly through the function of the "offspring" of the good, the sun, in relation to vision (506e ff). Things are visible to the eye when the light of the sun enters the relation as a third factor. The eye is the most sunlike of all instruments and receives its power of sight from the sun as it were through an influx. Moreover, the sun which lends to the eye the power of sight can by virtue of this power itself be seen (508a–b). These are the propositions concerning the sun which serve as the *analogon* (508c) to make intelligible the role of the Agathon in the noetic realm (*noetos topos*). The Agathon is neither intellect (*nous*) nor its object (*nooumenon*) (508c), but that what "gives their truth to the objects of knowledge and the power of knowing to the knower." The Idea of the Agathon is "the cause of knowledge [*episteme*] and of truth [*aletheia*] as far as known" (508e). The analogical elucidation of the Agathon by means of what is most like it (*eikon*) is then carried one step further. The sun not only provides visibility, but generation, growth, and nurture to the visibles, though it is not itself generation (*genesis*). And likewise the Agathon not only makes objects knowable, but provides them with their existence and essence, though it is itself beyond (*epekeina*) essence in dignity and power. The *epekeina* is Plato's term for "beyond" or "transcendent." The excellence created by the Agathon in the soul is not identical with any of the four virtues in the model (518d); Plato's preferred term for its designation is *phronesis* (518e).

The ascent to the vision of what lies beyond (*epekeina*) being, as well as the experience of the way, were expressed by Plato more than once, especially in the *Symposion* and *Phaedrus,* in grandiose symbols. The symbolic expressions differ because the forces that drive and drag on the way have a wide range from Eros and Mania to the desire for true knowledge. In the *Republic* it is the desire for truth that drives man on his way through the various forms of knowledge, from the less to the more perfect ones, until he sees transcendent reality which in its turn constitutes the objects of *noesis*, as well as the faculty of *nous* or *episteme.* There are various forms of knowledge because there are two realms of objects given to human understanding, the realm of becoming (*genesis*) and the realm of essence (*ousia*). Each of the realms, furthermore, has two subdivisions of objects. In the realm of becoming things are either shadows and reflections, or objects of sense perception; in the realm of essence they are mathematical objects or ideas proper. To the altogether four classes of objects correspond the four faculties of knowledge: *eikasia, pistis, dianoia,* and *noesis* or *episteme* (509d–511e). The transcendental constitution of the soul can be achieved when a man passes through the forms of knowledge, when he ascends from the realm of shadows (and the corresponding *eikasia*) to the realm of ideas (and the corresponding *episteme*) and ultimately to the vision of the Agathon itself. In order to express this way, Socrates tells to his friends the Parable of the Cave:

(1) Human beings are chained in a cave, with their faces to the wall. Behind them the cave rises towards an opening, with a blazing fire at a distance. Between the fire and the prisoners is a low wall, behind which persons are passing, holding up vessels, statues, and figures of animals so that they protrude above the wall. The prisoners see nothing but the shadows on the wall of the cave before them, their own shadows as well as the shadows of the objects protruding above the wall. To the prisoners truth would be nothing but the shadows of themselves and the objects (514–515).

(2) In the second part of the Parable one of the prisoners is released from his bonds and forced to stand up suddenly, to turn around to walk, and to lift his eyes toward the light. The experience is painful. The glare of the fire will dazzle him. And at first he will be inclined to consider the shadows true reality, and the real objects distortions (515).

(3) In the third part the prisoner is dragged up to the mouth of the cave and has to face the upper world and the light itself. He advances in his power of vision from the shadows to the real objects, and further to the source of light itself. And he finally recognizes the sun as the lord of the visible world and, in a sense, as the ultimate creator of all things which he saw in his prison (516). Once he has seen the light, he is reluctant to return to the cave and to his fellow prisoners. They had a practice of conferring honors on those who best observed the sequence of shadows and who could, on the basis of their observations, guess the ones that would appear next. He no longer has the taste for such wisdom and such honors; and he endures anything rather than return to that miserable life.

(4) In the fourth part, however, the prisoner is taken back to his former seat among his fellow prisoners. He finds it difficult to adjust himself again to the darkness. He is a ridiculous figure among his companions who never left their places, for he no longer is as alert as they

are at the game of the shadows. They scoff at him because he has lost his sight in the ascent; they think it better not to ascend at all, than to return in such a condition. And if he tries to loosen others from their shackles they lay hands on the offender if they can, and put him to death (516–517).

The meaning of the Parable in general is clear and needs no elaboration. It is an allegory of the philosopher's education, as well as of his fate in the corrupt society, with a concluding allusion to the death of Socrates. We can turn, therefore, to the special purposes for which Plato introduced it at this point of the dialogue.

The Parable, first of all, prepares a clarification of Paideia. A man's education to the full understanding of reality is incomplete as long as he has not undergone the turning around of the soul, the *periagoge* in the Parable. The *periagoge*, however, poses a problem to education different from the problems of Paideia developed in the earlier Socratic purification of traditions. For all the virtues of the soul, previously described in the models, have something in common with excellences of the body, in so far as they can be created by habituation (*ethesi*) and training (*askesesin*) where they do not already exist (518d). To that limited extent, therefore, one can say that virtue can be taught. In so far as the "professions" of the sophists (for instance of Protagoras in the dialogue bearing his name) go beyond that point, however, and assert that true knowledge, *episteme*, can be put into the soul, they are in error (518b–c). For the kind of vision (*opsis*) that enables a man to see the Agathon must exist in a soul, as a man must have eyes to see (518c). The educator can do no more than turn this organ of vision, if it exists in the soul of a man, around from the realm of becoming toward being and the brightest region of being—"and that, we say, is the Agathon" (518c). Hence, Paideia (518b) is "the art of turning around [*periagoge*]" (518d).

Paideia, Periagoge, and Agathon, thus, are intimately connected; and that connection, established by Plato himself, must be kept in mind if one wishes to avoid the extravagant interpretations which so easily suggest themselves, because in Christianity the *periagoge* has become conversion in the religious sense. To be sure, the Platonic *periagoge* has the overtones of conversion; but no more than the overtones. The experience remains essentially within the boundaries of the Dionysiac soul, as the various formulations in the context of the Parable make it clear. Man should engage in a course of study, from mathematics to dialectics, that will "facilitate the apprehension of the idea of the Agathon." That tendency is to be found in all studies which force the soul to turn away from becoming toward being, and ultimately toward the region where dwells "the most eudaimonic being" (526e). Once they have engaged in such "divine contemplation" (517d), men will want to stay "up there forever" (517c), for there they will feel eudaimonic themselves (*eudaimonizein*) (516c) and as it were "transported to the Islands of the Blessed while still living" (519c).[19] Hence, the beatitude of the Eudaimonia is not a beatific vision in the Christian sense, but literally a heightened state of Daimonia, which the Daimon in the psyche of man will reach when he engages in cultivation (*paideia*) through association with the eudaimonic Agathon.

The philosopher who has reached the state of Eudaimonia will be inclined to linger at the height of contemplation. He will be reluctant to return to the darkness of the Cave and to dispute shadows with the prisoners. Hence, as far as the order of the polis is concerned, the means of its salvation seems to be self-defeating. When the only men who can establish good order withdraw into the life of contemplation, the government will be left to the unenlightened politicians, or to those men who strive for *phronesis* but never reach it. Socrates must impose, therefore, on his reluctant philosophers the duty of returning to the Cave.

But why is this duty incumbent on them? Why should the philosopher sacrifice himself to co-citizens who would rather kill him than follow him? The question of apolitism becomes acute; and Plato qualifies the duty to return, indeed, by distinguishing between various situations in which the philosopher may find himself. Return is a duty only in the polis of the *Republic*, not in the surrounding corrupt society. For the polis of the *Republic* is based on the principle that the happiness of the individual is subordinate to the happiness of the whole (419ff; 519e). Each class of the citizens must contribute its share, "by persuasion or by constraint" (519e). And the polis has a right to demand the philosophers' sacrifice, because it has provided the course of education that should enable them to bind the polis together (519–520). In other poleis, where men have achieved the contemplative life spon-

---

[19] For further passages of this nature from other dialogues, see Friedlaender, *Platon*, I, 81.

taneously (*automatoi*), without aid of the community or even in opposition to it, however, they have no reason to be zealous about the
payment of a nonexistent debt of gratitude (520a–b). We are again
touching the previously discussed possibility of ultimate withdrawal
from the polis and attendance to the politeia in the soul, with the perspective that this course opens into existence in a spiritual community
beyond temporal organization of government. Nevertheless, that problem is no more than touched in the context of the Parable. The order
of the *Republic* contemplates no such differentiation of existence into
spiritual and temporal. The philosophers of the good polis, once they
have received their education, are under the stern decree: "Down you
must go [*katabateon*]" (520c). The decree resumes the opening theme
of the *Republic*, the "I went down [*kateben*]" of Socrates; and perhaps it recalls Orphic associations of a *katabasis* to Hades to aid the
souls in the underworld. For the philosophers must go down, as the
saviors like Socrates, in order to help the prisoners in the Cave. Since
they have seen "the truth of the beautiful, the just, and the good,"
they can discern much better than the dwellers "There" the obscure
things, the shadows (*eidola*) of the real things. Since they have seen
the Agathon, the polis under their rulership will be governed with
a wake mind (*hypar*) and not be ruled, as most poleis are today, darkly
as in a dream (*onar*) (520c–d).

§ 5. THE DISINTEGRATION OF ORDER

The order of the good polis, even when at last it is established, will
disintegrate. Part III of the *Republic* (543a–576b) studies the causes
and phases of disintegration, as well as the forms through which soul
and society pass when they decline. The general meaning of the study
derives from its position in the dialogue as a whole, as we have set it
forth in the opening section of the present chapter. With regard to its
form we should note that the process of decomposition is told as a story,
in the same manner in which the formation of the paradigm of good
order unfolded as the story of its creation. The tale of the successive
bad forms of government is the counterpart of the poleogony in which
the good forms succeeded each other. No question, therefore, can arise
as to whether the sequence of forms is meant as a history of decline.

To be sure, historical questions arise as topics within the tale; but the time of the tale itself is the time of a mythical narration, just as in the poleogony, not the time of history.

1. *The Somatic Unity of the Polis*

As a study of the disembodiment of the Idea, Part III balances the embodiment of the Idea in Part II. The language of embodiment and disembodiment has its pregnant meaning because Plato makes the body in the biological sense the sound somatic basis, a condition for the establishment of the good polis, in the opening section of Part II (449a–466d). Part III correspondingly opens the study of disembodiment with the causes of disorder in the somatic basis which in its turn will lead to disorder of the psyche (545b ff). We shall, therefore, begin our analysis with the project for securing a sound somatic basis for the good polis.

The project, to which we have referred several times previously, envisages the community of wives and children among the guardians and rulers, as well as a program for eugenic mating. Socrates approaches the subject with some hesitations because the idea runs counter to what is ordinarily accepted as the nature of things in matters of family relations. In order to understand the motivation of the strange program, we have to recall the fundamental problem of all Hellenic politics, that is, the inability to overcome the gentilician cohesion and to create political institutions on a regional or national scale. The polis, we remember, was constructed out of families and tribes. No direct membership in the polis was possible; citizenship in Athens could be acquired through birth or through adoption into one of the phratries or demes. The idea of personal membership in a community of the spirit, irrespective of family ties, was still in its infancy; it had just begun to express itself, in the fourth century, in the form of philosophical schools. In this historical situation we have to understand the Platonic project of a community of women and children as an attempt to overcome the disruptive family divisions by transforming at least the ruling class of the polis into a single family. The profound sentiments arising from sex relations, as well as the parent-child relations, will no longer be contained by the small family but will be "communized" (Plato uses the verb *koinoneo*) among the whole group of guardians (464a–b).

While the motivation of the proposal is furnished by Plato himself, we are on less safe ground when it comes to the question why this particular project should have been chosen as a solution to the problem. The question is especially intriguing because Plato, one should think, had at his disposition the means of overcoming disruption through family relations in his idea of a spiritual community united by the Agathon. The formation of a mystical body through a common spiritual substance living in all members has, in fact, become historically the solution to the problem of forming communities beyond real or fictitious family relationships. Plato evokes, as one should expect him to do, the idea of good order through a Paideia which inculcates the same spirit in the citizenry; but then he projects, in addition, a concrete somatic substance as the basis for the spiritual community. And that is not a passing idea in the *Republic;* for the same concern about proper mating as the condition of spiritual balance reappears in the later *Statesman.* The enduring concern about the somatic basis, we suggest, reveals the degree to which the Platonic notion of a spiritually formed personality is still embedded in the compact myth of nature. Body and psyche, in spite of their admitted separability, are still fundamentally inseparable. Hence, a true order of the spirit cannot be realized in community unless supported by eugenic selection of right bodies; and the means to overcome the disruptive exclusiveness of the family bond is found in the projection of the family on the scale of the polis. The polis is man written in larger letters in more than one sense.

We have recognized the limitations of the family and tribal units as the fundamental problem in Hellenic polities; and we have noted the desire to overcome such limitations as the motive of Plato's construction. However, as soon as we accept this desire as the motive, we are faced by the fact that the solution is of doubtful value. What Plato ultimately wants is the unified, spiritually well-ordered, national community of the Hellenes—but the order which he actually evokes is that of a polis, strengthened in its exclusiveness by the sentiments which inevitably must arise from the emphasis on somatic unity.

Plato is not unaware of the difficulty, for he lets the project of the eugenic communal family be followed by a brief discussion on the rules of war (466d–471c). He distinguishes between wars against barbarians and wars among Hellenes. The latter he considers not to be wars in a strict sense but rather cases of civil strife. In such civil wars with other Hellenic cities, the rulers of the polis will have to observe special rules which prohibit all cruelties, destruction of cities, enslavement or wholesale killings, for the Hellenes will fall into bondage to barbarians unless they spare their own race (*genos*) (469b–c). Again, this conception is not a passing idea; it blossoms out, in the *Critias,* into the myth of the federated Hellenes under the hegemony of Athens. The insistence on the polis as the unit ordered by the idea is self-defeating if a unified Hellenic nation is the ultimate political aim, and the further aggravation through insistence on somatic unity for the polis is certainly baffling; it must have deeper roots than mere conservatism or lack of imagination. And we find, indeed, that the very insistence on this aggravating somatic unit is the key to the understanding of a problem which has occupied Plato even in his old age and which has found full expression only in his last work, the *Laws.*

The problem that occupies Plato from the *Republic* to the *Laws,* and even casts its shadow on the *Politics* of Aristotle, is the size of the polis. One of the principal purposes in Plato's organization of the polis as a "single family" is the control of the rulers over the population figure: the polis should not become too big or too small. In the *Laws* Plato decides on a fixed number of family heads; while Aristotle in the *Politics,* develops the limitative category of autarky for the polis, and even finds the Platonic figure of approximately five thousand for the number of family heads too high. From the point of view of practical politics, in the face of the Persian danger and of the rising power of Macedonia, this insistence on the small size of the polis was fatal, and, as we have seen, Plato was aware of the problem. If he insists nevertheless, the reason has to be sought in the conception of the political entity as an embodied Form. The Form, or Idea, cannot organize any amount of matter into an order; the body which the Form creates for itself has to be suitable as a vessel for the Form. The Form is a limitative principle, a Measure, a *metron,* in the cosmos; and the body has to fit the clear, finite Measure. This conception of the Form as a limiting principle is not an inevitable ingredient in all civilizations on the level of the cosmological myth, but a specifically Hellenic trait. In spite of parallels with Hellenic civilization in other respects, as for instance in the inability to overcome the limitations of the family, the ancient Chinese thinkers, for example, could conceive of a political unit as a cosmic empire which in its universality was an analogue of universal Heaven. Moreover, we have seen conceptions similar to the Chinese prevalent in the ancient Near East. The general causes of the Hellenic peculiarity have been discussed previously. In the present context the peculiarity must be accepted as a fact. In the civilization in which Plato lived Form was experienced as the Measure of finite, visible, clearly delimited objects in the world. Hence, the "body" had supreme importance as the medium in which the Measure was visibly realized.

The conception of Form was completely articulated only in the *Laws*. In his last dialogue, Plato indeed constructed the polis as a mathematical crystal which in its proportions reflected the numerical relations of the cosmos. Nevertheless, the problem is present in the *Republic* even though in Book V, in the section on the community of women and children, the problem of the Measure does not yet appear quite clearly. To be sure, we find provisions for keeping the population figure stable; but the further provisions for maintaining and continuing the "body" of the polis remind us more of a digression into animal husbandry than of a metaphysical discussion of the cosmic Measure. As a consequence, this section with its emphasis on genetics and eugenics has frequently been criticized as something like a race theory. That the meaning of the provisions is not "biological" in the modern sense, but cosmological, appears only in the opening pages of Book VIII, where the discussion of their cosmological meaning is the starting point for the theory of the sequence of bad political forms.

2. *The Mythical Failure of Incarnation*

Socrates raises the question how the good polis can ever begin to dissolve and start on the path from the original monarchy or aristocracy to the first of the bad forms, that is, to timocracy (545c). The question is crucial because the earlier discussion in Book V had assumed that the establishment of the "single family" would result in complete peace among the members of the ruling class. And peace in the well-ordered ruling class is the guarantee of stability, since no dissension of the lower classes is to be feared as long as the rulers do not quarrel among themselves (465b). The discussion in Book VIII takes up this argument. If any change in the good polis occurred it would have to originate in an internal dissension of the ruling class. As long as the ruling class is of one mind (*homonoia*), it cannot be upset, however small it may be (545c–d). How then can the polis be moved out of its stable order? (545d). The question cannot be answered directly because it concerns the mystery of iniquity, that is, the instability of cosmic Form itself. Plato mediates the question, therefore, by a mock-Homeric appeal to the Muses, and supposes them to answer in a teasing manner, as if they were talking to children, jesting, with a pretense to being in earnest (545d–e).

What has been born, the Muses answer, must perish. The good polis seems unshakeable, but even this fabric, in time, must suffer dissolution (*lysis*). Its decay is inevitable because it is beyond the powers of man at all times to observe the rhythms of the cosmos. All creatures, plants as well as animals, have periods of fertility and sterility both of psyche and body. In the case of the human species, even the wisest of rulers, in spite of their calculations and observations, will sooner or later miss the propitious time for conception (*eugonia*), and children will be begotten out of due season (546a–b). Then follows a disquisition (in its detail obscure) on the mathematical properties of periodic numbers for that "which is of divine birth" (probably the cosmos) and that "which is of human birth" (546b–c). When the Guardians miscalculate the right time (*kairos*) for mating, the quality of the children will not be perfect (*euphyes, eutyches*) (546d). And, once the initial misconception has occurred, the further course is inevitable. The next generation of Guardians will neglect the Muses and the education of young men; when they become rulers in their turn, they will not too well discern "Hesiod's and our races" of gold, silver, brass, and iron. And thus the movement has started toward the dissolution of the likeminded ruling class (546a–547a). Dissension will arise between those Guardians who have brass and iron in their souls and the others who still have gold and silver. The first will be drawn toward money-making and the acquisition of property; the second, desiring only the pure metals in their souls, will be drawn toward virtue and the old customs. In the end they will compromise and agree on private ownership in houses and land; they will enslave the people who formerly lived freely under them, devote themselves to war, and establish their rule by force. That is the starting point of transition toward oligarchy; and that intermediate state is the form of timocracy (547b–c).

The good polis is not exempt from the cosmic mystery of Being and Becoming. The Form that has been embodied will be disembodied;

it is beyond the powers of man to overcome the transitoriness of the flux and to create eternal Being. The eternal Form in Becoming is a fleeting moment between creation and dissolution. To realize that Plato holds this position even in the *Republic* is of importance for the continuity of his thought. *Phaedrus, Theaetetus, Statesman, Timaeus,* and *Critias* vastly enlarge the horizon of problems; but the philosophy of history which Plato gradually unfolds in the later dialogues does not imply a break with the *Republic*.

3. *The Sequence of Political Forms*

Timocracy, oligarchy, democracy, and tyranny are the stages through which the good polis passes on its way of decline to the "ultimate malady of the polis" (544c). Since the sequence has its origin, not in an historical event, but in the mythical failure of the incarnation of Form in Becoming, questions concerning the precise nature of the sequence will inevitably arise. Plato himself has given a few indications concerning the meaning of the sequence through his definition of criteria for (1) the selection of the four forms (*idea, eidos*), and (2) the order in which they follow each other. The four types are selected because they have distinct names in common usage and are clearly distinguishable species (*eidos*); and their order is determined by the valuation put on them by popular consensus (544c).

At this stage of the argument, Plato does not claim that every historical polity is bound to pass through the sequence of forms. On the contrary, the selection of examples, as well as the surrounding remarks, seem to exclude the notion. As examples of timocracy are mentioned the constitutions of Crete and Sparta; but there is no suggestion that either of them has fallen off from a previous more perfect form, nor that they will have to develop into oligarchies, democracies, and tyrannies. For the latter three types, Plato gives no example at all, presumably because a sufficient number of instances would occur to every Greek reader. Moreover, other types, as hereditary monarchy or a form of government in which the highest office can be bought, are mentioned though excluded from consideration because they are "intermediate" between the distinct species. But again no claim is made that in transition from one clear type to the next a concrete polis has to pass through the intermediate phases (544c–d).

The taxonomic nature of the sequence is further accentuated through the discussion of the characters that correspond to the political forms. Plato reaffirms the anthropological principle which dominated the exposition of the polis of the idea. There must be as many types of characters as there are types of political forms. Constitutions do not "grow out of trees and stones," they grow out of the characters of the men who live under them (544d). Hence the description of the four political forms will be combined with the description of the four corresponding characters, descending from the competitive and ambitious type, which is the highest in value, to the despotic type, which is the lowest. As a result of such a survey, we shall arrive at a full understanding of the completely unjust type, so that we can compare it with the perfectly just type of the well-ordered soul; and the comparison will enable us to answer the question whether happiness is to be found in the just life rather than in the unjust life (545a). The exposition of this program ends with the agreement that such a review and appraisal would indeed be "systematic" (*kata logon*) (545c). It would seem the sequence has nothing to do with history at all.

The nature of the sequence appears in a new light, however, when Plato proceeds to the execution of the program. The four types, as well as the corresponding characters, are not simply described in succession; Plato presents them in the form of a "tale" in such a manner that in time they develop intelligibly one out of the other. We have referred already to this problem when we indicated that the time in which the four forms follow each other is primarily the time of the mythical narration, not the time of history. Nevertheless, the problem is not exhausted by this formula. Let us observe in a concrete instance how the transition from one form to the next is effected. When the cosmic mishap in mating has occurred in the good polis and, as a consequence, the first symptoms of disorder begin to show, the stage is set for the appearance of the timocratic man. He is assumed to be the son of an excellent man of the old school. The father himself will hold aloof from public life and rather forego some of his rights and opportunities than debase himself by participation in the shabby scramble for advantages. The character of the son, however, will be influenced by the inevitable domestic difficulties. The mother complains that her prestige among women suffers because her husband does not hold high office; and the financial affairs of the family decline. The mother finds her husband absorbed in thoughts and somewhat indifferent to her; she

makes remarks to the son that his father is not much of a man, that
he takes things too easy, and so forth. The servants talk in a similar
vein out of loyalty to the family interest; they urge the son not to
emulate his father but to stand up for his rights when he is grown up.
Outside the house the young man observes that a man who minds his
own business is not much respected, while people admire a busybody
who has his fingers in every pie. His views of life inevitably will be
affected by such influence, and the father who wishes to cultivate his
son's mind cannot outweigh them. The result will be a compromise
between the *logistikon* and the *epithymetikon* in the character of the
young man; he will be dominated by the *philonikon*; and that means
that he will become arrogant and ambitious (549c–550b).

From the analysis emerges the principle by which Plato constructs
the several political forms and corresponding characters, as well as the
principle of transition from one to the other. The characters and their
political forms are determined by the predominance of one or the
other of the three forces of the soul. The polis is good when the
logistikon predominates in the souls of the rulers; it is a timocracy when
the *philonikon* predominates; an oligarchy when the passions of the
epithymetikon and *philochrematon* predominate. In order to derive
the further forms of democracy and tyranny, Plato subdivides the
passions (*epithymia*) into the necessary and wholesome, the unnecessary
and luxurious, and the criminal ones (558c–559d). In the oligarchy,
the necessary desires which induce a restrictive, parsimonious, miserly
life predominate. In the democracy the unnecessary passions which lead
to insolence, anarchy, waste, and impudence are let loose. In the despotic
soul this pluralistic field of passions is dominated by a champion lust
of a criminal nature which induces men to translate into reality the desires which they experience in dreams.

Plato uses the anthropological principle in order to make the transitions intelligible. Characters and forms do not simply correspond to
each other but the various social forces (father, mother, servants,
friends, acquaintances, and so on) struggle in the soul of the individual; and they can struggle within the individual soul because they
are psychic forces. The psyche is a society of forces, and society is the
differentiated manifold of psychic elements. The forms can follow
each other intelligibly in time because their sequence as a whole is a
process within a soul, that is, the process of gradual corrosion in which

the elements of the psyche are one after the other loosened from their "just" position in the integrated, well-ordered soul, until the passions without a higher ordering principle range freely without restraint.

The passions in the soul, however, do not range quite freely even in the last stage of moral confusion. The order of the soul through predominance of the higher forces is gone, but a new order of evil has taken its place. The analysis of the transition from the democratic to the despotic soul may well be considered the masterpiece of Platonic psychology. In the democratic state of the soul all appetites are on the same footing and compete with one another for satisfaction. The state may even have certain advantages not realized in the oligarchic state, in that the soul is at least not warped by the singleness of the acquisitive desire, but freely indulges in pleasures and luxuries with a degree of sophistication. This state of an amiable, and perhaps aesthetic, rottenness, however, exhausts itself, and now the last abyss of depravation opens. For beyond the ordinary luxuriance of desires lie the ultimate lusts which "stir in a soul in its dreams" but ordinarily are kept down in waking life by the controls of wisdom and law. In dreams the beast goes on its rampage of murder, incest, and perversions. The wise man knows about these possibilities and their source. He will not go to sleep before he has awakened the *logistikon* in his soul and fed it on noble thoughts in collected meditation. He will have seen to it that during the day his desires were neither starved nor surfeited, so that neither their delights nor griefs will disturb his contemplation; he will now soothe his passion in order not to fall asleep with his anger aroused against anyone. Thus, having put to rest the two lower forces of his soul and having awakened the highest one, his sleep will not be disturbed by bad dreams (571d–572a). The procedure of the despotic man is the very opposite of that of the wise man. Far from attempting a catharsis of his soul, he will, on the contrary, go beyond the confusion of conflicting desires and give the mob of rival appetites a master by letting the lust of his dreams enter his waking life.

Plato's term for this deepest lust which casts a glow of evil over the life of passions, is Eros. That Eros he sees under the image of a Great Winged Drone, surrounded by the buzzing swarm of pleasures of a dissolute life until the sting of desire has grown in the Drone into a craving that cannot be satisfied. Then, at last, when the master-passion has acquired its full *mania* it breaks out in frenzy; it purges the soul of its last remnants of shame and temperance, and subordinates all actions to the satisfaction of its insatiable craving (572d–573b). The *Eros tyrannos* (573b; d) is the satanic double of the Socratic Eros. The *enthousiasmos* of the Socratic Eros is the positive force which carries the soul beyond itself toward the Agathon. The *Eros tyrannos* is winged like the good Eros but parasitical (the Drone); he has no productive *enthousiasmos* but a sting (*kentron*) which insatiably drives to waste the substance. Nevertheless, both Erotes are modes of *mania*. The desire which turns the soul toward the Good and the desire which succumbs to the fascination of Evil are intimately related; the *mania* of the soul can be its good as well as its evil daemon. Even in the *Republic,* where the Agathon holds the center, the problem of cosmic dualism cannot be quite suppressed. We can go even further and say that in the dualism of Eros the dualism of Good and Evil is reduced to its experiential basis. For the good and the bad Eros lie close together in the soul as its potentiality either to gain itself by transcendence, or to lose itself by closure and reliance on its own resources. The dualism of the Erotes, closely related to the Christian dualism of *amor Dei* and *amor sui,* receives its specific color from the experience of transition from one mode to the other. Even the tyrannical Eros with its *mania* is an ordering principle; and while the substance has changed, the style of order is retained. The decomposition of the well-ordered soul leads, not to disorder or confusion, but to a perverted order. It seems that Plato was acutely aware of the spirituality of evil and of the fascination emanating from a tyrannical order. The *Eros tyrannos* is dangerous and evil, but it is not contemptible—just as the order of Atlantis, in the *Critias,* has its qualities of luciferic splendor. In this conception of tyranny, as related to the foundation of the perfect polis through a metamorphosis of Eros, we touch perhaps upon the most intimate danger of the Platonic soul, the danger of straying from the difficult path of the spirit and of falling into the abyss of pride.

The analysis has come to its end; and we are still faced by the question whether the theory of the successive political forms has any bearing on the interpretation of political history. While nothing was expressly said on the point in the *Republic,* one could sense that the problem of historical sequence was somehow involved in the theory.

Not only Hellenic civilization, but civilizations in general, show something like a sequence of political forms which begins with heroic monarchy and aristocracy, then moves on to the rise of the Third Estate with its oligarchic problems, further on to the entrance of the masses into politics, and issues forth into the forms of plebiscitarian democracy and tyranny. However blurred the pattern may be in the various civilizations, it nevertheless is there. Moreover, the sequence is, on the whole, irreversible. Civilizations do not begin with a plebiscitarian tyranny and then move on to heroic aristocracy; they move from the rule of the Third Estate to mass democracy, but not in the opposite direction, and so forth. Obviously, an irreversible pattern exists.

The cycle of political forms in this sense has remained a problem in the theory of history and politics through the ages. It will be sufficient to recall the names of Aristotle, Polybius, Machiavelli, Vico, Spengler, and Toynbee. None of the sequences evolved by the various thinkers can be called satisfactory, though all of them have absorbed a sufficient amount of historical materials to prove that the problem is not vain. The main reason for the failure lies in the disregard for the principles which Plato has evolved for the treatment of the problem. Plato achieves the intelligibility of his sequence through the use of the anthropological principle. No attempt is made to construct the pattern by an inductive method that would generalize historical observations; the intelligibility is achieved through the interpretation of the psyche as a manifold of social forces, and of society as a manifold of psychic forces. The analysis is in substance a theory of the decomposition of the soul through the metamorphosis of Eros.

If we accept the Platonic terms of the problem, the consequences for the interpretation of history are clear. On the one hand, the sequence can be found if political history contains processes of psychic decomposition; on the other hand, the clarity of its appearance will depend on the extent to which extraneous blurring factors are involved in the process of decomposition. Assuming that a good many extraneous factors are involved, and that these factors show a considerable variety in the various civilizations, the attempt to construct the pattern inductively through generalizations on the basis of empirically observed political institutions must remain abortive because inevitably the peculiarities of the civilizational process which has served as the primary model for the generalization will enter into the construction of the pattern—as for instance the peculiarities of the Roman civilizational process have colored the construction of Vico's *storia eterna ideale.* Nevertheless, while the extraneous factors vary and blur the pattern considerably, they do not blot it out completely. The historical process of a civilization seems, indeed, to have for its nucleus a process of psychic decomposition. Again, the Platonic theory points the way to a treatment of this problem. The process of decomposition, if and so far as it exists, presupposes an initial order of the soul. The empirical investigation of a civilization and its political phases must, therefore, clarify this initial order of the soul, its growth and ramifications, and then study the phases of its decomposition. The approach to the problem will rest on the assumption that a political society, in so far as its course in history is intelligible, has for its substance the growth and decline of an order of the soul. The problem of the political cycle, we conclude, cannot be solved through generalization of institutional phenomena, but requires for its solution a theory of the ordering myth of a society.

§ 6. THE EPILOGUE

The Epilogue of the *Republic* is a carefully constructed work of the Art of Measurement, the *techne metretike,* that measures life in the perspective of death (602c–603a). It consists of four sections:

(1) The good order of the soul, its politeia, must be established and continuously preserved through right Paideia (608a–b). If the soul is regularly nourished by influences that play on its passions, the strength of the rational element, the *logistikon,* will be dissolved (605b) and with it the faculty of measuring rightly (603a); instead of the good a vicious (*kake*) politeia will be set up in the soul (605b). In the surrounding society, the principal source of the vitiating Paideia is mimetic poetry, represented by Homer and Hesiod, by tragedy and comedy. The attack on Homer, for the reasons indicated, forms the first section (595a–608b).

(2) "Great is the struggle" that determines whether a man will become good or bad; "justice and all Arete" must be continuously guarded against the lure of honor, wealth, office, and even poetry; that is an end in itself (608b). While justice must be achieved in life for its own sake, the end receives a literally infinite dimension of importance

through the fact that the soul is immortal, so that its problems cannot be conveniently solved through bodily death. In "proof" of the immortality of the soul Socrates reflects on the respective effects of disease on body and soul. Everything has its specific goods and evils. Grain will mildew, wood will rot, iron will rust, and the body of man is affected by diseases. In the case of all bodily things in this wider sense, their specific evils will waste and ultimately destroy the things. In the case of the "thing" that we call soul, however, the specific evils, its vices, have no destructive effect on the thing itself. No soul has ever died from vice, as a body has been destroyed by disease. Hence, there is no reason to assume that external events, such as the destruction of the body, will ever destroy the soul. Since the soul is neither destroyed by its own nor by alien evils, it is everlasting and immortal (609a–611a). Only if the soul is considered under the aspect of its immortality can its true nature be discerned as something akin to the divine (611e). If it is viewed only in its sufferings through community with the body, its distorted appearance may be mistaken for its nature (611d). And a clue to that true nature, covered as it were by the barnacles, and crushed by the waves, of existence, is given through the soul's love of wisdom (*philosophia*), which is the yearning for its true company, the eternal. When in this life the soul strives for justice for its own sake, it follows that gleam of immortality toward a more perfect order, after the obstacles of bodily existence are removed (611d–612a).

(3) Glaukon and Adeimantus wanted to hear the praise of justice as a good in itself. Their request has now been fulfilled. The nature of the soul, as well as the reasons why it should and does pursue a course of justice, have been clarified without side glances at rewards and advantages. "The soul ought to do what is just, whether it possesses the ring of Gyges or not" (612b). Now that the condition has been met the question of rewards can be treated without danger of misunderstandings. And it should be treated, because the common opinion that justice will cause nothing but trouble for a man is erroneous. In fact, the just man, who by the practice of virtues makes himself like to God as far as that is possible for man, will be loved by gods and men. The gods will surely not neglect a man who is willing and eager to be righteous; and men will honor them with offices and family connections. The unjust man, on the contrary, may have a good start, but in the

end he will be found out and suffer punishment and contumely (612a–614a).

(4) The prizes and rewards of justice in life are nothing, in numbers and magnitude, compared with those in afterlife (613b–614a). The brief announcement is followed by the Pamphylian Myth which describes rewards and punishments for the good and bad souls in Hades, as well as the consequences which their previous cultivation of Arete has for the choice of a future life.

The four sections, thus, deal with the nature of the soul and its justice in life and death, and correspondingly with the rewards of justice in life and death.

With the main construction is interwoven the "old quarrel between philosophy and poetry" (607b). In the third part of the Poleogony Socrates had excluded from the good polis various "types" of mimetic poetry because of their bad influence on the soul. Improper conduct of gods, heroes, and men, if represented by poets with the splendor of their art, can appear as model conduct to the unwary reader or listener; and even if not imitated outright, the regular imaginative occupation with it will work as a dissolvent in the soul. In speaking of the Socratic Paideia in the good polis, we remarked that the disintegration of the people's myth assumes two principal forms. On the one hand, the symbols of the myth are exposed to misunderstanding by enlightened fundamentalists who take a mythical tale as a realistic story. That was the misunderstanding against which the Socratic Paideia offered the remedy of radical banishment. On the other hand, the myth, even if not misunderstood, had become improper in the Xenophantic sense and could no longer be used as an instrument of expression for the experiences of the philosopher's soul. That Xenophantic impropriety of *mimesis* in art becomes the primary problem of the opening section of the Epilogue.

Plato is not at war with poetry as an art. On the contrary, he speaks of his love and reverence for Homer which even now makes him hesitate to talk (595b) of the "mighty spell" of rhythm, metre, and harmony (601b), and of the pleasure aroused by realistic representation (605c–d), and he calls Homer the "most poetic of poets" (607a). The philosopher objects to the poets because of the mimetic character of their work. Mimesis, imitation, is reprehensible for two reasons. In the first place, imitation is not the original, and the philosopher is in search of "original" being, of the idea. The craftsman incorporates the idea in his product, as for instance the idea of a table in a table, in a sense imitating it; and the painter who represents the table in his painting will, therefore, be the imitator of the imitation. The work of the artist, thus, is reality "at the third remove" (596a–597e). In the same sense the maker of tragedies is "three removes from the king and the truth" (597e). In the second place, the imitator is not familiar with the "original," but will be guided in his production by the user of the object. The mimetic artist makes no attempt at representing, even at a third remove, the truth of the original, but will represent the appearances of the original that will please his public. And the multitude is less interested in the true nature of things than in passions and colorful characters (605a). Such "realism" in the representation of the unrestrained, confused, and fretful soul, however, will inevitably corrode the soul of the spectator and listener, though only a few are aware that what we enjoy in others will of necessity react upon ourselves (605c–606b). Hence, all such mimetics are ruinous to the mind of the listener—unless he has, as an antidote, an understanding of their real nature (595b).

In the general charges against mimetic poetry is embedded the great attack on Homer (598d–600e). Homer, as well as the mimetic poets deriving from him, both tragic and comic, pretend to the knowledge of all arts in so far as they represent them in their work. But no reckoning will be demanded for the pretense in general; the argument will be sharpened to the question whether Homer really knew anything about the most important and beautiful of all arts: the defense of the polis in war, the administration of justice in peace, and the education (*paideia*) of men. If Homer was more than a creator of phantasms, a mimetic poet at the third remove of reality; if he only held second place, and knew what pursuits made men better or worse in private or public life, then the "fair question" (599d) would have to be asked: To name the polis that owes him a debt like Lacedaimon to Lycurgus, or Italy and Sicily to Charondas, or Athens to Solon. Or, was there a war in Homer's time, well conducted by his command or counsel? Or, are there any inventions reported of him, useful for the arts and practice of life, as of Thales or Anacharsis? Or, if public service was not his strength, do we hear of friends and disciples of Homer who loved his company and learned from him an Homeric way of life, like the Pythagoreans, who through their order celebrate the greatness of their founder to this day? (599–600). We hear none of these things. Homer was indeed a mimetic poet at "the third remove" from reality; and no claim that he is the educator of Hellas (606a) will gain his work admission to the good polis (607a).

The attack on Homer, in order to be intelligible, must be understood in the context of the "old quarrel" (*palaia diaphora*) between philosophy and poetry in which it is placed by Plato (607b). The discoverer of the psyche and its order is at war against the disorder, of which the traditional education through the poets is an important causal factor. The philosopher's Paideia struggles for the soul of man against the Paideia of the myth. In that struggle, as we have seen, the positions changed more than once. The Homeric epic itself, with its free mythopoeia, was a feat of criticism in a situation of civilizational crisis. Hesiod's new truth had its point against the old myth including Homer. For the generation of the mystic-philosophers both Homer and Hesiod had moved into the sphere of untruth, to which they opposed the truth of wisdom, of the soul and its depth. Aeschylus created the dramatic myth of the soul, superseding the epic myth in general. For Plato, finally, the tragedy and comedy of the fifth century became as untrue as Homer from whom the chain of Hellenic poetry descended. The discovery of the soul, as well as the struggle for its order, thus, is a process that extends through centuries and passes through more than one phase until it reaches its climax in the soul of Socrates and his impact on Plato. The attack on mimetic poetry from Homer to the time of Socrates pronounces no more than the plain truth that the Age of the Myth is closed. In Socrates the soul of man has at last found itself. After Socrates, no myth is possible.

Nevertheless, an age of order and its symbolization cannot be relegated to the past through declaration. Whether it has objectively the characteristics of a past depends on the existence of a present with an order of its own. The banishment of mimetic art as the instrument of Paideia makes sense only if there exists an effective, alternative instrument of the new Paideia. What new symbolic form will take the place, or rather, has already taken the place of epic and tragedy in forming the order of the soul? The answer is obvious; but because it is obvious Plato cannot give more than hints.

There are three such hints offered in the Epilogue. The first of them is given in the address to "Dear Homer" (599d). The "fair questions" are asked of him under the assumption that he is not an artist at the third remove from reality, but a creator on the second level. Over the question who is an original artist, that is, a firsthand creator of the idea, Plato spreads silence. But into this silence are spoken the words of Socrates that no polis will ever be eudaimonic unless its lineaments are traced "by draftsmen who use the divine paradigm" (500e), by the philosophers who have associated with divine order until they have themselves become orderly and divine in the measure allowed to men (500c–d). In the course of their work they glance, alternately, at the virtues as they are in the nature of things, and at that which they try to produce in man to make him in the image of God; and from their efforts will result the Schema of the Politeia (501b–c). The draftsman of the Schema is the original artist; and he is at work in the *Republic* itself.

The other two hints are given when Socrates admits to the good polis no poetry but "hymns to the gods and encomia of noble men [*agathoi*]" (607a). We do not have to look far for examples of either category. The Pamphylian myth, at the end of the Epilogue, is a hymn to the gods who are just and guiltless. And the *Republic* is the encomium of a noble man—of Socrates.

CHAPTER 4

Phaedrus *and* Statesman

§ 1. THE PHAEDRUS

In the event that true philosophers should come to power in a polis, Socrates suggests in the *Republic,* the whole population over ten years of age should be sent out of the polis to the countryside. Then the philosophers should take over the children under ten years of age and raise them after their own manner or character, and in their own institutions (*nomoi*). This would be the surest and quickest way to establish the politeia among a people (541a). The program is ingenious and eminently practical. We see it followed almost to the letter in our own time when bands of sectarians gain power in a country and begin to reconstruct the people according to their own manners and character by eliminating the older generation from public life and by bringing up the children in the new creed. The program has only one flaw: it cannot be executed by true philosophers. For any attempt to realize the order of the idea by violent means would defeat itself. The authority of the spirit is an authority only if, and when, it is accepted in freedom.

Hence, the passage in question is not a Platonic program for political action in the historical environment. Plato is not the speaker; he presents to the reader a report, made by Socrates to an undetermined audience, of a dialogue in the course of which Socrates had made this remark to his partners in the conversation. This threefold mediation is the most important element in the meaning of the passage. After the sacrificial death of the historical Socrates, no attempt at direct action will be made. The Socrates-Plato of the dialogue evokes the idea of the right order; those who have ears may listen. The passage has no other function than to show that technically it is not impossible to translate the idea into reality, and to forestall the facile assumption that the Socratic politeia is an impractical daydream. The idea *can* be realized if the people *want* to realize it; the philosopher-king is present in their midst, waiting for their consent. Beyond this appeal, however, no attempt either will or can be made to force the consent; if no response is forthcoming, that is the end of political action. The appeal went unheard, as might have been expected.

The lack of response had important consequences for Plato's future life and work, for he washed his hands of Athenian politics definitely. It meant the end of the philosopher-king who would realize the idea in Athens or anywhere else. While the idea was not to be revised, a revision imposed itself with regard to the relations between Plato, the idea, and history. The work of revision on principle is the *Phaedrus,* completed perhaps not much more than a year after the *Republic*.

The analysis of this masterpiece of Platonic art will confine itself to the points which have a direct bearing on the revision of Plato's position. First, we have to consider the revision of the problem of withdrawal and return. In the Parable of the Cave the philosopher was enjoined to return to the cave and to enlighten his fellow prisoners. Plato has discharged this duty through the *Republic;* the prisoners have turned out to be an incorrigible lot; now he has left the cave for good. Through his return from the return, however, Plato has not condemned himself to solitude and silence. He has entered the upper world, the realm of the idea in communion with other souls who have seen the Agathon. In the *Phaedrus,* therefore, the rigid parallelism between the "model" of soul and polis recedes into the background, while the relation between idea and soul becomes so close that the two seem to merge. The problem on this new level is expressed in the formula: "All that is soul is deathless" (*psyche pasa athanatos,* 245c); and the soul is deathless in so far as it sees, and through vision participates in the Idea (247).

The "participation" seems to establish a difference between the soul and the idea in which it participates; but then again the difference is abolished in that the "soul" is not the individual human soul but a cosmic substance. The "soul" is the idea or form of the cosmos itself, articulated into nobler and less noble souls which, according to their rank, animate parts of the cosmos itself or merely human bodies (246). The ranks of these member-souls, furthermore, are not immutable, as the souls migrate from one existence to another and can perfect themselves. The cosmos as a whole thus is an entity, engaged in a pulsating movement of perfection and decline throughout its psychic articulation. Hence, the "participation" of the individual soul in the idea means the rank of perfection which this specific particle of the total psychic substance holds at the moment in the pulsation of the world.

The Idea has the character of a dynamic principle which determines a pulsating movement of the cosmos in psychic expansion and contraction. The rank of the member-souls of this total soul is, therefore, no longer determined by the vision of the Agathon, but through their psychic tension or tone, the higher or lower intenseness of their animation by the cosmic fundamental force. The higher degrees of such psychic animation Plato calls *mania*. The highest degree is the erotic madness, the *mania* of the lover (245). In the state of the erotic *mania* man lives in the dynamic substance of the cosmos and the substance lives in him; and since this substance is the "order," the Idea itself, we immerse ourselves in *mania* in the Agathon and, reversely, in *mania* the Agathon fills the soul. All such formulations, however, are inadequate because the language symbols distinguish between soul and idea, while in fact the process should be understood as an impersonal pulsation of the cosmic force, a flow and ebb of the cosmic rhythm in that particular part of the total psychic substance which for the time being gives form to a particular human body. The manic relation between the lover and the loved thus is eminently the *locus* at which the Idea gains its maximum intenseness of reality. In the communion of the manic souls the Idea is embodied in reality, whatever may be its status of embodiment in the polis. In the community of the erotically philosophizing companions Plato has found the realm of the Idea; and in so far as, in the Academy, he is the founder of such a company, he has, indeed, embodied the Idea in the reality of a community.

The field of Plato's philosophizing has enlarged from the polis to the realm of the soul, which is identical with the universe from its all-embracing *anima mundi* to the lowliest sub-souls in the hierarchy. For the purpose of systematic classification, however, a great dividing line is drawn through the realm. On one side of this line lies nature; on the other side lies man in society and history. It is the dividing line which, in the later work, determines the organization of the poem of the Idea into the *Timaeus* and the *Critias*. In the *Phaedrus* we are concerned primarily with the realm of the human soul.

With the shift of the scene from the polis to the realm of the psyche, a further position of the *Republic* has to be revised. The hierarchy of the wise, the spirited, and the appetitive souls, which determined the social stratification of the Socratic polis, does not render adequately the ranks of the new realm. Hence in the *Phaedrus*, Plato presents a new hierarchy of the souls, classified in nine groups and ranked in the following manner (248d–e):

(1) The philosopher, the *philokalos*, the music and erotic soul
(2) The law-observing king, the soul of the war leader and the ruler
(3) Statesmen, economic administrators, traders
(4) The trainers of the body and the physicians
(5) The seer and the priest
(6) The poets and other mimetic artists
(7) The artisan and peasant
(8) The Sophists and demagogues
(9) The tyrannical soul

Plato does not add any commentaries to the list. Nevertheless some of its implications are fairly obvious. Above all, the philosopher-king has disappeared. The highest rank is now held by the philosopher, *i.e.*, the music and erotic soul, while the king who rules according to the law, the ruling soul, has moved to the second place. This redistribution of ranks reflects the new position of Plato. The embodiment of the Idea in the polis is no longer the absorbing interest; the Idea will be embodied wherever such embodiment is possible; and it is embodied most intensely in the souls who are possessed by the erotic mania. That all other souls have to rank lower is clear. The actual classification and ranking, however, is somewhat puzzling at first sight. Still, we can discover the principle of the hierarchy if we reflect on what has happened to the poets.

We find the poets relegated to the sixth place, together with other mimetic artists. That in itself is no more than we might expect after the attack in the *Republic*. We find also, however, that not all poets are relegated to this low rank, for in the first group there appears, side by side with the *philosophos*, a new figure, the *philokalos*, the Lover of Beauty; and we find this new figure characterized, together with the *philosophos*, as a soul which is inspired by the Muses and by Eros. This *philokalos* is the new poet, truly possessed by the *mania*. If any proof were required, the classification shows definitely that the conflict in the

Republic is not a quarrel between "philosophy and poetry" in the modern meaning of the words, but the conflict between the poets of the decaying Hellenic society and the true poet of the newly discovered realm of the soul, who is a twin brother of the philosopher, if not identical with him.

Once we recognize the double appearance of the poet, as the old and the new type, we can understand the structure of the hierarchy, for the poet is not the only figure who appears twice. We further recognize the pairs of philosopher and sophist, of king and tyrant, of statesman and demagogue. The conflict between the idea of the polis and the declining historical polis that animated the *Republic* is translated in this list of the *Phaedrus* into the hierarchy of souls in the realm of psyche. The first rank of the manic soul is followed by three ranks of souls which participate in the idea in a supporting mode. The law-observing king, the administrators, and the trainers of the body are a group that could be the nucleus of the well-ordered polis, if it ever should be realized. The next three ranks—the seers and priests, the mimetic poets, the artisans and peasants—are the souls which constitute the decaying Hellenic society. The last two ranks—the sophists, demagogues and tyrants—are the active element in the decaying society, the carriers of the corruption, the enemies of the manic soul and its supporters.[1]

In the history of Athens the *Phaedrus* is the manifesto which announces the emigration of the spirit from the polis. The historical Socrates had attempted to save the polis through direct action on the individual citizens, in obedience to the command of the gods. The Plato of the *Republic* issued the appeal of the Idea, and was still bound to the polis through his hope for a response. The Plato of the *Phaedrus* is resigned to the fact that the polis has rejected his appeal. The resignation, far from being a private affair of Plato's, has as its consequence a restructuration of Athenian society. For Plato, while not ceasing to be an Athenian, is now an Athenian who, in full consciousness, goes through the hard experience that the public order of his country is so rotten that it can no longer absorb and use the substance of its best men. Athens, as a political order in history, has ceased to be representative of the idea of man which has grown in Athens as a civilizational

[1] The interpretation follows Kurt Hildebrandt, *Platon*, 294f.

order. The polis is rapidly losing its "style" in the sense of a perfect interpenetration of substance and form. The form continues to exist but it has become a worn-out garment, hanging badly around the human substance of the community. In this phase, a civilizational order undergoes a profound change. The public order which formerly was fully representative becomes now, together with the social forces which support it, one element in an open civilizational field in which grow other forces with a rival, and superior, claim to be representative. The co-existence of a public order and of civilizational forces which it does not represent is what may be technically called the state of disintegration.

Whether the situation is accepted by the philosopher, as the bearer of the unrepresented forces, with bitterness, or with resignation, or with indifference—in any case he is compelled to reinterpret the problem of politics. The dissociation of Athenian society into an unrepresentative public order and an unrepresented spiritual substance is expressed, in the *Phaedrus,* in the new hierarchy of souls. The "model of the polis" in the *Republic* evoked the idea of the integrated, representative polis; the list of the *Phaedrus* surveys the field of actual disintegration. This attempt at an empirical description, however, raises the serious epistemological problem of a critical foundation for the categories used in the description. We may assume that the Athenian politicos and average citizens did not acknowledge the validity of the description, any more than our politicos and average citizens will accept the proposition that the movement of the spirit is not to be found in the gigantomachia of rivalling world powers; they probably saw in Plato just another speech-making sophist over whom the course of history would pass on—an opinion which they must have voiced freely if we interpret correctly *Phaedrus* 257d. Such conflicts of interpretations are inevitable in an age of disintegration; and the critical foundation of the theoretical position outside the decaying order becomes, therefore, an urgent necessity. Plato solved the problem—as it must be solved, and as it was solved again in Christianity—through a new ontology. He removed reality from the hands of the politicians by denying the status of ultimate reality to the collective body politic on principle. The Idea when it leaves the polis, does not leave man. It goes on to live, in individuals and small groups, in the mania of the erotic soul. Both situation and solution resemble the Augustinian; but the withdrawal of reality from a declining world cannot issue in the symbol of a *civitas*

Dei; on the level of the myth of nature, the result has to be a *civitas naturae.* The Idea is reborn, and the position of the philosopher is authenticated, through the communion with a nature that is *psyche.* That is the ontological foundation for Plato's late political theory; and the communion is the source of the "truth" of the mythical poems in which the late Plato symbolizes the life of the Idea.

Nature still is *empsychos* and the hierarchy of souls, extending from the human sphere into the cosmic, permits a gradual transition from human to divine nature. An imaginative realization of the pre-Christian life of the soul in nature, and of nature in the soul, is necessary if we want to understand the process of divinization which becomes increasingly marked in the late work of Plato. The dissociation of society into the *città corrotta* and the erotic souls engenders a tension of such sharpness that the common bond of humanity between the lost souls and the manic souls is almost broken. The difference between the souls tends to become a generic difference between a lower type of human beings, close to animals, and a higher type of semi-divine rank. This divinization, which seems absurd in the realm of Christian experience, is inherent in the logic of the myth of nature. If the particle of substance which animates a particular human individual happens to be of high quality, there is no objection to recognizing its semi-divine character. The obstacle to such recognition which in the Christian orbit stems from the experience of creaturely equality before a transcendent God, does not exist in the Platonic experience.

This survey of the principal features which characterize the new position of Plato after the *Republic* will enable us now to deal with the problems of the *Statesman.*

§ 2. THE STATESMAN

Through the *Phaedrus* Plato had acknowledged the state of disintegration as irreparable. In the following dialogues, in the trilogy of *Theaetetus, Sophist,* and *Statesman,* he formulated the problem of politics from the new position.

1. *The Trilogy of Dialogues*

The *Theaetetus* opens on a scene in Megara, in front of the house of Euclid the philosopher. Euclid comes home and finds a friend who is just inquiring after him. He explains to him that he is returning from the harbor where he has seen Theaetetus off to Athens. Theaetetus had come back from a battle near Corinth, badly wounded and diseased, with little hope of recovery; Euclid tried to persuade him to stay in Megara at his house, but Theaetetus had pressed on for home. Euclid was reminded on this occasion of the prediction of Socrates concerning the future of Theaetetus, and he remembered a conversation which had taken place between the two shortly before the death of Socrates. Euclid has written down this conversation as it was reported to him by Socrates, and now he orders his slave to bring the scroll and to read it to him and his friend. The notes of Euclid are the three dialogues. The *Theaetetus* ends with the agreement of the participants in the dialogue to meet on the next day and to continue the conversation, and they plan to extend it to the three topics: the Sophist, the Statesman and the Philosopher. The *Sophist* and the *Statesman* are the report of the conversation which took place on the next morning. The third dialogue was never written by Plato.

The construction resembles in some respects that of the sequence *Republic–Timaeus–Critias.* The first of the dialogues is not an original conversation but a report, while the second and the third dialogues are linked to the first as its continuation on the following day. Moreover, the last dialogue, the *Philosopher,* is announced by the interlocutors but not written by Plato, and the same is true for the *Hermocrates* of the other series. The parallel construction deserves some attention because in the case of the *Philosopher* we have good reason to suspect that its announcement by the *dialogi personae* does not express a plan of Plato but has to be understood as part of the internal meaning of the dialogues; we shall have to remember the point when we approach the problem of the missing *Hermocrates.* And, finally, both in *Theaetetus* and the *Republic,* that is, in the first dialogues of the two series, Socrates is the main speaker, while in the subsequent dialogues, though Socrates is silently present, the rôle of the speaker is assigned to other men.

In both cases the construction serves the purpose of mediation. Through the form of the dialogue, Plato creates a distance between himself and the propositions of the speaker; through the device of letting second and third dialogues emerge from situations of the first, with different persons in the rôle of the main speaker, he removes himself one step farther from a direct address to the reader; and through the device of embedding the dialogues in reports, one more degree of mediation is added. In the series *Theaetetus-Sophist-Statesman* the mediating form is of particular importance because the dialogues communicate sentiments of an intenseness that would burst the form if they were expressed directly. And even if their direct expression had been technically possible without destroying the situation of the dialogue itself, it would have senselessly drawn on the head of Plato the fate of Socrates.

The dialogues are characterized by a strong undercurrent of violence. The hope for a regeneration of the polis through the spirit is gone, and the gulf between the condemned public order and the representatives of the spirit has become unbridgeable. In the dialogues themselves this new rigidity of the conflict leads, on the one side, to the heroization of the semi-divine, manic souls, while, on the other side, the lost souls of the polis appear ominously under the symbol of the beast (*thremma*). Nevertheless, the parties in the conflict are chained together by the historical fate of being Athenians. Plato never surrenders the *imitatio Socratis;* neither for himself nor for the members of the Academy does he reject the duty to die in obedience to the law of Athens. The dialogues are placed at the very time when Socrates is occupied with the preliminaries of the trial that will lead to his murder; and his partner in the first dialogue is Theaetetus, one of the hopes of the younger generation, who now is returning to Athens, dying from the wounds received in battle for a polis which rejects his soul but uses his body in defense like a piece of inorganic matter. We have to realize this situation in order to understand the cold rage of Plato who is compelled to live in obedience to a government of the beast which makes the best die by the beast and for the beast.

2. *The Diversion of the* Theaetetus

The rejection of, is not an escape from, the polis. Plato neither develops his position into a philosophy of apolitism like the Cynic school, nor will he engage in conspiracies with foreign powers, nor show any disloyalty to the constitutional authorities. The disorder of the polis cannot be repaired by descending to the level of disorder, by adding a new faction to the existing ones. The tyranny of the rabble cannot be transformed into freedom by countering it with a tyranny of the spirit.[2]

---

[2] Today we live in a situation similar to Plato's. The response of a contemporary philosopher to the problem will further clarify the Platonic position. In Karl Jaspers, *Die geistige Situation der Zeit* (Berlin-Leipzig, 1931), we find the following reflections on the conflict of mass and nobility: "We are faced today by the last campaign against nobility. The campaign is con-

The pathos of Platonic existence at this stage finds its expression in the great diversion of *Theaetetus* 172–77.

Again, the literary form of the Diversion enters into the argument. The men engaged in philosophical discourse are freemen, they are men of leisure who can interrupt their argument in order to follow a side issue at their discretion; they are not men of affairs who have to conform their conduct to the social conventions in a public meeting or to the rules of procedure in a court. The man of leisure and the man of affairs are the two types to be characterized by means of the Diversion as a literary form:

(1) First Plato characterizes the man of politics. He is always in a hurry and pressed by the situation. He is engaged in lawsuits, speaking with an eye on the clock that he may not overstep his time limit; he is faced by an adversary and his objections, and in debating his case he is bound by the strict rules of procedure. He is in the rôle of a servant quarreling with a fellow servant before a seated master; the point in question is never one of indifference but it touches his personal existence. Engaged in such pursuits he has become shrewd and cunning, he flatters in word and deed, and his soul is small and crooked. His slavish condition from early youth has warped his inner growth and freedom; fears and dangers have stunted and botched him; and they have engendered

---

ducted not on the political or social fields but in the souls themselves. Man wants to reverse an evolution in which we see the essence of a modern time that now is past, that is, the development of personality. The seriousness of the problem of how we can take care of the mass-man—who is not willing to stand in inner independence—leads to the revolt of existential plebeianism in every one of us against the duty of being ourselves which God in His inscrutability has imposed on us. The potentiality of man to gain himself through following his destiny, is about to be destroyed. . . . This is the ultimate revolt against the real nobility in man. The earlier political revolts could succeed without ruining man; this last revolt, if it were to succeed, would destroy man himself" (p. 174). This is the Platonic conflict between *psyche* and *thremma*. On the solution of the problem through elitarian activism we find the following passage: "Exclusive minorities, in the consciousness of their nobility, can seize the power in the state under the name of a vanguard, or of the most progressive, or of the most energetic, or as the followership of a leader, or by the historically inherited rank of blood. They organize themselves in analogy to earlier sects: with rigorous selection, high demands, severe discipline. They experience themselves as an elite; and after the seizure of power they try to perpetuate their elitarian character through the education of a youth that will continue them. Nevertheless, even if in their origins the strength of personality (as the nobility of man) may have played a rôle, and even if this strength continues to play a rôle in the decisive individuals, the group as a whole soon turns out to be a minority with all the characteristics of a new, and not at all aristocratic, mass. In an age which is determined by the masses, it remains hopeless to represent the nobility of man through a ruling minority" (p. 177). On the potentiality of human existence in this politically hopeless situation—where the public order has become unrepresentative and the nobility of the soul cannot find public representation—the reader should refer to the pages on the "Heroism of Man," *ibid.*, 157–59.

habits of deception and revenge. Thus he has grown into an unhealthy manhood and believes himself to be a miracle of wisdom.

(2) Then Plato characterizes the philosopher. From his early youth he has never found the way to the agora, the court, or a political assembly; he does not participate in the legislature, nor in the social activities of clubs, of luncheons, and of entertainments with wine, women, and song, which are the means of winning an office; he never has heard of the latest news which is so terribly important, nor is he acquainted with the *chronique scandaleuse*. This attitude is not a pose for gaining a reputation.[3] He is sincerely unaware of what is going on, "for his body only dwells in the polis," while his mind roams earth and heaven, and reflects on the things above and below it, but never will stoop to anything within reach (172–173). In illustration, Socrates, the speaker, recalls the anecdote of Thales who fell into a well while looking at the stars, much to the exhilaration of his Thracian servant girl. Such is the philosopher who hardly knows whether his next-door neighbor is man or animal while he is inquiring into the nature of man (174).

The ancedote of Thales and the Thracian servant girl places the philosopher and the people into their mutual presence. Within the Diversion it forms the transition from the characterization of the types to the characterization of their social reactions to each other:

(1) First, the philosopher in the company of the men of affairs. In such company the philosopher is the laughingstock not only of Thracian servant girls but of the rabble (*ochlos*) in general, for he tumbles into wells and into every sort of trouble through his inexperience. He will look awkward and sheepish to the point of imbecility. When men of distinction are praised he will fall into fits of laughter and appear an idiot. When they praise the rulers of men he will fancy to be listening to the praise of shepherds, with the exception that the human herd from which these shepherds squeeze their wealth is more invidious of nature than sheep or cattle. When they praise the great landed proprietors, that will seem to him a trifle, for he is accustomed to thinking in terms of the whole universe. And when they praise men of noble lineage he will think of the indefinite line of ancestors who preceded the noble ancestor and who were not quite so noble. The philosopher will be derided and distrusted by the vulgar for he seems to despise them and to be ignorant.

(2) The situation changes, however, when the philosopher dominates

---

[3] Probably a fling at philosophers who cultivate apolitism by principle, like the Cynics.

the scene. When he can drive the man of affairs out of his specious arguments and draw him into an inquiry of the justice and injustice in his
own soul, and from the trivialities about the happiness of common men
and kings into a serious reflection on politics, then the man of affairs
is dismayed and lost; he will begin to stammer and become a source of
laughter, not for Thracian servant girls but for the men who are not
slaves.

These are the two characters: the philosopher who appears a simpleton
at menial tasks; and the regular citizen who is smart and neat at these
tasks but does not know how to carry himself as a gentleman and cuts
a sorry figure when it comes to joining in the hymnic discourse on the
true life of the gods and the men who are blessed by them (*eudaimonon*)
(174–176).

Is there an escape from such evils? The power of Evil can never be
abolished, for the evils, since they cannot dwell among the immortals,
have to swarm around mortal nature. The only relief from this necessity
is offered by the flight from mortality to immortality. We must achieve
"god-likeness according to our power" (*homoiosis theô kata to dynaton*)
by becoming "just and pious with insight" (176b). This regeneration of
the soul in the likeness of the immortals is decisive, not the external
virtuousness of conduct. The *homoiosis theô* is the criterion of true
reality and strength in man (*deinotes*), or of his nothingness (*oudenia*)
and want of manhood (*anandria*) (176c). There are set before man the
two eternal models (*paradeigmata*) after which he can form himself:
the models of godly blessedness or of godless wretchedness (176e). Man
can grow with his deeds into the likeness of one or the other of these
models. It would be supremely important to impart this insight to the
wretched people but if you try to explain it to them, in their superior
wisdom they believe they are listening to an idiot. Strangely, however, if
you talk to one of them in private, and if he has the courage to listen to
you and does not run away, a curious disquiet begins to stir in him; his
rhetoric fails and he becomes small like a child (177).

The form of the Diversion is lucid but its meaning is complex and
subtle. We shall begin with the relationship between the Diversion and
the Parable of the Cave.

The Diversion is a repetition of the Parable on the new level of politics, after the appeal of the *Republic* has been rejected. In the Parable,

as we have seen, the problem of the return of the philosopher to the Cave was in suspense. It is his duty to return, but only under the condition that he would be the philosopher-ruler of his fellow citizens. The condition has not been fulfilled; the idea has not been realized in the historical polis. As a consequence of this failure the field of politics has assumed the open, pluralistic structure which Plato has expressed in the hierarchy of the souls in the *Phaedrus*. Now, in the Diversion, the issue of the new situation is formulated in its full sharpness. If the historical polis resists its regeneration through the Idea, that is a misfortune for both the polis and the philosopher; but the historical resistance invalidates neither the Idea, nor the position of the philosopher whose soul is ordered by the Idea. The understanding of this tension is the key to the understanding of Plato's work after the *Republic*. Formerly, the historical reality of Athens was the adversary to be overcome and replaced by the reality of the idea. Now the inimical reality not only becomes an integral part of the field of investigation, but it even gains a certain preponderance because the reality of the idea is clarified, once and for all, in the *Republic*. The theory of politics is now enlarged to encompass the reality which is not ordered by the idea.

As a consequence of this enlargement of the horizon, the return to the Cave appears in a new light. It is a return deprived of hope or intention of reform, a return "in body only," for only the body of the philosopher will live in the historical polis in which his soul has no part. The scurrilous and dangerous character of the situation, which in the Parable was envisaged as temporary, has become permanent; and the Diversion elaborates this character with so much detail that even the urbanity and irony of Plato can hardly veil the stigmatization of historical reality as a caricature of true reality. The construction of the three dialogues is now revealed in its full importance: The element of murder in the situation is confined to the enveloping reminders of the fate of Socrates and Theaetetus, while the dialogue itself retains only the elements that will appear as scurrilous to the exoteric reader because his sense of reality is so perverted that he cannot recognize the implications of murder in the atrocities on the spiritual and intellectual level.[4]

[4] In our time we can observe the same phenomenon in that people are shocked by the horrors of war and by Nazi atrocities but are unable to see that these horrors are no more than a translation, to the physical level, of the spiritual and intellectual horrors which characterize progressive civilization in its "peaceful" phase; that the physical horrors are no more than the execution of the judgment (*krisis*) passed upon the historical polity.

In spite of these precautions the situation is clear. The philosopher and the Athenian *homo politicus* are contrasted as freeman and slave. Since the philosopher is not permitted to be present in the polis with his soul, he is not quite sure whether his neighbor is "man or animal." With great circumspection Plato stigmatizes the various types who are "big shots" for the rabble, that is, the rulers of men, the rich, and the socialites; while the people at large is the flock—through its intractability and invidiousness worse than animals—that is fleeced by its shepherds. The anecdote of Thales and the Thracian handmaid, finally, suggests, as clearly as Plato could dare, that the Hellenic Athenians have become barbarians. Further implications could be clarified through a comparison of the Diversion with its great counterpart in modern political literature, that is, with the *Vorrede* to Nietzsche's *Zarathustra*. Sometimes the formulations are almost identical, as for instance in the reaction of the *homo politicus* to the exhortation of the philosopher. Plato's man of affairs listens, firm in his superior cunning, and knows that he is listening to a madman; it is the same reaction as that of Nietzsche's Last Man: "Formerly all the world was demented—say the most cunning and squint."

The enlargement of the field of investigation compels a theoretical revision. The categories of order developed in the *Republic* cannot be used in an analysis of disorder. Moreover, the myth of the Socratic soul can no longer be used as the only source of theory when it comes to the theoretization of the un-Socratic souls of the *ochlos*. In the Diversion, therefore, appears the "power of Evil" as the counterforce to the Agathon; and the paradigm of true order that is laid up in heaven is parallelled by the paradigm of "godless wretchedness." The nature of this second paradigm is not sufficiently clarified by Plato. Certainly, the "evils" are not simply the burden of earthiness; they hover around mortal *physis*, but they are not *physis* itself. The evils are psychic entities like the psyche which, after many a rebirth, will finally gain immortal status. Since psyche and idea are interchangeable in this phase of Plato's work, the question arises whether Plato, perhaps under Persian influences, wanted to develop a metaphysics of two hostile psychic forces in the cosmos. The question can hardly be settled on the basis of the scant references to the problem in Plato's work. There is, of course, the passage in *Laws* 896e, where Plato, speaking of the world-soul, questions whether

one soul can be responsible for both good and evil and assumes the existence of at least two souls. Nevertheless, the conclusion, already drawn
from this passage by Plutarch, that Plato had assumed two conflicting
world-souls, is not compelling.[5] If we read the passages from the Diversion
and from the *Laws* in the light of the theory of psyche developed in the
Phaedrus, Plato seems rather to have assumed a pluralistic structure of the
psyche in the universe, and perhaps even a pluralistic structure of the
human soul. This latter assumption seems to be indicated by the concluding sentences of the Diversion, where Plato presents the philosopher in
intimate conversation with the man of affairs. With the tenderness of a
Pascalian *directeur de l'âme*, Plato describes the strange disquiet which
befalls the wordly souls when *in camera* they are shaken out of their
cunning and complacency. The abyss of nothingness, in the Pascalian
sense, opens for a moment, from which the order of the psyche, which
is present even in the "beast," may break forth. Nevertheless, we should
not talk away the focussing of the forces of good and evil in the two
paradigms. The tendency toward a dualistic conception of the psyche-
idea is definitely present; and if the recognition of evil has not issued in
a clear metaphysical construction, at least the new dimension of reality
is henceforth noticeable in the Platonic philosophy of order.

3. *The Obscuring Devices of the* Statesman

The Diversion has established a field of politics in which the reality
of the idea and the reality that is not ordered by the idea coexist. The
apparently static character of the situation is broken in the *Statesman*
through a philosophy of history which reduces the conflict to a transitory moment in the cyclical history of the cosmos. A perspective of
future development is opened.

Perhaps Plato was afraid an exoteric reader would misunderstand
the opening of a perspective as a plan for revolutionary action. Whether
this was the reason or whether other motives have played a rôle, at any
rate the *Statesman* is one of the most obscure of the Platonic dialogues,
not because of its subject matter, but because it is made obscure, with
great skill and labor, by various devices of indirection. We shall briefly
indicate the obscuring devices, and then proceed to the analysis of the
core of meaning itself.

Sophist and *Statesman* are twin dialogues. On the day after the

[5] *The Laws of Plato*, trans. by A. E. Taylor (London, 1934), 289, n.1.

Theaetetus the partners of the earlier dialogue meet again, and the company is enlarged by the Younger Socrates and the Eleatic Stranger. This larger company discusses the topics of the sophist and the statesman in succession, and it plans to discuss the philosopher as the third topic. As a first device of indirection Socrates, the main speaker of the *Theaetetus,* lapses into silence, and the Eleatic Stranger becomes the dominant figure. The topic is the Statesman, that is, the philosopher-king of the *Republic* faced by a reality that is not ordered by the idea. We remember the identification in the *Republic* of the speaker with the philosophic ruler of the polis: If Socrates-Plato were himself the speaker in the *Statesman,* the situation would acquire an atmosphere of direct, political action; with the Eleatic Stranger as the speaker this danger is averted. The philosopher-statesman is now transformed into an innocuous object of logical inquiry: We know already what a philosopher-king is; we do not have to *explore* his nature and function; we are engaged in an exercise in logical classification with the purpose of *defining* the concept of the statesman as one specimen of the genus "shepherds of flocks." The long-drawn exercise, with its amusing incidents, serves as a screen which makes us almost forget that the object of the discussion is silently present.

This obscuring effect of the logical inquiry is intensified, furthermore, by the device of letting the company project a third debate, the dialogue on the Philosopher. The reader is induced to believe that the discussion of the problems is incomplete, and that only the remaining debate on the Philosopher will fully reveal Plato's position. As a matter of fact, the problems are completely rounded out; the Statesman is the Philosopher himself, and the Philosopher is present. No third dialogue is to be expected. Hence, the title of *Statesman* which Plato has given to the dialogue should perhaps be taken more seriously than is usually done. If the project of the third dialogue is no more than an obscuring device, there is no distinction to be drawn between the Statesman and the Philosopher. The Statesman corresponds to the philosopher-king of the *Republic,* but while in the *Republic* the royal philosopher is envisaged as the ruler in the polis of the idea, he is now, under the name of the Statesman, envisaged as the representative of the idea, as a savior with the sword, who will restore order to society in its time of troubles.

The mythical character of this figure, finally, is revealed, and again obscured, by Plato's device of interrupting the logical exercise at the decisive point through one of his mythical poems. As the process of logical classification cannot supply the substance of the subject matter, that substance has to be injected from the outside. The myth of the cosmic cycles serves this purpose while, at the same time, it removes a rich body of meaning from the field of explicit statements. And its meaning is, furthermore, kept obscure through its fragmentary form, for precisely at the point where the future course of history would have to be revealed in symbolic form, the myth breaks off. This fragmentary form deserves our particular attention because it recurs in the *Critias*. In the case of the *Statesman* the literary form leaves no doubt that the myth was meant to be a fragment; in the case of the *Critias* the dialogue simply breaks off in the middle of a sentence and the literary form does not reveal the reason. In the light of the intentionally fragmentary form of the myth in the *Statesman*, we shall have to consider the question whether the *Critias* is perhaps intentionally a fragment, too.

4. *The Myth of the Cosmic Cycles*

We shall begin the analysis itself with the myth of the cosmic cycles (*Statesman* 269–274). The myth is organized in two main parts. The first part develops the general myth of the cosmic cycles; the second part deals specifically with the present cycle. The first part is further subdivided into the myth of the cycle in nature and into the myth of the cycle in society; this subdivision adumbrates the division of the late mythical poem into the *Timaeus* and *Critias*. Between the two subdivisions of the first part is inserted a reflection on cosmic youth and age; into the second subdivision of the first part is inserted a reflection on the value of the social phases of the cycles. We shall follow the myth through these several parts.

At one time the Cosmos is conducted and rolled on its path by God Himself, while at another time, when the periods of its measured time are completed, it is released from the divine control and then proceeds to revolve by itself in the opposite direction. The autonomous, opposite movement is possible because the Cosmos is a living creature, endowed with intelligence at its original creation. And the alternation of movement is inevitable, for only divine nature is privileged with changeless identity, while the Cosmos, since it partakes of bodily nature, must submit to the law of change. Nevertheless, since it was endowed at its creation with unusual qualities, its change is reduced to revolution in reverse as this is the least deviation from its proper motion. No other explanation of the alternation of movement is permissible. Neither must we assume that God Himself would move the Cosmos first in one and then in the opposite direction; nor must we assume the existence of two Gods who rotate it with contradictory purposes.

The alternation of movement affects, not the realm of nature only, but also the realm of man in society. In the first cycle God Himself superintended the Cosmos, while the various parts of the Cosmos were placed under the superintendence of lower divinities. Divine spirits were assigned to tend the various herds of living creatures; and each of these good shepherds had the power to care effectively for the creatures in his charge, so that there was no violence, no devouring of one another, and no war or discord among them all. God Himself was the shepherd of men; at that time there was no government (*politeia*) nor separate possession of women and children, for all men rose from the earth without memory of the past. The earth furnished them with food in abundance; they needed neither clothing nor shelter, as the climate was tempered to their constitution. Such was life in the Age of Cronos.

When the period had been completed and the time for change had come, the divine Helmsman let go the rudder and the Cosmos began to rotate in reverse direction by Fate (*heimarmene*) and Innate Desire (*symphytos epithymia*). The lower divinities who were advised of what was coming left their charges. Then, as the Cosmos reversed its motion it was shaken by earthquakes which worked destruction among the living creatures. At last, however, the Cosmos settled down into its new motion under its own authority, following the instruction of its Creator (*demiourgos*) and Father to the best of its recollection. At the beginning it performed its function with comparative precision; in the later course the performance became clumsy. The cause of degeneration was the bodily element in its composition. Originally, before the cosmic order had been imposed upon it, this element had been in an utterly chaotic state. From its Creator the Cosmos had received its good qualities; but from its previous state it had retained, and reproduced in its living creatures, the disorderly and obstreperous (*adikos*) qualities which arose from the World of Space (*ouranos*). When the Cosmos was superintended by the divine Helmsman it injected into the living creatures only a trifle of evil while predominantly they were good; and when it embarked on its own course, it performed its function of order best in the beginning. However, as time went on and forgetfulness invaded the Cosmos, the primordial malady of disorder gained the upper hand and in the final phase broke out openly. The danger of complete destruction approached.

At this juncture, God resumes the control of the Cosmos so that it will not fall again into the abyss of incommensurability. He reverses the tendencies towards sickness and dissolution and restores the order of the Cosmos to immortality and lasting youth (*ageros*).

One of these reversals of motion occurred at the beginning of the present period. The Cosmos was left to itself. Deprived of the care of the spirits man became weak and defenseless, exposed to the wild beasts and destitute of resources; he was in the direst straits until, under the stress of necessity, he learned to provide for himself. This situation is the origin of the legendary gifts of the gods—of Prometheus, Hephaestus, and other benefactors. As a matter of fact, all the civilizational inventions and achievements were the work of man himself who now had to live by his own efforts and to keep over himself the watch that had been abandoned by the gods, exactly as the Cosmos as a whole which we imitate and follow in its changes.

A myth of Plato becomes a trap for the interpreter—as the Egyptian myth has become a trap for the explorers of Atlantis—if he takes it literally. The propositions of the myth have to be established with precision because they are the basis for the meaning which is to be derived by interpretation; but they do not themselves contain a "philosophy" of Plato. In the case of the myth of the cosmic cycles we must beware in particular of mistaking it as an overt philosophy of nature and history, and assuming that Plato was waiting for another reversal of cosmic motion that would bring back a Golden Age of Cronos. In order to arrive at the meaning we have to reduce the myth to its experiential basis; and we can find this basis if we reflect on the hierarchy of gods in the myth. The lowest level, occupied by the symbols of the people's myth, that is, by Cronos, Prometheus, Hephaestus, and a host of good daemons, we have to discard for the moment as irrelevant for the principal meaning. The next higher level is occupied by the One God who imposes order on chaos, maintains and restores it. In reflecting on the ordering work of this God, Plato sheds some light on the problem of the two paradigms in the Diversion. There is only one God but he is not omnipotent; he is opposed by the primordial force of chaotic matter; and even when order is imposed on matter, there still remains the Innate Desire which, if it follows its own tendency, will revert to chaos. The rejection of a second God seems to suggest rather that in his *analogia entis* Plato was willing to ascribe personality to the force of order but not to the forces of disorder. The position is comparable to the Christian with its construction of evil as nothing. This interpretation is confirmed by the assumption of a highest divinity, on a third level of the hierarchy, who governs the rhythm of order and disorder in time, *i.e.*, of Heimarmene. The static order of the cosmos is supplemented by a time order which determines its rhythm in such a manner that, on the one hand, the divine order of the idea does not last undisturbed forever but that, on the other hand, on the brink of destruction through the forces of chaos, the cosmos will regain the youth of its order. The trinity of the right order of God, of the Innate Desire, and of Heimarmene marks the border beyond which lies the mystery of iniquity.

Around this center of theodicy are arranged the other parts of the myth.

Plato is not yearning for the return of a Golden Age. Between the descriptions of the ages of Cronos and Zeus a reflection on their relative values (272b–d) is interjected. If we assume that the men of the Saturnian age, with their boundless leisure and their power to hold intercourse not only with men but also with brute creation, had used these advantages for the purpose of philosophizing and of increasing wisdom, then we would have to say that the age was happier than ours. Until we have found, however, satisfactory witnesses of the love of that age for wisdom and discourse, we had better drop the matter. The paradisic myth of the Golden Age is thus dismissed as part of that old myth which has become untrue for the philosopher who has grown to his full spiritual stature. The idyll of unproblematic happiness is unworthy of man. This rejection, however, destroys the overt meaning of the myth, for: What purpose does the myth of the cycles serve if we are not interested in the alternative to the present cycle? What sense have the complaints about the misery of the present age if we prefer it to the Golden Age? The construction of the myth does not seem to make sense.

This impasse can be broken by the method of translating the overt symbols of the myth into processes of the soul. The myth of the cycles will render a philosophy of history if the several levels in the hierarchy of the gods are treated as symbols for the evolution of the soul. The rejected Age of Cronos and the accepted Age of Zeus symbolize stages in the evolution of consciousness from the myth of the people and the poets to the level of the philosopher. The age of the older myth has come to its end. The tension between order and disorder, which is always part of the structure of reality, can no longer be expressed in the form of complaints about the present and of a projection of the right order into a paradisic Golden Age. The omnipresence of the tension is now symbolized by Heimarmene, the highest divinity who governs the process of history; the age of the people's myth is symbolized through the cycle in which the life of man is superintended by the divine spirits of the old myth; the new age is symbolized through the cycle in which the gods have withdrawn from the Cosmos and watch its rotation from afar. In this new age, the present one, the Cosmos moves autonomously; and man, following its example, moves autonomously, too. Plato rejects explicitly as legendary the fables of the gods who aided man in his predicament through civilizational inventions. Civilization and its order is the work of man. In the beginning of civilization this order emerged from the recollection of the instructions imparted to the Cosmos and man by the gods, that is, from the unconscious. With the exhaustion of these forces the disorder of desire begins to gain ascendancy, and society will revert to a chaotic state unless a new irruption of divine order checks the forces of disorder.

But how will these forces of order operate—in the history of the soul, and not in the overt story of the myth? At this point the myth breaks off deliberately and the solution of the problem is pressed into one sentence, so carefully embedded in the story that it may easily be overlooked. For between the first and second parts of the myth (273e) there is injected the sentence: "Thus we have told the whole of the story; and its earlier part is sufficient as a presentation [apodeixis] of the royal ruler [basileus]." This earlier part of the story cannot be the description of the Age of Cronos that Plato has rejected; it must be the myth of the "God" of order who holds in the hierarchy the rank between Heimarmene and the divinities of the popular myth. This "God" will now restore order, not through the restoration of a Golden Age but through the instrument of the royal ruler who is the vessel of divine order in the present age.

This interpretation does not exhaust the myth. It would be tempting to enter into the technical details of overlapping meanings and of symbols with double functions which lend to the myth the qualities of a

dream-play. We have to confine ourselves, however, to the problems of
more immediate political relevance. As far as these immediate problems
are concerned the philosophy of history which we could disengage from
the myth is rich in suggestions and associations. The emergence of the
age of autonomous man from the age of the people's myth reminds us
strongly of Vico's philosophy of history. With the clarification of his
own position Plato seems to have gained a clearer view of the meaning
of the people's myth as the ordering force of the community preceding
the differentiation of the philosopher's consciousness. Moreover, he seems
to have clearly understood the problem of the exhaustion of the myth
(which plays an important rôle in Vico's philosophy) and the impossibility of returning to the former level once the spell is broken. When
the new consciousness of the spiritual soul is gained, the indulgence in
paradisic symbolizations becomes unbearable; the myth of the Golden
Age is rejected because the paradise implies the renunciation of philosophic consciousness. The misery of consciousness is preferable to the
bliss of unconsciousness. Nevertheless, the misery of consciousness, which
increasingly characterizes Hellenic civilization since the Age of the Sophists, can go too far. The release of desire which accompanies the exhaustion of the myth leads to the disintegration of society; the increase
of desire characterizes the old age of a civilization.

The idea of an aging world suggests the Augustinian *saeculum senescens* in which the misery of the Graeco-Roman world has found its final
expression; but this suggestion also draws our attention to Plato's entirely different spiritual situation. For Plato could neither, like St.
Augustine, throw the arch of waiting for the Second Coming over the
senescent age; nor could he split the historical process into a profane
history and a transcendental history of good and bad souls. Though
torn by the struggle of Good and Evil, there is only one historical reality
for Plato; and unless the idea is the order of reality it is not an order of
anything. In this situation originates the conception of the cycle of which
the myth of the cosmic cycles is the poetic symbol. The idea of the cosmos as a pulsating psychic substance, which Plato had evoked in the
Phaedrus, is now developed into the idea of a pulsating history. By the
inscrutable mystery of Heimarmene, the psyche-idea has its periods
of decline and recurrence in history. In the age of differentiated consciousness, however, these periods do not overcome man unknowingly.

While the source of divine order is still beyond consciousness, and while the idea has to be recovered through anamnesis, its human manifestation is no longer the people's myth but the divinely ordered man who has realized in himself the *homoiosis theô*. The cycle of decline does not reverse itself automatically; it has to be reversed by the man who is the vessel of the idea.

This situation which determines Plato's evocation of the royal restorer of order resembles in many respects that of Joachim of Flora. At the end of the twelfth century A.D. the tension between the Augustinian idea of the *saeculum senescens* and the experience of an actually growing civilizational order reached the breaking point. The consciousness of a new epoch manifested itself, in Joachim of Flora, in the announcement of a new Christlike leading figure, the *dux,* whose appearance would inaugurate the new age of spiritual order. The parallel between the Platonic royal ruler and the Joachitic *dux* does not, however, extend to all the aspects of the two evocations. Within the Christian style of eschatology the *dux* has to inaugurate the final realm on earth. Within the style of the myth of nature the restoration of the idea does not have the character of finality; the restored idea will decline again and the cycles will roll on indefinitely. Moreover, the Joachitic *dux* arises from the tension between a growing civilization and an idea of decline, while the Platonic ruler arises from the tension between a real political decline and a new spiritual substance. As a consequence, the Joachitic evocation finds its fulfillment in representatives of civilizational pride and of immanent perfection of society, from the progressivists of the eighteenth century, through Comte, Marx, and Mill, to Lenin and Hitler; while the Platonic evocation finds its fulfillment in the increasing spiritual ordering of a disordered world, through the figure of Alexander, through the soteriological kingship of the Hellenistic age, the Roman imperial order, and through Christ.

5. *The Royal Ruler and Political Reality*

Without the myth of the cosmic cycles, the theory of politics which Plato develops in the dialogue proper is difficult to understand. Certain modes of misunderstanding have even become so well established that it is worthwhile to begin the analysis with an exposition of the most frequent misinterpretation.

In the course of the dialogue, the Eleatic Stranger develops a classification of the forms of government (*politeia*). Governments can be divided into those of the one, of the few, and of the many; and the three types can be further bisected according to the rulers' obedience or disobedience to true law and custom. From the divisions results the famous classification of the forms of government:

Lawful	*Lawless*
Monarchy	Tyranny
Aristocracy	Oligarchy
Polity	Democracy

The six types, moreover, are ranked according to their values. Lawfulness or lawlessness will be realized most thoroughly if the government is in the hands of a single ruler; it will be realized least thoroughly if the government is in the hands of the many. Thus monarchy becomes the best form of government, tyranny the worst; aristocracy the second best, oligarchy the second worst; in the case of democracy the lawful type will not be realized too well because of the conflicting interests and opinions of the many, while lawlessness will be handicapped by the same conflict of the many. This classification and evaluation seems to cause great satisfaction to some modern interpreters, for at last Plato admits, not only that a government of laws is better than a government of men, but that democracy is a better form than oligarchy.

Regrettably, we cannot join in the rejoicing. In the first place, Plato would have "admitted" these points even at the time of the *Republic,* if he had cared to express himself on the subject matter. The *Statesman* does not revise an earlier opinion, but deals with a new subject matter, that is, with historical reality and the nature of its resistance to penetration by the idea. Second, the classification of the forms of government has nothing to do with our current "descriptive institutionalism." For in the very middle of the *Statesman* Plato has placed a disquisition on the art of measurement (*metretike*). There are two ways of measuring things. By the one method we measure them according to number, length, breadth, depth, and velocity; by the other method we measure them according to a standard of fitness, appropriateness, and right timing (*pros to metrion kai to prepon kai ton kairon kai to deon*), in brief, by a standard of the mean (*meson*) that is removed from the extremes (284e). In politics we classify the types of reality by reference to a standard of the mean, supplied by the "trueness" of the law which the rulers obey or disregard. We shall see later what is meant by the trueness of the law; for the moment we have to stress that the division of political forms into lawful and lawless concerns the "spirit" of the laws, not the institutions of government. A Platonic tyrant, on the one hand, is not obliged to indulge in misdeeds through individual acts without a basis in positive law, but is permitted to use the more efficient method of enforcing general rules which suit his purpose. A democracy, on the other hand, does not become lawful in the Platonic sense by virtue of its accoutrements of a popularly elected legislative assembly and of courts which observe due process of law. And third, the main topic of the *Statesman*, as the title indicates, is the royal restorer. The classification of political forms is introduced incidentally, with the purpose of characterizing the types of rulers who are *not* Statesmen. In relation to the "true" political order all six of the enumerated forms are "untrue" (*ouk orthos*, 302b). The episode of the classification closes, therefore, with the remark that the artless (*atechnos*) drama is now played out; the swarm of Satyrs and Centaurs can be chased off the stage because, at last, their antics have been separated from the true art of politics (303d). Hence, the realm of the six forms is the counter-realm to the idea; it is the happy playground of Satyrs and Centaurs, that is, of sophistic intellectuals and politicians; it is the realm, not of Statesmen, but of factious partisans (*stasiastikos*), of the upholders of nightmarish idols, and themselves such monstrosities (303c).

We turn from the satyr play to the serious drama. In the economy of the dialogue the myth of the cycles was introduced for the purpose of clarifying the concept of the royal ruler. Up to the point of its introduction the ruler had been defined as an instance of the genus "shepherds of flocks." The myth has revealed the definition as insufficient; for the shepherd of the human flock would correspond to the divine spirit who superintended the human herd in the Age of Cronos. In the age of autonomous man, however, the situation of the shepherd has changed in so far as all men are his rivals for the position of rulership (275b). The great theme of the *Statesman* is formulated: the royal ruler in his struggle with an obstreperous society.

The contrast between the two partners to the struggle is drawn sharply, without a touch of compromise. The rule of the divine shepherd (*to schema to tou theiou nomeos*) is the highest political form, higher even than the rule of the lawful king, while the statesmen whom we find now in power resemble rather their flock in habits and breeding (*paideia*) (275c). Royal power in the strict sense, as distinguished from political power in the declining historical polis, is the existential state of a wisdom both judicious and authoritative (*kritikos, epistatikos*) (296b). Hence, the distinguishing character of true rule cannot be found in the institutions of aristocracy or democracy, of consent of the people or compulsory obedience, of wealth or riches of the ruler, but must have something to do with science (*episteme*) (292c). Such science, however, is the privilege of one or two, or, at any rate, of a very few men; and—pointing to the silently present ruler—the few who possess the *logos basilikos* are the rulers whether they rule in fact or not (292e).

The possession of the *logos basilikos* characterizes the ruler existentially. The nature of true rule, thus, has been disengaged from the problem of institutional forms as well as from that of actual rule. The true political form can, therefore, now be defined as the form in which the ruler really possesses, and does not only pretend to possess, the royal science. Whether he rules according to law or without law, whether the subjects consent voluntarily or submit to compulsion, and whether the ruler is rich or poor, does not matter (293c–d). The guiding principle of the ruler's action is the good of the polis. For this purpose he may kill some of the citizens and exile others; he may reduce the size of the city by sending out colonies; or he may increase its size by settlements of strangers. As long as he acts according to wisdom and justice, the city over which he rules will have to be called the only "true" (*orthos*) polis. All other types of rule are not truly good and, while some of them are better than others, even the better ones are only imitations of the good one (293d–e).

The sketch envisages the royal ruler as a savior with the sword who will restore external order to a polis by a violent, short operation, preliminary to the establishment of a more permanent order. We have to understand the sketch against the background of contemporary events in Sicily where measures of this kind had become the routine of politics. In the most opulent region of the Hellenic polis world the distintegration had reached a point of physical destruction and depopulation, where only the most violent measures of deportation and resettlement could break up the party strife and restore a semblance of order. With the

Sicilian events before his eyes and the fear of their imminent spread to Athens, Plato envisaged the royal ruler as the alternative to the Sicilian tyrants and military adventurers. There is little of the "academic" in the atmosphere of the Academy; the scholastic exercises in classification are subordinated to the main purposes of penetrating a historical situation and of demonstrating the practical problems to which it gives rise. In the concrete situation the rule of law is an institution, not to be clarified and stored away as a permanent item in the knowledge of students, but to be questioned both as a source of disorder and as an obstacle to the restoration of order. When the spiritual and moral disintegration of a polity has reached the phase of imminent destruction, the time has come for emergency measures that will supersede all constitutional forms. Plato understood that the nature and acuteness of the crisis required an extra-constitutional government of men; this insight makes him a philosopher of politics and history superior to Aristotle, who, with a sometimes inconceivable complacency, could describe the nature and order of the Hellenic polis and give shrewd recipes for dealing with revolutionary disturbances at a time when the polis world came crashing down all around him and Alexander was inaugurating the age of empire.

The contemporaries of a crisis, however, are reluctant to recognize the magnitude of the problems. The sketch of the emergency powers accorded to the royal restorer is followed by the remark of the Younger Socrates that, on the whole, he agrees, but that a rule without law has a harsh sound (293e). The remark is the opening for a discussion of the problem of law. On principle, there is no merit in law as an order of human action. For law is a general rule while human action is personal and concrete. The discrepancy between the general and the personal makes it impossible to lay down a rule that will apply with justice to a class of cases at all times; for this reason a legal rule always has the character of an obstinate and ignorant tyrant who does not allow questioning of his orders. A simple rule cannot cover what is the reverse of simple. The best thing of all is that a man should rule, not the law, provided that the man is endowed with royal wisdom (294a–c). Nevertheless, law is an inevitable appurtenance of social order, because it is beyond the powers of even a perfect ruler to exhaust the vicissitudes of human life by individual decisions. Law is a technical expedient as a rough approach to a majority of cases; and the wise legislator will lay down such rules of expediency. Some of them will be newly written, some will enact the customs of the country (295a–b). The technical necessity of law and custom does not, however, abolish their character as expedients. It would be nonsensical to bind the legislator by his own rules; when circumstances change, or when the individual case requires it, he will change the law according to his wisdom; and he will even use violence, if compulsion is necessary to substitute the better for the worse. The general rule remains the expedient; in the perfect case the art of the ruler is the law (295d–297b).

The reality of politics in history does not have the structure of the model politeia in which the ruler possesses the *logos basilikos*. Nevertheless, reality is intelligibly related to the model, even though its mode should be one of derivation, or of a falling off. Plato indeed accords such a derivative mode of reality to the surrounding political structure and calls it *mimesis*. The term has an amplitude of meaning that embraces imitation and representation, as well as caricature, enactment on a stage, and satyr play; and it has become, therefore, a source of frequent misunderstandings. Moreover, matters are not simplified by Plato's device of embedding the discussion of the problem of law into a parable which illustrates the handicaps of the Statesman by the similes of the pilot and the physician. We shall try to translate this web of meaning, as far as possible, into systematic order.

The category of mimesis, now, applies to the whole sphere of historical politics. Both lawful and lawless governments are imitations of the true politeia of the royal ruler. The lawful government imitates the royal ruler in his enactment of written laws and customs; the lawless, tyrannical government imitates him in his power to change the laws out of the fullness of his wisdom, in case of an emergency. This differentiation on the mimetic level would be of little interest if it were understood as referring to institutional structures, for the institutions of government do not change in the transition from monarchy to tyranny, or from any of the lawful types to the corresponding tyrannical form. What changes is the content of the law. Throughout the dialogue the lawful and tyrannical types are understood as an historical sequence. The reality of politics moves from the order of law to the disorder of tyranny. Hence, the differentiation of the forms of government is part of the Platonic philosophy of history: The "true" substance, which lives in the order of the polis in its earlier phase, is exposed to gradual exhaustion until the time arrives when violent changes are necessary to maintain or restore order. Obviously the question arises: From where did the "true" substance of the law come in the earlier phase of the polis? And can it not be renewed from the same source? This is, indeed, the question which Plato raises under the title of mimesis. According to the *Statesman,* the mimetic character of actual politics is inevitable and cannot be radically abolished. All one can do is to inject as much of "true" reality as possible into the actual polis at times and then let it run its course until the misery has become great enough so that, let us hope, the people will prove amenable to another injection.

The cyclical injection of substance is the only possible mode of life for the polis because in the age of autonomous man the true order of the royal ruler is impossible as a permanent establishment. The men who possess the *logos basilikos* are always few in number. The royal art (*basilike techne*) or political science (*politike episteme*) will never be attained by the mass of the rich or by the common people (300e). Moreover, since this art and this science do not come within the range of their personal experience, it is difficult for the people to recognize it when they have it under their eyes; and it is even unbelievable to them that such a thing as a true ruler should exist. If a ruler appears who wishes to reform the polis the people cannot know whether he is indeed the true ruler or only his mimesis, the tyrant; they will be offended by his pretention because they cannot believe that anybody is able to rule in the spirit of virtue (*arete*) and wisdom (301c–d). The polis of man has no natural head, like a beehive, who would be recognizable at once as superior in body and mind (301e).

Since the royal rule is impractical, while the mimesis through tyranny is undesirable, all that is left for forming a polis is the mimesis through written law (301e). True order cannot be realized in the polis, human nature being what it is, but it can be approached if the laws and customs of the true polis are adopted and preserved unchanged. No citizens will be permitted to act contrary to them and infringements will have to be punished by death (297e). This will not be a particularly happy arrangement, for the circumstances of the polis will change and the laws will cause more and more disorder because of their unchangeability; but it is the best that can be had considering the impracticality of royal rule. And how can this true substance ever enter the laws of the mimetic polis? Through the precarious process of persuasion (296a). Such good as there is in the laws of the mimetic polis has come into it because the people at some time have listened to the wise legislators in their midst. Plato is not elaborate on this point but we may assume, from the references in other contexts, that he considered Solon one of the wise legislators who injected into the polis an order that lasted for a while. The laws would have to be copies of the truth (*aletheia*) which comes from those who have knowledge (300c). And once the substance of the law is acquired, the best a polis can do is not to do anything against the written laws and national customs (301a).

The conservative counsel that the polis will do best if it adheres to its ancient laws and customs does not mean, of course, that Plato has suddenly found good points in a government of laws but that he considers the mimetic polis so bad that, whatever the citizens will do, they will change things for the worse. Hence, the suggestion of a second best form of government is immediately followed by the parable of the pilot and physician which describes the disaster of the lawful polis with feeling. The Eleatic Stranger uses the similes of the pilot and physician in order to illustrate what will happen to an art if the people try to regulate it mimetically. The basis of the parable is the earlier mentioned impossibility for the ordinary layman to judge the decisions of the expert artist. The layman only sees that strange things happen to him at the hands of physicians and pilots. The physicians hurt him, take away his money out of proportion to the material value of the medicine, and frequently do not help him; and the pilots leave him ashore when the hour of sailing arrives, cause damages at sea, and throw his merchandise overboard in storms. Let us suppose that the indignant victims of such iniquities assemble and, in complete ignorance of the arts of medicine and navigation, resolve on a body of regulations which for the future will determine the actions of physicians and pilots to the last detail, without leaving room for discretion. At this point the Younger Socrates interjects: "You take pains to tell something that is silly" (298a–e). The Stranger then goes on to suppose that the artists from now on will be chosen from the rich or from the whole of the people and that they will be elected by lot; after their election they will have to heal the sick and to navigate vessels according to the written

rules. The Younger Socrates interjects: "That is even worse" (298e).
The speaker then goes on to suppose that at the end of the year of
office the incumbents will have to face a people's court of review, that
anybody may come forward and charge them with not having observed
the letter of the rules in the conduct of their business and that, if found
guilty, they will be sentenced to a fine or jail. The Younger Socrates
interjects contemptuously that a man who takes office under such conditions deserves any penalty. Even the boys of the Academy know
that no self-respecting person will take office under the contemporary
government of laws (298e–299b). But the Stranger continues to suppose strange things. He supposes an enactment that forbids anybody
to inquire into navigation or medicine, and if, nevertheless, he indulges
in such inquiries and arrives at new discoveries, he shall not be called
a pilot or physician but a prating sophist; and if he corrupts the
young by imparting to them his knowledge and tempts them to follow
the arts in an unlawful manner he shall be punished with the utmost
rigor. "For nobody should be wiser than the law" (299b–c). After this
culmination of lawfulness in the murder of Socrates the Stranger addresses the Younger Socrates directly and asks him what the result would
be if this procedure were extended to all the arts and sciences so as to
comprise all human activities; and he receives the answer—in one of the
rare instances where Plato speaks directly in the network of indirection
—"The arts would utterly perish and could never be recovered; and life
which is a burden even now would then no longer be worth living"
(299e).

Even if the marasmus and deadly paralysis of lawfulness are sur-
passed in evil by the crimes of a lustful tyrant, one can hardly say that
Plato has used the *Statesman* to sing the praise of the government of
laws. The laws of the polis may originally have been based on experience
and the recommendations of wise counsellors who persuaded the people
to enact them (300b), but in the course of history the mimetic character of political reality does its work. When the order of the polis is
founded on the letter only, and action is divorced from wisdom, we need
not be astonished at the miseries which befall the mimetic governments (301e). Rather we should wonder at the survival qualities of
the polity; for the political communities have always endured these
evils and some of them are still not overthrown, though they may
perish in the future. This is their fate because they are conducted by

the worst sort of ignorance, that is, by men who know nothing about politics and nevertheless believe they have mastered the political art to perfection (302a–b).

The diatribe against the government of law is followed by the classification and evaluation of the six political forms. Plato stresses that the classification is not pertinent to the main topic but that it has rather the character of a *parergon*. Nevertheless, he admits it into the discussion for it has a bearing on the whole scheme of our actions (302b). He does not elaborate the phrase, but it obviously refers to the bearing which the actual state of politics has on the life of the philosophers, both passively and actively. It has a bearing passively in so far as a state of politics which kills such men as Socrates and Theaetetus can make life unbearable and drive men to suicide; it has a bearing actively in so far as it determines the philosophers' withdrawal from public life, the organization of the Academy, and the attempt to counteract the horror of the age by the evocation of the royal ruler, whose rule is among governments what God is among men (303b).

The characterization of the royal ruler has not progressed hitherto beyond the first sketch of the savior with the sword who will restore external order to a community in an emergency. But as the emergency measures of the Statesman are not in themselves a guarantee of lasting order, the rapid, cathartic act of the ruler will have to be followed by the more arduous work of weaving the permanent fabric of the polity. Hence, the remaining part of the dialogue is devoted to the isolation and description of the royal art proper.

The isolation of the royal art is undertaken under the simile of refining gold. First, the workmen sift away earth and stones; then, a mass of valuable elements akin to gold is left (such as silver, copper, and other precious metals) which must be separated by fire. The preceding part of the dialogue has removed all alien matter from political science; now the metals of a kindred nature have to be distinguished from the pure gold. These substances kindred to royalty are the arts of generalship, the administration of justice, and rhetoric. All of them are necessary in support of the royal art, but they are not the art itself because they lack autonomy. They are ministerial and can function only under the direction of the Statesman. "For the royal art should not act itself but direct those who are able to act" (305d). The science which presides over all the subordinate functions, as well as over the laws, most properly will be called "political" (305e). The hierarchy of souls from the *Phaedrus* is resumed by the distinctions, with the significant change, however, that the manic souls of the *philosophos* and the *philokalos* have gained the dimension of political action. And we find, furthermore, one of the constant themes of Plato's political dialogues resumed, that is, the myth of the metal ages of Hesiod. In the *Republic* the metals signified the characters of the three classes in the polis of the idea; now they signify the ruler and his helpers in their struggle against the decaying historical polity. In the *Laws* we shall meet them again, in a last transformation, signifying the character traits of man in the polis which has become a cosmic analogue.

The royal art in action is described under the simile of the art of weaving. The Statesman must weave into a supple fabric the warp and the woof of the political texture, that is, the characters of men. Compared with the *Republic*, the psychology of Plato has gained a new subtlety. The somewhat rigid pattern of the soul as possessed of three virtues, with one of them predominating and thus determining the character of the whole, is now replaced by a more differentiated classification of types. Some men, indeed, can be distinguished by courage (*andreia*), others by temperance (*sophrosyne*), but the virtues have become ambivalent and may even operate against each other. We may praise the man who possesses courage because he is energetic, brave, quick, and vigorous; but on other occasions we may find him violent, brutal, and mad. We may praise the man who possesses temperance because he is steady, gentle, persevering, restrained, and considerate; but then again we may find him slow, cowardly, sluggish, meek, and silly. Moreover, the two types are antagonistic to each other; within a polis quarrels may easily arise between them, for each will consider its peculiar qualities superior to those of the other. Again, if in a polis one or the other type predominates, the existence of the polis is in danger. On the one hand, if the temperate type predominates, life will certainly be peaceful and quiet; and the polis will also live at peace with its neighbors. But peacefulness is sometimes out of season; the polis will pass imperceptibly from freedom to slavery if no resistance is offered to encroachments; and the unwarlike spirit will make it an easy prey to aggressive neighbors. On the other hand, if the courageous type predominates, the polis will be torn by internal strife and its ag-

gressiveness will raise up foreign enemies; the ultimate result will be
ruin and misery (306a–308b).

The virtues in themselves, without orientation and discipline, will
not amalgamate into a stable order. Before Plato enters into this problem, however, he considers a further variant of characters which has to
be faced by the Statesman who wants to create order out of a disinte-
grated multitude. He has to consider the men who do not possess any
virtue at all and hence are unusable as the raw material for a political order. The art of politics will not attempt to weave into an order
good as well as bad materials. The Statesman will have to begin his work
by testing human nature in play; only those who are found fit will be
entrusted to teachers for further education. Those who do not possess
courage and temperance or other inclinations to virtue (*arete*), those
who by an evil nature are carried away to godlessness, pride (*hybris*),
and injustice, the Statesman will have to eliminate by death or exile, or
by punishment with the greatest disgrace; and those who find their
happiness in ignorance and baseness he will relegate to a state of slavery
(308b–309a).

Only when the uneducable men are eliminated can the weaving
of the political fabric begin (309b). The Statesman will have to bind
with the cords of unity the two elements in men, that is, the element
which is born from eternity (*aeigenes*) and the element which is
born biologically (*zoogenes*). The first element, which is divine in
nature, he will have to bind with the divine cord of truth; the second
element he will have to bind with the human cord of appropriate
marriages (309c; 310a–b). The divine cord is the "true notion" (*alethes
doxa*) of the beautiful, the just, the good, and their opposites. When
the true notion is implanted, the soul will experience a rebirth in the
divine (309c). Only the Statesman who is inspired by the royal Muse
can work the transformation; and he can do it only in the noble souls
(*eugenes*) who are rightly educated (309d). In this process the
courageous man will become tempered and civilized so that he will not
derail into brutality; while the temperate man will gain strength and
wisdom so that he will not derail into silliness (309e). Still, the complete fabric will have to balance carefully the two types, as each left to
itself would cause the polis to degenerate into one-sidedness. And the
divine rebirth will have to be supported by the matching of the two
types in marriage, so that inbreeding of each type will not divide the

citizenry into two castes (310a–e). The royal art, thus, consists in weaving the characters into an order which receives its unity through the notions of the good and just held in common (310e). The work has been completed successfully when the two types are drawn into a community of like-mindedness and friendship (*homonoia kai philia*) (311b–c).

The royal ruler is the mediator between the divine reality of the Idea and the people; he is the Zeus who rejuvenates the order that has grown old; he is the physician who cures the souls (310a) by causing them to be reborn in the heavenly medium (*en daimoniô genei*) (309c); and in causing this rebirth of the souls he provides the polis with a new spiritual community substance (*homonoia*). It is superfluous to point out in detail the parallel of this Platonic evocation with the Pauline conception of the Christian community, bound into one mystical body through rebirth in the Spirit of Christ, deriving its coherence from the like-mindedness (*homonoia*) of its members and overcoming the difference of gifts and characters through *agape*. Rather, it is necessary to stress the fundamental difference that the Platonic rebirth of the community is not the salvation of mankind, but a return to the youth of the Cosmos that will be followed, under the inscrutable law of Heimarmene, by a new decline.

CHAPTER 5

Timaeus *and* Critias

When the philosopher opposes the order of his soul to the myth of the people, he discovers that he must use a new set of mythical symbols in order to express the source of his authority. For the soul is neither a subject, nor an object, but an entity, illuminated with consciousness from within, that explores its own nature by means of the Zetema. In the course of this exploration the soul will find its own depth (Heraclitus) and height (Parmenides); it will become conscious of the human essentiality and universality of its order (Xenophanes); it will understand action as attunement with the order welling up from its depth (Aeschylus); and it will, finally, discover itself as the entity whose experiences are expressed by the symbols of the myth (Socrates-Plato). When that level of consciousness is reached, the unconscious, or semiconscious symbols, comprehensively designated as the myth of the people, will acquire the characteristic of "untruth" in relation to symbols which express the experience of the more fully conscious soul. The conflict between levels of consciousness, from Homer to Plato, in which the higher level of the moment relegates the preceding lower levels to the realm of untruth, now reaches its climax in the radical conflict between the myth of the fully conscious philosopher's soul and all preceding symbolic forms. At the same time, however, the philosopher discovers that the myth is the ineluctable instrument for communicating the experience of the soul; for he must himself develop mythical symbols in order to express his discovery both as a process and as a result. And through that opposition of his conscious myth to the less conscious forms he becomes aware that the old myth also expresses the truth of the soul, merely on a less differentiated level of consciousness. The soul as the creator of the myth, and the myth as the symbolism of the soul, is the center of the philosophy of order. That center, the philosophy of the myth, is reached by Plato in *Timaeus* and *Critias*.

The twin dialogues are an accomplished work of art. They treat of the myth in the form of a myth; and they explain their own organization in the form of an introductory myth. Nothing can be said discursively about the meaning of the dialogues that would not presuppose the presentation of the myth itself. Hence, the analysis cannot start with a brief survey of their organization, or with the burning problem of their fragmentary character. We must start, as Plato does, with a presentation of the Egyptian myth that serves as an introduction to the problems of the dialogues.

1. *The Egyptian Myth*

The *Timaeus* presents itself as a sequel to the *Republic*. The earlier dialogue had been cast in the form of a report made by Socrates to an unnamed audience. Now, in the opening pages of the *Timaeus*, the listeners are revealed as Timaeus, Critias, Hermocrates, and an unnamed person. Socrates and the company that listened to his report assemble again, with the exception of the unnamed person. It is the evening after the *Republic*, and the company of four continues to discuss the topic of the previous evening. Socrates summarizes the elements of the good polis and expresses his dissatisfaction with the state in which the description of the Politeia was left. It is like seeing beautiful creatures at rest; one feels a desire to see them in motion, engaged in action suitable to their build. In the case of the polis we should like to hear of its struggles with its neighbors, or a war in which it puts to the test the qualities ascribed to it in the painting. In brief, we should like to have an epic celebrating the historical struggles of the polis. Socrates feels himself unable to sing the praise of the polis in action. And he has no confidence that either the poets or sophists would be equal to the task. The poets, with their mimetic art, are good at narrating the spectacles among which they are brought up; but it is not for them to imagine the epic of the idea. And the sophists are vagabonds, not rooted in any polis, and therefore unable to master a task which requires a whole man, that is, a philosopher who is engaged in the affairs of his polis (19). Hence he is handing on the task to his companions who are most suited by their qualities to accomplish it. They are Timaeus, from the well-governed city of Locris in Italy, a philosopher who has conducted with honor the affairs of his polis; [1] Critias, the member of a noble

[1] Timaeus of Locris, for all we know, is a fictitious person invented by Plato for this

Athenian family; [2] and Hermocrates, the Sicilian aristocrat, who had dis-comfited the Athenian expedition of 415–413 against Syracuse (20).

The companions are quite willing to attempt the task. As a matter of fact, the night before, after they had left Socrates, on their way home to the house of Critias where the other two live as his guests, they had already discussed the possibilty; for Critias, while listening to the report of Socrates, had been strongly reminded of an old legend of earlier ex-ploits of Athens, at a time before the present historical aeon, when Athens had a constitution surprisingly similar to the one developed by Socrates in the *Republic*. Critias had heard this legend from his grandfather, the older Critias; and the older Critias had heard it from Solon himself, a friend and relative of Dropides, the father of the older Critias; and Solon had heard it from the priests at Sais when he travelled in Egypt. And the present Critias is now ready to relate the legend, as reported by Solon, to the company of this evening (20–21).

When Solon travelled in Egypt he learned that the city of Sais had as its founding deity a goddess who, the Egyptians said, was identical with Athena. The Saites believed themselves to be related to the Athe-nians. Moreover, the priests of Sais had a knowledge of antiquity far be-yond the remotest memory of the Hellenes. On one occasion, when talk-ing about the great Deluge and the survival of Deucalion and Pyrrha, one of the priests said to Solon that the Hellenes were like children; there was not one old man among them. The reason why is that, at long intervals, the earth undergoes certain catastrophes through fire or water, as a consequence of a deviation (*parallaxis*) of the celestial bodies. When the deluges or conflagrations occur civilization becomes extinguished on the earth so thoroughly that only a few persons survive who possess little, if any, memory of the past. Only Egypt, because of its peculiar climatic conditions, escapes the general destruction. Hence in Egypt the memory of many of these catastrophes is retained, while elsewhere civilization has to start anew and history is not remembered beyond the last deluge. Thus the Athenians do not know that in the period before the last deluge their country was peopled by the best and most beautiful race of men, that their polis was distinguished in war, well governed, and equipped

---

occasion. After Plato a Pythagoraean philosopher of this name is mentioned, and works are ascribed to him; but most of what we learn about him seems to stem from Plato's *Timaeus*.

[2] Plato does not characterize him more closely. By chronology he might be the grandfather of the poet and statesman Critias, one of the Thirty Tyrants. The family was related to Plato's.

with the best constitution of which tradition tells. This former Athens was founded 1,000 years before Sais, and the registers of Sais go back for 8,000 years. Moreover, the institutions of Sais even today reflect in many respects the constitution of the former Athens which the founders of Sais imitated. The Athens of 9,000 years ago had a class of priests separate from all other classes; it had separate classes of artisans, shepherds, hunters, and husbandmen; and the class of warriors again was distinct from all others. The laws of the city were ordered by wisdom (*phronesis*) as are the laws of Egypt to this day. The history of the Athens of old was as distinguished as its order; and the most brilliant of its feats was the victory in the war against Atlantis. For at that time there existed in the west, beyond the pillars of Heracles, the island of Atlantis. It was a huge island, as large as Libya and Asia together, and on it had developed a mighty power which prepared to conquer Europe and Asia. In the great defense against the Atlantian invasion the Mediterranean peoples remained ultimately victorious because Athens held out, after all the allies had succumbed, and won the last battle. The peoples within the pillars owe their freedom to Athenian valor. Some time after this war, violent earthquakes and floods occurred, and when the deluge had subsided, the island of Atlantis had disappeared in the sea (21–25).

Thus far goes the account of Solon's story in the *Timaeus*.

The motive that drives beyond the *Republic* into the problems of the *Timaeus* is the concern about the status of the idea. In the *Republic* the idea of the good polis had, ontologically, its status, first, as the paradigm laid up in heaven and, second, as the politeia of the well-ordered soul. Its status on the third ontological level, as the order of an actual polis in history, was never satisfactorily clarified. The elaboration of the good polis in the poleogony would perhaps best be designated as a "projection" of the well-ordered soul, if a modern term be allowed. The uneasiness about the status of the idea becomes articulate in the *Timaeus*.

In the *Republic* we heard one of the participants refer to the good polis as existing only *en logois;* in the *Timaeus* we find, correspondingly, the polis in the *Republic* characterized as given *en mythô* (26c), as a story, or fable, or fiction. This *mythos* is in need of transposition into a state which can be characterized as *alethes*, as true, or genuine, or real (26d). How can that transposition of the story into truth be achieved? In the *Republic* the question could remain in suspense if the dialogue was understood as a moment of suspense between the evocation of the idea and its realization in political action; the appeal *might* be successful; the evocation *might* flow over into the spiritual regeneration of Hellas. But what was the status of the evoked idea if it failed to be embodied in an historically real order? What was the meaning of the well-ordered polis when its evocation was not the first step to its embodiment in reality? Was it, after all, an irrelevant velleity, the impractical program of a philosopher dabbling in politics? And, more fundamentally, what kind of an entity is an idea that neither remains set up in heaven, nor becomes the form of some piece of reality in the cosmos? Is it an idea at all? Or perhaps no more than a subjective opinion? Metaphysically, the *Republic* ends with a great question. And this question is now solved by the *Timaeus* (and the following *Critias*) through the myth which transposes the well-ordered polis of the *Republic* from the status of a story to the status of an order in historical reality.

Systematically, the mythical transposition corresponds to the Christian construction of sacred history in the Augustinian sense, or to the construction of historical dialectics in the Marxian sense. Plato, however, had at his disposition neither the idea of a transcendental destiny of the soul, nor the idea of an intramundane, transfigured, ultimate history. His solution had to be found within the myth of nature and its cosmic rhythms. The idea of the well-ordered polis is not embodied at present in an historical society; if we ascribe to it, nevertheless, objective status as a form of reality, the ascription of objectivity must be based on an earlier or later embodiment of the idea. Moreover, a theory is needed which explains the temporary disembodiment. Into the creation of this myth of the polis as the measure of society which in its crystallization and decay follows the cosmic rhythm of order and disorder, has gone the ripe art of Plato the poet.

We have touched already on the ingenious device by which the basis of objectivity is broadened beyond the evocative soul of Plato. The report of Socrates stirs the memory of Critias; his recollections lead us to the revelations of the older Critias; from there we go on to the story of Solon; from there to the tales of the Saitic priests; and the register of Sais, finally, leads us to the Athens of the preceding aeon. With each step the genealogy broadens the collective memory: from the lonely speaker Socrates to the contemporary Critias, from the contemporary generation to the generation of the forebears, from Solon beyond the Hellenic world into the Egyptian, and through the memory of the Egyptian register beyond the present aeon of the cosmos into the previous cycle. Moreover, the polis itself becomes saturated with reality in this process: from the evocation through Socrates, to the imitative reality of Sais, and, finally, to the full, original reality of the former Athens.

The ascent in time to the origins is skilfully interwoven with the motif of youth and age in the descent of the idea to the present, as well as with the principle of continuation of the dialogue. The wisdom, the *phronesis*, which descended from the founding goddess of Athens and Sais to the citizens, is handed on from the old men to the young. The Hellenes are children, civilizationally always young, because they lose the memory of previous cycles. The Hellenic child, Solon, receives the legend from the civilizationally old men of Sais; and Solon, the old man, hands it on to a boy, the son of his friend Dropides. At the next link in the chain, the transmission broadens out into a charming episode. The occasion is the festival of the Apaturia, of the admission of the boys to membership in the phratries. Among the elders who are present is the old Critias, aged ninety; among the boys are the young Critias and his friend Amynander. The boys recite poems, some of them by Solon, and Amynander takes the occasion to make a polite remark about the quality of Solon's poems to the elder Critias. The old man responds. He praises Solon, and in the course of the praise he tells the Eygptian legend, for he wants to show that Solon had excellent material at hand for a great epic but was prevented by his occupation with politics from using his talents to the full. In the *Timaeus*, the legend is embedded in the report of the present Critias of the conversation between the elder Critias and Amynander. We are only one step removed now from the Socratic present, and the transmission slips into the form of the dialogue which can be continued in further evocative dialogues. Critias, the listener, has preserved the memory of the dialogue between Critias the elder and Amynander; and Critias was present in the audience of the Socratic report of the *Republic*. On the present evening, in the *Timaeus*, the two dialogues blend and are continued.

At this juncture, when we enter the Socratic present, youth and age change their meanings. In the chain of transmission, the story went from the old to the young; but now, in the *Timaeus*, the chain comes to its end. The present Critias, who is now a man of ripe age, does not hand the story on to the younger generation for further transmission *in infinitum*. On the contrary, Critias had forgotten the story long ago; only the Socratic report of the previous evening had stirred his memory; and he has spent a good deal of the night in extracting the story, through anamnesis, from the memory of his youth. The account of this anamnesis is an essential part of the story, and he goes into details at some length. Immediately on leaving Socrates he had started to tell to his companions such parts of the story as he was able to recollect at the moment (20 c–d). While listening he had become aware with astonishment that "by some divine fortune" the Socratic polis remarkably resembled the vaguely remembered polis of Solon's story. He did not want to speak right away, however, because through the effect of time he had forgotten too much of it. The story began to come back during the conversation on the way home, and during the night he recovered it completely. "For it is true, what is said, that what we learned in childhood remains in memory in a surprising manner. I am not sure that I could remember all that was said yesterday; but I should be greatly astonished if I forgot any of the things which I have heard very long ago." He listened, at the time, with childlike fascination to the old man's narrative; he questioned him and let him repeat the details; and the words were branded in his memory like an encaustic picture (26b–c). The old man Critias, thus, is informed through the memory of the young Critias. Youth is the repository of the idea, and age can gain access to it through anamnesis. The symbolism finds its elucidation through the myth of the *Statesman* where the world, released in perfect state from the hands of the gods, becomes worse, in course of time, the farther it moves away from the divine origin. Youth is nearer to the divine origin, and the youth of the origin has to be recovered through the anamnesis of age. Age is the epoch in the cosmic revolution at which we have arrived in the *Timaeus*. From its divine youth the idea has declined during the 9,000 years since the war with Atlantis. For the world that has grown old has come the time for its return to the origin, the time for age to recapture the youth of the idea. Hence the evening of the *Timaeus* is an evening of the old men, of the men who have seen the Agathon; or rather, we should speak of the whole series of evenings which starts with the Socratic report as the evening of the old men. For in this series, Socrates is not the educator of the *Republic* who awakens in young men the understanding consent to his evocation; he is the reporter who evokes in his companions, not their youthful consent, but their ripe response and confirmation. The Egyptian myth of Critias confirms the Socratic polis. It is not the kind of consent given by Glaukon and Adeimantus in the *Republic*, but an independent confirmation which adds the historic dimension to the polis. The full idea appears at the intersection of the two co-ordinates drawn by Socrates, when he "projects" the order of his soul which has seen the Agathon, and by Critias, when he recovers the youth of the cosmos. The two poleis can now be identified.[3] Critias, who has given only a summary view of Solon's tale, is ready to report his recollections in full. "The polis and its citizens which you have described to us *en mythô*, we shall now transpose into the order of reality [*epi talethes*]. It will be the ancient polis of Athens; and its citizens, which you have imagined, we shall assume to be our ancestors in truth [*alethinous*]. All is in harmony, and we shall not be mistaken if we say that the citizens of the two poleis are the same" (26c–d). Socrates agrees readily, for what could be a better basis for further discussion than a narrative which is not an invented legend (*mythos*) but a true story (*alethinos logos*) (26e).

When Plato's ironic play with myth and truth has reached the point where the Egyptian myth has become a true story, most suitable to serve as a basis for further discussion, it is time to extricate ourselves from the fabric of the poem and shift the level of analysis. Up to this point we have followed the myth in order to establish its meaning as intended overtly in the work. Now we must take our position outside the dialogue and inquire into the meaning which the work has as a creation of Plato.

In order to arrive at this meaning, first of all, the apparent historical elements in the dialogue must be discounted. We have previously indicated that Timaeus of Locris is probably a fictitious person. Critias is barely a name; he functions generically as the respected member of an Athenian noble family. Hermocrates, the Sicilian, to be sure, is an historical personage, but the allusion can hardly imply more, as we shall see, than Plato's intention to hold up the menace of conquest to Athens. And the historical Socrates has disappeared almost completely behind the figure of Plato's creation. The irrelevancy of the historical element must be realized, in particular, with regard to the Egyptian myth itself. There

---

[3] In *Order and History* II, Ch. 6, 2, 4, we have studied the identification of the Milesian *arche* with the divine One that is experienced in the mystical leap of Xenophanes. The same problem now recurs on the level of the Platonic symbolization of the embodiment of paradigmatic order in the stream of history.

is no trace in history of an island of Atlantis, nor of a saga of Atlantis antedating the *Timaeus*. The myth of Atlantis seems to be invented wholly by Plato. Consequently the ascription of the narrative to Solon has no basis in fact. Solon, indeed, travelled in Egypt but there is no record that he brought back a myth of this kind. Hence, the story of the transmission of the narrative from the Saitic priests to Solon, and further on to the younger Critias, is without historical foundation. It is introduced exclusively for the purpose of conveying the meaning which it has within the fabric of the *Timaeus*.

Once we have realized the a-historical character of the *Timaeus*, as well as its relation to the *Republic*, we are prepared to interpret the dialogue as a drama within the soul of Plato. The Socrates who is dissatisfied with the polis of the *Republic* is Plato himself, and in search of the true or full idea we meet again Plato in the person of Critias. It is Plato who finds Atlantis through anamnesis, and the youth in which he finds it is neither that of Critias, nor his own in a biographical sense, but the collective unconscious that is living in him. The story of the transmission, furthermore, symbolizes the dimension of the unconscious in depth by tracing the myth through the levels of the collective soul of the people (Solon to Critias), and of the generic soul of mankind (the old Athens and Sais), into the primordial life of the cosmos from whose travail springs man (the level of the gods). The *Timaeus* has, indeed, moved beyond the *Republic* with its paradigm set up in heaven and beyond the forces of Thanatos, Eros, and Dike. For the paradigm in heaven now has to be authenticated by the assent of the unconscious; and the forces which orient the individual soul toward the Agathon are now supplemented by the forces of the collective soul which reaches, in its depth, into the life of the cosmos. The development was foreshadowed by the *Republic*, especially by the Pamphylian myth of the Judgment of the Dead, but only now, in the Egyptian myth of Athenian prehistory, has it reached full symbolic expression.

The transition from the earlier to the later phase is symbolized subtly by the distribution of rôles in the *Timaeus*. The life of the individual soul which animates the speculation of the *Republic* is identified now more closely with the symbol of Socrates. In the evocative dialogue with Socrates the Agathon has become visible; and his report is introduced in the *Timaeus* as the motive of the present gathering, that is, of the new dramatic evolution; the debt of gratitude to Socrates as the great mover of the soul is again acknowledged. Nevertheless, other forces appear now by his side. He is still present in *Timaeus* and *Critias* but he has become silent. In the dialogues which bear their names, Timaeus and Critias are cast in the rôle of the main speaker that formerly was given to Socrates; Hermocrates would have appeared in this rôle in the projected third dialogue. Timaeus, the astronomer, unfolds the creation of the cosmos down to the creation of man. That is Plato's acknowledgment of his debt to the Pythagoreans who awakened in him the sense for the fundamental measure and rhythm in nature. And then the task is carried on by Critias who relates the heroic prehistory of Athens and the war with Atlantis. That is Plato's acknowledgment of his debt to Athens and the aristocracy to which he belongs.

The idea of the polis has grown into its fullness, not because it has gained overtly the dimension of history, but because in the life of the soul the solitude of contemplation is now in harmony with the transpersonal rhythms of the people, of the human race, and of the cosmos. The age of intellection, precariously in revolt against the appearance of history, has found its strength and support in the youth of the unconscious.

The soul may become the scene on which a drama is enacted; but not of necessity does the drama find expression in symbols like the myth of the *Timaeus*. It requires the forming power of a personality to translate the movements of the soul into the intricate language of mythical symbols. We must now consider the rôle of Plato as the poet of the myth. The *Timaeus* gives more than one clue for the understanding of Plato's late creations. There is above all the remark of the elder Critias on the poetic work of Solon: "Yes, Amynander, if Solon had not made verse as a pastime but had applied himself to poetry like others; if he had worked out the tale which he brought here from Egypt, and had not been compelled by the revolts and other troubles which he found brewing on his return to neglect poetry completely, in my opinion, neither Hesiod, nor Homer, nor any other of the poets would have been as celebrated as he" (21c). Since the Egyptian myth is Plato's invention, Solon is Plato himself; and the passage must be considered as autobiographical. Plato himself is the poet who has shown his qualities in minor works (as Plato actually has done), who had to occupy himself with the political calamity of his country, and who did not become an epic poet in rivalry with

Hesiod and Homer though he had in his hands the story that most suitably could be worked out in an epic poem.

At first sight this confession is puzzling. Can it really mean that Plato had the ambition of becoming a poet in rivalry with Homer, but that he was occupied too much with political affairs, and now feels too old to embark on the adventure of an epic? That he renounces the dream of his youth and is resigned to write nothing better than philosophical dialogues? The sad story of ambition and failure would be in flat contradiction to the vehement attack on the mimetic poets in the *Republic*, and in particular to the famous address to "Dear Homer" (*Republic* 599d). Could Plato have reversed his judgment, so deeply rooted in his opposition of the myth of the soul to the myth of the people? But we know that Plato has not changed his position in the *Timaeus*, for the Socrates who did not feel equal to the task of singing the praise of the polis was sure that the mimetic poets, "past or present," were not capable of doing it either (*Timaeus* 19d). In this point no more than in any other does Plato reject the *Republic*.

The solution to the puzzle of this confession is to be found when we shift again from the overt identification Solon-Plato to the symbolism of the soul. The "Solon" of the *Timaeus* is rather close to the stratum in the life of the Platonic soul that otherwise is symbolized by "Socrates." The "Socrates" who has reported the *Republic* hands on the task to "Timaeus" and "Critias," that is, to the strata of the unconscious (the "Egypt," the "Youth") from which Plato has extracted, through anamnesis, the saga of Atlantis. Plato is far from renouncing the rank of the poet. He is not going to be a "Solon" who, under the pressure of affairs, leaves unused the treasure from Egypt. Through the *Republic* he is the lawgiver of his polis like Solon, through the Academy, the founder of a school like Pythagoras; in both respects he has succeeded where Homer failed. And now he will be the poet, not a mimetic poet "in the third remove from reality," but the poet of the idea itself. If there is renunciation in the *Timaeus*, and in particular in the autobiographical passage, then it is Plato's renunciation of politics: the Solonic life of the lawgiver, the phase of the Socrates-Plato who speaks in the *Republic*, is closed. Socrates-Plato lapses into silence, and in the *Laws* he will disappear altogether; but Timaeus-Plato and Critias-Plato will sing the poem of the idea.

2. *The Plan of the Dialogues*

The series of dialogues that begins with the *Timaeus* has remained a fragment. More than one reasonable conjecture is possible with regard to its continuation and conclusion; and the debate among Platonists has not achieved consensus. Since the interpretation of the fragment is seriously affected by the historian's conception of its place in the evolution of Plato's thought, as well as by his assumptions concerning the missing parts, we must briefly clarify our own position in the matter. For that purpose it will be helpful to ascertain what is really known about the plan, so that our certain knowledge can be clearly set off against the conjectures which must supplement it.

From the introductory part of the *Timaeus* we know that the whole series was supposed to be a continuation of the *Republic*. The polis of the idea that had been unfolded as it were in a static picture will now be shown epically in historical action. We know, furthermore, that the continuation was motivated by dissatisfaction with an idea that was not the form of any reality; hence, the historical embodiment of the idea will be the great topic of *Timaeus* and *Critias*. Closely connected with this problem is a further piece of information, contained in the remark of Socrates that his summary of the "chief subject" of the previous dialogue was complete (19a). As a matter of fact, the summary included the institutions of the good polis, to the end of *Republic* V, but did not include the subsequent parts culminating in the problem of the Agathon, nor the theory of the bad forms of government. The omission from the summary of this cardinal piece of the *Republic* on the Agathon has caused various conjectures. We prefer the assumption that no summary of the *Republic* was intended at all, but only a recall of the good polis, preparatory to the clarification of its ontological status through the myth of the *Timaeus*. No conclusions should, therefore, be drawn concerning an intended revision or rejection of the parts of the *Republic* omitted from the summary.

With regard to the plan of the whole work, we must beware of uncritically accepting the indications given in the dialogue as a plan of Plato's. They are pronounced by the *dialogi personae*, not by the author in direct speech. We only know for certain that two dialogues were planned—for the good reason that they were written. Whether Hermocrates, who is repeatedly announced as the third speaker after Critias, would have, indeed, delivered a third speech, and whether his contribution would have been embodied in a third dialogue, is rather doubtful. For according to the plan set forth in 27a–b, first Timaeus will speak on the birth of the cosmos and carry his account to the nature of man, and then Critias will take over mankind from him (though only that portion which have received from Socrates the perfect training), make them Athenian citizens, and tell their history according to the myth of Solon. No subject matter is left for Hermocrates; Timaeus and Critias would have exhausted the project of 27a–b.[4] The matter is further complicated by the mysterious unnamed person, prevented by an indisposition to be present. Why is he mentioned at all? Will he perhaps appear in the course of the proceedings and give them an unexpected turn? We do not know. The only fact to which we can cling is the person of Hermocrates himself. As we have suggested previously, the presence of the Sicilian victor over the Athenians can hardly imply anything but a threat to an unregenerate Athens. Which form, however, the threat would have assumed (perhaps that of a speech by Hermocrates, in conclusion of the *Critias*, in order to balance the Egyptian Myth at the beginning?) must remain impenetrable. For the purpose of our interpretation we shall assume that the meaning of the whole work is exhausted by the plan of 27a–b.

Finally, we have to consider the fragmentary character of the *Critias*. Again, we do not know why the dialogue has remained incomplete. Whatever the unknown reason was, the *Critias*, though breaking off in the middle of a sentence, does not break off at an accidental place. Before the fragment ends, the description of Athens and Atlantis is completed and the cause of the war in a divine resolution is explained. Moreover, the closing scene (Zeus addressing the assembly of the gods) marks a formal incision in the dialogue, and the corresponding scene in the *Timaeus* elucidates the meaning of the incision in the *Critias*. The dialogue, thus, is a formal fragment, not an accidental one; its meaning is rounded in itself and does not depend on what might have followed. In our interpretation we shall, therefore, act on the assumption that the inde-

---

[4] Platonists have availed themselves to the full of this opportunity for conjecture. A survey is given in the "Notice" of Albert Rivaud's edition of the *Timaeus* (Platon, *Oeuvres Complètes*, Vol. X, Paris, 1925), 15f. Cornford assumes that the topic of Hermocrates is probably to be found in Book IIIf. of the *Laws* (*Plato's Cosmology*, New York, 1937), 6f.

pendent meaning of the fragment reflects an intention of Plato, and not take into account any conjectures concerning the missing part.[5]

3. The Philosophy of the Myth

The philosophy of the myth is presented in the *Timaeus* in the form of an intricate myth of the myth. In order to make the rather difficult analysis of this part of the dialogue both adequate and convincing, it is advisable to have it preceded by a discursive statement of the problems involved. The summary given in the present section will extend, therefore, to the Platonic problem of the myth as it has evolved up to this point, as well as to several clarifying formulations of the later work.

At various points the summary will be slightly expanded beyond the immediate problems. The *Timaeus* marks an epoch in the history of mankind in so far as in this work the psyche has reached the critical consciousness of the methods by which it symbolizes its own experiences. As a consequence, no philosophy of order and symbols can be adequate unless the Platonic philosophy of the myth has been substantially absorbed into its own principles. It seems appropriate, therefore, to include a few hints concerning the importance of the *Timaeus* as a basis for every philosophy of the myth.

The *Republic* projects the soul on the canvas of society. The *Timaeus* projects it on the still larger canvas of the cosmos. In the *Republic* the psyche furnishes the model of order for the polis, in opposition to Thrasymachus who conceives social order materialistically as the successful imposition of the interest of the stronger on the weaker natures. In the *Timaeus* the psyche furnishes the model of order for the cosmos, in opposition to Democritus who conceives cosmic order as a harmony arising from the constellation of atomic elements. The realms of being are now penetrated to their limits by psyche. As far as metaphysical construction is concerned, no corner of the universe is left to the materialists as a foothold from where the order of the psyche could be negated on

---

[5] The indispensable bases for an interpretation of the Timaeus are Taylor, *A Commentary on Plato's Timaeus,* and Cornford, *Plato's Cosmology. The Timaeus of Plato translated with a Running Commentary* (New York, 1937). Of particular value for the interpretation of the *Critias* was the "Epilogue" of Cornford's work. Of the older literature, the treatise by J. A. Stewart, *The Myths of Plato* (London, 1905) is still important for the *Critias*. For the theory of the Idea in the *Timaeus* Erich Frank, *Plato und die sogenannten Pythagoreer* (Halle, 1923) is the most lucid presentation. The best analysis of the political aspects of the *Timaeus* is to be found in Kurt Hildebrandt, *Platon.*

principle. The order of the cosmos has become consubstantial with the order of the polis and of man.

While the extension of the order of the psyche to the cosmos is important for the systematic perfection of Platonic metaphysis, it contributes little to the crucial problem of the embodiment of the idea in historical reality. The projection of the psyche into the order of the polis was the point of doubtful legitimacy in the *Republic,* and it does not become less doubtful by a projection of the psyche on a still larger scale. For the cosmos is not a datum of immanent experience; the philosopher, as a consequence, cannot advance verifiable propositions concerning the psychic nature of its order. That is the difficulty which Plato solves by means of the myth. The analysis of the Egyptian myth has shown that the "truth" of the myth will arise from the unconscious, stratified in depth into the collective unconscious of the people, the generic unconscious of mankind, and the deepest level where it is in communication with the primordial forces of the cosmos. On this conception of a cosmic *omphalos* of the soul in the depth of the unconscious rests Plato's acceptance of the myth as a medium of symbolic expression, endowed with an authority of its own, independent of, and prior to, the universe of empirical knowledge constituted by consciousness in attention to its objects.

The omphalos, through which the cosmic forces stream into the soul, has a twofold function in the formation of the myth. It is first the source of the forces, of the sentiments, anxieties, apprehensions, yearnings, which surge up from the depth and roam in the unconscious, urging toward assuaging expression in the imaginative order of mythical symbols. The fact of this openness toward the cosmos in the depth of the soul is, second, the "subject matter" of the myth, broken by the finiteness of human existence into the spectrum of birth and death, of return to the origins and rebirth, of individualization and depersonalization, of union or re-union with transcendent reality (in nature, erotic relations, the group, the spirit), of suffering through temporal existence in separation from the ground and of redemption through return into eternal communion with the ground. The myth itself authenticates its truth because the forces which animate its imagery are at the same time its subject matter. A myth can never be "untrue" because it would not exist unless it had its experiential basis in the movements of the soul which it symbolizes.

While a myth cannot be "untrue" in itself, it can become "untrue" historically. The dynamic, which determines the historical spectrum of the myth, has two principal sources: (1) the rise of spiritual consciousness to new levels, and (2) changes in the relation between man and his environment, including the changes in man's knowledge of himself and of his environment. In concrete analysis, the two sources can hardly be separated clearly because, on the one hand, a differentiation of spiritual consciousness is in itself an increase in human self-knowledge with far-reaching consequences for the understanding of man's place in his environment, and because, on the other hand, an increase of environmental knowledge may be a ferment that causes a differentiation of spiritual consciousness. The myth-creating forces of the soul, while retaining the identity of their origin and subject matter, have to express themselves in symbols which correspond to the level of spiritual consciousness, as well as to the degree of differentiation which the self-understanding of man in his environment has reached. Hence, within Hellenic civilization we have to discern several successive levels of the myth. On the most archaic level the mythical forces express themselves in symbolic actions, *i.e.*, in the form of rites. On a higher level the myth appears in the narrower sense of a *mythos, i.e.*, of a tale of anonymous origin which interprets the rites; these are the people's myths, of the kind that were collected and organized by Hesiod. On the third level the anonymous, collective character of the myth begins to break and the personal psyche makes its appearance, transforming the symbolic material of the preceding level into instruments of expression for the spiritual movements (the "wisdom through suffering") of the individual soul; this is the level represented by the tragedies of Aeschylus, in particular by *Prometheus* and *Oresteia*. The free use of the more archaic symbolic materials by the artist on the higher level of spiritual consciousness, however, changes the attitude of man toward the mythical symbols. For when the myth need no longer be taken "literally" (if it ever was), the symbols can be manipulated and transformed deliberately in order to fit the exigencies of differentiated, personal experiences. This is the fourth level, represented by Plato, where the myth retains the seriousness of its "truth" but is at the same time consciously an imaginative play.[6]

[6] On the "rite" as the most archaic level of mythical expression and on the *mythos* as a tale which interprets the rite, cf. the pioneer studies by Jane E. Harrison, *Prolegomena to the Study of Greek Religion* (Cambridge, 1903), and *Themis, A Study of the Origins of Greek Religion* (Cambridge, 1912). On the transition from the level of the archaic *mythos* to the myth of

The new dimension of conscious play is the characteristic of Plato's mythical creation. Such play is possible only under certain conditions which are present neither at all times nor in all men; and we have to be clear about these conditions if we wish to understand the function of the myth in Plato's late work. First of all, the nature of the myth must be understood by the creator or poet as the upwelling, from the unconscious, of psychic forces which blossom out into assuaging expression. An awareness of this nature of the myth is probably always present in mythical creation, even on the most archaic level; for without this assumption it would be difficult to account for the range of imaginative play which is considerable even on the ritual level, and it would be quite impossible to account for the bewildering richness of the play on the level of the mythical tale. What is new on the level of Plato is not the element of play itself but rather the inner freedom of the play, engendered by the growth and differentiation of the personal psyche from the sixth century onward. While the inner distance from the myth inevitably destroys the naïveté of the play, and the myth consequently becomes for Plato a work of art, it must not destroy the "truth" of the myth. This is the second condition of the conscious play. Plato knows that one myth can and must supersede the other, but he also knows that no other human function, for instance "reason" or "science," can supersede the myth itself. The myth remains the legitimate expression of the fundamental movements of the soul. Only in the shelter of the myth can the sectors of the personality that are closer to the waking consciousness unfold their potentiality; and without the ordering of the whole personality by the truth of the myth the secondary intellectual and moral powers would lose their direction. It is, on principle, the insight that has found its classic expression in the Anselmian *credo ut intelligam.*

If the inner freedom toward the myth degenerates into the postulate of a freedom from the myth, serious consequences for the stability both of personality and society will ensue. If the meaning of history is seen in the overcoming of the myth through "positive science," as it is

---

Aeschylus cf. Gilbert Murray, *Aeschylus, The Creator of Tragedy* (Oxford, 1940). The consciousness of imaginative play in the creation of a myth is an intricate problem which recently has received elucidation through Jan Huizinga's *Homo Ludens. Versuch einer Bestimmung des Spielelements der Kultur* (Basel, 1944). Huizinga traces the consciousness of play back to the most archaic levels of mythical creation and would even assume "play" as a substratum, reaching down into the animal world, on the basis of which the differentiated human creations like rites, myth, law, speculation, etc., have to grow.

for instance in Comte's philosophy of history, the problem of mythical truth changes its aspect completely. If empirical science is made the model of true knowledge the myth obviously does not conform to it; it will appear as a "primitive" or "anthropomorphic" type of knowledge, perhaps not entirely without value in its time, but certainly imperfect and irrational in character if compared with the equations of mathematical physics.

The model of positive science destroys the understanding of the myth for the past as well as for the present. With regard to the myth of the past the symbols and dogmas that have grown historically will be misunderstood as concepts and verifiable propositions and will inevitably be found of doubtful value. The symbols of the myth are cut off, through this attitude, from their basis in the unconscious and are required to legitimate themselves as if they were propositions concerning objects. The myth is erroneously supposed to be meant "literally" instead of symbolically, and consequently appears as naïve or superstitious. With regard to the myth of the present the result is equally destructive. The myth has a fundamental function in human existence and myths will be created no matter what anybody thinks about them. We cannot overcome the myth, we can only misunderstand it. With regard to the contemporary myth, of the eighteenth century and after, the positivist misunderstanding has the consequence that the mythical symbols are claimed to be what the symbols of the past are charged not to be, that is, "science" or "theory." Such symbols as "reason," "mankind," "proletariat," "race," "communist society," "world-peace," and so forth, are supposed to be different in nature from pagan or Christian symbols because their mythical truth is covered and obscured by the superimposition of the additional myth of science.

Since the myth does not cease to be myth because somebody believes it to be science, the telescoping of myth and science has a peculiar warping effect on the personality of the believers. As long as the movements of the unconscious are allowed to express themselves in myth in free recognition of their nature, the soul of man preserves its openness towards its cosmic ground. The terror of an infinitely overpowering, as well as the assurance of an infinitely embracing, beyond as the matrix of separate, individual existence, endow the soul with its more-than-human dimension; and through the acceptance of the truth of this dimension (that is, through faith) the separateness of human existence

can, in its turn, be recognized and tolerated in its finiteness and limitations. The acceptance of the myth (or, on the Christian level, the *cognitio fidei*) is the condition for a realistic understanding of the soul.
When the balance of openness and separateness is destroyed through the
telescoping of myth and science, the forces of the unconscious will stream
into the form, not of the myth, but of theory or science. The symbols of
the myth become perverted into intramundane, illusionary objects,
"given," as if they were empirical data, to the cognitive and active functions of man; at the same time the separate, individual existence suffers
an illusionary inflation because it absorbs into its form the more-than-
human dimension. Man becomes anthropomorphic—to use a phrase of
Goethe's. The symbols of the myth are translated into realities and aims
of anthropomorphic man: The nature of man is basically good; the
source of evils is to be found in the institutions; organization and revolution can abolish such evils as still exist; the powers of man can create
a society free from want and fear; the ideas of infinite perfectibility, of
the superman, and of self-salvation make their appearance.[7]

The Hellenic period of enlightenment resembles in many respects the
Western age of reason and science. The disintegration of the old myth,
as well as the advancement of science, causes an illusionary inflation of
the individual that is in substance, though not always in the phenomena,
the counterpart of the Western inflation. In its historical situation the
myth of Plato has, therefore, more than one function. First of all, it
supersedes the disintegrating old myth of the people and discounts it
as "untrue"; it, furthermore, opposes itself to the warping of personality
through enlightened materialism; and it, finally, regains the truth of the
myth on the new level of the differentiated consciousness of the mystic.
The plurality of functions determines a variety of Platonic attitudes toward the old myth which must appear as contradictory as long as the
source of their logic in the problem of the new myth is not realized.

In the *Republic* we could observe the hardness of Plato in discarding
the old myth, and in the *Laws* we shall see the provision for a censorship
that will prevent elements of the old myth from entering the polis of
the new myth. In his hardness Plato even goes to the extreme of rejecting
the glory of the Homeric epic. If we search for the motives of the attitude we shall not find them on the level of a conflict between dogmas.
The issue, as the *Statesman* has revealed, lies between two experiences
of order. On the level of the old myth, order is experienced as humanly

---

[7] For an expansion of these problems see my *New Science of Politics* (Chicago, 1952).

anonymous. The gods will have to repair it if it falls into decay; and the hope for redemption from evil crystallizes in the paradisic myth of the Golden Age. On the level of the new myth, order is experienced as the embodiment in community of the living order in the soul of the philosopher. The differentiated spiritual consciousness, in its conflict with a less differentiated state of the soul, has to be protected against the danger of being dragged down again to the more archaic level.

In Plato's work the attitude of protective hardness seems to be contradicted by the frequent manifestations of ironical tolerance for the gods of the past, of sincere admiration for the rejected poets as artists, and by the generous reception of figures of the Hellenic pantheon into the symbolism of the new mythical poems. This contradiction, however, is only apparent, for as long as the spiritual order of the soul is not endangered, there is no reason for harshness against the symbols of the past. Their imagery is precious to the artist. Moreover, they are authentic symbols of movements of the soul, and their truth, while superseded by the new myth, cannot be invalidated on its own level. The wider and more grandiose perspective that has opened in the soul does not abolish the reality of the archaic experiences; it will embrace them but relegate them to a humbler distance.

An illuminating instance of such treatment of the old gods is to be found in *Timaeus* 40d–41a. In this passage, after Plato has related the creation of the celestial gods, he reflects on the generations of the old gods from Gaea and Uranus to Zeus and Hera. He finds it beyond his powers to give an account of that part of the theogony and is willing to rely on the stories of the Orphics who relate it in detail. For certainly, since they are descendants of the Olympian gods, they must be well acquainted with their own ancestry. We must follow custom and accept what they say for we cannot mistrust "the children of gods though they speak without probable or certain proof." The irony of this passage is directed, not against the gods, but against the Orphic sages who claim to descend from the gods and to know all about their family affairs. Plato wants to ridicule, not the old myth, but the men who have left its truth so far behind that they treat the myth "literally" as if it were an empirical account of historical events. Even in the flat literal account, however, it still communicates a truth and should not be entirely omitted, therefore, from the theogony.

In the *Laws* Plato explicitly distinguishes between the archaic truth

of the myth and its effects on those who take it as a piece of moral advice. He cautions against easy judgments concerning the good or bad
effects of the theogonic narratives on those who hear them, "for they
[the narratives] are old." And then he complains bitterly about the bad
effects on young people who take the tales of divine misdemeanors as
an invitation to follow their example. Even at this point, however, when
Plato recognizes that a myth which has become untrue historically can
no longer mould the souls of the young, he respects its inherent truth
and counsels: let the old stories be told "as it pleases the Gods." The real
danger to the soul does not come from the ancients (*archaios*); it comes
from the enlightened moderns (*neos kai sophos*) who not only misuse
the old myth but also in their illusionary inflation through science have
lost the truth of the myth altogether (886). When speaking of such
enlightenment, which does not supersede the old myth by a new one but
loses the myth itself, Plato becomes passionate and eloquent: for how
shall we plead for the existence of gods dispassionately? "No one can
help feeling resentment and disgust with the parties who impose the
burden of argument on us by their want of faith in the stories heard so
often in earliest infancy. . . . At rising and setting of sun and moon,
they have heard and seen the universal prostrations of mankind, Greeks
and non-Greeks alike . . . with their implication that gods are no fic-
tions but the most certain of realities. . . . When we see all this evidence treated with contempt . . . and that, as any man with a grain
of intelligence will admit, without a single respectable reason, how, I
ask, is a man to find gentle language in which to combine reproof with
instruction" (887).[8] The myth authenticates itself; its existence is the
evidence of the existence of the forces which create it. Nevertheless,

---

[8] The translation is Taylor's *The Laws of Plato*. The process of enlightenment is described
admirably by Gilbert Murray in his *Aeschylus*, 79f.: "Vigorous minds begin to question the conventions in which they have been brought up and which they have now outgrown. They
reject first the elements in them that are morally repulsive, then the parts that are obviously
incredible; they try to reject the husk and preserve the kernel, and for a time reach a far
higher moral and intellectual standard than the generations before them or the duller people of
their own time. Then, it seems, something is apt to go wrong. Perhaps a cynic would say—
and it would be hard to confute him—the element of reason in man is so feeble a thing that
he cannot stand successfully except when propped in the stiff harness of convention. At any rate,
there is always apt to come a later generation which has carried doubt and scepticism much
farther and finds the kernel to consist only of inner layers of husk and then more husk, as
the place of George IV's heart, according to Thackeray, was supplied by waistcoats and then
more waistcoats. First comes inspiration and the exultation of the breaking of false barriers: at
the end comes the mere flabbiness of having no barriers left to break and no talent except for
breaking them."

times of transition are a real danger to man for they may cause him to lose the truth of the myth. Hence, in the *Epinomis,* Plato suggests that the lawgiver "who has any intelligence at all" will refrain from innovations in religious matters; he will beware of turning his city toward a new cult that quite probably will be supported less solidly by piety; and he will not dare to change the ancient rites for he ought to know that our mortal nature has no certain knowledge in such matters (985c–d).

The various passages illuminate the facets of Plato's attitude toward the myth. He rejects the old myth because it has become historically untrue; but he defends it, nevertheless, against the enlightened materialists who, from the historical untruth, will draw the conclusion that a myth as such has no truth. He will ban the old myth, when its truth has become unintelligible, from the polis of the idea because the opaque symbols expose it to ridicule and engender agnosticism in the people; but he will enjoin the legislator not to change a myth when it is still accepted by the people, because changes may engender distrust against the truth of any myth. He evokes the new myth of the soul; but he preserves an ironic tolerance toward the old myth, even in those instances where quite probably it has become unintelligible to him, because there is a truth in it even if it is no longer quite understood.

The variety of attitudes reveals Plato's freedom toward the myth. It is a freedom of the play with symbols, which increases rather than diminishes the seriousness of the myth since it permits a more careful rendering of the movements of the unconscious. On the level of the symbols this flexibility may result in contradictions which in their turn may arouse questions with regard to the "real" intentions of Plato. We could observe instances of such contradictions in the *Statesman:* Is there one supreme God or do we have to assume at least the two ultimate forces of good and evil? What is the relation of Heimarmene to the One God who regulates the periods of the cosmos? Why do we need the host of divinities in the Age of Cronos if it is the purpose of the myth to show that the age of popular conceits belongs to the past? There can be only one answer to such questions: The "real" intention of Plato must not be sought in any one of the conflicting symbols but in the recognition that the complicated structure of the unconscious in depth and time cannot be harmonized into a system. On this occasion we might recall the confession of Goethe: "As a naturalist, I am a pantheist; as an artist, I am a polytheist; as a moralist, I am a monotheist."

The freedom of the play is not licentiousness. There is an order in the game in so far as the myth symbolizes the forces which stream into its creation from the cosmic omphalos in the ground of the soul. Freedom of the myth means a keener awareness of the movements in the ground as well as of their specific autonomy, a willingness to bend over the ground and to apprehend most faithfully whatever emerges from it, however untranslatable it may be into coherent, rational discourse. It, furthermore, implies the recognition that the conscious subject occupies only a small area in the soul. Beyond this area extends the reality of the soul, vast and darkening in depth, whose movements reach into the small area that is organized as the conscious subject. The movements of the depth reverberate in the conscious subject without becoming objects for it. Hence, the symbols of the myth, in which the reverberations are expressed, can be defined as the refraction of the unconscious in the medium of objectifying consciousness. What enters the area of consciousness has to assume the "form of object" even if it is not object. The symbols, therefore, do not denote an unconscious reality as an object, but, rather, are the unconscious reality itself, broken in the medium of consciousness. The freedom of the play is possible only as long as the creator of a myth remains aware of the character of the symbols as a nonobjective reality in objective form. If he loses the sense that dangerous forces are playing through him when he plays with the myth, when perhaps he goes out in search of the object expressed in symbols, or attempts to prove or disprove its existence, not only his labors will be lost, but he may lose his soul in the process.

In spite of the fact that symbols do not refer to objects, their meaning is intelligible. The intelligibility of mythical symbols, their "truth" in the Platonic sense, is the crucial problem of a philosophy of the myth. The myth is unintelligible if we apply to it an epistemology which has been developed for the case of our knowledge of the external world. The attempt to extend an epistemology of the sciences to the myth would imply the assumption that the soul has throughout the structure of "intentionality," that is, of a consciousness intending its object. We would fall into the anthropomorphic fallacy of forming man in the image of conscious man.

Before a philosopher can even start to develop a theory of the myth, he must have accepted the reality of the unconscious as well as of the relation of every consciousness to its own unconscious ground; and he cannot accept it on any other terms than its own, that is, on the terms of the myth. Hence, a philosophy of the myth must itself be a myth of the soul. That ineluctable condition is the chief obstacle to an adequate philosophy of the myth in an age in which the anthropomorphic obsession has destroyed the reality of man.

The task, however, is at no time easy. The coincidence that the creator of a myth is at the same time a great philosopher who knows what he is doing, as in the case of Plato, is unique in the history of mankind. Even in the case of Schelling, who ranks next to Plato as a philosopher of the myth, his achievement is marred by the gnostic inclination to intellectualize the unconscious and to reduce its movements to the formula of a dialectical process. Schelling cannot be quite absolved of the charge levelled by Irenaeus against the gnostics of the second century A.D.: "They open God like a book" and "They place salvation in the gnosis of that which is ineffable majesty." Plato's philosophizing is free of such inclinations—perhaps because he shared unreservedly the common Greek conviction that things divine are not for mortals to know. Whatever may have been the respective shares of tradition and active insight in Plato's attitude, even in the moments of a most awesome intimacy with cosmic mysteries the veil which separates the myth from knowledge is not torn. Plato's myth always preserves its character as the transparent flower of the unconscious. Its symbols are never broken, with the intention of letting the glare of consciousness penetrate into their beyond, or with the result of letting the unconscious flood and destroy the finite subject. The difference in the attitudes of the two philosophers is perhaps most clearly revealed in Schelling's criticism that Plato had to use the myth for expressing the fundamental relations of soul and cosmos because dialectical speculation could not yet serve him as the instrument for sounding the abyss. The criticism characterizes as a shortcoming in Plato, though as one that was conditioned by his historical position, precisely what we consider his greatest merit, that is, the clear separation of the myth from all knowledge that is constituted in acts of consciousness intending their objects. On the level of the myth of the soul, this separation corresponds to the Christian distinction between the spheres of faith and reason.

4. *The Myth of the Myth in the* Timaeus

The uniqueness of Plato's myth of the myth makes it of the utmost importance not to lose the slightest detail of its execution. The Egyptian myth had symbolized the descent to the "Egypt" of the soul from which, through anamnesis, was brought back the "true story." We have availed ourselves gratefully of the suggestion and expressed the ultimate point to be reached by the descent as the "cosmic omphalos" in the ground of the soul. Thus we have accepted the ineluctable condition and used a mythical symbol in philosophizing on the myth. We shall now follow Plato further into the problems of the myth as they are unfolded in the preliminary remarks of Timaeus (27c–30c).

Timaeus opens his account of the cosmos and its creation with an invocation both of the gods and of human powers. The account will be satisfactory to us only if it is pleasing to the gods (27c); but we must appeal to the human powers, too, since the account must be clear in expression and communicable (27d). Thus, in a preliminary fashion, the place of the myth is fixed at the intersection of the assent of the unconscious and the forming action of consciousness. Timaeus, then, proceeds to determine more closely the conditions under which a myth of the cosmos is possible. He distinguishes between that which has eternal being without becoming, and that which is becoming without ever having eternal being (27d). Eternal being can be apprehended by the intellect (*logos*); what changes and becomes can be apprehended by belief and sensation (*doxa; aisthesis*) (28a). What then is the nature of the cosmos? Is it Being or Becoming? And will it have to be approached by intellect, or by belief and sensation? The answer seems to favor the second alternative: For the cosmos can be seen and touched, it belongs to the realm of becoming, and it is an object for belief and sensation (28b–c). This decision seems to ignore the problem of the myth, since the cosmos would become an object for the human subject to be apprehended in acts of nonmythical cognition. And indeed, more than one Platonist was induced to isolate the epistemological strand from the fabric of the *Timaeus* and to find in this passage Plato's intention to distinguish between the "final" exactness of mathematics and the "provisional" character of propositions in the empirical sciences.[9] The epistemological argument, however, is interwoven with the evocation of the myth. The cosmos, to be sure, belongs to the realm of becoming; yet it participates in the realm of eternal being because the Demiurge has fashioned it as an image (*eikon*) after an eternal model (*paradeigma*) (28a–b; 29a). Plato takes particular care to clarify the relation *eikon-paradeigma*. He raises the question whether the Demiurge has really fashioned the cosmos, after an eternal, not after a generated, model. And he decides on the first assumption, because the cosmos is the most beautiful of all things that have become and the Demiurge is good; the contrary supposition would be blasphemous (29a). We are beyond empirical knowledge of sense or belief; the appeal goes to the spiritual sensitiveness, *i.e.*, to the assent of the unconscious.

The account of the cosmos has ceased to be a problem for objective cognition; as a consequence of the assent it has shifted to the plane of mythical symbolization. If the cosmos were fashioned after a generated model, then, and only then, would it really belong to the realm of becoming; but since it is fashioned after an eternal model, it is an *eikon* of that which is comprehensible by intellect and insight (*logos*; *phronesis*) and which exists in permanent sameness (29a). Being and Becoming have subtly changed their meanings. They no longer signify classes of objects which are accessible, respectively, to intellect and belief, but components of an entity which is neither quite Being nor Becoming. The *paradeigma* cannot be seen by the *logos* of man in its eternal being but only as embodied in the cosmos. And the cosmos, since it is an image of eternal being, is more than a perishable thing in the flux of becoming. The *eikon* is being-in-becoming. Hence, the cosmos is itself a symbol, emerging into the world of objects, but transparent toward its eternal ground. Moreover, we have advanced one step further toward clarifying the problem of intelligibility. The cosmos is intelligible, and we can give an account of it, because the being which manifests itself in becoming is of the kind that can be known by intellect—though it is fully known only by the *logos* of the Demiurge, not by the *logos* of man. The creative ground of the cosmos, while

[9] That has happened even to an authority of the rank of A. E. Taylor. See his *Commentary on Plato's Timaeus* under 27d5–29d3 (pp. 59–61).

surpassing the consciousness of man, is kindred to the finite mind and hence can be understood by it.

We must be aware of this change of meanings when we interpret the concluding remarks of this section. An account, says Timaeus, is kindred (*syngenes*) to the things which it sets forth (29b). If the thing is abiding and discoverable by *logos,* then the account itself will be abiding and conclusive; if the thing is a likeness (*eikon*), then the account itself will only be likely (*eikos*). For as reality is to becoming, so is truth (*aletheia*) to trust (*pistis*) (29c). We seem to have returned to the epistemological distinction—unless Plato wished to indicate by the change of terminology from *doxa* to *pistis* that the problem had been modified. The return, however, is only apparent, for we must not forget that in the context of the argument the *aletheia* is God's and the *pistis* is man's. We are not faced by the alternatives of true and likely accounts; the alternative lies between the truth that is visible to God and the likeliness of the account that is the share of man, precisely because there is the truth of God in the cosmos. The account of "gods and the generation of the universe" will be no more than likely because the speaker and his listeners are no more than "human in nature" (29c–d). Nevertheless, the conclusion that we have to accept the *eikos mythos,* the likely story, seems to imply a lesser degree of "truth" than the earlier assurance that we are going to hear an *alethinos logos,* a true story.

The apparent conflict is solved in the following pages when Timaeus begins the account of creation itself. The Demiurge is good and desires all things to become as nearly like himself as possible (29e). Since order is better than disorder, the god took over discordantly moving primordial matter and brought it from disorder (*ataxia*) to order (*taxis*) (30a). He, furthermore, considered it better to have intelligence (*nous*) than to be without it, and that intelligence cannot be present anywhere apart from soul (*psyche*). Hence he fashioned *nous* within *psyche,* and *psyche* within *soma* (body), so that the cosmos would reflect as closely as possible the supreme goodness of its creator (30b). Thus, "according to the likely story," the cosmos is "in very truth" a living creature endowed with soul and intelligence (*zoon empsychon ennoun*) (30b–c).

In the present context we cannot deal with the passage exhaustively, but must confine ourselves to the points that have a direct bearing on the theory of the myth:

(1) First of all, the problem of *eikon-paradeigma* has undergone a modification. The Demiurge creates the cosmos after a model (reaffirmed in 31 and *passim*). But now he himself has become the model, at least for certain general elements, of cosmic order. He creates the cosmos in his own image with regard to *taxis* and *nous*, and, since *nous* cannot exist apart from *psyche*, probably also with regard to *psyche*. These elements are not the forms of the cosmos in its physical aspect; we might characterize them as the purposive and dynamic elements of cosmic order, providing its goodness and intelligibility. Hence we may say that Plato, in the symbol of the Demiurge, has concentrated the elements of "ordering force" which bridge the gulf between the eternal being of paradigmatic forms and the reality in which they have to be embodied. The Demiurge is the symbol of Incarnation, understood not as the result of the process but as the process itself, as the permanent tension in reality between the *taxis* of form or idea and the *ataxia* of formlessness.

(2) Second, the principle that binds form to the discordant movement of matter is named as intelligence-in-soul. Psyche, as we know from other contexts, is "the mover that moves itself"; movement or process is psychic in substance; and psyche is not blind but made luminous by the *nous* that is fashioned into it. Form (*idea*) has its being in eternal sameness; it is drawn, through intelligence-in-soul, into the process of embodiment in nature, man, and society. Psyche, in a sense, is the intermediate realm between disembodied form and the shapeless movement of matter; but then again we might say it is the only reality in a dynamic sense, for disembodied form and shapeless matter would never coalesce into a "world" without the cosmically creative force of psyche. Moreover, the psyche is the pervasive substance of the cosmos. It animates not only the cosmos itself into a *zoon empsychon* but is the creatively ordering substance in all its subdivisions down to man; for the Demiurge fashioned the cosmos as a living creature with all things in it "kindred to it with regard to their substance" (30d–31a).

(3) This argument brings us, finally, to the concluding sentence of Timaeus: that "according to the likely story" the cosmos is "in very truth" a living creature. The likely story, the *eikos mythos*, renders something more than mere likeliness; it renders the very truth

(*aletheia*). The passage corresponds to the earlier one in the Egyptian myth where the invented story became all of a sudden an *alethinos logos*. After the prolonged teasing with the epistemological distinctions of *logos* and *doxa,* we can see in this sudden reversal hardly anything else but a pointed irony that the humble instrument of "unscientific" myth is the source of the only truth that matters. In this irony, however, there is no confusion. The *aletheia* of the myth is not the *aletheia* of the *logos*. The paradigm still dwells in its eternal sameness, inaccessible to the *logos* of man; we still have no other knowledge of it than "likeliness." What the myth can disclose "in very truth" is the psychic nature of the cosmos as a whole and in its parts. The myth does not render the truth of the idea; it renders the truth of its Incarnation.

We can now summarize the general theory of the myth as it emerges from the *Timaeus*. The substance of the cosmos, including man and society, is psyche illuminated by intelligence. Psyche is the force which transforms the disorder of matter into order by imposing on it the paradigmatic form. The paradigm of the cosmos itself is inaccessible to the intellect of man; we see it only in the image created by the Demiurge. Nevertheless we can give a likely account of the likeness because our psyche is part of the cosmic psyche, and in the medium of our individual psyche we respond with the *eikos mythos* to the cosmic eikon. And how do we know that all this is true and not perhaps an unfounded construction? Because the symbols used in the account originate in our psyche. We receive the myth from the unconscious, that is, from the cosmic depth of our soul that reverberates into the field of consciousness and intelligible communication. The *eikos mythos* carries its own *aletheia* because in it we symbolize the truly experienced relation of our separate conscious existence to the cosmic ground of the soul. The theory of the myth is itself a myth; its truth is not the truth of the intellect but the self-authenticating truth of the psyche.

The systematic place of the *Timaeus* in Plato's philosophy of politics has become clear. The order of the soul, in the *Republic,* was authenticated well enough through the ascent from the Cave to the intelligible realm of the Idea. The *Republic* had not, however, authenticated the paradigm of the good polis as the form of society in history. That second step required the insight into the consubstantiality of soul and society, and ultimately of the cosmos. The myth of the soul can be the myth of the polis only if both individual soul and the polis in history can be embraced in the psyche of the cosmos. The Statesman who imposes the *taxis* of the idea on the *ataxia* of recalcitrant historical matter derives his authority from the Demiurge who imposes the paradigmatic order on the discordant movement of cosmic matter.

5. The Myth of the Incarnation in the Timaeus

The main body of the *Timaeus* elaborates the myth of the cosmos that has been justified in the introductory part. Its ramifications into the details of a philosophy of nature are not our concern. We shall restrict our analysis to the central symbols which support the incarnation of the idea in history.

In order to penetrate to the meaning of the symbols we must again reflect on the relation between the overt story of the creation which the *Timaeus* narrates and the drama of the soul which it symbolizes. For there is conducted a serious debate among commentators on the *Timaeus* on the question whether Plato actually intended to advance a "doctrine" of creation in time, or whether he assumed the existence of the cosmos from eternity. Considering the superb clearness of the dialogue we can hardly admit that such a question may be raised. The symbol of "creation in time," of a "beginning" of the cosmos, is necessitated by the literary form of the mythical "tale." Whatever Plato's "doctrine" of creation would have been, if he had ever thought of having one, in the story the creation inevitably must occur as an event in the inner time of the tale. For the rest, there is no doubt concerning Plato's position, as he has set it forth explicitly in *Timaeus* 37d. According to this passage, time is the *eikon* of eternity. The paradigm is eternal (*aionios*); since the Demiurge could not simply transfer this quality of the model to the image, he created in the cosmos a moving likeness of eternity; this likeness is time. Time is the everlasting (*aionios*) likeness of eternity, "moving according to number." Time, thus, is a quality in the *eikon*; and creation, therefore, cannot be a process in time; and the formula of a "creation in time" is senseless. This solution is, in substance, the same which St. Augustine offers for the problem of time and eternity: "If before heaven and earth there was no time, how can one ask what Thou didst then? For there was no Then, when there was no time. . . . Thou hast made all times and before all times Thou art; and not at any time was time not." [10]

The distinction between the time of the tale and the time of the cosmos further clarifies the relations between Being and Becoming, as well as between myth and knowledge of objects. The time of the tale is neither the eternity of the paradigm nor the everlasting time of Becoming. It symbolizes the in-between of time and eternity. Being does not precede Becoming in time; it is eternally present in Becoming. The flux of Becoming with its transitory objects, as we have seen, is not merely a series of data given to belief and sensation; it has a dimension pointing out of time toward eternal Being. Along this dimension moves the process of Incarnation, intersecting at any given time with the process of Becoming. This process which intersects the time of Becoming at the point of its present, but is not part of the process of Becoming itself, is the process of the psyche; and the time of the tale is the "form of the object" into which consciousness casts this timeless process.

The distinctions of the *Timaeus* with regard to the problem of time lend theoretical support to the method which we have used hitherto in the interpretation of the several Platonic myths. The interpretations of meaning through shifting from the overt meaning of the "tale" to the drama of the soul which it symbolizes, finds its justification in the relations between the timeless process of psyche, the time of Becoming, and the time of the tale.

In the following analysis of the myth of Incarnation, we shall neglect, therefore, the "story" itself, and present its elements in such a fashion that the drama of the psyche emerges from them.

The agency which creates the cosmos is designated as the Demiurge. He creates the cosmos for a reason (*aitia*). The reason is his goodness. And since the good is free of jealousy, he desires all things to be like himself. This goodness, free of jealousy, is the "supreme principle [*arche*] which governs the coming-into-existence [*genesis*] and the order of existence [*kosmos*]" (29e). The divinely creative substance in the Demiurge is the Nous; hence the building of the cosmos in the

[10] St. Augustine, *Confessions*, XI, 13.

likeness of the god becomes a work of the Nous.[11] The total cosmos, however, is not a work of the Nous alone; for Plato's Demiurge is not the omnipotent Christian creator of matter. The Demiurge can build an ordered cosmos, but he has to impose his order on a pre-existent material. The pre-existent substratum of the cosmos follows its own movements, and the critical work of creation consists in bending the substratum to the order of Nous.

The substratum is difficult to describe because it is not given to the cognitive faculties of man. Not even *pistis* will assure us of it; such knowledge as we have of its existence we achieve through a kind of "bastard reasoning" (*logismo notho*) (52b). Plato circumscribes it through a considerable array of mythical symbols and similes which touch on the various aspects of the substratum in the process of creation. In so far as the substratum limits the creative power of the Nous by its own character, it is called Ananke (47e–48a). In so far as it has to enter into the form imposed by the Demiurge, it is likened to a plastic material which can assume any shape without losing its specific nature (50a–c). In so far as it receives the form from the Demiurge, Plato speaks of it as the "nurse of Becoming" (*geneseos tithene*) (49a). Moreover, he symbolizes the creative process as a begetting of the offspring, *i.e.*, of the cosmos, through form as the father and the substratum as the mother (50c–d).[12] The substratum has no qualities of its own, but is of such a nature that the qualities of form can be bestowed upon it. Thus it is neither earth nor air nor fire nor water, nor any other formed element; yet it partakes of their nature; for otherwise the elemental forms could not be imposed on it (48b–d; 50d–51b). Finally, Plato gives a name to the substratum: he calls it Space (*chora*), "everlasting and not admitting of destruction" (52a–b).

The drama of creation is enacted in an uncreated realm which precedes creation—though not in time. The Demiurge operates under the conditions which are prescribed by eternally being Form, by Space, and by Genesis. The triad of Being, Space, and Genesis existed before the cosmos was created (52a). Creation itself, that is, the imposition of Form on Space and Genesis, becomes possible through an interaction or

---

[11] It is better to retain the Greek term. Any rendering by a modern term (such as intelligence, reason, *Geist,* spirit) would fragmentize the compact meaning of Nous.

[12] Quite possibly this symbolization leans on an interpretation of the Pythagorean **Tetraktys.**

agreement (*systasis*) between the ordering will of the Nous and the Ananke of Space. "Since Nous prevailed upon Ananke, persuading her to lead most things in becoming toward the best, the universe originated through Ananke's submission to reasonable persuasion [*peitho*]" (48a).

It is not difficult to discern in this symbolism a further development of the myth of the *Statesman*. The Demiurge corresponds to the Royal Ruler; he has to impose the order of Nous on a recalcitrant material, as the Statesman has to impose the order of the idea on a recalcitrant historical reality. Again we are faced with the dichtomy of good and evil. This time, however, Plato has endeavored valiantly to clarify the problem which formerly he symbolized by the two paradigms. For the force of resistance is now located in the substratum of Space with its movements of elements which are no elements but nevertheless have their qualities to the degree that elemental form can be imposed on them. The recipient of form, furthermore, has become a female principle, *chora*, which is everlasting like form. Its everlastingness, finally, is that of a material movement, of a chaos before form, and Plato uses the term genesis in order to distinguish its eternity of movement and change from the eternity of changeless Being.[13]

The new dichotomy represents a considerable advance over the *Republic*. The resistance to the idea has now become as eternal as the idea itself; and to overcome this resistance in creation is the permanent task of the Nous. In the Parable of the Cave the emphasis was on the ascent of the soul from the Cave to the intellection of the Idea; the emphasis has now shifted to the descent and the imposition of the Idea on formless reality. The problem of the ascent to the Idea, however, has not disappeared completely; for, in discussing the difference of belief and intelligence, Plato remarks (51e) that true belief is shared by all men, but the Nous only "by the gods and a small number of men." The descent of creation is feasible only because there exist the gods and the "small number of men" who are able to see the Idea itself in its eternal Being. Nevertheless, the descent has now become the crucial problem, and Plato for the first time gives full attention to the force of the soul which carries the Idea from Being into Becoming. In the *Statesman* this force had been suggested incidentally; now, in

---

[13] We have retained the Greek term *genesis* on this occasion and have not translated it as Becoming in order to avoid confusion with the Becoming of the cosmos after creation. The genesis of the triad (*on, chora, genesis*) is a Becoming which precedes the Becoming of the cosmos. The Becoming of the cosmos can be apprehended through belief and sensation; the precosmic genesis is apprehended *logismo notho*.

the *Timaeus*, it becomes the great central symbol under the name of Peitho, of Persuasion, which induces the Ananke of the chaos to submit to the Nous.[14]

In the *Statesman* Persuasion appeared in the discussion of the mimetic polis. The law of the polis should imitate the "true" law, and the question was how such imitation could ever be achieved in practice. Plato's answer was that, short of violence, the injection of truth into the polis could be achieved only by persuasion. In the *Statesman* these remarks are embedded in the extended discussion of the lawful polis, and their incidental character is probably the reason why this key problem of the embodiment of the Idea is usually overlooked. In the *Timaeus* Persuasion is placed in the systematic center so that no doubt can remain about its importance as the force of the soul which embodies the work of the Nous in reality. Moreover, the problem of Persuasion receives a new sharpness through the change in the symbol of Necessity. In the *Statesman* Necessity appeared as Heimarmene, the goddess who determines the periods of the cosmos; in the *Timaeus* Necessity has become Ananke, the limitative force of *chora* which yields to Persuasion. The Nous of the Demiurge overrules Ananke through Peitho, and the cosmos is created as the permanent structure of Becoming.

In the cosmos, at least, Nous has prevailed over Ananke and imposed the order of the idea. The task of the Statesman can now be conceived as the creation, in politics, of an order analogous to the order of the cosmos. This last step, the evocation of the polis as a cosmic analogue, Plato has taken in the *Laws*.

Through the force of Eros the soul rises to the intellection of the Agathon; through the force of Peitho the soul incarnates the Agathon in reality. Eros and Peitho are the forces of the ascent and descent, and, under this aspect, the *Timaeus* is the counterpart to the *Symposion*. Considering the parallel rank of the two forces, it is perhaps curious

---

[14] The passage concerning the Nous, shared by "the gods and a small number of men" who can see the Idea itself, reintroduces the "epistemological strain" into the argument. There seems to be possible, after all, a direct knowledge of the Idea, unbroken by the myth. Precisely the occasion, however, on which this epistemological strain reappears, should warn against extracting an epistemology in the modern sense from the work of Plato. Plato's "man" is not a modern *Subjekt der Erkenntnis* which has absorbed the Christian tradition of creaturely finiteness. Plato's "man" is a psyche; and we have seen in the *Phaedrus* that the psyche in man has a range from ordinary humanity to semi-divinity. The epistemology of Plato presupposes a myth of man which differs fundamentally from the Christian idea.

that Plato should have so little to say about Peitho as compared with the
great hymn to Eros. The quotation that we have given practically exhausts what we find in the *Timaeus* on the process of Peitho. Whatever else the reasons for such briefness may have been, one reason certainly was that every Greek knew what was meant by Peitho, while
Eros was the new daemon of the Platonic circle.

When Plato introduces the force of Peitho he recalls a theme of
the other great spiritual thinker of Hellas, of Aeschylus. The theme of
the *Oresteia* is the yoke of Ananke and its breaking through the wisdom that has come by suffering. The generations of the gods follow
one another, each doing penance for the violence of its rule by falling
a victim to the successor, until Zeus breaks the chain through his personal rise to a just rule of constraint and wisdom. Likewise the mortals,
as Agamemnon, bow to Ananke and commit misdeeds, to be followed
by avenging misdeeds in horrible succession until the chain of vengeance
is broken, in the *Eumenides,* by Athena who persuades the Erinyes to
accept the acquittal of their victim and to change their own nature
from vengeance to beneficence. The closing scene of the *Eumenides*
brings the clash between the two generations of gods, representing stages
of development in wisdom. Athena represents the new wisdom and
justice of Zeus; the Erinyes represent the old order of justice through
vengeance. The Erinyes do not yield easily, for the old order has its
reason and justification; and Athena insists that she does not wish to
show disrespect to her older sisters. She holds the thunder of Zeus in
reserve to beat down resistance, but she does not want to use violence.
She appeals to the Erinyes to respect "the majesty of Peitho" (885); and
she rejoices when the *Zeus agoraios* has triumphed and the victory of
the *agathon* is secured (973ff.). The parallels between Plato and Aeschylus are so close that they hardly can be accidental. The *Zeus agoraios,*
the Zeus of persuasion over the assembly of the people, is next of kin to
the Demiurge and the Royal Ruler. The victory of Nous over Ananke
in the *Timaeus* must be seen against the Aeschylean background of the
victory of the new wisdom over the older mythical forces. If such support were needed, this relation between the *Timaeus* and the *Oresteia*
would further confirm the systematic place of the *Timaeus* in Plato's
philosophy of history and politics.[15]

[15] On the *Oresteia* see Murray, *Aeschylus;* on the relation to the *Timaeus* see Cornford,
Plato's Cosmology, 361ff.

6. *The* Critias

Timaeus has told the story of the cosmos and of man. Now Critias succeeds him in the role of the speaker and tells the story of Athenian prehistory.

The fragment of the *Critias* contains a brief description of ancient Athens and a longer one of Atlantis. It breaks off at the point where the god resolves on the necessity of war. Even so the interpretation is hampered more by wealth of meaning than by the fact that the story does not go beyond the exposition. For Plato has given full play to his imagination, and the work, if completed, would have been one of the most grandiose poems of antiquity.

In the *Critias*, with its story of a war between Athens and Atlantis, we are in the realm of history. The memory of the Persian War furnishes the background for an Athens that remains victorious against an overwhelmingly strong barbarian power and saves Hellas, with its superior civilization, from destruction. Geographically, however, the barbarian power has shifted from east to west. Perhaps Plato wanted to allude to the western danger from the Sicily that is represented in the dialogue by Hermocrates. But we must also consider that the war of the *Critias* takes place in the preceding aeon of the cosmos. Hence, the inversion of directions perhaps has something to do with the inversion of the cosmic movement in the cycles of the *Statesman*. At any rate, it seems more sensible to search for the place of Atlantis in the logic of the myth than in the western ocean.

The Athens-Atlantis aeon is not in every respect the Golden Age of Cronos which, in the *Statesman*, preceded the Age of Zeus, but it retains from it the tutelage of the gods over man. According to the story of Critias, the regions of the earth were distributed among the gods by Dike (109b). Athens had fallen to the lot of Athena and Hephaestus (109c), Atlantis to the lot of Poseidon (113c). When the regions had been distributed the gods created the order for their domains and the men in them. They did not rule their herds by violence, however, like shepherds who use the stick, but directed the souls of men, according to their plans, by Peitho (109c). The Peitho of the gods established the order of an Age that had advanced beyond the direction of the cosmos by the Demiurge, but not yet become the realm of autonomous man. The story of the *Critias* unfolds in a twilight realm between nature and full human history.

We must remain aware of this intermediate status of the aeon; for the story will lose its point if we forget that Atlantis, too, is an order of the gods, while Athens is no more than an order of the gods. On the one hand, the order of the idea is incarnate in prehistoric Athens by grace of the gods, not by virtue of man. The order of Atlantis, on the other hand, falls from grace because the admixture of mortal elements makes human weaknesses prevail over the virtue which stems from divine institution. Within the enchanted precinct of the mythical aeon, Athens incarnates the order of wisdom without the alloy which causes decline, while Atlantis incarnates the order of wealth and power fraught with the temptations of greed and *hubris*. We might say that Plato has split the problem of order and distributed the rôles. Being is Athens, Becoming is Atlantis. The *Critias* deals, indeed, with the problem of incarnation, but the idea is fully incarnate neither in Athens nor Atlantis. The drama of incarnation assumes the form of the war between the two poleis of Being and Becoming, and in this mythical struggle Being remains victorious over Becoming. The victory, however, is not final, for in the realm of history, decline and disembodiment is the fate of every incarnation. Hence, in the mythical tale, Athens and Atlantis do not exist happily ever after but are both destroyed by the catastrophes which mark the end of the aeon. By transposing the problem of order into the mythical aeon Plato, thus, could separate the elements of the concrete order into the Being of Athens and the Becoming of Atlantis; he could, furthermore, translate the drama of incarnation into the story of the war between the two poleis; and he could, finally, translate the decline into the symbol of the end of the aeon.

The myth of the prehistoric aeon of Athens and Atlantis has the same relation to the problem of political order in history as the myth of the precosmic struggle between Nous and Ananke to the problem of cosmic order. The parallel is suggestive; it encourages us to pursue the meaning of the myth one step further. The *Timaeus* marks an advance in Plato's thought beyond the *Republic* because the resistance to the idea is treated with a new seriousness. The blindness for the idea, the shapelessness of chaos, are not to be overcome by contempt; the victory of the idea cannot be secured by merely evoking the right order of the polis. The chaos has become co-eternal with the idea, and only through the *systasis* of Nous and Ananke can the cosmos gain form. Even an advancement beyond the *Statesman* is noticeable. In the trilogy of *Theaetetus-Sophist-Statesman*, the recalcitrant historical reality was treated as the force of evil, as the *thremma*, the beast. In spite of the attention to the problem of Persuasion, the atmosphere of the earlier trilogy was fraught with violence. The *Timaeus* shows a new respect for the other half of the elements which go into the making of a cosmos. Punishment is still provided for the bad souls; but, on the whole, invective ceases when Nous is faced by the a-noetic, primordial substratum. The same change of tone can be observed in the *Critias*. While Atlantis is the counter-polis to the Athenian polis of the idea, characterized as wealthy and powerful, as barbarian and perhaps as sinister, her order is willed by the god and is by no means contemptible.

Since the myth of the great struggle is strongly touched by the memory of the Persian Wars, it is quite possible that the new atmosphere of respect in the *Critias* reflects an Aeschylean influence as does the symbol of Peitho in the *Timaeus*. The *Persae* of Aeschylus is the unique instance of a war play which celebrates the victory of a people by dramatizing the tragedy of the defeated enemy. Less than a decade after Salamis and the destruction of the city, there could be written in Athens and performed the drama which describes the defeat of the Persians, without hatred or triumph, as the tragic fall of a great nation through pride and *hubris*. The defeat is caused, not by a superiority of Hellenes over barbarians, but by the fall of the Persians from their right order. The gods resolved on their defeat. The fate of the transgressor is the lesson held up to the Athenians. In the *Critias* it is Atlantis that experiences the Persian fall and defeat. "When the divine element in them began to diminish . . . they became unable to bear their prosperity and behaved unseemly. To those who had eyes to see, they appeared ugly for they were losing the most precious of their gifts. But to those who had no eyes to discern the life of true *eudaimonia*, they appeared most beautiful and happy at this time when they were full of unjust will to power [*pleonexia*]" (121b). Zeus, who rules according to law, perceived the miserable condition of a once excellent people and resolved on their defeat in order to chastise them and bring them back to moderation (121b).

The parallel again is so close that it can hardly be considered an accident. It seems permissible to assume for the *Critias,* as for the *Timaeus,* an Aeschylean influence in the new and deeper understanding of the fall from the right order. This influence does not express itself, however, in the mere repetition of an Aeschylean dramatic situation, for the war between Athens and Atlantis is not a transposition, into another historical time, of the conflict with Persia. Atlantis is the component of Becoming in historical order, so that the fall of Atlantis is the fall of Athens from true Being. The *hubris* of the Persians and their subsequent defeat could be held up to Athens, by Aeschylus, as a tragedy that might befall any people. In the *Critias* the fall from the right order has become the fate of Athens herself and the physical disaster (as symbolized by the presence of Hermocrates) has become imminent. In the rich symbolization of the *Critias* at least three motifs are intertwined: (1) the internal fall from the right order, (2) the external disaster which may be the consequence of the fall, and (3) the hope of regeneration. The internal decline and regeneration of a polity and the external rise and fall of historical powers are of the same substance and are interrelated in their meaning. Plato has come, through his myth, as close to a philosophy of world history as a Hellenic thinker within the firm horizon of the polis could come.

In the *Timaeus* and *Critias,* the world of Plato has increased in content over the *Republic.* To the realm of the idea has been added the co-eternal realm of Becoming. Plato has recognized that there is more than one principle on which a political order in history can be built. The order of the idea remains the highest, but other orders of no mean quality can be in conflict with it. Beyond Hellas in space lies the world of Persia; beyond Hellas in time lies the world of Crete; and beyond the realm of the idea lie realms of social organization which draw their inspiration from other sources. Considerable importance is attached, therefore, to the principles on which the rival orders of Athens and Atlantis are constructed in the *Critias.* In particular the order of Atlantis has its fascination because Plato here actually does what he is so frequently and erroneously suspected of doing in the *Republic*—he is constructing a "Utopia." The procedure is engrossing because, in this case, a political thinker of the first rank constructs a Utopia, not with the intention of evoking the image of an ideal state, but with the purpose of evoking a rival order to the good polis. Moreover, he does not solve the problem by simply heaping evils on the rival order. The Atlantis of Plato could, indeed, pass as a Utopia written with the intention of evoking an ideal, prosperous, happy community, under the rule of benevolent despots whose principal concern is the welfare of the people. The Atlantis is the unique instance of a Utopia written "in bad faith" by a master of political psychology. In his construction Plato uses the materials which a Utopian writer might have used "in good faith"; and he does it so skillfully that the account of Atlantis does not degenerate into a satire on dreamers of ideals. For the dream of Utopia, that is, the dream of achieving the perfect society through organizing men according to a blueprint instead of forming them in an educational process, is a serious affair; it is something like the black magic of politics. Most appropriately, therefore, the dream of Atlantis rises in luciferic splendor.

The description of Athens precedes that of Atlantis. The two accounts belong together and elucidate each other.

The region of Athens, as we have seen, fell to the lot of Athena and Hephaestus. Their natures of brother and sister are united by the common love of wisdom and the arts (*philosophia, philotechnia*); that is why they received a region which is naturally adapted to *arete* and *phronesis*. In this country they implanted children of the soil, of good nature, and created the order of the polis according to their insight (109c–d). On the institutions Plato is brief because, on the whole, they correspond to the polis of the idea as described in the *Republic* (110d). Topographically, Attica had not yet suffered the consequences of erosion through the great floods. The hill of the Acropolis was much larger than it is today; its plateau was sufficiently extended to serve as the residence of the guardians. The country was still fertile, rich in woods, sources, and rivers (110d–112d). The guardians of Athens were at the same time the freely accepted leaders (*hegemones*) of Hellas; and they ruled their polis, as well as the other Hellenes, everlastingly with the same justice (112d–e).

To the lot of Poseidon fell an island in the western ocean. It was peopled by men born from the earth. One of the families lived on a mountain that rose in a plain located at the middle of the length of the island and open toward the sea. Poseidon took pleasure in a daughter of the mortals and had by her ten sons. The oldest was named Atlas. He and his nine brothers were the ancestors of the ten kings of Atlantis. The god protected the mountain of his love by drawing around it circles of sea and land—three circles of sea, separated by two ring-formed islands. The descendants of the divine-mortal couple developed the site into the city of Atlantis. The island-mountain itself and the ring-formed islands were surrounded by huge walls. The outermost wall was covered with brass, the second with tin, the wall of the island-mountain with the red-flaming orichalcum. The stones for the wall and for the city were broken from the circular islands; their colors were white, red, and black; and the color pattern of the stones decorated the city. At the center stood the temple of Poseidon, covered with silver except for the pinnacles which were covered with gold—"a barbaric spectacle." The palace of the kings, on the main island, was the work of generations, each king trying to surpass his predecessor by the splendor of his embellishments. The circular islands were pierced by canals so that ships from the sea could pass through, and the canals in turn were spanned by magnificent bridges. The circular strips of sea between the islands were, thus, transformed into safe harbors, and the cavities from which the stones for the walls had been taken were transformed into subterranean docks, and so forth.

This should be enough of the details to show the scale and style of Plato's account. Let us be briefer on the other points. The island abounded in natural resources, mineral as well as vegetative and animal, and the people increased their wealth through extended trade. The systems of transportation, canals, of territorial organization, revenue, and the military are described in detail as following a rigid rational plan like the topography of the island. For governmental purposes the island was divided into ten provinces, ruled by the descendants of the first ten kings, the oldest always ruling the city itself and its surroundings. Within the provinces the kings were the supreme masters of their subjects; the relations between the kings were governed by the Commandments laid down by Poseidon himself and preserved in the sacred precinct on the island-mountain. Among these commandments or decrees were the rules that the kings should not make war against each other; that they should mutually come to each other's aid if the subjects in a city tried to expell the royal dynasty; that they should take counsel together on war and other matters; that they should always preserve the rule of the line of Atlas; and that none of the kings must be sentenced to death unless five of the ten kings supported the judgment.

Every five or six years, alternating the periods of odd and even years, the kings foregathered in a ceremonial meeting for the purpose of discussing their affairs, of investigating whether they had violated the Commandments, and of judging anybody who had committed an infraction. The ceremony consisted of three parts: a sacred bullfight, the sacrifice of the bull, and the session of judgment proper. First, bulls were released in the sacred precinct of Poseidon; the kings prayed that they might catch the acceptable victim for the sacrifice and then they started the chase with wooden spears and nets. When a bull was caught, he was sacrificed at the column on which the Commandments were inscribed, with a ritual which included the common drinking of the blood of the sacrificial animal. After dark had fallen the kings donned robes of a dark blue color, and, sitting on the embers of the sacrifice, with all lights extinguished, opened their judicial session. At daybreak the sentences were engraved on a golden tablet, and the tablet together with the robes were dedicated as a memorial of the session.

Allowing for a considerable freedom of imagination with regard to the details, the account shows that Plato has constructed his Atlantis rather strictly so that the image of a counterorder to the polis of the idea would emerge. The rulers of Athens are autochthones, of a nature which is pliable to the agathon; and the gods have formed them through *philosophia* and *philotechnia*. Their rule over the polis as well as their hegemony over Hellas is freely accepted by the subjects and federated poleis as the rule of virtue and wisdom. The rulers of Atlantis are of semidivine origin, so that their quality depends, not on the formation of their personality, but on the divine element in their substance; if the divine element is diluted, their quality will weaken. The order of their government does not spring from *arete* and *phronesis*, but from the decrees of the god, and the subjects do not accept the rule freely but bow to the pleasures of the order and to the force which maintains it. Plato makes it a point that the Atlantian kings are surrounded in their palaces by the most reliable of their troops; and among the decrees of the god we noted the obligation of mutual aid against rebellion. The natures of the regions are similarly distinguished. Athens is "naturally appropriate" to a rule of *arete* and *phronesis*, while the rational topography of Atlantis with its circular seas and islands is created by Poseidon. In the description of the city, the system of communication, and the financial and military organization of the country, Plato has indulged in an orgy of rational planning. This section may have been inspired by the work of Hippodamus of Miletus, the city planner and architect of the Piraeus with its long walls, and also the author of a model constitution—an ancient precursor of our modern engineers who display a devastating readiness to transfer their proven ability to organize concrete and iron, to the organization of mankind. This rational planning of Atlantis, which expresses "barbarian" expansive power and wealth, contrasts with the modest arrangements of Athens, which express the order of a stable society, with its arm-bearing population kept at a maximum of twenty thousand and with propertyless rulers who conduct their lives on a subsistence level. The Atlantian rationality and planning, thus, is characterized as the expression of phenomenal power, the Athenian arrangement as the expression of substantive order.

The periodic meetings of the kings, with their ritual of bullfight, sacrifice, and nocturnal judgment, finally, deserves more attention than the usual antiquarian remarks about the probable origin of details in the surviving memory of Cretan ceremonies. In the context of the trilogy *Republic–Timaeus–Critias* these rites with their chthonic associations are the counterpart to the ascent to the Agathon. The polis of the idea is ordered by the wise rulers; and the rulers are wise because their Eros has led their souls to the vision of the Agathon. The community of the erotic souls is the nucleus of the well-ordered polis. The rulers of Atlantis also participate in a divine principle; but their participation does not take the form of a transformation of the soul by the Idea. The rulers are not human, but semidivine in their origin, and they preserve their divine substance through the periodic ritual communion with their origin, that is, through the sacrifice of the bull-god and through partaking of his blood. The chthonic symbolism of the night and the dark blue robes emphasizes the ritual as a communion with a divinity of the nether regions—in contrast with the Agathon, the sun of the intelligible upper realm. Moreover, the subjects who are ordinary humans cannot participate in the communion. Hence the virtues of temperance and justice cannot furnish a bond between rulers and people. The rule of the dynasty has to be maintained by body-guards and the mutual support which the kings give to each other. The order of Atlantis has its origin in divine lust, the order of Athens in divine wisdom. In this opposition of the lower to the higher mysteries we probably touch the core of the symbol of Atlantis.

The lust of existence is as ultimately divine as its overcoming through the ascent to the intelligible realm. Yet the lust of the god cannot create more than the appearance of form. His order is vitiated from the beginning by its compromise with mortality and in the end it will return to formless flux. We have seen the fall from order through the gradual admixture of mortal elements. The *Critias* concludes with the intervention of Zeus.

The god of gods perceived the impending disaster and wanted to restore moderation through chastisement. "For this purpose he assembled all the gods in their most noble habitation, which is situated at the center of the cosmos and overlooks from on high all that participates in Becoming, and having them assembled he said. . . ." At this point the *Critias* breaks off. We have noted previously, however, that assembly and address of the *Critias* correspond to the assembly of the gods and the address of the Demiurge in the *Timaeus* (41a–d). When the Demiurge has completed his work to the point where man and the lower natures remain to be created, he assembles the gods and tells them that mortal creatures of three kinds have not yet been brought into being. Without them the cosmos would be imperfect. "But if I myself give them birth and life they would be equal to gods." He will, therefore, create only the immortal part of man while the gods who themselves are created will have to weave the immortal element into the mortal ones and to create of this fabric man and the lower creatures. "Bring them into existence, feed them and cause them to grow; and when they perish, receive them back again." The souls created in this manner would each be put on a star as in a chariot, shown the nature of the cosmos, and taught the laws of Heimarmene. Then each soul would be incarnated in a body, with the freedom of conducting its life in such a manner that after death it would either return to its star and to eternal happiness or sink down to lower incarnations (41e–42d). The address of the *Timaeus* and the subsequent arrangements thus account for the birth of the human soul and for its freedom to fall or to rise. The corresponding episode in the *Critias* would signify, so it appears from the context, the rebirth of man when society as a whole has fallen from grace. Moreover, this rebirth of fallen man through the intervention of Zeus parallels, on the level of the myth of prehistory, the closing pages of the *Statesman* with their account of the rebirth of man in society through the intervention of the Royal Ruler. In spite of its fragmentary form, the meaning of the *Critias* thus is clear as the myth of decline and rebirth of the idea in history, and more specifically as the rebirth of the idea in the form of an Hellenic empire.

CHAPTER 6

The Laws

When Plato died in 347 he left his last work, the *Laws,* in an unfinished state. Though in a formal sense it is complete to the last word, it contains a number of stylistic defects and minor inconsistencies which betray that it has not undergone a final revision. While this state of things is unsatisfactory, as we do not know to what extent eliminations of details and prolixities would have changed the general complexion of the work, it is not necessary to exaggerate the problem. It is hardly justifiable to speak of the state in which the work is preserved as that of a "first draft," as has been done on occasion. If we mention the problem at all, the reason is that criticisms concerning the style of the *Laws* have entered the larger pattern of charges against this last work of Plato. As in the case of the *Statesman,* a block of misconceptions has become solidly standardized; and while some dents have been made in it in recent years, it still obstructs an adequate interpretation. It will have to be our first task, therefore, to remove these obstacles to a critical analysis of the *Laws.*

1. *Misconceptions about the* Laws

The first of the charges is levelled against the style of the work. We hear that the *Laws* is garrulous and rambling, that it is poorly organized, that the rigidity of old age makes itself felt in the treatment of the problems; and we hear signs of regret that Plato did no longer possess the powers of construction that went into the *Republic.* To criticisms of this type we can only answer that, setting aside the minor defects due to a lack of final revision, the accusations are entirely unjustified. The *Laws* is a work of old age indeed, but not in the sense that it betrays a weakness or decline. The work rather glows with a ripeness of style that is peculiar to some of the greatest minds when their vitality remains unbroken into the later years. The subject matter is now entirely at the disposition of the master; the process of creation seems effortless;

and the conspiracy of content and expression is so subtle that the creator almost disappears behind a creation that resembles a necessary growth.

While the charges are unjustified, they nevertheless have an intelligible cause in that the critics have not understood the formal organization of the *Laws*. This problem of form may be characterized, in a preliminary fashion, as the shift from an external organization of the material, through divisions and subdivisions, to an internal organization through the recurrence of dominant motifs in a flow of associations. The *Laws* has only one major, external incision—the one that separates the first three books from the subsequent nine. And this incision serves precisely the purpose of articulation through dominant motifs in as much as the first three books marshal the motifs, while Books IV–XII apply them to the exposition of the *nomoi* of the polis. Within the nine books the subject matter itself is distributed in a roughly systematic sequence from the choice of site and population for the polis, through social institutions, magistracies, education, and festivals, to civil and criminal law—but this systematic order is subordinated to the order of the dominant motifs. The high points of this internal organization are to be found in Books VII (Education) and X (Religion) with the recurrence of the principal motif of Book I, that is, with the symbol of the God who plays the game of order and history with man as his puppet. Hence, the reading of the *Laws* becomes a fascinating experience if one understands its organization. In associating chains of thought, dependent from the dominant symbols, Plato has poured out his mature wisdom on the problems of man in political society. This *Summa* of Greek life embraces in its amplitude the consequences of the Trojan war and the Doric invasion, it analyzes the failure of the Doric military kingship and the horrors of Athenian theatrocracy, it reflects on the effects of harem education on Persian kings and on the preservation of art styles in Egypt, on the consequences of enlightenment and the inquisitorial enforcement of a creed, on the ethos of musical scales as well as on the undesirability of fishing as a sport. To some critics this associative outpouring may seem rambling; to us it seems that there is not a dead line in the work; every fact and argument adduced serves its purpose in adding to the grand view of human life in its ramifications from birth to death.

Two other misconceptions deserve no more than bare mention. The *Laws* develops fully the religious position of Plato; the polis whose foundation and organization is described may be characterized as a theocratic state. In the liberal era a work of this kind could only arouse grave misgivings among scholars for whom the separation of church and state was a fundamental dogma, and for whom a theory of politics had to be defined in terms of the secular state. The liberal prejudice remains evident even in recent interpretations of the *Laws*. Plato is at best a "reactionary," and becomes at worst a "totalitarian," because of the provisions for the enforcement of a creed and punishment for utterances of an antireligious nature. Others again find extenuating circumstances in the old age of Plato: When a man becomes old, as we know, he becomes religious; the veil of charity should be drawn over the weakness of an otherwise great mind. That one cannot approach the problems of Plato from a dogmatic position of this kind is obvious; further discussion is unnecessary.

The second of these elementary misconceptions crystallizes in the formula that the *Laws* is a treatise on "jurisprudence." The assumption is not entirely wrong. The *Laws,* indeed, contains sections which have to be classified as jurisprudence in the modern meaning of the word; and one may even say that Plato's contributions to the advancement of criminal law and the improvement of judicial procedure have not yet received all the attention which they deserve. The assumption, however, becomes erroneous when the formula is meant to convey the idea that the whole of the *Laws* is a treatise on these subjects. The error is in part induced by the translation of the title *Nomoi* as *Laws* with the implication that the laws of Plato mean laws in the sense in which the word is used in modern legal theory. Plato's *nomos*, however, is deeply imbedded in the myth of nature and has an amplitude of meaning which embraces the cosmic order, festival rites and musical forms. The assumption that the *Laws* is a treatise on "jurisprudence" ignores this range of meaning, and inevitably destroys the essence of Plato's thought. The evasion of this essence (and that is the other source of the error) is again caused by the secularist inclinations of modern historians and their unwillingness to follow Plato in a theory of politics which bases the order of the community on harmony with the divine Measure.

A third group of misconceptions touches a more complex problem. It concerns Plato's designation of the *Laws* as the second-best plan for a polis. We hear that Plato had developed in the *Republic* his plan for the ideal state, that his project was utterly unrealistic, that he himself

became convinced of its Utopian character and finally, that, in the
Laws he developed an ideal which took into account at least some of
the exigencies of human nature. Moreover, the *Laws* is distinguished
from the *Republic* by its recognition of historical traditions and customs as well as of the necessity of legal institutions. While the *Republic*
still envisaged something like a dictatorial government without laws,
the *Laws* embodies the more mature conception of a constitutional
government under the laws. The appraisals frequently have overtones
of rejoicing (which occurred also in the appraisals of the *Statesman*)
that Plato at last had to surrender his idealistic demands and come
down to the level on which his more solid and experienced compeers
in political science are moving all the time.

In order to dissolve this network of misconceptions we shall start
with the point, previously discussed, that the good polis is not an ideal
state; and even more, that the word "ideal" has no meaning in a
Platonic context. The Idea is Plato's reality, and this reality can be
more or less well embodied in the historically existing polis. Once this
point is understood, the problem of the "compromise with reality" has
to be reformulated. A compromise certainly is implied in the plan
of a second-best project, but it is a compromise concerning the degree
of intensity and purity with which the idea can be embodied in an
obstreperous material. The idea remains the reality as before, and the
good polis of the *Republic* remains the "first best," but the human raw
material—which in itself is no reality at all—may to a greater or lesser
degree prove fit to become the vessel of reality. If it is supremely fit,
then the reality of the idea may become embodied in it to the degree
which Plato had envisaged in the *Republic;* if it proves less fit, at least
the embodiment to the degree of the *Laws* may be possible; if it should
be even worse, Plato envisages third and fourth degrees of embodiment.
We shall discuss this question in more detail presently. First, however,
we have to clarify another aspect of this misconception.

The plan of a second-best polis seems to imply a transition from
the "ideal" of dictatorship by the philosopher-king to the "ideal" of
a government by law with constitutional consent of the people. In
this instance we have to unravel a whole series of misunderstandings.
First of all, the laws to which the people are supposed to give their
consent are not just any laws which please the people, nor are they
made by the people. They are still the laws of the philosopher-king, the

laws which Plato has given for the polis. Any other laws, which might perhaps be more to the liking of the people, would not characterize the second-best polis, or even the third or fourth; they would characterize no polis at all that could be considered an embodiment of the reality of the idea. "Constitutional government," without regard to the spirit of the laws, is no reality for Plato, but the corruption of reality.

Moreover, the conception of a transition from the dictatorial rule of a philosopher-king to a government by law with the consent of the "people" disregards the actual content of both the *Republic* and the *Laws*. The *Laws* is not a compromise with the "people," formerly submitted to a dictatorial rule, and now to a rule of law. Plato's sorrow is less that he can find no people that would submit, but, rather, that he can find no philosopher-kings who could rule. If we compare the social stratification of the *Laws* with that of the *Republic*, we observe a scaling down of the quality of the strata with regard to their ability to embody the idea. In the later work the communal organization of the guardians of the *Republic* has disappeared; the highest social stratum consists now of a citizenry of petty landholders. Correspondingly the economic class of peasants and artisans of the *Republic* has disappeared in the *Laws*; it is replaced by slaves and alien residents. Diagrammatically we gain the following picture:

	Republic		*Laws*
(1)	Guardians	(1)	——
(2)	Economic Class	(2)	Free Citizenry
(3)	——	(3)	Slaves and Alien Residents

In the *Republic* Plato has abolished slavery; in the *Laws* he has reintroduced it. This change on the institutional level best characterizes Plato's lowering of the standards of embodiment. He now admits a stratum in society which he considered unfit even for the elementary formation and education that was to be the privilege of the ordinary free citizens of the *Republic;* and correspondingly he has lost the hope of finding men who could be the guardians, in sufficient numbers to form the ruling society of a polis.

Finally, we have to consider the assumption that Plato's thought has evolved from the "dictatorial" idea of the *Republic* to a "government by law" in the later work. As a matter of biographical record it is highly doubtful that any such evolution took place at all. The assumption of an evolution of Plato's thought with regard to this particular point seems to have no other basis than the further gratuitous assumpion that between two ideas must lie an evolution in time if the dates of their publication are a good number of years apart. In the case of Plato we possess biographical indications that the time at which an idea is expressed in an exoteric work does not of necessity correspond to the time of its conception. We are informed, for instance, through the *Seventh Letter,* that the idea of the philosopher-king has to be dated at a time which precedes the completion of the *Republic* by perhaps more than twenty years. In the same manner, we learn from the *Seventh Letter* that the idea of the philosopher-king must have been interwoven with the idea of the "rule of law" at least as early as the time of Dion's appeal to Plato to come to Syracuse; and quite probably the interweaving of the two ideas did not take place on this particular occasion, in 367, but was preceded by a period of gestation the length of which we cannot surmise. In the *Seventh Letter,* at any rate, Dion is designated as the man who could have united in his person "philosophy and power" (335d); and the rule of the philosopher-king is characterized as the establishment of an order in which man attains happiness through the conduct of his life in the light of justice "whether he possesses this justice himself or whether the guidance of holy men has nurtured and formed his habits to the way of righteousness" (335d). And how can the philosopher-king establish this order? By using "all means to bring the citizens under the discipline of the best and appropriate laws" (336a). These laws will not consist merely of a code containing legal rules and sanctions. The legal provisions themselves will be preceded by discourses, the prooemia, which set forth at length theological and ethical foundations of the rule. The laws will become, by means of the prooemia, the instrument of education for the citizenry. The idea of the prooemia, of the literary form of the *Laws* in which Plato expresses his thought in long systematic digressions, thus, had already been conceived at the time of his occupation with the Sicilian problems. In the *Third Letter,* addressed to Dionysius and to be dated *c.* 356, Plato reminds the tyrant specifically of their preparatory work on the prooemia for the laws of Syracuse in 367 (316a). And, as we suggested earlier, it is hardly probable that Plato should not have conceived the idea before this date.

From the beginning, therefore, the idea of the philosopher-king must have been considerably more elastic than it would appear from the *Republic* alone. While in the *Republic* the guardians are assumed to be numerous enough to form a ruling class which can furnish an army, there seems to have been also present in the mind of Plato the rather obvious possibility that their number might be somewhat less adequate. Hence we can define the variants for the embodiment of the idea (best, second best, and so forth) as determined by the number of persons who can be truly called a *nomos empsychos*. If they are numerous enough, a whole ruling class of a polis can be a *nomos empsychos*, as is the plan of the *Republic*. If the numbers are small, the citizenry of a polis can embody the idea only in the secondary form of habits inculcated by education and permanently supported by legal institutions which actually comprise a treatise on the life of a polis in partnership with God. The philosopher-king enters the structure of this secondary embodiment of the idea only as the *nomothetes*, the lawgiver, and as the author of the prooemia. That would have been Plato's rôle in the attempted reform of the Sicilian constitution, and that is his rôle in the *Laws* where, at a further remove, under the guise of the Athenian Stranger, he instructs the lawgivers for the polis of Magnesia on the principles on which they ought to build their constitution, while the future citizens of the colony have to do nothing but consent.

In the light of this highly flexible conception of the philosopher-king and of his functions in the polis we have, finally, to raise the question whether the transition from the *Republic* to the *Laws* can at all be characterized as the transition from a dictatorial rule to a rule of law. On various occasions we have already pointed out that the polis of the *Republic* is not a polis "without laws," as is so frequently asserted. As a matter of fact, it contains the constitutional law as well as a good deal of the civil law of the polis. The notion that, from the earlier to the later work, Plato's thought has "evolved," or "matured," towards a recognition of constitutional government and the rule of law must be dropped. The difference between the two models has to be sought on the existential level. The *Republic* is written under the assumption that the ruling stratum of the polis will consist of persons in whose souls the order of the idea can become reality so fully that they, by their very existence, will be the permanent source of order in the polis; the *Laws* is written under the assumption that the free citizenry will consist of persons who can be habituated to the life of Arete under proper guidance, but who are unable to develop the source of order existentially in themselves and, therefore, need the constant persuasion of the prooemia as well as the sanctions of the law, in order to keep them on the narrow path. In conclusion we may say that the *Republic* and the *Laws*, while they both provide legal institutions for a political society, provide them for two different types of men; the differentiation of rank as the "best" and the "second best" is determined by the quality of the men whom Plato envisages as the vessel of the Idea.

We have concluded our analysis of misconceptions, and in particular the misconceptions with regard to the nature of the "second-best" polis. Nevertheless we should not close this section without consulting an authority who usually is forgotten in the mêlée of conflicting opinions, that is, Plato himself. In the *Laws*, Plato has written a page (739b–740a) on the meaning of the terms "best" and "second-best" polis. The best "polis and constitution and set of laws" exist when the polity is pervaded by the principle that among friends (*philos*) all things are in common. This means that "women, children, and all possessions" should be held in common; that things which are by nature private, such as "eyes, ears, and hands" should seem to see, hear, and act in common; that all should approve and condemn in common and should experience joy and sorrow on the same occasions. If the *nomoi* of a polity unite it to the utmost in this sense, then we have the polis which is "truer, better, and more exalted in *arete*" than any polis which is constructed on a different principle. If such a polis should ever exist "where gods, or sons of gods live, many or one," the citizens will have achieved the truly happy life. For a "model of a constitution" we should look nowhere else, but cling to this one and strive to come as near to it as possible in our construction of a constitution. The constitution which the interlocutors of the *Laws* are discussing will be, if it ever will be established, the closest approach to the model; hence it will be "nearest to immortality [*athanasia*]" and for this reason it must be called the second best.

Immediately following these explanations Plato begins to elaborate the property division of the second-best polis (740). Land and houses should be divided among the citizens; they should not till the land in common—for that would go beyond their assumed "origin, breeding, and education." Nevertheless, when the distribution is made, the owners should be made conscious that their individual lots are portions of the common substance of the polis, and so forth.

These passages should suffice for the elucidation of the problem. The order of the best polis presupposes that it is given for a community of *philoi*, that is, of persons who are bound together by the existential bond of *philia*. Only under this condition can the true *koinon* be realized, that is, the *koinon* not of women, children, and possessions only, but a *koinon* of ethos and pathos. The men, however, who are capable of being true *philoi* are rare; so rare, indeed, that Plato speaks of them as "gods, or sons of gods." Only when, by some miracle, such semidivine beings should live in a polis could its life be ordered by the *nomoi* (739d) which the *Republic* has evoked. Ordinarily we have to assume a human raw material of a somewhat less perfect nature (*genesis*). In ordering the social life of such more common human beings we must be satisfied with the *nomoi* that are classified as second best. The second-best order, however, is closely related to the first best in so far as the idea of existential community which is expressed in the *nomoi* of the first order should also be expressed in the *nomoi* of the second one. The difference will be one of intenseness only; the second order will embody as much of the substance of the first as the weaker human vessel can bear.

2. *The Platonic Theocracy*

The evolution of Plato's conception of order toward the position of the *Laws* must be understood in the context of Hellenic politics. The poleis had never found their way toward unification on a national, territorial scale, even though the threat of the Persian great power was clear to everybody. The need for a more comprehensive organization must have been so obvious at the time, that Plato's vision of an Hellenic empire had nothing extraordinary on principle. It was so close indeed to the trend of pragmatic politics that it barely anticipated the solution which the problem found, in the generation after his death, in the imperial foundations of Alexander and the Diadochi. And his evocation of the philosopher-king is, under one of its aspects, no more than the expression of the search for an Hellenic figure that would correspond to the savior-kings and pharaohs of the Near Eastern empires. The vision is so unextraordinary that it is even difficult to imagine how a political thinker in this situation could demand less than Plato does. For what he envisaged was in fact no more than a federation of Hellenic poleis under the leadership of an hegemonic polis; what was realized institutionally in the various hegemonic leagues, like the Spartan or Athenian, he wanted to extend to the whole of the polis world. The Platonic problem is not the end but the means. For the failure of the leagues, and the cause of the failure in the insuperable parochialism (some call it love of freedom) of the gentilitian poleis, was all too clear. A plain demand for an all-embracing Hellenic federation might as well be left unspoken in view of the situation. A solution had to come through force, or through the spirit, or through both.

The solution through force alone, setting aside the doubts about its desirability, was hardly practical. If Athens and Sparta were not strong enough to impose a federation, no other polis was in a position to undertake the task. On the level of power politics the problem resembled that of German kingship in the high Middle Ages: none of the old duchies was strong enough to impose effective order on the others; the attempt could be made only from a new and larger territory (such as Upper Italy, Sicily, Bohemia, Austria, Brandenburg) as the basis of operations. In the Hellenic case, the unification was undertaken from Macedonia and ultimately from Rome. Observing the political events of his time, Plato must have considered the Macedonian solution as a possibility, but in his work, if we except the doubtful *Fifth Letter* to Perdiccas III, the idea of a unification by force alone is never touched. Plato preferred a combination of force and spiritual reform.

In the *Seventh Letter* he fairly clearly set forth his ideas concerning the strategy of unification. The process should begin in Syracuse with the conquest of the city by the party of Dion. The victory should be followed by the imposition of a constitution, guided by the principle of *isonomia*. In the context of the *Seventh* and the *Eighth Letter isonomia* means an "equitable" constitution that would establish something like a condominium of the former parties in the civil war. The content of the new legislation should be determined by a constitutional assembly drawn from other Hellenic cities in which members of the Academy would play a decisive role. The blessings of this constitution Plato expected to be so great that a federation of the Sicilian poleis would soon follow the establishment of order in Syracuse. And the success of the federation, finally, would exert an appeal of such strength that a pan-Hellenic federation might be formed.

This peculiar combination of power politics with spirtual reform causes the difficulties which unsettle Plato's earlier position and urge him on toward the position of the *Laws*.

The formulation of the difficulties will be best prepared by stressing the ineluctability of the position. The alternative of imposing a cosmological order of the Near Eastern type on Hellas could not be envisaged by Plato. In the first place, the idea was impractical. When Alexander displayed tendencies in this direction, his Macedonians simply did not follow suit. And even after the unification had become a fact on the level of power politics, the moderately successful Orientalization of Mediterranean rulership, the so-called pseudomorphosis, was accomplished only when the Roman Empire was already deep in the shadow of the threat by the Great Migration. And second, a debouchment into the Near Eastern imperial order could not be Plato's intention, because his myth of the soul, while it was bound by the myth of the cosmos, had absorbed the differentiation of the autonomous psyche which had occurred in the world of the polis since the sixth century. For Plato there was no way back to the collective salvation of a people through a mediator-king, halfway between God and mankind. The problem of regeneration had become personal. The other alternative, the course followed by Machiavelli in a comparable situation, could not be considered by Plato either. The Italian thinker was also faced by the problem of unifying a world of city-states on the higher national level so that it could hold its own against the national states of France and Spain; and he also knew that a true order was impossible without a spiritual reform. Since he found the spiritual resources neither in himself nor in anybody else, he confined himself to the evocation of the Prince who would achieve unification through tactical means in power politics. This component of the Prince, to be sure, is present in Plato, but it never becomes dominant. For the tyrannical alternative would have meant, as it did for Machiavelli, the renunciation of the spirit and the fall into demonism.

This last observation will allow us to distinguish more clearly the various aspects of the Platonic difficulties. Power and spirit can indeed not be separated. The violent, tyrannical solution, which at first sight might appear as a solution by power alone, involves in fact the corruption of the spirit, for the soul of the tyrant would have to close itself demonically against the law of the spirit that doing evil is worse than suffering evil. A Plato will be tempted, but he will not fall. The radical alternative would be the withdrawal from the sphere of power, if not into solitude, at least into the restricted community of those who are responsive to the appeal of the spirit. This tendency, which is also present in Plato along with the temptation of tyranny, has expressed itself in the foundation of the Academy. But then, again, the Academy is conceived as the institutional instrument by which the spirit can wedge its way back into the political arena and influence the course of history. The ambiguousness of the position becomes manifest, especially in the *Statesman,* in the admixture of a heavy dose of violence to the Persuasion of the royal ruler. Plato is not a Christian saint. To be sure, he wants to persuade, but he also wants to embody the Idea in the community of a polis. And in order to give the visible form of institutions to the invisible flow of the spirit, in order to enlarge the erotic community of the true *philoi* into an organized society in politics, he is willing to temper persuasion with a certain amount of compulsion on the less responsive and to cast out the obstreperous by force. He could not know that he struggled with a problem that had to be solved through the Church. The theocracy, therefore, remained the limit of his conception of order.

Within the boundaries drawn by the myth of the cosmos, the position of Plato evolves from the *Republic* to the *Laws* in a manner that can be best elucidated by comparison with the evolution from the Sermon on the Mount to the function of the institutionalized Church. The counsels of the Sermon originate in the spirit of eschatological heroism. If they were followed by the Christian layman to the letter among men as they are, they would be suicidal. The Sermon is addressed to the disciples of the Son of God, to his *mathetai,* much as the *Republic* appeals to the disciples of the son of god Plato. While the counsels of the Sermon cannot become rules of social conduct in the world as it is, they are nevertheless the substance of Christian doctrine. If they and their guidance were removed from Christianity, the power center that makes it an effective historical reality would be destroyed. Since the Sermon is unbearable in its purity, the Church infuses as much of its substance as men are capable of absorbing while living in the world; the mediation of the stark reality of Jesus to the level of human expediency, with a minimum loss of substance, is one of the functions of the Church. Likewise, in the *Republic* Plato speaks with divine authority when he calls up his disciples for the radical conversion, the *periagoge,* a call which presupposes that man is capable of following it. This conviction that the appeal can find response is waning in his later years. An evolution takes place which parallels in Christianity the transition from Jesus to St. Paul; in the *Laws*

Plato has arrived at the Pauline, ecclesiastic compromise with the frailty
of man. In the heroic appeal of the *Republic* Plato himself appeared as the
leader of his people; his own divine reality was to guide them toward
their regeneration. Now Plato has proved too great. The people cannot
stand the naked reality; their existential potency is so low that they
can look at it only through the veil of his prooemia. In the *Laws* Plato
appears as the ecclesiastic statesman. He has withdrawn the direct existential appeal; his own person is blotted out; an "Athenian Stranger,"
a man "who has knowledge of these things," develops a plan and the
motivations for theocratic institutions that will be bearable to men as
they are. All that is left of the *Republic* is its spirit; the divine sermon
recedes into the place of the heroic counsel; and of the spirit there will
live in the institutions no more than is possible.

Plato's position evolves from heroic appeal to ecclesiastic statesmanship, as we have said, within the boundaries drawn by the myth of the
cosmos. The Idea waxes and wanes in the rhythms of incarnation and
disembodiment; and the form of the polis is the reality of embodiment.
The theocracy is the limit of Plato's conception of order, because he
does not advance to the distinction of spiritual and temporal order.
Plato's experience of the life of the spirit as an attunement of the soul
with the divine Measure is essentially universal; and in the *Laws* we
sense the idea of a universal community of mankind in the spirit lying
just beyond the horizon; but the last step is never taken—and was not
to be taken by man without revelation. For Plato the spirit must manifest itself in the visible, finite form of an organized society; and from
this tension between the universality of the spirit and the finiteness of
its embodiment follow, as the characteristics of Plato's politics, the supplementary use of violence as well as the Puritanic touch of a community
of the elect. The tendency is toward ecclesiastic universalism; the result
remains theocratic sectarianism.

We have reached the limits of the Platonic conception of order—but
the limits of the symbolism are not the limits of Plato. As previously
suggested, the *Laws* is not a political *livre de circonstance*. The genesis
of the *Laws*, it is true, is intimately connected with Plato's participation
in Sicilian affairs. If we compare the *Letters* on this subject with the
content of the *Laws*, there can be no doubt with regard to the parallelism
of institutional projects. It would be rash, however, to conclude that the
work is no more than a code of laws that could serve as the model con-

stitution of a polis. For the *Laws* is a work of art; and specifically it is
a religious poem. If the work were no more than a code, our interest in
it would not extend beyond the limited pragmatic value of the legal
provisions; as the poem, in which the Platonic art of letting the form
interpenetrate with the content has reached a new height, it has its supreme importance as a manifestation of the spirit. As the religious artist
Plato has reached the universal level which as a theocrat he did not reach.
As the lawgiver for the Hellenes he has narrowed the spirit to its finite
embodiment in a political organization of the elect (leaving to one side
that he failed in practice); as the creator of the poem he has entered,
if not the Church, the universal community of the Spirit in which his
guidance is as authoritative today as it ever was in the past.

3. *The Dominant Symbols*

The organization of the *Laws* does not depend on the external division and subdivision of its subject matter. The interrelation of form and
content as an associative stream, articulated by dominant motifs results in a network of subtle relations that would require a treatise for its
exhaustive analysis. I shall attempt no more than to trace the main
lines which run through the work; the infinite richness of detail must
of necessity remain ignored.

The dialogue opens on a scene in Crete. Three elderly gentlemen
set out in the morning for the long walk from Cnossus into the hills
to the temple and cave of Zeus. They are an Athenian Stranger, the
Cretan Cleinias, and the Lacedaemonian Megillus. The way is long and
they resolve to while the time away, most suitably, with a discussion of
the Cretan constitution and laws, of which the author is the god to whom
they are ascending. At this point the form of the dialogue begins to
emerge from the scene. The ascent will be long but leisurely. The goal
is certain, it is the god; and this end is linked to the beginning, for the
first word of the dialogue is *theos*. Between the beginning and the end
in God rises the path, ardous and sun-scorched, but interspersed with
groves of cypresses of a rare height and beauty and with meadows where
the wanderers may rest in conversation. God is the motif that dominates
all others; and the dialogue, while winding its path through the world
that is embraced by God, will not lose its direction in spite of the long
digressive rests in the groves.

The day is hot—and not by accident. We are near the longest day

of the year, the day of the solstice (683). The theme of the beginning
and the end is continued with this introduction of the sun as a motif.
The beginning and the end may be the distant points between which a
course extends; and they may be the point of coincidence at which one
epoch ends and a new one begins. The solstice is the symbol of the turning point in the rhythm of the cycles. The choice of the symbol is not
arbitrary; the sun symbolism of the *Laws* continues that of the *Republic*.
In the earlier dialogue the Idea was the sun of the intelligible realm;
now we are in the visible realm of institutions which embody the Idea;
of this realm the visible sun is the ruler. Its revolutions determine the
sacred rhythm of the polis; the solstice marks the end of a year; on the
day following the solstice the calendar of the sacred festivals begins
anew; and on this day the highest judicial magistrate is chosen for the
polis (767). The symbolism, however, is carried further into the structure
of the dialogue itself. The three wanderers are old men. They have set
themselves the task of creating the laws for a new colony; but their
work would be incomplete and futile if it provided only for the structure of a polis and did not provide for the education of men who can
keep the laws intact and renew them. The spirit must be transmitted
from the old men "whose day is setting" to the younger men who will
have to continue their work (770a). The *Laws* is an ending at which the
wisdom of age is transmitted to the future generations. The principal
instruments for this transmission are the great prooemia, the main body
of the *Laws* itself. And indeed, "a divine *afflatus*" seems to have guided
the wanderers and their conversation on this longest day (811c). The
discourse had begun "at dawn," and now, in the middle of the way
(the passage is to be found actually at approximately the physical center
of the *Laws*), the Athenian Stranger becomes aware that, under the
divine guidance, "this compact discourse of his composition" has become
"rather like a poem," that he has created a form of spiritual poetry that
most suitably will furnish the model for the sacred art of the new
polis, the art in which the spirit will be kept alive (811). The distention
of the way between the beginning and the end in God thus becomes
focussed in the center of a divinely inspired poem, created at the solstice
when Plato's life declines, marking an end and a beginning in the spirit's
process.

The three wanderers themselves are symbolic figures.[1] The Cretan

---

[1] One aspect of this symbolism has been discussed in an earlier context. Cf. *Order and History* II, Ch. 1, 2, 4.

institutions were reputed to be the oldest in Hellas, and the constitution of Lacedaemon was closely related to them. In the three persons of the Cretan, the Lacedaemonian, and the Athenian there is reflected the course of Hellenic history. Crete is the omphalos at which the Hellenic world is bound to its Aegean prehistory; the return to Crete is the return to the youth of Hellas. Now, at the end of Hellenic history, we return to its beginning. The symbolism of a return to the youth of the cycle that we have encountered in the *Statesman* and the *Timaeus* is resumed and focussed, as in the instance of the solstice, in a symbolic presence through the simultaneity of the three wanderers who mark the end and the beginning.

The distention of the discourse is bound up in the integral form of the poem; the revolution of the sun is focussed in the solstice; and the extension of Hellenic history is brought, through the three wanderers, into the presence of a conversation. This contraction of extended time into a symbol of timelessness is not a mere artistic device; it is Plato's new technique of symbolization. A movement of the soul that formerly had been expressed in myths of cosmic cycles and in the "time of the tale" has now come to its rest in the art of the timeless poem. The suspension of time in the eternal presence of the work of art has become a conscious principle in Plato's last creation. We can observe this process of suspension best in the great symbol of the god who plays with men as with his puppets, for in this symbol Hesiod's myth of the Metal Ages, the myth which stands at the beginning of Hellenic speculation on the cycle in politics and history, comes to its end.

In the Hesiodian form of the myth the ages follow each other down to the present and last age of the world, the iron age that is pregnant with the expectation of a catastrophic end and a new beginning. In Plato's work the myth undergoes a contraction of its time dimension through a series of steps from the *Republic* to the *Laws*. In the *Republic* the myth symbolizes the simultaneity of social stratification in the good polis. The three classes are bound together in their order by the myth that a god has mixed gold in the souls of the rulers, silver in the souls of the warriors, and brass and iron in the souls of the lower class. The principle of contraction is already at work. The golden age of the past is drawn into the present of the polis through the evocation of the philosopher-king; and the inferiority of the lower element is restrained by its subordination to the rule of the higher. In the logic of a myth of the soul, however, the contraction is not yet perfect. While the hierarchy of virtues that was projected by Hesiod into the sequence of ages is drawn back to its origin in the psyche, the virtues are still distributed over the individuals and classes of the good polis. The elements, which in principle are the elements of every psyche, are arranged as an externalized pattern so that only the polis as a whole represents the tensions of the soul. While the time sequence is contracted into the simultaneousness of a social structure, this structure itself is still an externalizing projection. In the *Statesman*, then, the metals are used to symbolize the royal art proper (gold) and the supporting arts of the true polis (other precious metals). But it is doubtful whether this further transformation is a serious advance beyond the *Republic*. A hint of the impending contraction is to be found only in the subsequent description of the royal art as the art of weaving together the elements of the soul and of binding them by the divine cord of truth. In the *Laws*, finally, we reach the stage where the elements, symbolized by the metals, are contracted in the individual soul and their interplay becomes the truly human problem.

The perfectly contracted symbol appears in the *Laws* in the context of the anthropology which characterizes the late work of Plato. A human being is considered to be one whole person. This person, however, is divided within itself by two conflicting foolish counsellors, joy and sorrow (or pleasure and pain: *hedone, lype*). Besides these fundamental feelings there are to be found in the soul furthermore their corresponding apprehensions (*elpis*). The apprehension of sorrow is a movement of shrinking back in fear or aversion (*phobos*); the apprehension of joy is a movement of audacious and confident reaching out (*tharros*). And beyond the feelings and their apprehensions, finally, lies the reflective insight and judgment (*logismos*) concerning the better or the worse of the basic movements. The description of this organization of the soul is then connected with the problems of order in society in that a reflective insight regarding the better or the worse, if sedimented in a decree of the polis, is called a *nomos* (614c–d).

This is the structure of the soul which Plato symbolizes through the myth of God as the player of the human puppet. Let us imagine, the Athenian Stranger says, that we living creatures are puppets of the gods, perhaps created as their playthings, perhaps created for some more serious purpose—we do not know which. But certain it is that all these sentiments or apprehensions are the cords or strings by which we are worked. Their tensions pull us in opposite directions and therein lies the division of vice and virtue. One of these cords is made of gold and is sacred; it is the cord of reflective insight or of the communal *nomos* of the polis. The other cords are made of iron and various lesser materials. The pull of the golden cord is soft and gentle; in order to become effective, it needs the support of man. The pull of the other cords is hard and violent, and man has to resist it or he will be drawn away by it. The man who has understood the truth of this *logos* will understand the game of self-rule and self-defeat and will live in obedience to the pull of the golden cord; and the city that has understood it will incorporate it into a law and will live by it in domestic relations as well as in relations with other poleis (644d–645b).

The myth unfolds its full meaning approximately midway in the *Laws*, in Book VII. The Athenian Stranger is about to discourse on the subject of instrumentalities and methods of education. He apologizes for elaborating the problems in so much tedious detail; and he pleads that the keels must be laid carefully for the vessels that will carry us through the voyage of life (803a–b). Then he goes on to say that human affairs certainly should not be taken too seriously, but that unfortunately we cannot help taking them in earnest, considering that the ways of man have become corrupt in our time. True seriousness should be reserved for matters which are truly serious; and by nature, God alone would be the worthy object of our most serious endeavors. In these our days, however, men have forgotten that they are the playthings of God and that this quality is the best in them. All of us, men and women, should fall in with this rôle and spend our lives "in playing the noblest of plays." The current sentiments among the people, however, go rather in the opposite direction; hence we have to take seriously the affairs of this otherwise insignificant plaything (803b–c). The problem thus, arises through the popular inversion of the order of relevance with regard to human affairs. According to the prevalent misconception the serious work must be attended to for the sake of the play; thus people think that war is serious work that ought to be well discharged in order to secure peace. As a matter of fact, however, there is nothing serious about war at all because in war we find neither play (*paidia*) nor formation (*paideia*), and these two have to be counted the most serious for us human beings (803d). Hence we should spend our lives in the pursuits of peace, and that means in "playing the plays [or games]" of sacrifice, song, and dance so that we may gain the grace of the gods and shall be able to vanquish our enemies (803e). Thus we shall live our lives as what we really are, "as puppets for the most part, though having a little bit of reality [*aletheia*], too" (804b).

The dimensions of meaning in the symbol begin to become clear. First of all we have to note the advance in the analysis of the psyche beyond the *Republic* and the *Statesman*. The rigidity of characterizing the types of souls through the virtues has disappeared. Plato penetrates now beyond the virtues into the movements of the soul, into the realm of *pathe*, and into the consciousness of values, the *logismos*. Virtues and vices are no longer elemental characteristics; they have become the resultants of the interplay between the forces in the deeper stratum of the soul. Plato has found the common denominator of traits which formerly seemed ultimate. With the rigidity of characterization, furthermore, the rigidity of the characters themselves has disappeared. The inequality of the basic human types has dissolved into a gamut of variants, resulting from the play of forces in a psychic constellation which is basically the same for all men. This change in the anthropological conception from inequality to equality corresponds to the lowering of the existential level in the transition from the *Republic* to the *Laws*. The philosopher-kings of the *Republic* differed existentially from the rest of mankind in that in their souls the divine order itself could be realized; the *nomos* could enter their souls so that they would become a *nomos empsychos*. The men of the *Laws* are equal because the *nomos* is equally beyond them all. What they have in their souls is the *logismos*, the ability to discern values, but whether they will follow the pull of this golden cord or, rather, the pull of another one, is uncertain. One of the several meanings of *nomos* emerges now more clearly: the meaning of the *nomos* as the presence of the divine spirit. This spirit is not present in the souls of the equal men; it has solidified into a decree (*dogma*) of the polis; and this *dogma*, while it may be renewed and expanded by the citizens of the polis, is not created by them; they find themselves equipped with it, at the foundation of the polis, through the lawgivers. We can see now that the development of the symbol of the player and the puppets lies in the logic of the development of Plato's philosophy of existence. The gentle pulling of the golden cord which man should follow has replaced the ascent from the cave to the immediate vision of the Idea; the full stature of the man whose soul is ordered by the vision of the Agathon has diminished to that of a plaything (*paignion*) of conflicting forces; the sons of god have become the puppets of the gods.

And what has become of the philosopher-kings? Gone is the hope that their numbers could unite in the erotic community of the *philoi* and be the ruling society of a polis. Their number is sadly diminished; the formulation suggests repeatedly that there is only one "who has knowledge of these things," that is, Plato himself. And because of the lack of companions, this one cannot form a community; he has become anonymous, the "Stranger." All he can do is to provide the *nomoi* that will exert the divine pull on the lesser souls who in this, their lower rank, are all equal.[2] The "one" is withdrawing from the community of men because the community of equals has failed to be his equal; and he is withdrawing toward the divinity, into the neighborhood of the God who pulls the strings. The symbol gains its intensity because it is drawn, not from the experience of the puppet only, but of the player too. No doubt, there is a touch of contempt for man in the symbol. His partners in the discourse are quick to catch this tone: "You give us a very low opinion of the race of men, O Stranger" (804b). The Stranger begs forgiveness and pleads: "Toward the God was looking and feeling when speaking, who just spoke"; and then he adds soothingly (for those who do not look and feel in this direction with the same intenseness): "Let us grant, if so it pleases you, that our race is not so bad, but worth some consideration [*spoude*]" (804b). It sounds as if the Stranger, in his transport, had for a moment forgotten that even his fellow wanderers are not quite his equals and that one must speak to them with a little caution.

[2] The experiences which determine the conception of human equality in the great spiritualists merit closer investigation. In the case of Plato, as in the case of St. Thomas, the original sentiment seems to be the generosity of the aristocratic soul that is ready to accept everybody as its equal. A considerable amount of sad experience is required before a man of higher quality realizes with finality that men, on the whole, are not his equals, and before he is ready to draw the consequences, as did for instance Nicolaus Cusanus when he surrendered his optimistic faith in the possibility of parliamentary self-government for the Church and became a "monarcho-optant." A last phase may bring the return to the sentiment of equality when the inequalities become insignificant in view of the equidistance of all men from God. The Myth of Nature, however, offers an alternative to the Christian final equality. The idea of an hierarchically differentiated psyche, with gradual transitions from humanity to divinity, allows for divinization in this last phase. And this has been the solution of Plato in the *Laws*. The current interpretations, which want to see in Plato a development from a more autocratic to a more populist or democratic position, miss this decisive point. The atmosphere of the *Republic* is still that of an appeal to the equals of Plato; in the *Laws,* on the contrary, Plato has accepted the distance which separates him from other men; he now speaks as the divine lawgiver to men who are equal because they are equidistant from him.

Throughout the passages which deal with this symbol runs the word pattern of *paidia* and *spoude*. We must consider the shades of meaning of these terms. The field of the play is the soul of man, in which feelings, apprehensions, and *logismos* pull in different directions. The play is played by the gods in whose hands man is the *paignion*. Man, however, is not an automaton; he himself, in so far as he "is one," has a part in the play; he has to play the rôle which is assigned to him of supporting the pull of the golden cord and resisting the drawings of the lesser cords. Then the field is enlarged to the polis. The *nomos* becomes the pull of the golden cord; the play becomes the ritual "sacrifice, song and dance" of the citizenry; and, correspondingly, the conversation in which the *nomoi* are created becomes, in the words of the Stranger, "a grave [*emphron*] play of the old men played well up to this point" (769a). This play, then, is serious because it is ultimately directed by God, "the most serious." Man's part in it is equally serious because in this serious play he attunes himself to the divine direction. No other preoccupation of man's life, not even war, can be as serious as the ritual play in which he plays out his life. Men, however, in their spiritual confusion, lose sight of what is "most serious." Hence human affairs, which otherwise would not be so important, have to be taken seriously by the wanderers, and the play of creating the *nomoi* becomes itself a serious play. Nevertheless, sometimes the contempt for this childish race of men, who do not know what is serious and what is not, breaks through; then the Stranger pulls himself up and admits that man, after all, has to be accorded some seriousness, for, in spite of his fall, he is destined to play the serious play.

The serious play is enacted by every man in his personal life by supporting the pull of the golden cord; it is enacted by man in community by celebrating the rites of the polis in conformity with the *nomoi*. Nevertheless, man, in enacting the play, exhausts it neither in his personal nor in his social life. Man can only act the part that is assigned to him by God. Ultimately the cosmic play is in the hands of God, and only He knows its full meaning. The lawgivers must use persuasion on the young agnostics in order to convince them that the gods are not unconcerned about human affairs. In the face of the frequent wordly success of the wicked and the equally frequent external misfortunes of the good, in the face moreover of the rabble's praise of action which destroy the true *eudaimonia*, the young may fall into moral confusion and believe that all this can happen only because no god is watching over the events in the human sphere. Against this error the lawgivers have to insist that the cosmic process is penetrated by divine ministration to the smallest and most insignificant particle, such as man. For the cosmos is psyche throughout, and the life of man is part of this animated nature (*empsychos physis*); all living creatures, however, like the cosmos as a whole, are the treasure (or: possession, *ktemata*) of the gods (902b). The lawgivers must persuade the young men that the god who has created the cosmos has disposed all things for the weal and virtue of the whole. Action and passion of the smallest particle are governed by divine powers to the minutest detail for the best. The annoyance of the young has its cause in the fact that all the parts are ordered toward the whole and that the whole does not exist for the sake of one of its parts; this order of the whole is in the mind of God, it is not intelligible in its details to man; hence the grumbling at events which make sense only in the economy of the cosmic psyche, but seem to lack meaning in the perspective of the finite human psyche.

This argument is climaxed by the vision of the creator-god as the player at the board who shifts the pieces according to the rules. When he observes a soul, now in conjunction with one body and then with another, undergoing changes through its own actions as well as through the actions of other souls, there is nothing left for the mover of the pieces but to shift the character (*ethos*) that has improved to the better place and the one that has worsened to the worse place, thus assigning to each the lot that is due its fate (903b–d).

The Mover of the Pieces (*petteutes*) is the last and most awesomely intimate revelation of the Platonic God. The Player of the Puppets is a symbol whose meaning is easily understandable through the experience of the pulls in every soul. The Mover of the Pieces—this vision of the God who broods over the board of the cosmos and moves the particles of the Great Soul according to their relative merit, distinguished from the puppets by His perfect will of fulfillment under Fate—is drawn from the cosmic depth in the soul of Plato.

The *Laws* opens with the sentence: "God or some man, O strangers, —who is supposed to have originated the institution of your laws?" This sentence opens more than the immediately following conversation on the origin of Cretan institutions in the oracles of the Zeus, to whose cave the wanderers are ascending. The sentence opens and governs the organization of the whole dialogue. The symbol of God as the author of institutions dominates the first three books. The first and second books deal with the orientation of man and his communal institutions toward God. The third book surveys the course of political institutions in history, their defects and failures, and draws the historical lesson. This survey is also under the sign of God, for the course of history is the cycle that begins after the god-sent catastrophes which have destroyed the previous civilization. Moreover, this course is ending now in a twilight of decline because men have fallen from the divine order through their self-willed factionism. History shows the destruction that is worked when the parts want to govern the whole; and the lesson is the insight that a stable order can be restored only if the self-willed particularism is overcome and the parts fall again into their proper places through their orientation toward God. The purpose of the three books has been to learn "how a polis is administered best and how the individual man may best conduct his personal life" (702a). This purpose has been achieved and the exposition of the subject matter has come to its end.

The dialogue is set moving again through the consideration that hitherto only principles have been developed; a real result could be achieved only if the principles were put to a test (*elegchos*) (702b). But what form could such a "test" assume? At this point the Cretan intervenes and reveals that he is a member of a committee of ten, entrusted by the city of Cnossus with the foundation of a new colony. His charge extends to the material organization (choice of site, assembling the settlers, and so forth) as well as to the drafting of a code of laws. He suggests that the wanderers serve the purpose of the Stranger's test as well as of his own foundation by elaborately constructing the order of a polis based on the principles that have been developed. Now it is man who has to show his skill in lawgiving, not God. This construction of the polis by man begins with Book IV and fills the rest of the *Laws* through Book XII. The incision after Book III, as we have said, is the only external division of the *Laws*; and it is governed by the opening formula.

The construction is now in the hands of man; but that does not mean that God has no part in it. The Stranger embarks on a reflection which leads to the question whether man can really legislate at all. Circumstance and chance are such pressing factors in politics that one might almost say laws are never made by man but rather result from the determinants in a situation (709a–b). Nevertheless, while God is all and while, under God, *tyche* and *kairos* govern our lives, there is still an important rôle left for human skill if it knows how to co-operate with *kairos* (709b–c). In particular the skilled artist in every field, and so the lawgiver, will know for which conditions to pray, that he may exert his art most successfully.

What then are the conditions which God should provide so that the work of lawgiving may succeed? The first condition would be the existence of a polis under a tyrant, preferably young, with a good memory and readiness to learn, courageous and magnificent, and equipped with temperance; for under an autocratic government any reform can be achieved more easily than under conditions where a greater number has to be consulted (709e–710). The tyrant alone, however, would not achieve much of a reform. God must provide for the coincidence that among his contemporaries there is a lawgiver of distinction and that chance has brought the two into contact (710c–d). Even the two together, however, will not yet achieve the great work. The greatest difficulty is the third condition which has been fulfilled rarely in the whole course of history: the awakening of the "divine Eros" for temperance and justice in the occupants of places of great power. Of such instances we hear in Trojan times, but nothing of that sort has happened in our times (711d–e). The enumeration of the conditions concludes with the oracular formula: When wisdom and temperance are combined with the greatest power in a man, then the best of constitutions and of laws will be born (712a). The wanderers will assume that God has provided the *kairos* of these coincidences; and under this assumption they will embark on the description of their constitution.

What kind of constitution will it be? A democracy, an oligarchy, an aristocracy, or a monarchy? The Athenian Stranger rejects these possibilities suggested by the Cretan, for none of them is a "real" constitution. All of these types are settlements enslaved to the despotic rule of one of their parts and they take their names from these despotic parts. If, however, a polis must take its name from its ruling part, then it should properly be called by the name of the god who rules over wise men, that is, over men who possess the Nous (712e–713a).

This somewhat enigmatic demand is clarified, by the Stranger, by means of a myth. There is a tradition that in the blissful Age of Cronos all things were spontaneous and abundant, for Cronos, who knew that no human being could be entrusted with control over all mankind, had set divine spirits to tend the human flock. They gave peace, order, and justice, and kept the tribes of man in concord and happiness. This *logos,* "which flows from truth," is still valid today; it tells us that a polis which is ruled not by God but by a mortal has no escape from evil. Hence we should do our utmost to imitate the Age of Cronos and to order our private and public life in accordance with the immortality (*athanasia*) within us. And, therefore, we should call by the name of *nomos* the order of *nous* (713c–714a).

The symbol is constructed under the previously discussed principle of contraction. The elements which in an earlier myth were distributed over the time sequence of a tale, are now contracted into a mythical present. We recall the myth of the cosmic cycles, of the ages of Cronos and Zeus, from the *Statesman.* And we furthermore recall that the Age of Zeus was not to be followed again by an Age of Cronos, for in the Age of Zeus there had arisen a new factor, *i.e.* the autonomous personality of the philosopher, which made the return to the Golden Age both impossible and undesirable; the redemption from the evils of the Age of Zeus would have to come from a human agency that would take the place of the shepherd-god, that is, from the Royal Ruler. Now, in the *Laws,* the ages of Cronos and Zeus both belong to the past; Book III of the *Laws* has given the historical survey which closes the Age of Zeus and shows the necessity of a new start. And at this end, as in the other symbols of the dialogue, we return to the beginning; the new life beyond the Age of Zeus will imitate the Age of Cronos in so far as it will reabsorb into its human institutions the guidance of the god. This god, however, no longer is Cronos; he is the new god of the Platonic *kosmos empsychos,* the creative and persuasive Nous. The constitutional order, which the wanderers are about to create, will have to be called by the name of *nomoi* because this name is associated with *nous.*[3] The *nomoi* themselves thus become one of the new contracted symbols; in the *nomoi* the movement of the cycles has come to its end.

---

[3] It should be noted that the end of the sentence in which Plato associates *nomos* with *nous* is a pun: ". . . *ten tou nou dianomen eponomazontas nomon*" (714a).

4. Political Form

The method employed in the construction of the dominant symbols affects the structure of the dialogue at large. When the symbols that govern the meaning of the dialogue are formed under the principle of contraction, the exposition of meaning through the distended form of the mythical tale, or through the dialectical questioning of a Socrates who drives toward an issue, must give way to the associative exposition of a theme in dependence on the governing symbols. The resulting literary form will best be illustrated by an example.

In the first two books of the *Laws* an extraordinary amount of space is given to the customs of social drinking, a digression and a topic which has frequently baffled the interpreters. The digression is, indeed, baffling if one insists on reading it as a disquisition on drinking and ignores the various symbolic functions which it serves. The drinking itself is introduced, in the course of a discussion of educational problems, as the most convenient and inexpensive test for the resistance which a man can offer to the temptations of excessive relaxation. This problem is, then, interwoven with the symbol of the Player and the Puppets: the puppets should be "plied with drink" in order to test the firmness of the control of the *logismos* in their souls. This, however, is not a temptation to which the young should be exposed; it is reserved for those of riper age, over forty. For these men of riper age, however, convivial drinking under a master of the ceremony is more than a test, for the "plying with drink" is also supposed to remove the rigidity and inhibitions of age and to restore something of the flexibility and insouciance of youth. Hence, the test of the *logismos* in the puppet becomes ambivalent in so far as the relaxation will also increase the faculty of participating in the choric rituals in honor of the god; the drinking will enable the puppets to perform better their rôles in the "serious play." While the children and the younger people will be governed in their choric performance by the Muses and Apollo, this third chorus, that of the older men, will be governed by Dionysus. In this respect the digression on drinking serves to introduce into the choric ritual of the polis, the Dionysian principle by the side of the Apollinian. In another respect, however, the introduction of Dionysus is linked with the construction of the whole dialogue. The *Laws* opens with a reference to Zeus and Apollo, the gods who have originated the Cretan and Lacedaemonian institutions, represented by Cleinias and Megillus. Athena, the goddess of the Stranger, is only mentioned by courtesy; she does not reappear in a major function in the dialogue. The place of the third god is taken by Dionysus, the god who inspires the older men to the perfect performance of the ritual. These old men, finally, are not only choric performers; they are also the critics of the musical and dramatic performances in the polis of the *nomoi*. They have to watch over the selection of the *nomoi*, in the musical sense; they are the critics of their public execution—in contrast to the Athenian theatrocracy of the rabble; and since music and dramatic performance are one of the principal instruments of *paideia*, of the formation of character, they are the guardians of the *nomoi* of the polis against corruption. The serious play of sacrifice, song, and dance is under the supervision of the elders in order to prevent the corruption of the polis right at its source, that is, in the corruption of the ritual culture of the community. Dionysus thus governs the *nomoi*; he supersedes Zeus and Apollo.

We have selected the digression on drinking as an example of Plato's new technique of presenting his problems. To a superficial reader it might look like a weakness in the construction of the work, or even, in some details, like a joke in poor taste. In fact, the digression is representative of Plato's mastery in handling his new literary instrument. The example shows that it is impossible to isolate topics for special study without doing violence to the whole structure. Wherever one tries to draw a strand from this associative network for closer inspection, the whole fabric follows the pull. When we enter now, nevertheless, on the analysis of such special topics, rude cuts will have to be made in the operation, and the sequence in which the topics are presented is more or less arbitrary. We shall start with the problem of governmental form for no other reason than its associative proximity to the problem of the cycles which we discussed at the end of the preceding section.

Plato develops the problem of governmental form out of the theory of the cycle in politics. At present we are at the end of a cycle which began after the last great catastrophe sent by the gods, the great flood. Only a few men escaped the disaster, and with them human civilization began anew (677). Book III is devoted to the description of this cycle of political culture. It runs its course through the phases of growth, of climax and failure, and of decomposition—until the decline has reached the point where the time has become ripe for the new beginning of the *nomoi*.

In the period of growth the following development of political form is to be observed:

(1) After the flood only scattered remnants of humanity survived in the mountainous parts of the earth. The single homestead and family was the social unit. The way of life was rugged and primitive, but in its simplicity in many respects superior in character to more complicated civilizational conditions. There was no need for lawgivers in this simple state. Men lived by custom and the traditions of their fathers (*patriois nomois*). Nevertheless, even this state had a political form; it consisted in the rule of the elders. This form may be called *dynasteia*, that is, patriarchal chieftainship or lordship (677b–680e).

(2) With the lapse of time (to be counted in tens of thousands of years) and the multiplication of the race new forms developed. The next step will be the getting-together in greater numbers and the increase in the size of the polis beyond that of a clan settlement. The various clans who compose the village settlements will bring with them their traditions, and only now does the need arise for a lawgiver who will harmonize and weld the various traditions into a common law for the city. The governmental form will spring from the origin of the settlement: The rulers of the composing lordships will form the new aristocracy; or perhaps, if one of them should be given a pre-eminent magistracy, the form might be a *basileia*, a kingship (680e–681d).

(3) We have knowledge of the early developments only through incidental references by the poets, as for instance through the Homeric account of the life of the Cyclopes. With the next step, the descent from the mountains to the plains, we come closer to the light of history. The mountain villages are followed by the foundations of larger poleis in the plains, such as Ilium and the Greek poleis that were at war with her. Under the constitutional form (*politeia*) of the polis of the plains are comprised all the forms and vicissitudes (*pathemata*) of historical political societies and their constitutions (681d–682e).

(4) For the fourth phase in this development Plato relies on a mythical tradition concerning the Doric invasion. During the ten

years of the Trojan wars various domestic revolutions occurred in the Greek poleis. When the war bands returned they found a younger generation in power and they were not welcome in their homes. The exiles organized under the leadership of a certain Doriaeus, reconquered their hometowns, and proceeded to organize a powerful federation among the Peloponnesian poleis of Lacedaemon, Argos, and Messene. The members of this federation were under the rule of the Heraclidian royal house. This fourth type of organization Plato calls an *ethnos*, a nation (682d–683b). The new people called themselves the Dorians, and their national federation was powerful enough to afford adequate protection not for the Peloponnesians alone but for the Hellenes at large against provocations of the type which they had suffered from Troy. The Trojans would not have dared their outrage unless they had reckoned with the support of Assyria, a power which at that time was as great and as feared as the Persians in Plato's time. The new nation was a match for the Asiatic power of the time (685b–e). The power, in fact, was so great that, had it succeeded, it could have dominated mankind at will, Hellenes as well as barbarians (687a–b).

With the development of a national federation the growth of political form nears its climax. In this series of steps we can again sense Plato's dream of an Hellenic empire that would be a match for the Asiatic empires, and perhaps even more than a match. This potentiality of the Doric federation, however, was not actualized. We have reached the turning point of the cycle, the point where the decline will set in. In the construction of the dialogue this turning point is marked by a conversational reference to the fact that the wanderer's discussion is taking place at the time of the summer solstice (683c).

The Doric federation seemed to its founders an excellent political organization. Three kings and their peoples entered into a covenant to uphold and respect their positions as circumscribed by the law; they would, furthermore, come to each other's aid if any of the kings should encroach on the rights of his people, or if any of the peoples should encroach on the privileges of its king. Why did this admirable construction fail? It failed because in two of the three member polities of the federation the lawgivers had committed "The Greatest Folly" (*megiste amathia*) (689a), that is, they had not taken the precaution of providing either a well-balanced man for the royal function, or constitutional balances that would offset the foolishness of an autocratic ruler. The meaning of foolishness is defined in terms of the new psychology previously discussed. If a man hates what his insight recognizes as noble and good, and if he loves what his insight recognizes as ignoble and wicked, there exists in his soul a discord (*diaphonia*) between the feelings and the *logismos*; this discord is foolishness. A government must never be entrusted to a man who is foolish in this sense even if otherwise he should be highly informed, clever, and an expert; on the other hand, the government may safely be entrusted to a sane man even if he should be deficient in other qualities (689a–e). If no precautions of this kind are taken the chances are that the constitutional order will come to grief. This inclination toward foolishness is present in every man, and in absolute rulers it is fostered by the temptations of their position—so much so that it may be called the specific "disease of kings" (691a). The kings of Argos and Messene were no exceptions to this rule; their reckless foolishness caused wars in the federation and its destruction.

Lacedaemon survived the disaster and subjugated the ruinous confederates because, by divine providence, its constitution contained the balances which made for stable order. The first of these balancing devices was the double kingship; the second was the Council of Elders which had equal voice with the kings in affairs of importance; the third was the democratic ephorate, an office that was practically filled by lot (691d–692a). In the hour of the national danger, however, in the Persian Wars, the conduct of the Peloponnesian poleis was anything but glorious. Even in the best case, the Lacedaemonian, the development of political form had ended in stagnation (692d–693a).

From the national failure and the Lacedaemonian success a lesson can be drawn: governments will be stable only if they are organized as balances of certain elemental factors. All variants of constitutions are derived from two "mother forms" (*materes*). The first can be seen in its pure form in the Persian, the second in the Athenian constitution. All other constitutions are woven from these strands in various patterns. The existentially stabilizing core of government, which consists in the combination of freedom (*eleutheria*) and friendship (*philia*) with wisdom (*phronesis*), can be secured only by means of these two institutional forms (693d–e). Neither in the Persian nor in the Athenian case do we find this mixture; as a consequence, decomposition has been their lot. While the Spartan case could serve as the example of stagnation, the Persian and Athenian pure cases of governmental form will appropriately serve as examples for the dissolution of political form in the declining branch of the cycle.

For the historical details of Persian and Athenian decline the reader should refer to the *Laws* itself. What is relevant for us is primarily the criterion of decay, for it implies the standard of right order that is to be realized in the polis of the *nomoi*. The analysis of the Persian case provides occasion for establishing the standard by which honors should be awarded in a society and men be elevated to high rank. Goods can be ordered hierarchically in the following manner: The highest place in the hierarchy is held by the goods of the soul, in particular by the virtue of temperance; the second place is held by the goods of the body; the third place by substance and wealth. If a legislator gives first rank to wealth, or in any way promotes to the higher place what belongs to the lower, he does something which violates the principles of religion as well as of statemanship. In the Persian case this rule was violated, with the result that the perverse autocrats have no regard for the rights and welfare of the people, but inflict every kind of harm on them if they can reap an immediate material advantage for themselves; and with the further result that the people hate the government and are disloyal to the point that mercenary armies have to be employed in case of war (697a–698a). In the Athenian instance the decomposition is due to the increasing and excessive liberty of the people. The origin of dissolution can be traced to the disregard for the old musical order of the polis. The judgment of performances was in the older period the privilege of the educated ruling class; children and rabble had to refrain from applause until the officials had given their decision. This state of things was gradually superseded by the theatrocracy in which the people at large arrogated to itself the right to applaud what pleased and to criticize what displeased without regard to quality. From this assumption of judgment according to pleasure without insight results the general impudence of disregard for the judgment of one's betters. The further steps on this path are unwillingness to submit to the magistrates, resistance to paternal authority, and disobedience to the law. At the end comes disregard for oaths and pledges and contempt of the gods. This, in a sense, is also a return to the beginning, for the old Titanic nature breaks through, and the Titanic fate of a life of endless evil is re-enacted (700a–701c).

Plato's description of the political cycle in a civilization has exerted a paradigmatic function in the history of political ideas whch is so obvious that the mere mentioning of the two main lines of influence will be sufficient. The first and straight line of influence goes into Aristotelian ethics and politics. The sequence of phases in the growth of the polis is resumed by Aristotle in his sequence of family unit, village, and polis—with the decisive difference, however, that the fourth phase, the enlargement into the Hellenic empire, is discarded. In the same manner we find the hierarchy of goods as the nucleus of Aristotelian ethics. The other main line of influence goes into the cycle theory of history. The articulation of the cycle into the period of growth, that of climax and failure, and that of decomposition calls immediately to mind Vico's *storia eterna ideale* with its growth, acme, and decline, as well as the theories of Vico's more recent successors. With the third element of paradigmatic importance, that is, the theory of the mixed form of government, we shall deal presently.

The vast exposition of the structure of the cycle is not an independent piece of Platonic doctrine. Within the economy of the *Laws* it is the great preparation for the principle that will govern the institutions of the *nomoi*. This principle, the balancing of autocratic and democratic elements in a constitution, usually goes by the name of the mixed form of government. Nevertheless, we have to be cautious in the use of this term when speaking of the new polis which the wanderers are projecting. If we use it without further qualification for the designation of the constitutional project, we drag Plato's problem down to the level of an institutional device. Extreme forms, the argument would run, like the Persian and Athenian, have not functioned too well; a constitution like the Lacedaemonian, which uses the device of balancing the elements, has functioned better; as a consequence, let us project a balanced form. If there were no more to the *Laws* than this argument the work would hardly merit much attention, for this wisdom was probably voiced wherever Greeks met for a bit of political gossiping. The assumption that Plato had thought for a moment that the political problems of a civilization in crisis could be solved by tinkering with constitutional provisions would pervert the meaning not only of the *Laws* but of the whole work of Plato. Moreover, we have seen in the analysis of the cycle that Plato, while praising the balances of the Lacedaemonian constitution, has left no doubt about the stagnation of a polis which is organized for war but not for the serious play of the spirit in peace. The idea that the blueprint for a constitution without regard for the spirit that lives in the community could be Plato's solution for spiritual disorder is quite as wildly erroneous as the idea that Plato could ever have advocated a constitutional government under the law, with consent of the people, without regard for the spirit that lives in the law and in the people.

The institutional order of a community is not its spirit; it is the vessel in which the spirit lives. Neither must we search for the spirit in the mere pattern of institutions, nor must we accept such a pattern as a spiritual solution. Nevertheless, the institutions are instrumental in the actualization of the spirit, and some institutions are better instruments for this purpose than others. The mixed form of government has its importance for Plato because he considers it the more adequate instrument for the embodiment of the spirit. We remember from the *Statesman* Plato's distinction between the one "true constitution" and the several untrue ones. The distinction is still valid in the *Laws*, though now with certain qualifications which accentuate the instrumental character of institutions. In 712d–e Megillus finds it difficult to characterize adequately the Lacedaemonian constitution because the various elements are mixed in it. The Stranger gives the reason: it is a "real polity" (*politeia*) and not one of these so-called polities which in fact are no more than settlements enslaved to the domination of one of their component parts (713a). A few pages later (715a–b) the Stranger again insists that such communities should not be called polities at all, for they have no "true laws." And in a later context he calls democracy, oligarchy, and tyranny "these no-constitutions" (*tas ou politeias*) (832b). The members of such settlements should be called partisans rather than citizens (*stasiotes, polites*) (715b).

The solution, *i.e.*, the mixed form of government as the only true form, is carefully prepared in the description of the cycle. The period of growth lets us ascend to the promise of an Hellenic empire, to the failure of the federation and the stagnation in the balanced Lacedaemon; in the period of decline the fundamental ingredients of the true constitution are shown in their separate decomposition. At the apex between the ascending and descending branches of the cycle occurs the symbolic reference to the solstice—we are "near the point where the God turns from summer to winter." At this apex, furthermore, Plato introduces the theory of the two *materes* of all constitutions, the monarchic and democratic factors. From the solstitial apex of the cycle arises the institutional solution of the *Laws*, the idea of a constitution that will carry the polis beyond the spiritual stagnation of Sparta while preventing, by its balance, the decomposition of Persia and Athens. The cycle will be overcome by the timeless symbol of its apex. The problem of governmental form, thus, is drawn into the symbolic play of the *Laws*. Like the other symbols of the dialogue, the mixed form of government is a contraction of elements which formerly were distended in time. We may speak of a solstitial form.

The contraction of elements is the first characteristic of the institutions which are the appropriate vessel of the spirit. In the discussion of elections for the Council of the polis, the Stranger indicates that the method of election which he has devised will strike a mean between monarchy and democracy, "as a constitution always should do." Only by striking the mean (*meson*) can the lawgiver achieve the cohesion of the polis in true *philia*. There never can be *philia* between the slave and the master, between the base and the noble, if the two receive equal honors in the community, for to unequals equality becomes inequality unless a measure (*metron*) is preserved. Equality and inequality are the two rich sources of discord in a polis. The old saying that equality begets friendship is true, if the meaning of equality is properly understood. This meaning, however, is ambiguous. We have to distinguish between two types of equality: the mechanical and the proportional. The mechanical equality, that of "number, weight, and measure," can be realized easily in any society by simply distributing distinctions and offices by lot. The other equality springs from "the judgment of Zeus"; it is not so easily realized, but wherever it penetrates public or private affairs the results are blissful. This proportional equality metes out the greater awards to those who are distinguished by virtue and breeding, and the lesser awards to men of the opposite nature. A just order can never be established by catering to a few tyrants or to the populace, but only by meting out this true equality to the unequals. While no order can be just without the realization of proportional equality, the lawgiver nevertheless has to take care of the need for mechanical equality, too. The principle of proportional equality cannot be applied in a political community without some qualifications because the strict application would arouse the resentment of the masses to such a degree that rebellion would be inevitable. Equity and indulgence certainly are infractions of the strict order of perfect justice—but that is precisely the reason why they must be injected into the order. The masses, who cannot arrive at a place of honor by their personal qualifications, must have a way of arriving at it by other means in order to keep them satisfied. Election by lot must supplement the aristocratic election according to personal distinction as a safety valve for the resentment of the masses. Such a concession, of course, is fraught with dangers, but all the statesman can do is "invoke God and fortune" that they may direct the lot in such a way that the least damage is done to the right order (756e–758a).

The purpose of the construction is the creation of *philia* as the bond of cohesion in the community. By this purpose the Platonic conception of the mixed form is distinguished from a mere institutional device which looks for stability to a balance of power between the component parts of the system. The conception of a balance of power would rest on the assumption that the members of the community are fundamentally bent upon dominating each other and are prevented from realizing their desire only by the check of the opposing power. The Platonic conception, however, does not strike a balance between rulers and subjects; it rather strikes the balance between the noble and the vile. Plato goes behind class structures and the balance of interests in a society into the deeper problem of balancing the sentiments of a social group in such a manner that the inflexibility of the spiritual postulate shall not lead to an explosion of the lower instincts of the mass, while at the same time the inevitable concession to the mass shall not destroy the spiritual substance of the community. By assuaging the lower instincts through concessions, which, however, must not go so far that they become an insult to men of quality, a bond of *philia* will be created between heterogeneous elements.

In this construction the symbol of the mixed form closely follows the symbol of the puppet. In the *Republic* the lower elements in the community were kept in their place by the myth of the rigid distribution of the metals among the three social strata. In the symbol of the puppet the elements of the psyche were contracted into the tensions of feelings, apprehensions, and reflective insight within each individual soul. The soul now comprises the gold of rulership together with the lesser metals. In the same manner the community as a whole is now contracted from its distention through the shift in the meaning of *philia*—from that of a sentiment which binds in existential community the equals in the spirit, to that of a sentiment which binds into a communal whole the noble and the vile. The institutions which create this state of sentiment are the vessel that will hold the spirit and not burst under its pressure.

The interweaving of the monarchic and democratic *materes*, with a preponderance of the monarchic, however useful in projecting the institutions of a polis, does not deliver the institutions in their concrete detail. When we now approach the problem of the institutions themselves we again have to beware of pragmatic misunderstandings. Plato was not obsessed by the superstition that the blueprint of a constitution will deliver the world from evil. There is no magic quality in the institutions which he projects that would solve the political problems of Hellas. As a matter of fact, his institutions do not differ from those of the historical Hellenic poleis. There is a popular assembly, an elected council, and a board of chief magistrates. The population is of limited size, probably around 40,000, including women, children, slaves, and foreign traders. It is divided into tribes, there are priests, there is an army with elected generals, and so forth. The external aspect of these institutions will no more furnish the key to the meaning which they have in the context of the *Laws* than the principle of the mixed form of government in the abstract furnished a key to the symbolic meaning of the solstitial form. Hence it is quite beside the point to weigh with care, as is frequently done by interpreters, the question whether the institutions lean more toward the oligarchic or the democratic side in pragmatic politics and to draw conclusions from the analysis with regard to Plato's personal political position in the struggles of his time. Such an attempt is particularly reprehensible in the face of Plato's explicit declarations that the problems of the "true constitution" lie on a plane which is not that of the no-constitutions in the historical cycle.

The meaning of the institutions as the vessel of the spirit arises from a play with cosmic numbers. For the background of this play we have to look beyond the *Laws* to the *Timaeus*. The idea of the cosmos as a great self-moving psyche and of the celestial bodies as

divine souls in perfect movement leads to the further idea of the
numerical relations in nature as the structure of the psyche. The structure of the human soul is in its pre-existence related to the perfect
relations and periods of the cosmos; but the birth into a body disturbs
these motions and thus a soul is born as if it had no intelligence (*anous
psyche*) (*Timaeus* 44a). Only in the course of life can the order of the
Nous be recovered, and the most important means for the anamnetic
recollection of the cosmic order is the observation and study of the
order which actually prevails in the visible cosmos. "There is but one
therapy" in such matters: the nourishing of the ailing part on such
substance as is akin to its own. "The motions of the divine element in
us" have to be nourished by the thoughts and motions of the universe.
These motions every man should study, and thereby correct the motions
(cycles, *periodos*) in his head that were deranged at birth. In this
manner he will bring the noumenal part in his soul into accord with
his noumenal pre-existence as well as with the noumenal part in the
cosmos; and thereby he will achieve "the best life" that God has held
out to man in the present time as well as in the time to come (*Timaeus,*
90c–d).[4]

   In the late phase of Plato's thought the ideas which create the
form of the cosmos are numbers. The form as number is the principle
which Plato has applied in the construction of the institutions of the
nomoi. Through the numerical relations between the institutions, the
political form of the polis becomes a crystal of numbers reflecting the
mathematical structure of the cosmos itself. Concretely, the numerical
relations of the political form are governed by the sun symbolism. The
key number is 12. This is the number of the tribes in the polis, and each
such division of the people must be considered "a sacred thing, a gift
of God, corresponding to the months and to the revolution of the
universe" (771b). This key number 12 determines the form of the
polis throughout. The number of citizens who are householders and
own a portion of land is fixed at 5040. The number is chosen because it
is divisible by 12 as well as by all the integers from 1 to 10; it thus
permits the division of the population into twelve tribes. The first number, however, which fulfills the condition of being divisible by 12, as

---

[4] For the problems of the numerical structure of the cosmos and the psyche see Frank, *Plato
und die sogenannten Pythagoreer,* in particular pp. 105–107. See also for further elaboration of
this problem *Epinomis* 990–92.

well as by the integer series from 1 to 10, would be 2520. Plato chose the double, 5040, because as a consequence the number of citizens in each tribe will be 420, which is again divisible by 12. 5040 is the first number which also fulfills this second condition. The choice of this number may have been influenced, furthermore (though Plato does not mention it), by the fact that 5040 is equal to 7! (the product of the integers from 1 to 7) and thus implies a relation to the number of days in the week.

The Council of the polis has a membership fixed at 360, that is, 30 for each of the twelve tribes. The number is found by the multiplication of the number of the months (12) by the number of days in the sun-month (30). The members of the Council do not all serve at the same time; only one-twelfth of them, 30, serve each month. The number 360 is chosen, furthermore, because it is divisible by 4. The divisibility is of importance because in the election of the councillors the polis proceeds by election in property classes. The citizens are divided into four property classes, the first one possessing, over their land lot, once again the value of the lot, up to the fourth class which has the maximum property of four times the value of the land lot. No larger amount of property is allowed. The division of 360 by 4 results in 90 councilmen to be elected from each property class. The election is subdivided into two phases: in the first phase 180 men are elected from each class and in a second phase 90 from the 180 are chosen by lot.

The highest magistracy is the board of the Guardians of the Law. Their number is fixed at 37. In this case the election procedure has three phases. In a first phase 300 names which have received the highest number of votes emerge from the scrutiny; in a second phase there emerge the 100 who have now received the highest votes; and from these 100 are finally chosen the 37. Plato does not give any reason for the choice of the number 37; perhaps the explanation can be found in the fact that 37 is the twelfth prime number, not counting the 1.

Finally, we have to consider the predominance of the numbers one, two, three, and four, the numbers of the Pythagorean Tetractys. The indirect election of the Council has two phases; that of the Guardians of the Law has three phases. There are four property classes, which in relation to the twelve tribes, give the number three. The number 5040 stands in the relation 2:1 to the first number fulfilling the condition of being divisible by 1 to 10 and 12. In the election of the councilmen the number elected in the first phase stands in the relation 2:1 to the number finally chosen by lot. If we consider that the relations of the first integers, that is, the relations 2:1, 3:2, 4:3, are also the mathematical relations which determine the octave, the fifth, and the fourth, it seems to have been Plato's intention to create the form of the polis as a musical symbol and thus to relate it to the cosmic harmony.

5. Revelation at Noon

The political form is designed to serve the actualization of the spirit in the life of the community. The spirit lives in the laws. Hence the highest magistracy is devised as the board of the Guardians of the Law. At this point of the construction several motifs are interwoven. Through the guardianship of the laws, the true form of government is distinguished from the untrue forms. In the no-constitutions one of several conflicting claims to rulership is satisfied by making the people, or the wealthy, or the strongest, or the oldest, the rulers of the polis. In the true constitution the highest office is held by the men who are most obedient to the laws. The fulfillment of this condition alone, however, would not suffice to make the constitution a true one. To guard the laws would be of little avail if the laws themselves were bad. The guardianship of the laws acquires its full meaning through the earlier discussed association between *nomos* and *nous*. Only when the divine spirit of the *nous* lives in the *nomoi* will obedience to the laws result in the *eudaimonia* of man and the community. Office in the polis of the *nomoi* thus becomes a "service to the gods" (*ton theon hyperesia*), and the high magistrates are servants of the gods in so far as they are servants of the laws (*hyperetai tois nomois*) (715a–d).

But how can such *nomoi* which contain the spirit ever be instituted in a polis? Obviously they cannot originate in the people; for, if the people were able to give itself such laws and live by them no problem of civilizational decomposition would arise and there would be no need for a lawgiver. In searching for a solution the Stranger envisages the situation of the colony in process of foundation. When the future citizens are assembled one should address them on the purpose of life and on the nature of that conduct (*praxis*) that is dear to God and a following of Him (716c). This suggestion is then followed by the great address on this subject, divided into two parts: 715e–718b and 726d–734e. To the principles developed in the address we have referred frequently in various contexts of the present study. It will be sufficient to recall them briefly:

(1) In the first part Plato formulates the word that separates him from the Age of the Sophists, the word that marks the beginning of a science of order: "God is for us the measure of all things, of a truth; more truly so than, as they say, man" (716c). This is the conscious counterposition to the Protagoraean *homo-mensura*. Plato clarifies the opposition between the two principles carefully. He appeals to an old saying that God holds in his hands the beginning and the end of all that is; He moves towards the accomplishment of his purpose on a straight course, as his his nature; and ever by his side is Dike, ready to punish those who disobey the divine ordinance. Those who want to live harmoniously will follow closely and humbly in the train of Dike; but those who are puffed with pride—of riches, or rank, or comeliness—believe that they do not need a guide; they rather will want to be guides for others. The proud are abandoned by God; in their state of abandonment they will collect a company of others around them who are equally abandoned; they will embark on a frantic career and work general confusion. To the mass a man of this kind will seem to be a great man; but in a short while he will have to pay his debt to Dike through the ruin which he brings upon himself, his family, and his country. What line of conduct (*praxis*), then, could be called dear to God and a following of Him (*phile kai akolouthos Theo*)? It is a conduct that tries to be in harmony with Him. "Like is dear to its like, and measure to measure." Things that have no measure do not agree with each other, nor with things that have a just measure (*emmetros*). In order to be loved by a divine being man would have to strive with all his might to become like it. Thus the man who is temperate and ordered (*sophron*) will be loved by God, for his measure is attuned to God's measure; while the disordered (*me sophron*) man is unlike God.

(2) The second part deals with the psyche of man. The psyche is the most divine part in man, and the insight into the superiority of its rank over goods of the body and material goods is the first condition for the conduct in which man "likens" himself to God. Man must establish the true order of temperance and justice in his soul; he must then apply these principles to the order of his personal life, to the domestic order of the community, and to the relations both with strangers in the polis and with foreign poleis.

The two parts of the address are separated by an interlude. The Stranger renders the text of the address to his companions while the wanderers are resting in the shadow of one of the groves of cypresses. The conversation has begun at daybreak; by now it is noon. When the Stranger has finished the first part (on God and the conduct that is dear to Him) he is struck by a thought. Is it not, on principle, one of the doubtful aspects of a law that it is terse in its provision? That even a man who is most willing to obey is left in doubt as to what precisely is its intention and how it should be understood in a concrete case? The law deals with the citizen like a physician with an ignorant slave: he tells the slave what to do but he does not discuss with him the nature of his disease, nor does he give him the reasons for the treatment. Like such a physician, the lawgivers have hitherto relied simply on command and sanction. The address, however, of which the first part was now delivered, suggests another means that the lawgiver could employ to secure obedience. He could appeal to the intelligence and good will of the citizens by explaining to them his motives in formulating a law. He could, as the Stranger has just begun to do in his imaginary address, awaken their understanding for the spirit of the laws by informing them of the nature of God and of the friendship between God and man. In brief, he could use persuasion supplementary to coercion. We recall the appearance of *peitho*, Persuasion, in the *Statesman* and in the *Timaeus*. The Demiurge cannot impose form on the formlessness of Becoming by force; he has to use Persuasion to bend Ananke to Nous. Now Persuasion reappears as the means of bending man, the "material," to the *nomoi* of the *nous* and thus imposing on him the form of the polis. This thought is placed symbolically into an interlude between the two parts of the address of which the first part deals with God and the second with the human material that has to be persuaded. The gap between God and man has to be filled by Persuasion; in the organization of the dialogue the gap between the two parts on God and man is filled by the interlude on Persuasion.

Persuasion holds the middle between God and man. The question arises: How can this Persuasion be actualized in a polity so that it will become a permanently effective force, mediating in a constant flow the *nous* of the *nomoi* to the souls of the citizens? In devising this instrument for mediating Persuasion Plato makes one further move in his symbolic play. The god who governs the play is the God of its end and its beginning as well as of its middle. We have followed the play with the symbol of the solstice, with the acme of the cycle, and with the middle of the discourse which has brought the revelation that the *Laws* is a religious poem. In the present interlude on Persuasion, the decisive speech of the Stranger is introduced by the reminder that we have arrived at the middle of this longest day. The conversation has taken such a course "under the guidance of God," from daybreak to noon, that now at the height of the day the means is revealed to the wanderers by which they can achieve the constant persuasion of *nous* in their polis (722c). The Stranger begins his reflections by saying that in this long conversation about the laws the wanderers have hardly begun to talk about the laws themselves; all they have talked about were preludes or preambles to the law (*prooimia nomon*) (722d). "Now why did I say this?" It is because discourses and vocal utterances of any kind quite generally have preludes which serve as an introduction to the main theme itself. Curiously enough, such preluding is to be found in music rather than in the important matter of legislation. Wonderfully elaborate preludes, prooemia, are prefixed to the *nomoi* for the kithara, and quite generally to the *nomoi* of musical compositions; only in the case of what we consider the real *nomoi*, that is, the *nomoi* of a polis, it seems to be taken for granted that they cannot have prooemia. Nevertheless, what the wanderers have done since daybreak has been precisely such a preluding to laws. They have developed in fact a "persuasive" (*peistikon*) for the citizens, like the physician who explains and gives reasons for his treatment to the freeman. Laws should consist in principle of two parts: a coercive part, the "dictatorial prescription," and a persuasive part, the expository prooemium. The citizen should be prepared to receive the legislator's enactment in a spirit of friendliness and graciousness, and that can be achieved by prefixing a prooemium in the tone of persuasion. The listeners agree with the Stranger and resolve that their legislation as a whole, as well as its major subdivisions, shall be equipped with prooemia, and that the great address which the Stranger has begun and now, after the interlude, is to continue, is the most fitting prooemium on the spirit of the laws, and shall be prefixed to the codification as a whole (722–724). The literary form of the Prooemium, thus, becomes the mediator of the *nous* for the polis of the *nomoi;* and the expansion of the meaning of *nomoi* to embrace the musical form associates the preluding work

of the prooemia with the cosmic harmony that has crystallized in the
numerical relations of political form. The Prooemium is the form which
Plato has created for his religious poetry; and the great prooemia, in
particular the prooemium which fills the whole of Book X, are the final
expression of Plato's thought on God and the destiny of man.

6. The Drama of the Polis

Throughout his lifetime Plato was preoccupied with the problem
of play. The dialogues themselves are plays under the aspect of literary
form and more than once we had occasion to observe Plato's mastership
as a dramatist. Moreover, the intellectual environment in which he grew
up was still archaic in its modes of expression. The Age of the Sophists
shows astonishing parallels to our "modernity" in the nature of its
problems, but the sophist himself still exhibits the traits of a poly-
historic "medicine man" who gives public performances of his won-
drous skills for a fee. The Greek word for demonstration or proof,
epideixis, has the primary meaning of a sophistic rhetorical performance, be it the delivery of a ceremonial speech or a game in
which two sophists match their skills before an appreciative audience.
The drama of the *Gorgias*, as we have seen, is developed out
of a situation of this kind: the migratory sophist has come to town
and holds open house; anybody who wishes may come and test him
in a match of wits. Plato is the deadly enemy of this sport; for the
sophists misuse the play of the intellect for the destruction of the
people's faith without putting anything in its place. Their play frivo-
lously destroys the spiritual substance of Hellenic culture. Nevertheless, Plato is not opposed to play as such; on the contrary, in his later
years we can observe his marked endeavor to replace the frivolous play
of the sophists by his "serious play" of the spirit. In the chapter on
the *Timaeus* we studied the problem of the play in Plato's attitude toward the myth; and in the present chapter we have already had occasion
to study the symbol of the Player and the Puppets as the dominant
motif in the organization of the *Laws*.

Some light has recently been cast on the problem of play in Plato's
work, as well as on the nature of play in general, by the *Homo Ludens*
of Jan Huizinga.[5] This study on the function of play in the growth of

[5] Jan Huizinga, *Homo Ludens* (Basel, 1944).

culture is strongly influenced by Plato's theory and in its turn adds greatly to the understanding of this element in Plato's thought and work. Huizinga finds that the function of play is fundamental in man in the sense that it cannot be reduced to another factor. Neither must play be interpreted in a utilitarian manner as serving a purpose, nor must its meaning be derived from the content which it presents; either attempt would destroy the independent meaning of play. Moreover, play is not a function specific to man; it is to be found fully developed already in the animal world; and it is precisely its appearance on the animal level of Being that gives a clue to its interpretation. "In play we recognize the spirit. For play is not matter—whatever its essence may be. Even in the animal world it breaks through the limits of mere physical existence. If we consider it in the perspective of a world determined by forces and their effects, it is a *superabundans* in the full meaning of the word, something that is superfluous. Only through the influx of the spirit, which abolishes absolute determination, does the phenomenon of play become possible, thinkable, and intelligible. The existence of play confirms again and again the superlogical character of our situation in the cosmos. Animals can play, hence they are more than mechanical things. We play and know that we play, hence we are more than merely reasonable beings, for play is unreasonable."[6]

In this interpretation, play is an "overflow" beyond the "normal" level of existence, a source for the creation of new worlds of meaning beyond the everyday world. By virtue of this quality of transcendence play could become the vehicle of cultural growth through the creation of spiritual worlds in religions, legal institutions, languages, philosophy, and art. The history of culture shows indeed that the spiritual worlds of the high civilizations grow out of archaic forms in which the origin in forms of play is still clearly discernible. In particular, play is the vehicle of religious expression from archaic rites to the subtleties of the liturgical drama and the symbolism of the dogma. The seriousness of play, which is mixed with its playfulness even in such exoteric forms as sports and entertainments, and expresses itself in the observation of the rules of the game or in the preservation of the illusion in a performance, is heightened to the sacredness of play when its content is a religious experience. Conversely, however, even in the serious play the element of playfulness is not quite atrophied—whether its

[6] *Ibid.*, 5f.

presence expresses itself in Plato's freedom toward the myth or in the free acceptance of constitutional provisions for serious observance.

Our analysis of the *Laws* up to this point has shown already that play is the all-pervasive category of the dialogue: God plays with men as his puppets or as pieces on a board; man conducts his life as a serious play in following the pull of the golden cord; and the dialogue itself is an elaborate play with various symbols. The consistency of Plato in weaving this motif through all the levels of the work is especially remarkable because the Greek language offers a not inconsiderable obstacle to the enterprise. In Greek, as in several other languages (but not in the modern Western languages), the word for play, *paidia,* is associated etymologically with the sphere of the child (*pais*). The meaning of the word, as we see in the *Laws,* can be extended beyond this sphere to embrace the sacred play, but the nuance of a game for children remains conscious even in Plato's own play, that is, in the creation of the *nomoi;* for in 712b the Stranger exhorts his companions to evoke the *nomoi* in their discourse "like old men acting like boys" (*kathaper paides presbytai*). Various types of adult competitive games and occupations for leisure time apparently developed into definite forms so early in Hellenic civilization that a comprehensive category for play or game could no longer absorb them all. This is true in particular of the fundamental phenomenon of Hellenic civilization, the *agon,* which has acquired a connotation of seriousness to such a degree that its character as a play is all but lost. It is also true, however, for the occupations of adult leisure at large. The terms for leisure, *schole,* and the occupation of leisure time, *diagoge,* lead to difficulties in various respects. On the one hand, leisure means freedom from work, and to that extent its occupation is not serious. On the other hand, it is not seemly for a freeman to waste his time; he is supposed to show himself worthy of his freedom by employing his leisure in dignified occupation. From the serious, formative study and occupation which fills leisure time, the *schole,* our meaning of *school* is derived. But then again, the association of nonseriousness with leisure is so strong that occupations which fill the leisure time, as for instance in Hellas the very important occupation with music, are in danger of acquiring a touch of this nonseriousness. Hence we find, for instance, Aristotle endeavoring to show that music is something more than mere *paidia,* with the association of childishness; that it is a serious occupation worthy of filling the *schole* of a freeman because it contributes to his *paideia*, his formation.[7]

In spite of such difficulties of meaning, Plato attacks the problem of play at its roots and lets the culture, the *paideia*, of his polis grow out of the play of children, the *paidia*. In the analysis of the child and his education, he employs the theory of the soul which appeared in the context of the Player and the Puppets. The sentiments, the apprehensions, and the *logismos* in their co-existence characterize the structure of the adult soul; in the soul of the child the first experiences are those of pleasure and pain, and in the medium of these sentiments the child has to acquire its first notions of virtue and vice; wisdom and true belief can be developed only in later life and their acquisition marks the growth of the soul to its adult stature. Between these two states extends *paideia*, formation or education. "By *paideia* I mean virtue [*arete*] in the form in which it is acquired by a child" (653b). If pleasures and preferences, if pains and dislikes are formed in children in such a manner that they will find them in harmony with insight once they have reached the age of insight, then we may call this harmony *virtue*; while the factor of training itself should be called *paideia*. Education or formation (in the sense of a right discipline of likes and dislikes) of pleasures and pains, however, is easily relaxed and diverted under the burdens of a human life. The gods, therefore, had compassion for the hardships of men and punctuated their lives with the rhythm of festivals; and as companions in their festivals they gave them the Muses, Apollo, and Dionysus, so that through the divine companions in the community the order of things might be restored (653c–d). After these preparatory remarks, the Stranger comes to the point: The festivals with their songs and dances can have the effect of restoring a *paideia* which is suffering from the hardships of life because these rituals are grafted on *paidia*, that is, on the play of the children. We know that the young of all creatures cannot be quiet in body or voice; they leap and skip, they frolic with abandon and utter cries of delight. With regard to these elementary movements and noises of play, however, there is a difference between animals and men in so far as animals have no perception of order and disorder in such playful actions, while to men the gods have given the perceptions of rhythm and melody. By divine guidance the elementary play, which is found also with animals,

---

[7] See on these problems *ibid.*, 47–50 and 256–61.

is led to choric form in the play of man. Hence *paideia* has to start from *paidia*, and it will do so most appropriately through the spirit of the Muses and Apollo (653e–654a).

The foregoing formulations concerning the relation between *paidia* and *paideia* contain the fundamental principle of Plato's philosophy of education. This problem of education had been discussed already in the *Philebus*, but now it is sharpened into its final form—*i.e.*, the potential discrepancy between the feelings of joy and sorrow (or: pleasure and pain) and the objective good. Likes and dislikes are no guidance to quality. We may take pleasure in what is bad; we may feel an aversion toward what is good. This conflict is of fundamental importance for the growth of culture because, on the one hand, what is bad in the arts, thought, and conduct seems to give more pleasure to the uneducated than what is good; while, on the other hand, it requires a long course of arduous training before a man can feel sincere and reliable pleasure in a work of art or thought that is good. Bad taste comes easy, good taste requires discipline and training. The cultural decay of Athens found its most revolting expression, as ours does, in the previously discussed "theatrocracy" (in our time we call it "commercialism"), that is, in the tyrannical imposition of the tastes of the illiterate rabble as the standard by which success or failure on the public scene is decided. This does not mean that the work of quality disappears—the very figure of Plato in the middle of the Athenian breakdown is proof to the contrary; it means that the tastes of the rabble dominate socially and that the consequent mass recognition given to trash makes the work of quality socially ineffective. The contemporary attempts at totalitarian control of the cultural sphere are no more than the systematic perfection of the ochlocratic tyranny which develops in the "free" societies in their late phase of disintegration.

Plato's insight into the nature and source of cultural disintegration has determined his concept of education. Children must be trained to associate pleasure with what is good. Such training, however, is impossible if the social environment stimulates children to associate pleasure with what is bad. Hence the environment must be institutionalized in such a manner that the "bad pleasures" will be repressed and the "good pleasures" will be favored in their development. Moreover, such institutionalization presupposes standards, as well as their cultivation and preservation. Hence the polis of the *nomoi* provides for public supervision of education from the earliest choric training for children; it provides, furthermore, for the cultivation of standards through the critical function which is accorded to the Dionysian spirit of the older men; and it provides, finally, for a ministry of education as the highest office in the polity. Education thus becomes "a drawing and leading of children" toward the standards which have been pronounced right by the voice of the law. The child's soul must never learn to feel pleasure contrary to the law; it must learn to take pleasure and pain in the same things as the old men who set the standards. The choric *paideia* of the polis has the purpose of forming the souls of the children so thoroughly that they become incapable of experiencing pleasure in what is bad. The songs of the community, the *odai,* thus become charms, *epodai,* for the souls (*epodai tais psychais*), producing the harmony of pleasure and the agathon. They are indeed spells of the soul, fitting it most seriously for the ritual play of life; but since children cannot bear too much seriousness, they must be spoken of as "plays" (*paidiai*) and practiced as such (659c–e).

From the play of children *paideia* leads us to the serious play of the adults, and further on to the play of the community under the *nomoi.* The pathos of the communal play breaks through magnificently on the occasion of the Stranger's reflections on theatrical performances in the polis. The presentation of burlesque and comic plays must be left entirely to aliens and slaves; no freeman of the polis must demean himself by appearing in a ludicrous performance in public. The problem lies differently with regard to serious plays, that is, with regard to tragedy. When tragedians approach the polis with requests for permission to perform and for a chorus of citizens, the magistrates who have to render the decision should answer in the following manner: "Respected strangers! We are ourselves the poets of a tragedy—and it is the best and noblest of all. In fact, our whole polity has been devised as the symbolic presentation [*mimesis*] of the best and noblest life, and we hold it to be indeed the truest of all tragedies. Thus you and we are both poets of the same style, rival artists and rival actors in the noblest of dramas which only a true *nomos* can achieve—or thus at least is our sentiment. So do not expect us easily to permit you to erect your stage on our public square and to let the melodious voices of your actors rise above our own in harangues to our women and children and to the

people at large on the same issues as ours and mostly to the contrary effect. For we would be raving mad, and so would be the whole polis, if this
request were granted to you before the magistrates have decided whether
your compositions are fit to be recited in public or not. Go then, you sons
and scions of the softer Muses, and show your songs to the magistrates for
comparison with our own; and if they are as good as ours or better then
we shall grant you a chorus; but if not, friends, then we cannot"
(817b–d).

7. The Creed

The play of the polis is serious because its measure is God. In the
polis of the *nomoi*, however, men are not the sons of God; they are his
puppets. On the lower existential level, which is presupposed for the
citizenry, the divine measure cannot be the living order of the soul; God
and man have drawn apart and the distance must now be bridged by
the symbols of a dogma. From the vision of the Agathon man has fallen
to the acceptance of a creed. Plato the savior has withdrawn; his polis
cannot be penetrated by the presence of his divine reality; Plato the
founder of a religion is faced by the problem of how the substance of his
mystical communication with God can be translated into a dogma with
obligatory force.

Plato was the first but not the last political philosopher to be faced
by this problem. The modern system which comes nearest to his treatment of it is the *Tractatus Politicus* of Spinoza. If we consider the position of the Maranic Jew who had broken with the orthodoxy, who tried
to regenerate a religious creed out of his personal mysticism, who associated with the leaders of the Dutch aristocracy, who was interested in
the construction of a politico-religious government that would secure
internal peace for Holland, we find a number of elements assembled
which make his position resemble in many respects the Platonic. Of
particular interest is his attempt to formulate a creed for the people. He
tried to solve his problem through the creation of a minimum set of
dogmas that would leave the utmost liberty to individuals who might
wish to embellish the bare structure with details of their own, while it
would be sufficient as a religious bond for the political community. Moreover, Spinoza the mystic needed the dogma for himself no more than
Plato, but created it deliberately, as did Plato, for the mass of men whose

spiritual strength is weak and who can absorb the spirit only in the form of dogmatic symbols.

Spinoza's solution, which we may briefly call the "minimum dogma," was also that of Plato. The Platonic minimum comprises three dogmas: (1) the belief that gods exist; (2) the belief that they take care of man; and (3) the belief that they cannot be appeased, or "bribed," by sacrifice and prayer (885b). The institutionalization of this minimum dogma will take the form of a *nomos*, consisting properly of the provision for the punishment of impiety itself (confinement or death) and of the prooemium. The provision for enforcement is no more than a sentence (907d–e); the prooemium fills the major part of Book X.

Since we have already dealt with the principal content of this prooemium in various contexts, we need do no more now than direct attention to the particularly marked "persuasive" character of this poem. Here, where the ultimate destiny of the soul is at stake, Plato attacks the agnosticism and the spiritual aberrations of the age for the last time and with bitterness in broad casuistry. Once more he surveys the decay of the old myth and the skepticism of the younger generation, the types of the *esprit fort,* the devastations that are worked in the minds of the semi-educated by the progress of natural science, the organization of sectarian communities and of private, esoteric creeds, and the extravagancies of hysterical women. It is a survey that could have been written today. His particular wrath is aroused by the type which combines agnosticism with rascality. The ordinary agnostic who holds forth against religious prejudices may otherwise be a respectable character and view with revulsion the possibility of committing a wrongful act. Much more dangerous is the agnostic who is at the same time possessed by incontinent ambition, by a taste for luxuries, who is subtle, intelligent, and persuasive; for this is the class of men who furnish the prophets and fanatics, the men who are half sincere and half insincere, the dictators, demagogues, and ambitious generals, the founders of new associations of initiates and scheming sophists (908d–e). In order to designate these evils of the age appropriately and comprehensively, Plato now uses the category of *nosos*, a disease of the soul (888b). The *nosos* of spiritual disorientation occurs at all times in individual cases; and most men are liable to be afflicted by it. Against the possibility of this affliction the epodic character of the prooemium, its character as a charm for the soul, should be the great preventive.

The polis of the *nomoi* cannot rely on persuasion alone for the preservation of its spiritual substance. When the disease breaks out in spite of all precautions, coercive measures have to be taken against the afflicted individual. The enforcement of the law against impiety is entrusted to a special magistracy, the Nocturnal Council. This Council consists of the ten oldest Guardians of the Laws, of distinguished priests, of the minister of education, of men who have been sent abroad in order to study foreign institutions, and of a number of younger members. These junior members, who are selected by the elders, serve chiefly as informants on the life and problems of the polis. The Nocturnal Council meets daily between dawn and sunrise, the time when the mind is least preoccupied with the affairs of the day. Its most important function is that of a spiritual court which passes judgment on offenses against the creed. Disbelievers in the gods will be confined for five years in a reformatory. In this seclusion they will receive visits only from members of the Nocturnal Council who will attempt to influence them and to awaken their spiritual insight. If the educational effort throughout five years has remained without effect, they will be sentenced to death.

The spiritual court completes the construction of the polis as a theocratic community. This institution and its function has aroused the serious misgivings of historians in the liberal era. We have touched on both aspects of this problem, that is, on the secularist prejudices of the liberals as well as on the theocratic limitations of Plato, in the earlier sections of our analysis of the *Laws*. We may, however, add the remark that in the light of contemporary experiences our insight into Plato's reasons for his construction has been sharpened. As long as one could believe in good faith that the alternative to spiritual control and enforcement of a creed should be the freedom of the spirit, the Nocturnal Council looked sinister indeed. Plato, however, could not consider this alternative, for the horizon of his experience was filled with the tyranny of the rabble and the murder of Socrates. Today our horizon is filled with similar experiences. We have good reasons to doubt that a project of the Platonic type would solve the problems of the age on the pragmatic level of history; but we have lost our illusion that "freedom" will lead without fail to a state of society that would deserve the name of order.

The code of the *nomoi* is substantially completed. But an enterprise has not reached its end with the mere performance of a task. We have not done all that we ought to do before providing a permanent guarantee for the preservation of our work. Like the thread of the Moirae, the weave of the *nomoi* must be made irreversible (960b–d). With this reflection Plato introduces the topic that fills the closing pages of the *Laws*, the topic of *soteria*, a word which oscillates in the context of these pages between the meanings of preservation and salvation. In the case of a polis, such preservation must extend beyond the bodily health and preservation of existence into the health of the soul. The souls have to remain attuned to the *nomoi,* and this state of attunement, the *eunomia* of the psyche, must be guaranteed by special provisions (690d).

The instrument for securing *eunomia* will be the Nocturnal Council. We have seen that the polis is composed of heterogeneous human material. The very function of the Nocturnal Council as a spiritual court presupposes that its members are men of a quality which enables them to be the judges and educators of the errant sheep. This higher quality will partly be due to their nature; however, it will also be due to a more rigorous education to which the future incumbents of this high office will have to submit. The citizens must not all be left on the same level of training (965e); those who are to become the guardians must achieve a more perfect mastery of *arete* in word and action than the mass of their fellow citizens (964d). Without such a provision, the polis would be a body without a head. The citizenry of the polis will be its trunk; the Nocturnal Council will be its head. The junior members of this Council, who serve as informants, will be the eyes in this head; the senior members will represent its directive understanding, the *nous* (964e–965a).

The more rigorous education for the guardians has the purpose of creating in them a critical consciousness of the reality of the spirit as well as the ability to express this reality and its problems in reasoned discourse. That state of a critical consciousness, while it is not the mystical vision of the Agathon, is considerably more than the acceptance of the dogma on the part of the ordinary citizen. The minimum dogma for the mass of the people, thus, is supplemented in the polis by a higher form of the creed for the spiritual and intellectual elite.

The consciousness on this higher level of the creed will extend to a definite number of doctrines. In the first place the guardians will have to be clear about the nature of *arete*. It will not do for them to know that there exist a number of virtues, courage, temperance, justice, and wisdom. They will also have to understand in what respect these many virtues are one. This oneness toward which the manifold of the four virtues converges is the *nous* which governs them all. The full understanding of the *nous hegemon* is the first requirement for the guardians (963a; 964b). The relation between *nous* and *nomos* is again subtly suggested by the hint that this requirement is ineluctable for the guardians of a *theia politeia,* of a divine constitution (965c). The same kind of critical understanding will have to extend to the other problems of the soul and its order, as for instance to the understanding of the *kalon* and the *agathon* (966a). Pre-eminently, however, what is required is an understanding of the things divine. For the ordinary citizen, conformity to tradition will be sufficient; to the office of a guardian, however, no man should be admitted who is not inspired and who has not labored at these problems (966c–d). The training in divinity will have to extend, in particular, to the understanding of two fundamental doctrines. The first is the doctrine that the soul is the oldest of all created things, that it is more ancient and divine than anything which derives its motion from a previous cause. The second is the doctrine that the order in the movements of the stars reveals the *nous* as their governing principle (966e). No mortal man can achieve true fear of God (*theosebeia*) who has not grasped these two doctrines of the soul as the deathless ruler of all bodies, and of the *nous* that is revealed in the stars (967d–e). In order to support their grasp of these doctrines the guardians must, finally, be well trained in the preparatory sciences; they must see the connection between the understanding of the cosmos and the problems of music; and they must be able to express themselves coherently on the connection between these various problems. A man who has not acquired critical understanding in addition to the ordinary virtues is not fit to be the ruler of a community; he will rather have his rôle as a subject (967e–968a).

This will be the last *nomos* to be added to the codification: The Nocturnal Council, consisting of members who are educated in this manner, shall function as the guardian of the polis for the purpose of its *soteria* (968a–b).

The wanderers have resolved upon the last *nomos*. But now the critical question arises: Who will educate the educators? At this point the conversation returns from the imaginative play to the reality of the situation. No statutory elaboration of this last *nomos* is possible. The foundation of the colony must take its origin in the existential communi-

cation between the founders and the first settlers; the founding commission will have to inject the spirit into the foundation through its
association with the future permanent guardians of the polis. And where
will the founding commission find its source of inspiration? In the present
conversation in which one member of this commission, the Cretan
Cleinias, participates. And the spiritual leadership in the existential community which has been established among the companions of this conversation lies undoubtedly with the Athenian Stranger—who now
declares that his exposition of his convictions concerning education and
breeding will be his share in the venture. The third companion, the
Lacedaemonian Megillus, completes the thought; he advises his Cretan
friend not to spare entreaties and inducements in order to gain the co-
operation of the Stranger in the foundation of the colony—for without
him they would have to give up their undertaking now that they have
understood its full meaning.

Plato died at the age of eighty-one. On the evening of his death he
had a Thracian girl play the flute to him. The girl could not find the beat
of the nomos. With a movement of his finger, Plato indicated to her
the Measure.

PART TWO

Aristotle

CHAPTER 7

Aristotle and Plato

1. The Evolution of Aristotelian Thought

Aristotle was born in 385 B.C., at Stagira, a little town on the Aegean coast east of the Chalcidice. As a youth of seventeen, in 367, he entered the Academy and remained a member of the school until the death of Plato in 348. After Plato's death he left Athens for Asia Minor. For three years he taught at Assos, and then for another two years at Mytilene, on Lesbos. In 343 he was called to the court of Pella as tutor to the young Alexander. When Philip died and Alexander succeeded in the kingship, Aristotle returned to Athens in 335 and founded his own school, the Lyceum. He taught until 323 when the death of Alexander caused a revival of Athenian nationalism, making it advisable for Aristotle to leave the city. He moved to Chalcis, on Euboea, and there he died after a few months, in 322.[1]

The dates will aid in understanding the development of Aristotle's thought. When he entered the Academy in 367 the school had been going for almost twenty years; Socrates had been dead for thirty years; and Plato was past sixty. The Socratic phase of Plato's work, including the *Republic*, had become a body of literature to be studied by the younger generation; and Plato himself was engaged in the work that was to result in the series of dialogues from *Theaetetus* to *Philebus*, as well as in the elaboration of his late theology in the *Timaeus*, *Critias*,

[1] Fundamental for the understanding of Aristotle is Werner Jaeger, *Aristotle*, (2d ed., Oxford, 1948). Indispensable is still Ulrich von Wilamowitz-Moellendorf, *Aristoteles und Athen*, 2 vols. (Berlin, 1893), and Eduard Zeller, *Die Philosophie der Griechen* II/2 (Leipzig, 1923). On the Aristotelian science of politics cf. the Introductions and Prefatory Essays in W. L. Newman, *The Politics of Aristotle*, 4 vols. (Oxford, 1887–1902); the early work of Sir Ernest Barker, *The Political Thought of Plato and Aristotle* (London, 1906), as well as the Introduction and Notes to his *Politics of Aristotle* (Oxford, 1946); Hans Kelsen, "The Philosophy of Aristotle and the Hellenic-Macedonian Policy" (*Ethics*, 48, 1937/38, pp. 21–64); furthermore the sections on Aristotle in Charles H. McIlwain, *The Growth of Political Thought in the West* (New York, 1932); George H. Sabine, *A History of Political Theory* (2d ed., New York, 1947); and Alfred Verdross-Drossberg, *Grundlinien der Antiken Rechts—und Staatsphilosophie* (2d ed., Vienna, 1948).

and *Laws*. Entering the Academy at this critical juncture, the young Aristotle was formed both by the Socratic tradition and by the new forces which tended to decompose it into its religious and intellectual components.

Of the early work of Aristotle only fragments are preserved. They were dialogues and their titles indicate that the young philosopher was conscientiously working through the Socratic problems. The *Eudemus or On the Soul* corresponds to the Platonic *Phaedo*, the *Gryllus or On Rhetoric* to the *Gorgias*, the *On Justice* to the *Republic*, and the *Sophist, Statesman, Symposion,* and *Menexenus* to the Platonic dialogues of the same title. The only prose work, the *Protrepticus*, was a discourse on the philosophical life addressed to Themison, a prince of Cyprus. The dialogue *On Philosophy* probably was written shortly after Plato's death, for it contained a criticism of Plato's theory of the Idea that parallels the criticism in *Metaphysics I*. The fragments are numerous enough to make it certain that the early works were not only formally related to the Socratic dialogues of Plato, but that Aristotle had absorbed and made his own the Platonic conception of philosophy as a movement of the soul. For the young Plato, as we know, philosophy consisted of an ordering of the soul by the three forces of Thanatos, Eros, and Dike; and, corresponding to the three forces, philosophy was the practice of dying, the erotic reaching out of the soul toward the Agathon, and the right ordering of the soul through participation in the Idea. The same conception of philosophy as a mode of life, in the most literal sense of true life in contrast with the death of passions, pervaded Aristotle's early, exoteric work. It is a continuation of Platonic-Socratic philosophizing, and as such it has exerted its influence throughout the Hellenistic period and beyond it. The subject matter of the *Protrepticus* was cast into dialogue form by Cicero in his *Hortensius;* and through the Ciceronian mediation it deeply impressed St. Augustine: "This book changed my affection, and it turned my prayers toward Thee, O Lord, and it changed my purposes and desires. . . . With an incredible heat of my heart I yearned for the immortality of wisdom; and I began to rouse myself that I might return to Thee. . . . And not its fine speech did persuade me, but what it spoke. . . . I was stirred up, enkindled and inflamed by the book; and that only dampened somewhat my burning zeal that the name of Christ was not in it." [2]

[2] Augustine, *Confessions*, III, 4.

Philosophy as a mode of life in the Platonic-Socratic sense had formed the soul of Aristotle; and the imprint was indelible. The notion that a great break separates Aristotelian from Platonic philosophy has various sources. With some of them we have to deal later in more detail. For the present let us only mention that our picture of Aristotelian philosophy, since the early work is almost completely lost, was mainly determined by the esoteric schoolwork of the later years.[3] On the other side of the imaginary gulf between the two thinkers, we were equally handicapped until recently because we had no clear understanding of the great development of the late Plato. If one compares the Platonic *Republic* and the Aristotelian *Metaphysics,* ignoring the road which leads from the one to the other, the two works seem indeed to represent two entirely different approaches to the problem of philosophy—especially if one overlooks such sections as *Metaphysics* XII where the transitions can still be sensed by the more imaginative reader. And, finally, in his esoteric work Aristotle was very explicit in his criticism of Platonic theories, and much less explicit in his recognition of what he took over and developed. In *Politics* II, for instance, the reader will find a well reasoned rejection of certain parts of the *Republic;* in the rest of the work he will hardly be aware to what extent Aristotle uses the *Statesman,* the *Philebus,* and the *Laws* in the development of his own political theory unless he has the Platonic dialogues well in mind.

What actually happened is not so difficult to understand if we remember the critical date of Aristotle's entrance into the Academy. He did not enter only into the way of life of the philosopher; he also entered into the debate on its results. The way of life had produced doctrinal symbols for its expression, such as the immortality of the soul, the right order of the soul, the true being of the Idea, and the order of reality through *methexis,* through participation in the Idea. An interpretation of God, man, and the world had been developed; and the terms of this interpretation could be submitted to critical inquiry under several aspects. One could examine the method which had led to the construction of the terms, one could examine their systematic consistency, one could test their value as instruments of empirical science, and one could examine them in the light of new discoveries in mathematics and astronomy and the increasing knowledge of Babylonian cosmology. The Academy was not an institution for the transmission of textbook knowledge; at its

[3] The reconstruction of Aristotle's development is the work of Werner Jaeger.

core it was a group of highly active scholars concerned with the development of problems. For twenty years Aristotle was a member of this group; and while the answers of his late work differed widely from those of Plato and of his co-disciples Speusippus and Xenocrates, they were answers to problems of the Platonic circle.

Let us take as an example one aspect of the problem of the Idea. In the Platonic conception the Idea was an *eidos,* a paradigmatic form in separate, transcendental existence. The assumption of forms in separate existence raised the question how the separate forms could be the forms of empirical reality. The Platonic answer that the flux of becoming has being in so far as it participates in the Idea, or in so far as the Idea is embodied in it, only led to further questions concerning the meaning of participation. Aristotle abolished these problems by abolishing the assumption of separate forms as an unnecessary duplication. The form is perceived as such in reality through a function of the mind, through *noesis.* There is no essential being except the essences which we discern as such in the stream of reality; and they do not enter becoming from a transcendental realm of being, but essence begets essence in the infinite, uncreated stream of reality itself. At one stroke we are rid of the realm of paradigmatic ideas, of speculations on the possibility that ideas are numbers of one kind or another, of *methexis,* of embodiment, of the creation of the world, of the demiurge, and so forth. And as far as the history of philosophy on the doxographic level is concerned, we now have a clear opposition between Platonic transcendentalism and idealism on the one side, and Aristotelian immanentism and realism on the other side. Plato and Aristotle have developed two entirely different metaphysical systems.

In fact, neither Plato nor Aristotle have developed systems; they were far too much engrossed with the discovery of new problems. What happened on the level of philosophizing must rather be described as a shift of attention, accompanied by a far-reaching differentiation of problems. Plato and Aristotle were in agreement on the presence of form in empirical reality. By withdrawing attention from the origin of realized form in a realm of separate forms, the formal structure of reality itself came into clearer view. A vast field of new problems opened, such as the problems of substance and accidence, of essence as the object of definition, of act and potentiality, of matter and entelechy, as well as of the logical problems that were collected in the *Organon.* When Aristotle's attention was turned in this direction, when his inquiry concerned immanent form and the immense ramifications of its problems, the Platonic assumption of transcendental form might indeed appear as an unnecessary, and perhaps unverifiable, duplication of that immanent form that was given with such certainty in the immediate experience of the soul. Nevertheless, we must be aware that Aristotle's criticism of the Idea is not a criticism of Plato's thought itself. Plato had not "duplicated" immanent form; he had discovered transcendental form as a separate substance when his experiential attention had been turned in a direction opposite to the Aristotelian. Aristotle's exploration of the field of immanent form is in itself not an argument against transcendental form. Hence the question arises: What has become of the problems that had been seen by Plato when the eye of his soul was turned toward the Agathon? Has Aristotle abandoned them?

The answer cannot be simple. The Platonic realm of changeless, eternal being was not a wanton assumption; it was experienced as a reality in the erotic fascination of the soul by the Agathon as well as in its cathartic effects. The realm of ideas was one of the symbols which expressed the philosopher's experience of transcendence. And Aristotle was not only aware of this origin but was able to participate in these experiences. One of the finest formulations of the problem of faith occurs in a fragment of his work *On Prayer*, on occasion of the mystery-religions: "Those who are being initiated are not required to grasp anything with the understanding [*mathein*], but to have a certain inner experience [or passion, *pathein*], and so to be put into a particular frame of mind, presuming that they are capable of the frame of mind in the first place." [4] The *cognitio Dei* through faith is not a cognitive act in which an object is given, but a cognitive, spiritual passion of the soul. In the passion of faith the ground of being is experienced, and that means the ground of all being, including immanent form. Hence, it is legitimate to symbolize the ground of being through immaterial forms, like the Platonic Idea. Being can be experienced either in its world-immanent articulation or through the *pathein* of the soul in openness toward its ground; and for expressing the relation between transcendental and immanent being we have no other means than the analogical use of terms derived from our experiences of immanent being. If in his interpretation of being a philosopher wants to account for the whole structure

[4] Jaeger, *Aristotle,* 160.

of being—that is, for immanent as well as transcendental being—he has not much choice. In one form or another, he must do what Aristotle accuses Plato of doing, that is, he must "duplicate" being. Hence, the Aristotelian criticism of the Idea is pointless as far as the question of duplication is concerned. It is not pointless, however, where it attacks the speculative use which Plato made of transcendental being in his interpretation of immanent being. The relation between transcendental and immanent being, as we just indicated, can be symbolized only analogically. Neither Plato nor Aristotle quite penetrated this problem of metaphysical speculation; and an approximately satisfactory formula was only found in the Thomistic *analogia entis*. Plato, indeed, hypostatized transcendental being into a datum as if it were given in world-immanent experience; and he treated absolute being as a genus of which the varieties of immanent being are species. Aristotle rightly criticized this part of Platonic speculation; and in eliminating this confusion he penetrated to the clearness of his own ontology. For this magnificent achievement, however, he paid the great price of eliminating the problem of transcendental form along with its speculative misuse.

Aristotle rejected the ideas as separate existences, but neither did he repudiate the experiences in which the notion of a realm of ideas originated nor did he abandon the order of being that had become visible through the experiences of the philosophers ever since Heraclitus, Parmenides, and Xenophanes. The consequence is a curious transformation of the experience of transcendence which can perhaps be described as an intellectual thinning-out. The fullness of experience which Plato expressed in the richness of his myth is in Aristotle reduced to the conception of God as the prime mover, as the *noesis noeseos,* the "thinking on thinking." The Eros toward the Agathon correspondingly is reduced to the *agapesis,* the delight in cognitive action for its own sake. Moreover, no longer is the soul as a whole immortal but only that part in it which Aristotle calls active intellect; the passive intellect, including memory, perishes. And, finally, the mystical *via negativa* by which the soul ascends to the vision of the Idea in the *Symposium* is thinned out to the rise toward the dianoetic virtues and the *bios theoretikos.*[5]

I have kept the analysis of the issue as close as possible to the form

---

[5] For the conception of the prime mover as the *noesis noeseos* see *Metaphysics* XII, 9, 1074b; for the *agapesis* see *Metaphysics* I, 980a; for the conception of the soul and its imperishable part see *De Anima* III, 5; for the *bios theoretikos* see *Politics* VII, 2, 1324a.

in which it emerges from the Aristotelian text. That was necessary in order to clarify the origin of certain post-Platonic problems of philosophizing, but it has the disadvantage that a derailment which, though present in Aristotle, was still restrained by his genius does not come fully into view either in its nature or its consequences. And since the derailment has become one of the principal modes of philosophizing after Plato —so predominant indeed that the history of philosophy is in the largest part the history of its derailment—a note of explanation will be indicated. I am speaking of the transformation of symbols developed for the purpose of articulating the philosopher's experiences into topics of speculation. The phenomenon as such does not occur, in the wake of Plato, for the first time. As a matter of fact, the study of the sophists in *Order and History* II, Ch. 11, was an analysis of the transformation of the Parmenidean Being into a topic of immanentist speculation. But the Platonic work had the purpose of reversing the derailment, and of reestablishing the philosopher's experience of the order of being as well as the symbolism for its articulation, in opposition to the sophists; and Plato went even so far as to develop the pairs of concepts that we have studied in the present volume, Ch. 3, 3, 1, for the purpose of averting the relapse into sophistic philodoxy. If the relapse occurred nevertheless in the generation following Plato, and precisely in the work of the disciples whom he himself had trained in the Academy, a reason suggests itself which is rooted in the structure of philosophizing itself and cannot be explained by the label of "sophistry"—for neither Aristotle nor Speusippos were sophists, and we hesitated to apply the label to thinkers of the rank of Anaxagoras and Democritus, though they were engaged in the topical transformation of Parmenides' Being.

Not much is to be said about the problem in principle because it is simplicity itself. The leap in being differentiates world-transcendent Being as the source of all being, and correspondingly attaches to the "world" the character of immanence. Since experiences of transcendence can be articulated only by means of language which has its original function in the world of sense experience, the symbols, both concepts and propositions, which refer to the *terminus ad quem* of an experience of transcendence must be understood analogically, whether they be symbols of the myth, of revelation, or of philosophy. The derailment occurs when the symbols are torn out of their experiential context and treated as if they were concepts referring to a datum of sense experience. The

structure of the fallacy is simple indeed; one can only say to a presump-
tive philosopher: Don't do it! If the error is committed nevertheless, even
by an Aristotle, one will look for its source not in a failing of the intellect
but in a passionate will to focus attention so thoroughly on a particular
problem that the wider range of the order of being is lost from sight.
The philosopher of history, when he encounters a derailment of this type,
will therefore be less interested in the fascinating problems in which the
respective thinker gets himself involved (for on the level of philosophy
they are no problems) than in the passionate experiences which motivated the mistake. Since problems of this nature will occupy us at length
in the subsequent volumes of this study, it will be sufficient for the present to adumbrate some of the world-historic conflicts which are transacted in the form of pseudo-philosophical debates. On one of them we
have touched in the Aristotelian misgivings about the Platonic separate
ideas. According to the philosopher's attention to the transcendent source
of order, or to the order in immanent being, or to the order as reflected
in science, the essences can be found in separate existence, or embedded
in reality, or in the concepts of science. Correspondingly one can develop "philosophies" which place the essence *ante rem, in re,* or *post rem;*
and the respective idealists, realists, and nominalists can criticize one
another's "position" to shreds *ad infinitum.* A rich source of conflicts
then opened with the introduction of philosophical categories into Christian theology. When the categories of nature and person were applied
to the mystery of Incarnation, the Christological debate raged through
centuries before an adequate philosophical formulation could be found
in the definition of Chalcedon in 451. When the categories of form and
substance were applied to the mystery of the Eucharist, the new problem of transcendental chemistry exploded in the struggle about trans-
substantiation between Catholics and Protestants. When the *scientia Dei,*
which includes God's foreknowledge of man's eternal destiny, was im-
manentized into man's foreknowledge of his destiny, the foundation was
laid for separate churches of the elect down to the contemporary degeneration into civic clubs for socially compatible families. When the Christian idea of supernatural perfection through Grace in death was imma-
nentized to become the idea of perfection of mankind in history through
individual and collective human action, the foundation was laid for the
mass creeds of modern Gnosis.

Though conflicts of this type can occur only after philosophy as a symbolic form has come into existence, and though the debates are conducted by means of philosophical categories, it would be manifestly senseless to enter into the debate with the intention of exploring the validity of the argument. If a study of order and history would assume the form of a history of philosophy, or even more specifically of a history of political philosophy, merely because after the creation of philosophy the Western debate about order is conducted in philosophical form, it would itself derail in following the derailments of philosophy. The "philosophies" of order must not be taken at their face value, but must be critically examined under the aspect whether the symbols used have retained their original meaning of symbols which express the experience of the transcendent source of order, or whether they are used as speculative *topoi* for purposes widely differing from the Platonic love of the divine Measure.

2. *The Literary Structure of the* Politics

The preceding reflections will guide us in fixing our position with regard to the problems presented by the literary structure of Aristotle's esoteric works. The early works, written for publication, are lost. The principal extant sources for a study of the Aristotelian political science are his *Politics* and *Nicomachean Ethics*. These works do not have the form of systematic treatises on the subject matter indicated by the titles, but are collections of *logoi*, of discourses or inquiries, to be used as the basis for oral teaching. While the various *logoi* of the collections cannot be dated exactly, we know that they belong to different periods of Aristotle's life. Some may go back (at least in their conception) to the time when he was still a member of the Academy, others doubtless belong to his last years. The *logoi*, thus, are distributed over a time of more than thirty years, and their content reflects the previously discussed shift of Aristotle's philosophical attention. To the earlier philosophical motivation belong the *logoi* in which the philosopher's experience of transcendence determines the choice of problems; to the later period belong the sections in which the structure of immanent form becomes the predominant interest.

Nevertheless, caution is necessary. The date of the motivation is no sure guide to the chronology of the various parts of the work. While we can be sure that the *logoi* which rest on a broad basis of empirical materials belong to the later period (such as *Politics* IV, V, and VI), we cannot always ascribe the other *logoi* with certainty to an earlier period. The intensification of concern about immanent form is an *addition* to the Aristotelian range; it does not *supersede* the earlier philosophical motivation. We must always be aware of the possibility that a *logos* which by the nature of its problems belongs to the earlier class—and probably in its conception goes back to the early period—has been reworked in later years without showing traces of the shift of interest. Aristotle, as we indicated, was not interested in systematic unification of his written thought; he was interested in the completeness of his problems. When his various inquiries led to conflicting results, he simply let the results clash; and the conflicting views were peaceably recorded side by side. The most famous instance of such a clash occurs in *Metaphysics* XII where the discourse developing the monotheistic conception of God as the prime mover and the *noeseos noesis* is interrupted by another discourse, the present Chapter VIII. In this later discourse, differing in style and elaboration from the rest of the book, Aristotle developed the conception of forty-seven divine prime movers, each governing one of the irreducible motions according to the new astronomy of Eudoxus. On the doctrinal level we thus find in the same book an earlier monotheistic and a later polytheistic theology; and Aristotle shows no intention either of abandoning the earlier view for the later one, or of subordinating both views to a higher systematic construction.

Aristotle is not a systematic thinker in the sense that he attempted to build a philosophical edifice free of contradictions. In fact, the word *systema* does not occur in his works as a technical term. The absence of systematic consciousness is probably the principal reason why the esoteric writings of Aristotle had such little influence even in his own school in the centuries following his death; when his living word had ceased to animate his lecture notes, apparently they became a dead letter. The effectiveness of the esoteric Aristotle does not begin before the publication of his work by the eleventh scholarch of the Peripatetics, Andronicus, in the first century B.C. With the publication begins the commentatorial work in the school, culminating in the commentaries by Alexander of Aphrodisias, toward the end of the second century of our era. From Alexander onward, the study of Aristotle became the basis of systematic philosophising in all schools, and the tradition went in continuity through the Arabs into Western scholasticism. The conception of the systematic Aristotle grew in the commentatorial tradition, and it has remained a serious obstacle to a critical understanding of Aristotle's work to this day—whether the prejudice assumes the form of an insistence that the works of Aristotle must have a systematic order at all cost, or whether it assumes the form of the belief in the late "real" Aristotle who at last disentangled himself from his dependence on Plato.

In the case of the *Politics,* which is our present concern, the situation is further complicated through anachronistic interpretations and translations of Aristotelian terms. The *Politics* consists of at least three clearly distinguishable literary strata. Book II surveys and criticizes the views of predecessors on the topic of the best polis; it obviously is the introductory book of an early study on this subject. Books III, VII, and VIII contain this study of the best polis itself. Between the present Books III and VII is inserted an extensive study of the relatively best constitutions that can be realized under given conditions, as well as on the causes of revolutions and the means of avoiding them. Some, however, are inclined to consider Books IV and VI on the relatively best constitutions as belonging together, and Book V on the revolutions as a further insertion into an original *logos* comprising IV and VI. Anyway, there is agreement that IV to VI are a later study. The present Book I, finally, is probably the latest part, prefixed to the other books at the time when the whole series of *logoi* was united into its present form.

The ordinary debate about the "systematic" order of the books is complicated in this case, as we have indicated, by dubious translations. The "best polis" which is the subject matter of III, VII, and VIII is rendered in our modern translations as the "ideal state." The translation is anachronistic with regard to both of the terms. Aristotle deals not with the "state" but with the "polis"; and what we would call a state, that is, a politically organized people on its territory, is expressly excluded from the study. Moreover, Aristotle deals with "ideals" no more than Plato does. The word does not occur in Greek; and its meaning does not fully crystallize before the sixteenth century A.D. The "best" has more than one meaning in the Aristotelian context. It can mean, among other things, "the strongest," "the healthiest," "the most stable," "the most suitable as an environment for the realization of the comtemplative life," "the one that will most adequately keep in check the men who are not capable of realizing the good life," and (under the aspect of historical dynamics) "the flowering of the polis," or "the high point in the realization of the essence of the polis." None of these

meanings has anything to do with an "ideal." The "best" is the hypothet-
ical maximum in a scale of realizations; and not in one scale only, but in a
plurality of scales. The seeker of "ideals" will be dismayed when he finds
that Aristotle has at least three "ideals" in his *Politics*: (1) the monarchy
of the virtuous man, (2) the aristocracy of a small group of men who
combine the virtues of rulership and civic obedience, and (3) the middle-class polity. The mistranslation seriously affects an understanding of
the work. Historians speculate on an evolution of Aristotle from his
"idealistic" youth to his "realistic" maturity; the "realism" of maturity
is supposed to represent the "real" Aristotle who has overcome his early
"idealism"; "idealism" and "realism" are considered to be different
"systematic" phases in chronological succession; the disordered state of
the *Politics* is supposed to be convertible into order by "restoring" the
original sequence of the books (so that we arrive at the sequence I,
II, III, VII, VIII, IV, VI, V); and so forth.

    This whole complex of conjecture seems to us inadmissible. To be
sure, the two phases in chronological succession can be distinguished.
But they do not reveal a "systematic" evolution from "idealism" to
"realism." The earlier *logoi* are nourished from the experience of the
mystic-philosophers. Once the Platonic-Socratic order of the soul, and
together with it the order of the polis, is created and articulated, the result can be transmitted as doctrine. We now know what is "best," and
this knowledge can assume the form of "criteria" or "standards," the Aristotelian *horoi*. The standards are derived from the Platonic through the
process of intellectualization that we described in the preceding section.
Aristotle knows that the *bios theoretikos* is the "best" and that, consequently, the polis is "best" in which the happiness of the *bios theoretikos* can be realized. To the eudaimonia of man corresponds the *polis
eudaimon* (1323b30). Through the standards Aristotelian politics is
linked with the Platonic; and this link is never broken. Nevertheless, the
Platonic problems have been modified. For Plato, form was transcendental and his problem was the incarnation of the Idea in historical
reality through the psyche of the philosopher and his circle. For Aristotle, form is immanent to reality; the essence of the polis is immanent
to reality in the same manner as the essence of an animal or vegetable.
Political existence, however, is distinguished from animal or vegetable
existence in so far as rational human action is a factor in actualizing the
essence of the polis. A polis does not just grow; within the limits set by

material and human conditions, man can contribute to a more or less perfect realization. Hence, the knowledge of standards will be an aid for political practice; and a political science (*architektonike* or *episteme politike*, N.E., 1094a 27ff.) can be developed as a body of practical knowledge for the "lawgiver" (*nomothetes*). Aristotle becomes the teacher of lawgivers—a function that was adumbrated by the Athenian Stranger in the *Laws*. There is a continuity of evolution from Plato, the founder of the good polis, through the Athenian Stranger, who transmits as much of his mystical knowledge as is bearable to the founders of a colony, to Aristotle, who formulates standards and devises means for their maximum realization under varying material conditions. The decisive point is that this development was completed by the time Aristotle wrote the earliest parts of the *Politics*. Even in the early *logoi* the polis is a world-immanent entity and political science is the art of maximal actualization of its essence. The later *logoi* do not break with the earlier position; they only add immensely to the survey of typical material situations under which the lawgiver has to operate, as well as of the devices for approximating an actualization of essence under unpropitious circumstances.

The several discourses collected in the *Politics* are all on the same "systematic" level. It would be futile to extract a new meaning from them by rearranging their sequence, or by paying too much attention to the time at which they were written. The order in which they are extant was determined by Aristotle himself, and he gave his reasons for the order in the closing paragraph of *Nicomachean Ethics*: "First, we shall try to review what has been well said by our predecessors who investigated the subject. Then, on the basis of our collection of constitutions, we shall consider what is preservative and what destructive of poleis as well as of their different constitutions, and what are the causes that some of them are well governed and others not. Having studied these questions, we shall be better able to understand what is the best constitution, and how each must be ordered, and what laws and customs it needs." This plan roughly describes the actual arrangement of Books II through VIII of *Politics*. The acceptance of the Aristotelian order, of course, does not abolish the numerous conflicts between the various parts of the work. An interpretation of the *Politics* cannot have the task of finding a closed theoretical system in the text itself. The fact that various theoretical intentions remain unreconciled must be recognized. Nevertheless, the discourses as they are preserved are all written by Aristotle and originate in the unity of his philosophizing mind. Hence, it will be legitimate to make an attempt at extrapolating the doctrinal content of the *Politics* and to explore the possibility of finding the center of thought that lies beyond the terse and sometimes fragmentary text.

3. *The Consciousness of Epoch*

The central experience of Platonic politics was the consciousness of epoch. The age of the people's myth was drawing to its end, and the new age of the philosophers, of the Sons of Zeus, was commencing with Socrates and Plato. The experience found its expression in the myths of the *Gorgias*, the *Republic*, and the *Phaedrus*, of the *Statesman*, the *Timaeus*, and the *Critias*; and it reached the doctrinal level of a theory of the historical cycle in the *Laws*. This consciousness of epoch is also present in Aristotle, but the experience has undergone an important modification. Plato experienced himself as the inaugurator and royal ruler of the new age; his evolution could be traced from the suspense of the *Republic*, apprehending that the spiritual foundation would overflow into historical reality and transform Hellas, to the *Laws*, where the expectation of the new realm was transfigured into the two cosmic symbols of the polis that was the subject matter of the work and of the form of the work itself. In Aristotle the experience has become objectified: He knows *about* the epoch and he knows that it is marked by Plato. The epoch has become an historical fact and its nature can now be discerned as an incision in spiritual history. With Plato as seen by Aristotle begins, not a new age of the regenerated polis (for the political events showed all too clearly that the polis was doomed), but a new spiritual aeon of the world. Plato's judgment on his age is confirmed, but his work is not invalidated by his failure to link spirit with power in pragmatic politics. The transfer of authority which Plato claimed in the *Gorgias* has become historical reality. The polis may decline, sink to insignificance and disappear, but the world will go on in a movement of which the meaning is determined by Plato.

In the epochal consciousness of Aristotle, Hellas has achieved spiritual rank on the world scene through Plato. As a spiritual power it is now the equal to the older oriental civilizations. A *rapprochement* of Hellas and the Orient has taken place, preceding in time the actual expansion of Hellenic power through Alexander and preparing the amalgamation of the Hellenistic period. In the dialogue *On Philosophy*, written shortly after Plato's death, Aristotle mentions that Zoroaster lived six thousand years before the death of Plato. The figure does not intend to give historically exact information; it, rather, wants to establish a relation between Zoroaster and Plato as symbolic figures in the cosmic drama. According to the Iranian myth of the great cycle, Ormuzd and Ahriman each rule the world for three thousand years; their alternative rules are followed by aeons of struggle between the two forces of good and evil, ending in the victory of the good principle; the whole cycle has a duration of nine thousand, or, in another variant of the myth, of twelve thousand years. The fragmentary sources do not reveal what precise function Aristotle would have assigned to Zoroaster or Plato in the world drama; all we know is that obviously he considered them important figures in the struggle for the victory of the Good in the world and that he accepted the Iranian idea of epochs in this struggle, spaced by multiples of three thousand years.[6]

While we have no precise knowledge of the rôle assigned to Plato in the cosmic drama, the literary environment furnishes at least some indications. A precious document for Aristotle's view of Plato as a spiritual guide is his *Altar Elegy* in which he speaks of his master as

> The man whom it is not lawful for bad men even to praise.
> Who alone or first of mortals clearly revealed
> By his own life and by the methods of his words,
> How a man becomes good and happy at the same time.
> Now no one can ever attain to these things again.

The terse lines define the identity of goodness and happiness as the core of the Platonic gospel; and the last line expresses Aristotle's feeling of the difference of rank between Plato and ordinary men.[7] Moreover, we know that the circle of the Academy was aware of an inner affinity between the Platonic dualistic metaphysics and Iranian eschatology even in Plato's lifetime. And it is quite possible that Plato himself was inclined, in his later years, to approach his own theology to Iranian symbols. In the *Laws* (896e) we find the famous passage:

> *Ath.* And as the soul orders and inhabits all things that move, however moving, must we not say that she also orders the heavens?

[6] On the ascription of the fragments and their meaning cf. Jaeger, *Aristotle*, 131ff.
[7] For ascription and translation of the *Altar Elegy* cf. *ibid.*, 106ff.

Cle. Of course.

Ath. One soul or more? More than one—I will answer for you; at any rate, we must not suppose that there are less than two —one the author of good, and the other of evil.

Whether this passage means that Plato really wished to adopt the symbol of the two world souls as the adequate expression of his own religiousness must remain doubtful; the formulation is inconclusive; but it certainly shows that he toyed with the idea.

The general tendency in the Platonic circle to increase the prestige of Platonism through association with Iranian ideas is attested by *Alcibiades I*. In this pseudo-Platonic dialogue Socrates describes the education of Persian royal princes. At the age of fourteen the young prince is handed over to four tutors. The four educators are chosen from the most excellent among the Persians. One of them is the wisest, the second the most just, the third the most temperate, and the fourth the most valiant. The first, the wisest, instructs his pupil in the wisdom of Zoroaster, that is, in the worship of the gods, and he teaches him the duties of his royal office; the most just teaches him to speak the truth; the most temperate teaches him to overcome his passions and to rule himself, so that he will be a lord and not a slave; and the fourth tutor trains him to be bold and fearless (*Alcibiades I*, 121–122). From the context it is clear that Persia is held up as a model civilization, materially and culturally, where ideas are socially realized which in Hellas have only reached the stage of aspiration and intellectual articulation. And in particular the Platonic wisdom is in Persia an old tradition, practiced in the education of the prince.[8]

In Plato, the consciousness of epoch was an immediate experience and expressed itself in the creation of the myth. For the younger generation the epoch had come into objective view and could be discussed as a subject matter. Moreover, through the enlargement of the horizon and the absorption of Eastern knowledge, the problem of the epoch dissociated itself from the political crisis of Hellas. The intimate con-

[8] On the influx of Eastern knowledge in the Academy cf. *ibid.*, 131ff. In view of the scantiness of direct sources it may be worthwhile to recall that the idea of Persia as the realm of a philosopher-king in the Platonic sense outlasted the centuries. When Justinian closed the Pagan schools at Athens in 529 A.D., a number of the scholars emigrated to Persia in the expectation of finding a more congenial environment in the realm of the philosopher-king. Most of them returned after having tasted the reality. On a possible connection of this emigration with the later flowering of a Neoplatonic school in Baghdad see Walter Scott, *Hermetica* (Oxford, 1924), I, 103f.

nection between the myth of historical cycles and the concrete corruption of Athenian democracy that we found in Plato, gave way to abstract speculation on historical cycles in general. In the *Problemata* (XVII, 3) Aristotle reflects on the formal aspects of the problem of cycles in a manner that is curiously detached, compared with the passionate sorrow of Plato about the fate of his polis. Aristotle inquires into the meaning of the terms "prior" and "posterior." Should we really say that the generation of the Trojan War lived prior to us and that those who lived earlier were prior to Troy, and so on *ad infinitum*? As always, Aristotle rejects the idea of an indefinite regression. The universe has a beginning, a middle, and an end. When we are near the end, we are actually nearing the beginning of the next period. The later we are, the nearer we are to the beginning; and, thus, we may be "prior" to Troy, if Troy lies at the beginning of the period that we are approaching. The process of genesis and disintegration, which is characteristic of perishable things, may be subordinate to a law of eternal recurrence, similar to the eternal circular motion of celestial bodies. It would be foolish to assume that the same individuals recur in numerical identity; but the theory that the species as a whole has a course with recurrent structure, would be acceptable. If we assume human life to be a circle of the species, then the problem of "prior" and "posterior" would disappear, for a circle has neither beginning nor end.

The formalization of the problem is driven a bit far in this passage. The symbol of the circle is taken in its strict geometrical sense so that indeed "we should not be 'prior' to those who lived in the time of Troy nor they 'prior' to us by being nearer to the beginning." Even the recurrence of the cycle of the species, however, would still make it possible to speak of earlier and later with meaning, if the cycle had in itself an intelligible structure of growth, flowering, and decay. And, as we shall see presently, the abstract speculation on the cycle must be qualified in the light of other pronouncements of Aristotle on the problem. Plato, after all, is not just any event in a cycle but marks a structural high point. Nevertheless, the problem of the cycle has now found its abstract formulation; and this formulation has become historically effective and permeates Western speculation in continuity, through Arabic mediation, into the high Middle Ages and into our present. In particular we should note that through the abstract formulation the problem was dissociated from a theory of catastrophes (though in other Aristotelian contexts the catastrophes reappear), and that the cycle was understood as a structural pattern in time that may recur in the life of the human species.

Plato marks an epoch in the historical cycle. The objectivation had a further consequence, profoundly affecting Aristotelian thought on political matters. Plato was engrossed in the crisis of the polis; he witnessed the decay of Athens; and, more than that, he passed the death sentence on Athens in the *Gorgias*. A world was dying. For the generation of Aristotle the daily events confirmed the judgement. The plight of Hellas, however, had become less engrossing because a new factor had entered the scene, perhaps outweighing in importance the Athenian misery; the proportions of the problems had completely changed because Plato had lived. The order of Hellas was dissolving; but civilizations, while dying, may set free human potentialities such as the Platonic. A crisis is not an absolute end. Various sectors in a society develop differently, and while disaster may overcome one of them, other sectors may flower into a new beginning. Plato still envisaged society as a compactly integrated unit of political, educational, and religious institutions. After Plato begins a clear differentiation into political, religious, and noetic areas of life. When this process of differentiation has set in one certainly may speak of the crisis or dissolution of the civilization; but the crisis, as it were, is concentrated in certain sectors, for instance the political, while other sectors, like the religious, show a life that points to the future. In such periods we then find bewildering political antagonisms which originate in the dogmatization of partial views of the total phenomenon. For Plato, the politicians of Athens were the gravediggers of Hellenic political freedom, suffocating the life of the spirit that would have regenerated Hellas. For the politicians of Athens, the tendency of the Socratic schools to withdraw from political life and their influence on the young appeared to be an undermining of political order. And this attitude was not confined to nationalists like Demosthenes; it was also shared by the venerable old Isocrates, a conservative traditionalist. It is probably inevitable that in a dissolving society the interactions between the differentiating positions are not seen by the living as part of a total process running its fated course, but are torn apart into independent causes. There can be no doubt, of course, that the withdrawal of the best people from politics (which is a typical feature in such periods) will aggravate the crisis because the worst elements have the field for themselves. And there can equally be no doubt that social changes which propel dubious characters in great numbers into ruling positions make the political environment unlivable for well-bred men with some self-respect.

Beyond such bitterness of civilizational agony lies the ineluctable schism of a society. The mood of thinking will change profoundly when the schism is accepted as a fact beyond anybody's range of action. In Plato's work we feel the somber tension that stems from his theocratic will to achieve the impossible and to restore the bond between spirit and power. In Aristotle we feel a coolness and serenity which stems from the fact, if we may express it drastically, that he has "given up." He can accept the polis as the adequate form of Hellenic civilizational existence; he can dispassionately survey the varieties in his vast collection of 158 studies of constitutions; he can formulate standards and give therapeutical advice for treating unhealthy cases; he has no dreams of a spiritually reformed, national Hellenic empire; such unification as Hellas is undergoing results from the Macedonian conquest which is enacted over his head and apparently does not interest him very much; only the Asiatic conquests of Alexander cause some worry because he disapproves of his former pupil's inclination to treat Asiatics like Hellenes and to foster an amalgamation of the two civilizations. His life is no longer centered in politics, but in his stellar religion and in the *bios theoretikos;* his soul is fascinated by the grandeur of the new life of the spirit and intellect; and his work, ranging over the realms of being, brings them into the grip of his imperatorial mind. For such a man the accents of the crisis will no longer lie on the misery of Athens; they will lie on the new life that begins with Plato. An epoch is marked but it has the character of a new climax of the intellect, of the *nous.*

We can now better understand the meaning which a *rapprochement* of Plato and Zoroaster must have had for Aristotle. The human species has cycles with a definite structure; but not of necessity do we have to look for the law of this structure in the political growth and decline of a specific civilization. The structure of the cycle may have a larger span so that one climax may lie in Iran while another may lie in Hellas. And the epochs will be marked by events in the spiritual history of mankind, not by events in the political sphere—though the polities may have their sub-cycles of growth and decline. We shall not be surprised, therefore, that on the five or six occasions where Aristotle specifically refers to problems of the cycle, he refers to discoveries and rediscoveries of scientific or philosophical insights. In the *Meterologica* (I, 3), for instance,

when speaking of his theory of the ether, he suggests that the idea is not
new but can be found in the mythical tradition; and then he continues:
"For scientific insights do not occur among men only once, or twice, or
a small number of times; but they recur an infinite number of times."
In *Metaphysics XII* (1074b) he speaks of the divinity of celestial bodies
and refers to the myth of remote ages which also assumes these bodies to
be gods. On this occasion, however, he goes a bit deeper into the problem
of the myth. Besides assuming the celestial divinities the myth also tells
us that the gods have human or animal form, and it goes into anthropomorphic details about their powers and actions. This part of the tradition "has been added later in mythical form with a view to the persuasion
of the multitude and to its legal and utilitarian expediency." If the addition be discarded, the thought that the first substances are gods will
appear as an inspired utterance and lead us to the reflection "that, while
probably each art and each science has often been developed as far as
possible and has again perished, these opinions, with others, have been
preserved until the present like relics of the ancient treasure." One must
not press this passage too far; nevertheless, it seems to contain the thesis
that insights may be divinely inspired and then become buried in the
historical process through political and utilitarian exigencies. If we take
Aristotle by his word, a civilization has a nucleus of divinely inspired insight which deteriorates under the pressure of necessities in ruling the
multitude, and then can be recovered when the philosophers free themselves from the political encumbrances. The cause of decay would have to
be sought in the political sector of a civilization.

Let us, finally, consider the appearance of the cycle problem in *Politics* VII, 10 (1329a40 ff). Aristotle speaks of the desirability of having
a society organized in hereditary castes or classes, separating the ruling
warriors from the husbandmen. With obvious reference to Plato, he
opines that this is no recent discovery but that Egypt was organized on
this plan for times immemorial. With a formulation that we know already from the other contexts he continues that such devices "have been
discovered repeatedly, or rather an infinite number of times, in the course
of ages." The "necessities" may be assumed to have been taught by need
itself whenever it made itself felt, while the things which adorn and enrich life grow up by degrees; and this general rule will hold good also
for constitutions (1329b24–31). Egypt is an old country; we should
avail ourselves of the discoveries already made by the ancients and then

pass on to the subject matters hitherto neglected (1329b31–35). In this case Aristotle deals with insights inspired not by the gods but by necessity. Insights into necessities of social order need rediscovery, too. As the inspired insights will be lost through an overgrowth of political expediency, so the necessities may become obscured in the history of a political civilization through the overgrowth of refinements and luxuries. Moreover, we sense in these reflections an undercurrent of criticism directed against Plato. The implication seems to be that the rediscovery of the necessities of order in the *Republic* is highly meritorious, but it would perhaps have been simpler in this case not to rediscover but to use the insight lying ready at hand in Egypt, to use the knowledge already in our possession as a starting point and to advance to the study of less well-explored problems—as Aristotle does himself. These undertones are confirmed by *Politics* II, 5 (1264a1–5), where the argument is used in reverse. In this section Aristotle criticizes as impractical the Platonic suggestion of a community of women and property in the upper class of the *Republic*. One of the motives for rejecting the idea is its novelty. We should not disregard the experience of mankind; if such projects were any good they would not have remained undiscovered through the ages. "For, almost everything has been discovered already; though not all that has been discovered has been properly collected and inventoried, and not all that is known has been put into practice."

The theory of the cycle is an essential part of the Aristotelian theory of knowledge. The history of the species moves in cycles, and the repetition of the cycles from infinity has created something like an authoritative memory of the species. All great insights, whether they be religious or whether they belong in the class of necessities of order, have been gained. The rediscovery can be aided by an inventory of myths (in which the relics of former discoveries are preserved) and by the study of longeval civilizations (in which previous discoveries are still embodied in the institutions). The complete absence of any traces of a former discovery, on the other hand, will be a strong argument against the value of a newly advanced idea. In this function of the cycle in the theory of knowledge we recognize again the peculiar style of an intellectual thinning-out, as compared with the Platonic fullness of experience. Plato had authenticated his insights, drawn from the unconscious, through the myth of the cycle; the descent to the cosmic omphalos of the soul assured us of the truth of the myth. For Aristotle the myth of the cycle has become a doctrine, and the unconscious as a source of truth is replaced by the memory of the species that can be recovered through historical studies. Plato's non-objectifiable unconscious is now spread out through the infinity of history; its content is exhausted in the infinite series of its historical objectivations. Only on rare occasions do we find in Aristotle a remark which indicates his awareness that historical materials do not divulge their truth of themselves, but that they in their turn need authentication through the assent of the thinker's mind. *Metaphysics* XII, 8 (speaking of the myth of the stellar gods), for instance, closes with the sentence: "Only thus far is the opinion of our ancestors and earliest predecessors clear [or intelligible] to us"—probably meaning that those parts of the myth which do not coincide with the insight of the philosopher are not clear (*phanera*).

Let us close with a sentence from a letter of the last years of the philosopher: "The more I am by myself and alone, the more I have come to love myths." This sentence recalls, over the years, a remark in *Metaphysics* that "the lover of myths is in a sense a lover of wisdom" (982b18–20). The old lover of wisdom, alone with the wonders of the myth—that is the sublime figuration of the infinity of time in which truth is found, lost, and recovered.

CHAPTER 8

Science and Contemplation

1. The Range of Political Science

The will of the spiritual founder endows Platonic politics with its theocratic compactness. Before the contemplative eye of Aristotle the product of Plato's creative will falls apart, and the *disjecta membra* become independent topics. Aristotle's criticism of the size of the polis as suggested by Plato in the *Laws* may serve as an example of the decomposition.

Aristotle is of the opinion that 5,000 citizens would be too large a number for a well-ordered polis. If so many persons are to be supported in idleness as a ruling class, the polis would have to have a territory as large as Babylon (*Politics* 1265a10–18). The decisive point is that Aristotle gives the number as 5,000 while Plato has 5,040. The number 5,040 was chosen by Plato because of its cosmological relations and it cannot be changed to 5,039 or 5,041 without destroying the musical and zodiacal implications of the numerical symbolism. That, however, is precisely what Aristotle does. He destroys the Platonic play with cosmic numbers; he divests the figure of its symbolic meaning and treats it as a statistical population figure. The population of the polis is the "topic"; the figure must be investigated under its practical aspects; and, hence, it does not matter whether one takes the "round" figure 5,000 instead of the symbolically exact figure 5,040. While the transformation as such is quite intelligible, it is a bit puzzling psychologically. Aristotle was a member of the Academy during the decades in which Plato worked on the *Laws*; and he must have been thoroughly acquainted with its symbolic problems. Granted that his interest in population figures was practical—why does he indulge in this criticism of a figure which he must have known was meant symbolically? We have no certain answer to this question but we should be aware that criticisms of this type occur so frequently in the *Politics* that we must assume in Aristotle's veneration of

Plato an admixture of subdued animosity, venting itself in misunderstandings that cannot be quite unintentional.

The decomposition of the symbols must not be interpreted as a failure of Aristotle, or as a lack of ability to continue Plato's work on the same level. The Polis of the Idea originated in Plato's will to regenerate Hellas spiritually. In the face of the events a stubborn perseverance in the attitude of the Platonic will would not have proved Aristotle the equal of his master; it would have been silly. In Plato's own late development the life of the spirit was on the point, as we have seen, of breaking away from the polis; one step further would have led to the vision of the universal community of mankind. Aristotle's contemplative life was one of the possible ways of meeting the actual differentiation of life in a society in crisis. And a critic could only raise the question whether Aristotle had gone far enough on his way; he might opine that the conquering pupil and the contemporary cosmopolitan philosophers had understood the signs of the time even better and acted more radically on their insight. If anything is characteristic of Aristotle as a political thinker, it is his conservatism, that is, his hesitation to break away from the problems that had become topical through Plato and to enlarge their range. We do not find in the Aristotelian work a systematic treatment of politics from the new contemplative position; we rather find the contemplative attitude at work on a variety of problems as they present themselves in the environment.

As a consequence of such hesitations Aristotle has never achieved a clear delimitation of the field of political inquiry. The work that bears the title *Politics* is in its extant form constructed as the second part of a more comprehensive treatment of "political science" which also comprises the subject matters of the *Nicomachean Ethics*. In the *Ethics* Aristotle sets out to define politics as the science (or art) of human action. Actions have ends, and the ends may be subservient to higher ends; hence, a regressus *ad infinitum* would ensue unless a highest good (*tagathon kai to ariston*) be assumed (1094a22). The science which explores the highest good and which is concerned with human action under the aspect of attaining the highest good is a "mastercraft"; and this mastercraft is the science of politics (1094a28). It is the ruling science not only in the sense of its hierarchial comprehensiveness, but also in the practical sense that it regulates the place of the other practical sciences in the economy of the polis. For it ordains which of the other sciences should be cultivated in a polis, what disciplines of knowledge the different classes of citizens should receive, and to what extent they should learn them. Moreover, this regulatory power extends to the skills which are held in highest esteem, such as strategy, management of estate, and rhetoric. For these reasons the end (*telos*) of political science is the good of man. We are justified in calling the science of the good of man "political science" because—even though the good of man is the same as the good of the polis, that is, eudaimonia—the good of the polis is greater and more perfect (in the sense of the more comprehensive *telos*); and while it is better to attain and preserve the good of one man than nothing at all, it is nobler and more divine to attain it for a nation (*ethnos*) or a polis (1094b1–11). In this comprehensive conception of political science we can sense the Platonic origins. The whole life of man in society is integrated in a hierarchy of goods. The good of man is the same as that of the polis. The anthropological principle in its reversible, Platonic form is presupposed. And Aristotle alludes to the *Republic* when he considers the realization of the good for one man better than nothing (the Platonic one-man polis), but the realization on the scale of the polis greater and more divine. The program is plainly a conversion of the idea of the *Republic* into a systematically organized science of politics.

Obviously, in the contemplative attitude such a program cannot be carried out. The tight co-ordination of subject matter in the *Republic* stems from the spiritual will of Plato. Historical reality, however, as it meets the gaze of the contemplator, is not ordered by this will. When Aristotle turns toward the reality of his environment he must recognize the state of social differentiation and dissolution; and in this not at all well-ordered field he will find the Platonic will (and its product, the Idea) only as one phenomenon among others. Nevertheless, since he does find it as one of the phenomena in reality, indeed, the program will not be devoid of meaning. The Platonic vision of order has become part of reality, and while reality resists an embodiment of the Platonic idea it cannot escape the fate of being judged by it. The idea has become a standard. While a political science which intends to explore the structure of political reality cannot be exhausted by the exposition of Platonic standards, it will have to contain such an exposition as part of a more comprehensive inquiry. And, while Aristotelian politics as a whole does not execute the program, we indeed find the program realized as part of the whole work in as much as *Politics* VII and VIII (the so-called "ideal state" of the translators) is an exposition of standards in conformity with the program outlined in the opening section of *Nicomachean Ethics*. If we accept the thesis that *Politics* VII and VIII are in continuation with II and III, we may say that these four books of *Politics* correspond to the programmatic intentions just outlined. We are able, therefore, to clarify their systematic place as that part of Aristotelian politics which transforms the ordering impulses of the Platonic idea into the standards of political science. These standards, then, become the instrument for classifying, evaluating, and therapeutically influencing the variety of phenomena in political reality.

Aristotle, though, did not elaborate even such a modified system. The program stands at the beginning of *Ethics*. The science which in the program is designated as "political" was actually subdivided by Aristotle himself into ethics and politics. We must explore the reasons which induced, contrary to the program, a contraction of politics to the subject matters collected in the treatise that specifically was called *Politics*.

The Aristotelian program, whether ultimately one of political science or not, gets off to a good start. The anthropological principle in politics as established by Plato requires that the idea of the perfect polis expresses (or that the standards developed by a political science are based on) the nature of man. We must have a systematic understanding of the nature of man if we want to have a systematic political science. In accordance with these requirements *Ethics* I gives a philosophical anthropology in brief outline. We are in search of the true nature of man in order to ascertain (in a science of action) what is the highest good. For the designation of the highest good we customarily use the term *eudaimonia* (happiness). While we may assume agreement on the term, there is definitely no agreement on the question wherein precisely the eudaimonia of man consists. Three principal opinions are in conflict with each other. Eudaimonia can be found, according to some, in a life of pleasure and enjoyment; or, according to others, in the life of politics in which pleasure is found and honor gained through the practice of excellence of character; or, finally, in the life of contemplation. Aristotle decides for the life of contemplation (*bios theoretikos*) as the way of life by which true eudaimonia can be achieved, and he supports his decision by an analysis of the faculties in the human soul.

The soul of man has an irrational and a rational part, and according to preferences of classification one can subdivide either the one or the other into two further parts. We thus arrive at a tripartite division of the soul into its vegetative and sentient faculties which man has in common with animals; into passions and desires which are not rational but through persuasion, in an educative process, can be made to obey reason; and into the rational faculties proper. If then the specifically human function must be understood as an activity (*energeia*) of the soul, the proper function of man (in actualizing his specific excellence) can be more closely defined as an activity of the soul in obedience to the rational principle (*logos*); or, the good of man is the function of his soul in accordance with its own excellence (*arete*), or if there should be a plurality of excellences, in accordance with the best and most perfect (or highest) among them (I, 7).

The last qualification proves necessary because in fact there are several excellences of man. There is, in the first place, the realm of ethical virtues. A virtue is neither a state of the soul (like pleasure), nor a faculty; it is a quality of the character (*ēthos*), inculcated by instruction and practice until it has become a habit (*ĕthos*). These excellences are defined as the habits of choosing the mean (*mesotes*) between excess and falling-short (to which our passions or pleasures might lead us) as a prudent man would choose it according to reason (II, 5 and 6). Such habituations to choose the mean are, for instance, justice, temperance, courage, liberality, magnificence, and good temper. Beyond these ethical virtues lie, second, the dianoetic virtues, *i.e.*, scientific knowledge (*episteme*), art or skill (*techne*), prudence (*phronesis*), wisdom (*sophia*) and intellection (*nous*). These are the excellences which enable us to attain truth in its varieties of first principles (intellection), universals and demonstrated truth (scientific knowledge), the mastery of a subject which results from a combination of the knowledge of first principles with scientific knowledge (wisdom), and the right means for attaining the good of man (prudence). The dianoetic virtues stand higher in rank than the ethical virtues; and through the practice of the dianoetic excellences man rises to the true eudaimonia of the *bios theoretikos*.

So far the program could be executed and Aristotle could expand it into the brilliant, detailed analysis of the various virtues that fills the main body of the *Nicomachean Ethics*. Beyond this point difficulties begin to arise. In the first place, there are considerable complications with regard to definitions. We started out with a definition of political science as the general science of human action, culminating in the exploration of the highest good for man; and the first part of this science, so we assumed, was the philosophical anthropology of *Ethics* I. Now we learn different.

The ethical virtues are desirable in man, but they are not natural faculties; they must be inculcated in man through processeses which for their effectiveness depend on a suitable institutional environment. It will be the art of the lawgiver to create the proper institutions; and in this sense it is the principal purpose of political science to produce a certain character in the citizens, that is, to make them good and capable of noble actions (1099b28–32). The meaning of political science is now contracted to the art of the lawgiver who must know which institutional arrangements will produce the desired ethical excellences and which will not. In this restriction of meaning we touch on the reason for the subdivision of the subject matter into *Ethics* and *Politics*. Ethics is the science of excellences; politics is the science of the institutional means which are apt to produce the excellences in the citizens.

This redefinition, however, is not the last one. Aristotle, futhermore, assigns to political science a place among the dianoetic virtues; the science which supposedly produced the classification of ethical and dianoetic virtues now becomes one of the virtues classified. Political science is the same state of mind (*exis*) as prudence. Prudence may be understood as a virtue with regard to private affairs, but it also concerns the polis. With regard to the polis there are two kinds of prudence. The first is legislative science (in the sense of nomothetical, constitution-making science); the second is concerned with particular actions of a deliberative, judicial, and adminstrative nature. The second one is usually called political science, though—as Aristotle remarks—the name properly belongs to both (1141b23–28). Moreover, prudence also embraces the science of household management (*oikonomia*). The complete subdivision of prudence, besides prudence in private affairs, thus gives us Household Management, Nomothetic Science, and Political Science, and the latter subdivided into Judicial and Deliberative (1141b28–34). This, however, is not the nomenclature which Aristotle finally uses in the *Politics*. On the one hand, the *Politics* does not contain the political science (in the narrower sense just defined) at all but only the nomothetic science. On the other hand, it is not confined to nomothetics, but also contains a lengthy discourse on household management in I, 3–13. Leaving aside this last mentioned economic discourse, we may say that the political science which ultimately emerges in the *Politics* is a prudential science of nomothetics, with a rich admixture of reflections on problems of ethics and philosophical anthropology.

We have started with the program of politics as a general science of human action, and we have traced the course of redefinitions. We shall now trace the course of a second series of difficulties intimately connected with the first, that is, of the difficulties which arise from the nature of politics as a prudential science. Politics in the narrower sense of nomothetics intends to teach the lawgiver how to create the institutions that will inculcate the ethical excellences in the citizens. Assuming for the moment that such a science of means for the desired end can be successfully developed, there remains the great question whether the desired end is valid in itself and whether we should invest any efforts in its realization. The value of nomothetics depends on the validity of the prudential science of ethics as developed by Aristotle. What if somebody should challenge the truth of the Aristotelian propositions concerning excellences? What if he should advance an alternative catalogue of goods to be realized in society? If, for instance, we should make a rising standard of living the supreme value to be realized, the governmental institutions favoring the realization of this end would diverge widely from the standards developed in *Politics* VII and VIII. In brief: Aristotle has to face the famous "That's What You Think!"

Aristotle realized the problem. In *Nicomachean Ethics* II, 3 and 4, he explains that political science (in the sense of a general science of action) has a lower degree of exactness than the demonstrative sciences. We can arrive at truth in a prudential science only by sifting opinions; and we must use some caution when we proceed from the general rules to a discussion of concrete cases. The reader should, therefore, receive the propositions in the same spirit in which they are made, "for it is the mark of an eduacted man to look for precision in each class of things just so far as the nature of things admits"—a golden rule which should be taken to heart by our contemporaries who feel unhappy because political science has not the same type of exactness as physics (1094b11–27). Moreover, in order to discuss ethical problems with discernment, one must be well acquainted with them; the disputants must have had an all-round education and considerable experience in life and conduct, for these experiences are the basis of the discussion. Young men will, therefore, not profit much from the study of political science; and it makes no difference whether they are young in years or youthful in character. Ethics is not a matter of abstract knowledge but of the actual formation of the man; hence, for persons lacking in self-restraint the mere knowledge of ethical

rules will be of little use, while critical knowledge will be of great benefit for men whose passions are guided by reason. The pupil must be in
possession of good habits in order to be an intelligent student of the noble
and just, and generally of political science (1095b6).

Still, we have not disposed of the problem that different people desire
different things as good. In the face of this fact we must either maintain,
so it seems, that each man desires as good what appears to him as good
and that, as a consequence, we have only apparent goods; or, that there
is a real good, but that the persons who choose wrongly do not really
wish what they desire. Aristotle solves the problem by defining as good
what is wished for in the true sense, while conceding that every man
wishes what appears to him as good. He distinguishes between "true"
good and "phenomenal" good; all goods are good in appearance, but only
that phenomenal good is the true good which is desired by the true wish.
The truth of the good is inseparable from the truth of the wish; hence,
a critical debate about the good can be conducted only by men who are
capable of desiring according to truth. Such a man Aristotle calls
spoudaios. The translators render the term as "the good man." It would
perhaps be more adequate to speak of the serious, or weighty man; or, in
order to oppose him to the "young man" who is unfit for ethical debate,
one might call the *spoudaios* the mature man, or the man who has attained full human stature. Such a mature man differs from others by
seeing the truth in each class of things, being as it were their *kanon kai
metron*, that is, their norm and measure (1113a29–35).

These reflections of Aristotle are perhaps the most important contribution to an epistemology of ethics and politics that has ever been made.
We remember Plato's problem of the truth (*aletheia*) of the myth. The
truth of the compact unit of wish-good is, in the contemplative attitude,
the problem that corresponds to the truth of the myth. In our preceding
analysis of the cycle theory we have, furthermore, seen that the memory
of the species in the infinite time of recurrent cycles takes the place of the
Platonic unconscious from which, through anamnesis, the myth is drawn.
The reflections of Aristotle are of priceless importance in the history of
ideas because here we can observe in the very act how the truth of the
prudential sciences emerges from the truth of the myth. The debate
about truth in action is neither a vain opining without verification, nor
is it an intuition of "values" in the abstract. It is a critical analysis of the
excellences in actual existence in an historical society. The prudential
science can formulate principles of action (such as the *mesotes*) accord-

ing to reason (*logos*) because it finds the logos of action embedded in the habits of man. The reality of habituation and conduct in a society has prudential structure, and a prudential science can be developed as the articulation of the logos in reality. From this fundamental insight, then, follow the corollaries. The analysis of excellences can be conducted only by men who know the material which they analyze; and a man can know the excellences only if he possesses them. Moreover, its results can be understood as true only by men who can verify them by the excellences which they possess, that is, by mature men—or at least by men who are sufficiently advanced in formation of character themselves to understand the problem. As a consequence, if we may adapt a famous formula, ethics is a science of mature people, by mature people, for mature people. It can arise only in a highly civilized society as its self-interpretation; or, more precisely, in that stratum of a civilized society in which the excellences are cultivated and debated. From such a social environment the analytical consciousness of the virtues can flower; and this consciousness, in its turn, may become an important factor in the education of the young.

The intimate connection of a prudential science with a society in which the excellences are actualized raises a number of problems. They are on principle the problems which also arose on occasion of the Platonic myth of the soul; but they have undergone certain transformations in the Aristotelian medium of contemplation. Plato could develop the good politeia, he could actualize it in his own soul and in the souls of his friends, but he could not actualize it in historical reality as the order of Athens or of an Hellenic empire. On the level of pragmatic history, the philosopher is not the ordering force of society; he is in competition with rival forces of various kinds. The Platonic vision of order is not a possession of mankind; it is the possession of a limited group; and the same holds true for the Aristotelian prudential science. Other groups, and they may be the majority in a society, will be less receptive, or not receptive at all, to such insights. Men differ from each other in a manner which Aristotle characterizes through a quotation from Hesiod:

> Far best is he, who knows all things himself;
> Good, he that hearkens when men counsel right;
> But he who neither knows, nor lays to heart
> Another's wisdom, is a useless wight.[1]

[1] Hesiod, *Works and Days*, 293ff. Translated by W. D. Ross in the Oxford translation of *Nicomachean Ethics*.

If we translate these lines (1095b10–13) into human types, we may distinguish between (1) men who have authority, (2) men who can recognize authority and accept it, and (3) men who neither have authority, nor can recognize and accept it. If we define a good society as a society in which the highest good of man can be realized, then we arrive at the proposition: The existence of a good society depends on the social predominance of a group of men in whom the excellences are actualized, or who are the "norm and measure" in the Aristotelian sense. When the predominance of such a group is endangered, for one historical reason or another, by the masses whose passions (*pathos*) are not restrained by reason (*logos*), then the quality of the society will decline. Political science, in the sense of a general science of action, thus, is inseparable from a philosophy of historical existence. The validity of its insights is not in question; but the validity will be socially accepted only under certain historical conditions. The previously adduced challenge of the "That's What You Think" is, therefore, of considerable importance in a theory of ethics. The challenge cannot affect the validity of prudential science but it brings home to us that the debate on ethics can be conducted only among the mature men, and that a comprehensive study of moral phenomena must include a study of the moral attitudes of the fools or wights (*achreios*) in the Hesiodian verse. A pathology of morals, in the most literal sense of a study of disorder through vagaries of passion (*pathos*), is quite as important for the understanding of political society as the prudential science of the excellences. If we understand the "That's What You Think" not as a challenge to validity, but as a manifestation of the revolt against excellence, we shall become aware how precariously balanced the good society is in historical existence. And we shall understand that a well-functioning society must provide institutions not only for the inculcation of excellences in the educable but also for the management of the ineducable mass.

Aristotle was aware of this problem. In *Nicomachean Ethics* X, 9, he reflects that the task of ordering a society would be easy if men could be taught virtue by discourse. Discourse can encourage a generous youth of inborn nobility of character; it cannot guide the masses toward moral nobility (*kalokagathia*). The many are amenable to fear but not to shame; and they abstain from evil not because of its baseness, but because they are afraid of sanctions. Living by passion, they pursue the happiness of pleasure; and they do not know about the noble pleasures because they have never experienced them. To change the firmly rooted habits of such characters by argument is difficult, if not impossible. For, generally speaking, passions seem not to be amenable to reason but only to force. This being the state of things, it will be necessary to support the personal educational processes in a society by compulsory processes. The impersonal pressure of the law must come to the aid of personal influence and model conduct. The law has compulsory power (*dynamis*), and at the same time it is a rule participating in prudence and intellect (*phronesis* and *nous*). A right system of laws, educating and enforcing the discipline of the young and sanctioning trespasses of the adult, is necessary for the stabilization of society. And the lawgiver is the man who knows how to devise institutions that will have the desired result of securing the social predominance of human excellence as understood by the *spoudaios*.[2] We arrive again at the definition of politics as the science of nomothetics but now under the aspect of a science that will provide the supplementary instrument of compulsion for keeping in line those members of society who cannot qualify as *spoudaioi*.

We are coming closer to the more subtle reasons that have motivated the subdivision of the general science of action into ethics and politics. After the pragmatic failure of Plato it was probably clear to everybody who cared about such problems that political society could dissociate into private circles in which the excellences were cultivated (as, for instance, the cult communities of the schools) and the politicians who pursued quite different ends. One still could develop a science of nomothetics as Aristotle did in his *Politics*, but whether the moulders of the political destiny would make any use of it, that was the great question, probably to be answered in the negative. In view of the threatening possibility that the course of political history would annihilate the actual formation of a polity through the mature men, it became desirable to articulate the wisdom of the excellences independent of the problem of its political actualization. Through the *Nicomachean Ethics*, rather than through the *Politics*, the prudential wisdom of Hellas has separated from the contingencies of actualization and become the possession of mankind, or rather of that part of mankind that can recognize authority and bow to it. The *Nicomachean Ethics* is the great document in which the authority of the *spoudaios* asserts itself through the ages, beyond the accidents of politics.

[2] In this context again the problem of the *spoudaios* is elaborated, 1176a15ff.

2. *The* Bios Theoretikos

The conception of politics as a general science of human action, as we have seen, was animated by the Platonic, theocratic impulses. In the contemplative attitude, however, the program could not be carried out because political reality in fact was not formed by the Platonic idea. What remained of the initial impulse was the sketch of a philosophical anthropology in the opening sections of *Ethics* and the conversion of the idea into standards in the closing sections of *Politics*. In between, before the contemplative gaze, reality fell apart into the society of the mature men and into the political organization that would provide a suitable environment for inculcating the practice of ethical virtues as well as for repressing the ineducable. Correspondingly the science of human action dissociated into a science of the excellences and a nomothetic science.

Even with these adjustments to reality the whole field of problems was not yet covered. The further complications of a science of politics were given with the classification of opinions concerning the nature of eudaimonia. According to the variety of opinion three types of life could lead to happiness: the apolaustic life (that is, the life of hedonistic indulgence), the political life, and the theoretic life (*N.E.*, 1095b14ff). This classification implied a specific correlation between politics and the practice of ethical virtues; the man of character will lead his life of action in the field of politics (1095b30). A political science, if narrowed down in this manner, would exclude the theoretic life from its scope. In the Platonic politeia the philosopher-kings were the rulers; in the empirical polis of Aristotle the philosophers are on the verge of removing themselves altogether from politics. Such a tendency must have been strong, indeed, in the Academy in the late years of Plato; for, in *Politics* VII, 2, Aristotle explicitly considers the question which mode of life is the most eligible: the participation as a citizen in the community of the polis, or the life of an alien who detaches himself from the political community (1324a13ff). In the Parable of the Cave Plato had weighed the reasons for the philosopher's return to the polis; in historical reality, in the practice of the Academy, the detachment was tending to become a mode of life. "It was this circle of students that gave birth to Aristotle's ideal of 'the theoretic life'—not, that is to say, the animated gymnasium of the *Lysis* or the *Charmides*, but the cabin [*kalybe*] in the secluded garden of the Academy. Its quietude is the real original of the isles of the

blest in the *Protrepticus*, that dreamland of philosophical otherworldli-
ness." [3] The life of the philosopher, with its a-politic tendency, becomes
a new factor, disrupting the conception of a general science of action as
a political science. The polis remains for Aristotle the comprehensive
form of human existence; but the true eudaimonia can be found only
by transcending the life of politics into the practice of the dianoetic virtues.

The definition of the *bios theoretikos* is closely connected with the
definition of eudaimonia. A man is to be considered happy when he is engaged in a life of action according to highest (*teleios*) virtue (*N.E.*,
1101a15). There are degrees of eudaimonia according to the ranks of
virtues realized in human activity. The highest happiness (*teleia eudaimonia*) will be reached through an active life according to the dianoetic
virtues; the fullest eudaimonia will be a form of contemplative activity
(*theoretike energeia*) (1178b7f).

In making this decision Aristotle reaches back to his philosophical
anthropology. The happiness of theoretic activity is highest because
contemplation is the highest function in man; and it is the highest function because it is the function of the highest part in the soul of man, that
is, of the intellect (*nous*). The activity (*energeia*) of the intellect is
identified as the theoretic activity (*theoretike energeia*) (1177a17ff).
The meaning of "highest" or "perfect" is further elucidated by the designation of *nous* as the divinest part (*to theiotaton*) in man; the activity
of the divinest part, thus, becomes the divinest activity; and the pleasure
accompanying it becomes the divinest pleasure, the true eudaimonia.
The designation as divine is supported by the characteristics of theoretic
activity. The action of the *nous* (1) extends to the best of knowable
things, in particular to things divine; (2) it is an activity that can be
maintained more continuously than any other human activity; (3) it
is accompanied by a specific pleasure of marvellous purity and perma-
nence; in contrast with activities of the practical life, it (4) is least dependent on external instruments and on the help of other men, possessing to the highest degree the quality of self-sufficiency (*autarkeia*);
(5) the theoretic life has no purpose beyond itself, and its activity is
loved for its own sake, while in all other activities we work for some gain
from our action; and (6) the theoretic life is a life of leisure (*schole*),
and the scholastic, leisured life is the purpose for which we undergo

[3] Jaeger, *Aristotle*, 96.

the work of our practical life. In view of these qualities, especially of self-sufficiency, leisure, and relative freedom from physical fatigue, the theoretic life is to be considered the highest, because it is the most divine (1177a17–1177b26).

Of such a life we must say that it transcends the merely human level. Man can lead it only in so far as he is more than man, only in so far as something divine is really present in him. Since this divine part in the composite nature of man is *nous,* the life of the intellect is divine as compared with life on the merely human level of the practical excellences. Hence we must not follow the advice of those who would enjoin us to think only of human things because we are men, and only of mortal things because we are mortals. It is our duty to make ourselves immortal, as far as that is possible in life, by cultivating the activity of the best part in us which may be called our better or true self. The *nous* is the orienting or ruling part in our soul (*to kyrion*), and it would be strange indeed if man should choose not to live the life of his own self but of that of something else. And, finally, Aristotle lets his train of argument debouch, beyond anthropology, into the general problem of ontology. The most suitable realization of each thing is the realization of that which is best in its nature (*physis*); the life according to *nous* is the best and pleasantest for man because *nous* more than anything else is the very nature of man. "The life of *nous* is therefore the happiest [*eudaimonestatos*]" (1177b27–1178a8).

The account given in *Nicomachean Ethics* makes the meaning of the *bios theoretikos* clear as far as its place in Aristotle's general science of action, in his anthropology and ontology is concerned. The idea of a life of the intellect, however, has certain religious ramifications which in the account in *Ethics,* though touched upon, are not sufficiently clarified. Obviously, the Aristotelian nous is more than the intellect that becomes active in the sciences of world-immanent objects. The nous as the *theiotaton* is the region in the soul where man transcends his mere humanity into the divine ground. In the activity of the nous man is concerned about first principles and things divine, and in such activity his soul partakes of the things divine and is engaged in a process of immortalization. In the *bios theoretikos* we have the intellectualized counterpart to the Platonic vision of the Agathon which, in beholding the Idea, transforms the soul and lets it partake of the order of the Idea. Moreover, the difficulties of the philosopher continue into the Aristotelian transformation of the problem. The Platonic struggle with the people's myth is still the struggle of Aristotle. He is compelled to tread cautiously and to be apologetic about the expression of his new religiousness in the face of a conservative opposition which considers the inquiry into divine affairs, a *theoria theou*, improper and impious for mortals. In *Metaphysics* I Aristotle considered this problem more elaborately. The inquiry into first principles, culminating in the inquiry into the nature of God as the first cause of all things, is the highest of all sciences because it deals with the ends of all things; and since the end of a thing is the good of that thing, the highest science culminates in the knowledge of the highest good in nature. This science of celestial phenomena and the genesis of the universe is historically the last of all sciences to develop; the sciences of necessary things are the first concern of man, and only when a certain level of comfort is reached can man begin to wonder (*thaumazein*) about problems for their own sake. The science of first principles does not look to an ulterior advantage but rests in itself; and "as the man is free, we say, who exists for his own sake and not for another's, so we pursue this as the only free science, for it alone exists for its own sake" (982b).[4] And again he feels obliged to defend his exaltation of the *philosophia prima* against the older poets who would say that "God alone can have this privilege." The Gods, he contends, are not jealous, and he relies on a proverb reported by Solon that "the bards tell many a lie" (982b 11–983a11).[5]

It is difficult to reconstruct the full meaning of the *bios theoretikos* from the esoteric work of Aristotle. The comparatively terse, late formulations presuppose a development that must have manifested itself more clearly in the early work of which only fragments are extant. In

---

[4] In this complex of freedom, science of first principles, activity of the true self in contemplation, and eudaimonia must be sought the origin of Aristotle's distinction between freemen and slaves. See, for instance, *Politics* III, 9: "A polis does not exist for the sake of life only, but for the sake of good life; if it were otherwise, there could be a polis of slaves or lower animals; but that cannot be, for they do not participate in eudaimonia and the life of freedom [*proairesis*]." If we consider the religious implications of the *bios theoretikos* it would seem that in Aristotle's distinction of freemen and slaves we have a classification of human types which later, in Christianity, develops into the distinction of *pneumatici* and *psychici* (St. Paul), and further on, in Gnosticism, into the spiritual ranks of a gnostic hierarchy.

[5] On the knowability of God in a science of first principles see Harry A. Wolfson, "The Knowability and Describability of God in Plato and Aristotle" (*Harvard Studies in Classical Philology*, Vols. 56–57, 1947). On the tension between Aristotle and the traditional Hellenic views on this point see Jaeger, *Aristotle*, 164, and Bruno Snell, *Die Entdeckung des Geistes. Studien zur Entstehung des europaeischen Denkens bei den Griechen* (2d ed., Hamburg, 1948), 53.

order to recover the peculiar flavor of the experience we must draw on
materials from the literary ambiance of the early Aristotle. In the
Tusculan Disputations (V, 3, 8) Cicero reports an anecdote about Pythagoras which stems from Heraclides of Pontus, a fellow student of
Aristotle. In the anecdote Pythagoras calls himself a philosopher and
explains the meaning of the word by comparing human life with the
festivals at Olympia. Various types of men come to the game: some in
order to trade and to enjoy themselves, some in order to compete in the
contests, and some merely as spectators (*theoros*). The anecdote seems
destined to endow the Aristotelian distinction of the apolaustic, the
political, and the theoretic life with the authority of Pythagoras. The
philosopher appears as the "spectator"; and the *theorein* of Aristotle is
still close in its meaning to the noun *theoros* from which it derives.[6]
Moreover, certain sections of the *Epinomis*, which closely approach the
formulations of Aristotle in *Metaphysics* and *Nicomachean Ethics*, in-
form us about the spectacle at which the gaze of the spectator was
directed. This spectacle was the Heaven with the stars and their movements. The stars are divinities; and the Heaven, the world-shell, is God
for whom we may also use the terms Cosmos or Olympos (*Epinomis*
977a–b). The measured movement of the "visible gods" (985d) will
be an object of marvelling admiration (*thaumazein*) for the blest man
(*eudaimon*); from such admiration he will proceed to a desire for understanding so much as is possible for mortal nature, believing that thus
he will pass through life most happily, and that at the end of his life he
will arrive at regions meet for virtue, where he will have gained his full
measure of wisdom (*phronesis*) and remain a spectator (*theoros*) of the
most beautiful spectacle forever (986c–d). The *theoros* will be the contemplator of Heaven in this life, and such activity of his soul will lead
him to the eudaimonia of eternal contemplation.[7]

In the subtle identifications of Olympos, Cosmos and Ouranos
(Heaven) we, furthermore, sense a deliberate attempt at religious reform. The transition from the old Olympian to the new stellar religiousness seemed to require some persuasion that the new attitude, with its

---

[6] Jaeger, *Aristotle*, 96ff.

[7] The reader should observe the progress from *thaumazein* (the Aristotelian origin of
philosophizing) to *theorein* in this passage. On the complex of *thaumazein, theastai,* and *theorein*
see Snell, *Die Entdeckung des Geistes*, 47f. On the connection of "theoretic" religiousness with
the Homeric religiousness of the emigrant aristocracy in the Asiatic poleis see the same author,
ibid., 50, and especially the reflection on the relation between the "theoretic life" and the
Homeric *thaumazein, ibid.*, 52f.

obvious absorption of Oriental elements, was not quite as revolutionary as it must have appeared to the contemporaries. And indeed, in the *Epinomis* we find a lengthy address to the reader, trying to persuade him that Hellenes are obliged, and capable of proceeding, to this reform. The Hellenes are reminded that their geographical situation is particularly favorable for human excellence, as Hellas lies midway between a wintry and a summery climate. That in itself is an advantage. Nevertheless, the discovery of the cosmic deities was made earlier in Syria and Egypt, because those regions are more suitable to observation of the stars. But now that this knowledge has reached the Hellenes, they should remember that whenever they acquired something from abroad they turned it into a nobler thing. There is hope that again this acquisition from the barbarians will develop into a nobler and juster cult of the new deities among the Hellenes, considering their civilization, their Delphic prophetic wisdom, and their present cult institutions (987d–988a). This program of blending Hellenic with Oriental religiousness corresponds in its intentions to the Aristotelian enlargement of the historical horizon through the speculations on cycles in which Zoroaster and Plato can mark epochs. The new stellar religion is a development in Hellenic culture, but it is also a development through which Hellas consciously enters the wider community of mankind. For in his praise of the new divinities, the author of the *Epinomis* recommends them as divine images (*agalmata*), the "most beautiful and most common to all mankind"; none are established in more various places, none more distinguished by their purity, majesty, and the whole of their living existence (984a). The divinity of the all-embracing cosmic shell tends to become the symbol of the unity of mankind. In Aristotle's esoteric work, this tendency has found its clearest expression in *Metaphysics* XII. Above the stellar divinities there rises the prime mover of the eternal cosmos, the self-sufficient *noesis noeseos*, into the one originating and maintaining principle of the world: "For the world does not have the will to be ruled badly: The rule of many is not good, one be the lord" (1076a3ff).[8] The political symbolism creeps into the speculation on the oneness of the divine actuality. The term "monarchy" of the world does not yet occur in Aristotle, but its meaning is present. We have reached the point from which the Hellenistic-Roman political theology of the world-monarchy will carry on.[9]

[8] The quotation from *Iliad* II, 204. Cf. *Order and History* II, Ch. 3, 2, 1.

[9] On the problems of *Metaphysics* XII see Jaeger, *Aristotle*, 219–27. On the later speculation on world-monarchy, starting from Aristotle, see Erik Peterson, *Der Monotheismus als politisches*

The theoretic transcends the political life in the narrower sense of the word; we see it expanding into the speculation on the divine prime mover and culminating in the idea of the monarchical order of the cosmos. The immanent logic of the theoretic life seems to drive speculation from the polis to the cosmos with a monarchical constitution. Nevertheless, in his *Politics* Aristotle does not follow this course; the polis remains for him the perfect form of political existence in history. His method of building the problem of theoretic life into a political science is somewhat complicated. Perhaps we can understand the peculiarities of the construction best by setting it off against alternative courses that would have been possible.

The most obvious course to be followed would have been the recognition of areas of human life beyond politics. The tendency toward such recognition was present even in the late Plato, as we have seen; it was even more marked in the Aristotelian generation of the Academy; and the formation of the "schools" was a momentous step toward the institutionalization that we find completed in the rise of the church. Such recognition, if it should not result in the sterile apolitism of "foreigners" which Aristotle dreaded, would have required, however, a redefinition of the spheres of political and theoretic life in such a manner that the political order would become a basis of human existence subservient to the spiritual life of the soul, to the sanctification of life in the Christian sense. Considering the historical situation, the course was hardly practical; an imaginative construction of this kind would have been anachronistically remote from the structure of historical reality.

We saw a second possibility on the verge of realization in *Metaphysics* XII. The theological symbolization of the new religiousness could have led to the political theology of a world-monarchy, construing a monarchy of mankind as the analogue of cosmic order. Aristotle refrained from such analogous construction in spite of the fact that under his eyes an empire was in formation. The reasons for this restraint we can gather from *Politics*. Aristotle had very precise notions about the formation of monarchies through conquest and violence. He reflects on the opinion that possession of supreme power is the best of all things as it would put at the disposition of the possessor the means for performing the greatest number of noble actions. If this were true then the man who is

---

Problem. Ein Beitrag zur Geschichte der politischen Theologie im Imperium Romanum (Leipzig, 1935).

able to do it should take power away from everybody else—neighbors, father, brother, and friends—and make himself the supreme lord. The opinion can be considered true, however, only if we assume that the highest good can be achieved through robbery and violence. If we do not make this assumption we must say that subsequent virtuous conduct cannot restore the excellence that has been lost through the initial departure from virtue (1325a34ff). Royal rule is justifiable only under the condition that a society produces a man or a family of outstanding excellence, surpassing by far the rest of the people. In this case it would be unjust to ostracize such a man or family, or to treat them as equals with the others; the people ought to bow voluntarily to such superiority of virtue and accept the man, or the family, as king or as the royal family (1288a7–33). The denial of royal dignity and the relegation of such a man to the position of a subject—"that would be as if men should claim to rule over Zeus, dividing up his ruling functions among them" (1284b30ff). In these passages we hear an echo of the Platonic "sons of Zeus." Aristotle recognizes their claims to rulership but he doubts that such a situation will arise with any frequency. Superiority of a single man is more apt to occur under primitive conditions. "Kingships do not come into existence nowadays"; and when they arise, they will rather be monarchies or tyrannies; for in our days numerous men are of equal quality and no single man is so outstanding that only he would fit the greatness of the office (1313a5). Nevertheless, the improbable may happen and the incomparably superior man may appear. In that case we would have to say that "such a man would justly have to be considered a God among men." Such divinely pre-eminent men, however, are a law unto themselves, and we cannot make laws for them. The science of nomothetics is applicable only to societies where general rules for equals are to be given; there is no rule for the exception (1284a3ff).[10]

When Aristotle disdains to enter into the problem of monarchy as a cosmic analogue, his rejection of the possibility is founded on methodical considerations. The Hellenic society of freemen remains the model of human existence in society; ethics is the science of human action based

---

[10] The passages on kingship just quoted have furnished the subject for a great debate ever since Hegel (*Geschichte der Philosophie*, II, 401) suggested that Aristotle was referring to Alexander. There is nothing in the text to support the suggestion. For the whole complex of the relations between Aristotle and Alexander, as well as for the literature on the subject, cf. Victor Ehrenberg, *Alexander and the Greeks* (Oxford, 1938), Ch. 3, pp. 62–102, "Aristotle and Alexander's Empire."

on the experiences of a society of this type; and politics (as nomothetics) is the science of the legislative means that will secure its stable existence. The *Nicomachean Ethics* limits the range of problems that are permitted to enter into a science of politics. The problem of the large territorial nation (the *ethnos*), even more so the problems of supernational empires or of a political unity of mankind, are excluded from consideration. The restriction of the range of politics is fortified by Aristotle's theory of the distribution of ethnic characters over the habitable world. The peoples living in cold climates and in Europe are full of spirit (*thymos*) but lacking in intelligence and skills; hence, they retain a rugged freedom but are unfit for political organization and incapable of ruling others. The peoples of Asia have intelligence and skills but lack spirit (*thymos*); hence, they find themselves continuously in subjection and slavery. But the Hellenic peoples, situated in an intermediate climate, participate in all of the qualities in good balance; hence they continue in freedom and are the politically best organized of all nations. "And, hence, they could well rule all the others—if by chance they would politically unite" (1327b20–33).

Only a survey and weighing of all the passages will allow a balanced judgment concerning Aristotle's attitude toward the problem of world-monarchy. And even with all care one cannot arrive at more than probabilities. One senses a thinly veiled animosity against certain favorite ideas of Plato. The man who surpasses all others by his excellence, and will voluntarily be accepted as king by freemen, is ruled out as an anachronism. Plato's dream of an Hellenic empire, especially the dream of a world-empire, is disposed of with a sneer at the actual Hellenic disunity that could not even ward off domination by the Macedonians. On the other hand, the Hellenic civilizational pride is strongly present, and one can imagine Aristotle's profound misgivings against an imperial adventure that would combine and amalgamate Hellenes and barbarians into one political unit. As far as a science of politics is concerned we are, thus, thrown back upon the polis.

Once the alternatives are eliminated, the construction by which the theoretic life is related to the polis is simple in itself, though somewhat surprising. Without much discussion, Aristotle relies on analogies. The general science of human action has clarified the meaning of true eudaimonia. We now have to ask whether the best way of life is the same for the individual men and for communities. This question must be answered in the affirmative, the basis for such affirmation being the common opinion of mankind. Once this answer is accepted without further debate, and once we are agreed on the Aristotelian conception of true eudaimonia, we arrive at the conception of a *polis eudaimon* (1323b31). Since eudaimonia is the same for man and polis, the ethical categories also become transferable. The truly virtuous man is the *spoudaios* in the sense of *Nicomachean Ethics*, and correspondingly we now can speak of a *spoudaia polis* (1332a33). On the level of concrete politics the eudaimonia of the polis is achieved when the citizens are trained in such a manner that all strata of human existence are properly developed—the economic basis, the practical and warlike virtues, and the art of peaceful, contemplative existence. "There must be war for the sake of peace, business for the sake of leisure, things useful and necessary for the sake of things honorable." And in order to achieve this proper ranking of goods in the polis, its educational system must train the children and men of every age to realize their human nature in its whole dimension (1333a32–1333b5). The Aristotelian construction, thus, on the whole is faithful to the Platonic anthropological principle. As in the *Republic*, the virtues of the polis are developed parallel to the virtues of man. "Thus the courage, justice, and wisdom of the polis have the same meaning and form as the qualities which allow us to speak of individuals as just, wise, or temperate" (1323b33–37). The theocratic idea certainly is converted into standards for judging the quality of a polis; nevertheless, it is surprising, as we suggested, that the conversion should not break with the analogical construction of an elaborate *polis eudaimon* in spite of the fact that the Platonic founding will is no longer a living force in the Aristotelian contemplative attitude.

This peculiar conservatism, the unwillingness to break with the Platonic form in dealing with politics, manifests itself even more strongly in Aristotle's speculation on the eudaimonia of the polis as a self-contained existent. The polis, in order to be active, need not of necessity engage in external relations; the activity of the polis can be an end in itself; it may be an action of the various "parts" of a polis on each other, reproducing analogically the self-contained action of the *bios theoretikos* as well as the activity of divine existence. The analogy of autarkous existence pervades the world from the individual, through the polis, to God (1325b14–32). In this speculative construction of the autarky of the polis as an analogue of divine autarkous existence, Aristotle continues the myth of the polis as a cosmic analogue as Plato had developed it in the *Laws*. In spite of the transition to contemplative speculation we see Aristotle retaining the forms of Platonic mythical creation in *Republic* and *Laws*.

CHAPTER 9

The Science of the Polis

1. The Nature of the Polis

The inquiry is narrowed down to the polis, and the first question to be answered concerns its nature.

Every polis is a community (*koinonia*); and every community is established with a view to some good, for men act in order to obtain what they think to be good. The polis aims at the highest good, in so far as it is the highest community, embracing all the others. The highest and all-embracing community is specifically called political community or polis (*Politics* 1252a1–6). Since the polis is a composite community the inquiry into its nature will have to proceed by analyzing the compound whole (*syntheton*) down to its uncompounded composing parts (*morion*). Such analysis will enable us to distinguish between the different kinds of community rule, the more elementary and the higher ones (1252a17ff). The fundamental community is the household (*oikos*), consisting of the elemental relationships between male and female, parents and offspring, natural masters and natural subjects (or slaves). The aim of the household is provision for the daily elementary needs of man. For the satisfaction of more complex wants men organize the next higher community, consisting of an association of households, the village (*kome*). The rule of the village will arise through transfer from the rule in the household; the rule in the household being royal, royal rule will be the most elemental rule. That is the reason why Hellenic poleis were originally governed by kings; and this form of primitive rule is still to be found among barbarians. An association of several villages in a higher community, finally, results in the polis, the complete (*teleios*) community, large enough to be nearly or quite self-sufficient (*autarkeia*). Such a polis exists "by nature" (*physei*) in so far as the original community, the household, existed by nature. For the household came into existence for the sake of life, and this elementary community has expanded until it has reached the existence for the sake of good life (*eu* zen). With the expansion into the polis the elementary community has reached its end (*telos*); and the end which a thing reaches when it has fully developed we call its nature (1252a24–1253a2). From this analysis depend the corollary formulations: "The polis exists by nature"; and "Man is by nature a political living being" (*politikon zoon*). Moreover, the man who is apolitic, not by biographical accident but by nature, is either low in the scale of humanity, approaching an unsocial, beastly state, or above it, an outcast and adventurous lover of war (1253a2–7).

In the actual delivery of a lecture these terse opening notes of *Politics* were probably no more than the text for a lengthy sermon. In fact, they touch on most of the fundamental issues of Aristotelian politics. First of all, we find the categories of nature, of potentiality and of actualization applied to the study of the polis. The experiential models for such categorization are phenomena of the organic world where indeed we can observe evolutions from the potentiality of a seed to the actualization of its nature in a full-grown tree. The legitimacy of this transfer is not at all certain because (and this is the second issue, making its inevitable appearance) the polis is not an organism but a composite being owing part of its existence to the will of the composing human beings. The growth of the polis is not an inevitable biological process; men are not forced into the polis by an urge or instinct. Man is not a gregarious animal (*agelaion zoon*); he is a *politikon zoon* and that means that the end, the *telos,* of the community lies in the realm of conscious, deliberate recognition of good and evil, of right and wrong. For, "it is the characteristic of man, as distinguished from other living beings, that he alone has a sense of good and bad and right and wrong." And precisely in the community of moral insights lies the community of a household or a polis (1253a7–18). The nature of man, while finding its fulfillment in the polis, does not produce the polis automatically. The impulse (*horme*) toward political community is present in all men by nature; but it required a founder to create the polis; and the man who first brought others together in political community was the "author of the greatest good" (1253a30ff).

The introduction of the "author" (*aitios*) of the polis shifts evolution from the organic realm to history. The briefness of the notes makes it hazardous to pry into Aristotle's intentions. We can only say that the sequence of household, village, and polis roughly reproduces the historical sequence of social forms in Plato's *Laws*. For Plato, the sequence from simple to more complex forms of social organization marked the phases in the ascending branch of the historical cycle. For Aristotle, they also mark such phases; but Plato's looser empirical description is now subordinated to the actualization of a "nature"; the historical phases have become "parts" of the polis. The tightening of the construction has its advantages as well as its disadvantages. It may be considered an advantage that the "meaning of history" comes into sharper focus. The phases do not simply follow each other by degrees of increasing social complexity; they are a meaningful sequence up to the fulfillment in the autarky of a community in which the *bios theoretikos* can be realized. Various forms of social organization do not have to be classified like botanic specimens; they can be arranged in the order of an intelligible process. We have seen already that this method permits Aristotle to interpret kingship as a form that belongs to a past phase of the historical cycle and need not be taken into consideration in the analysis of the polis proper. Moreover, Aristotle approaches the problem that has been elaborated with care by Vico, that is, the problem of the substance which undergoes the evolutionary changes in the course of a cycle. A growth and decay must be the growth and decay of something. Vico dealt with that something under the title of the *mente eroica;* Plato identified it, at least for the period of decay, as the order of the psyche; Aristotle identified it, at least for the period of growth, as the political *physis* of man. Through the transfer of the categories of nature and actualization from the biological model to the polis, Aristotle, thus, has incidentally raised the theoretical issue that must be faced by every thinker who is in search of finite lines of meaning in the stream of history. These advantages, however, are due to a rigidity of construction which, in other respects, defeats its purpose. The Platonic phases of the growth of political form were much richer in empirical detail, and Plato could continue his description beyond the polis to the federation of the nation, the *ethnos.* This elasticity of empirical description is lost in Aristotle's speculation on the *physis* of the polis. Curious as it may sound at first hearing, Plato is the better empiricist; Aristotle, who wants to find form in reality at all cost, can find it only at the price of losing such parts of reality as do not fit the pattern of his evolving form. The polis is a premature generalization from insufficient materials. Form, if it is to be found in the historical stream of political existence, will prove to be considerably more complicated than Aristotle envisaged.

Considering the serious simplification of the problem of form, we shall not be surprised to see that Aristotle explores other approaches to the question independent of the first attempt. In the analysis of *Politics* I, 1–2 it was perhaps unexpected to find historical phases as the composing parts of the polis. We should, rather, have expected an analysis of the static structure into its composing elements. Such an analysis we find, indeed, in the section on the household. Again, Aristotle announces his postulate of analyzing a thing into its first and fewest elements (*meros*) and recognizes as such elements, in the household, the three relationships of master and servant, man and wife, parents and children (1253b1–12). This enumeration of elements is the remnant of a more comprehensive enumeration given by Plato in *Laws* 690 a–c. Plato wanted to establish the "axioms" (*axiomata*) of rulership. The term "axiom" originally has the meaning of a "claim to own or possess," but is changing already in the late work of Plato toward the meaning of a first assumption which does not need proof.[1] Plato assumes seven such "axioms" of rulership, equally valid "for the great poleis and the small households." They are:

(1) Parents must rule children
(2) The wellborn must rule the vulgar
(3) The old must rule the young
(4) Masters must rule slaves
(5) The better must rule the worse
(6) The thinking (or knowing, wise) must rule the ignorant
(7) The man chosen by lot must rule the man who is not so chosen

Aristotle's three component relations of the household correspond to the Platonic axioms (1) and (4). In *Politics* I, 3 the analysis applies to the household only; but in *Nicomachean Ethics* VIII, 10 the three elements are used for the theoretization of forms of government in a polis, in conformity with the Platonic assumption that the axioms are equally valid for poleis and households. Aristotle speaks of the three types of constitutions (*politeia*) *i.e.* monarchy, aristocracy, and timocracy, and their corresponding perversions (*parekbasis*) *i.e.* tyranny, oligarchy, democracy (1160a30–1160b23). And then he continues that the paradigms of these constitutions are to be found in the household. Monarchy

---

[1] On the shift from the juristic to the theoretic meaning of the word "axiom" in this passage of the *Laws* see Jaeger, *Paideia*, III, 235.

has its paradigm in the relation between father and sons; aristocracy in the relation between husband and wife; timocracy in the relation between brothers. The corresponding perversions of governmental form have their paradigms in perversions of the fundamental household relations (1160b23–1161a9). The construction is so vague in execution that it is impossible to determine with precision what the paradigms are and what precisely the *tertium comparationis* is. Nevertheless, it is not without interest, because it raises the problem of the original experiences in which human relations under more complex social conditions are rooted. And again we should note that, in comparison with Plato's list of axioms, the Aristotelian construction impoverishes the much wider and richer empiricism of the *Laws*.

The characteristics of the best polis, the "standards," are intimately connected with the nature of the polis in so far as the best polis is the one in which its nature is perfectly actualized. The transition from the inquiry into the nature of the polis to the study of its perfect actualization is provided by Book II of *Politics*, in which Aristotle explores the lessons which may be derived from historical actualizations of poleis, as well as from the suggestions of other thinkers, for the development of standards. The materials studied fall into three groups. First, Aristotle discusses the suggestions made by other thinkers, specifically the suggestions made by Plato in *Republic* and *Laws*, as well as those of Phaleas of Chalcedon and Hippodamus of Miletus; second, he surveys the historical constitutions of Lacedaemon, Crete, and Carthage; and third, he briefly reviews the ideas of lawgivers like Solon, Philolaus, Charondas and Pittacus. The discursive criticisms of Book II clarify the brief introductory remarks about the nature of the polis on various points.

A first criticism is directed against the Platonic demand for maximal unification of the polis, as well as against the measures serving this purpose, such as community of women and children and of property. The demand raises the fundamental question whether the members of a polis should have all things in common, or nothing at all, or some things in common and others not. That they should have nothing in common is impossible because in that case the polis would be nonexistent. There must be at least a territory, recognized as the common possession by the members of the polis. Beyond such fundamentals of community, however, the degree of desirable unification is an open problem. "The polis is by nature a [diversified] multitude" (*plethos*) (1261a18–19).

If we try to unify it beyond a certain point it will cease to be a polis and achieve the unity of a family, and ultimately of an individual. Maximal unification destroys the polis, for the *raison d'être* of the polis lies precisely in its being an association of diversified human types; a group of like people is not a polis. The unification which by some is considered the greatest good of the polis, is in reality its destruction, "for the good of each thing is what preserves it" (1261b9). Autarky requires diversification; if autarky is to be desired, then a lesser is preferable to a higher degree of unification (1261b10–15). The community of women and children would produce an undesirable degree of unification, and, therefore, should be barred—setting aside the earlier discussed argument that novelties of this kind should be distrusted on principle.

Such intense community is undesirable for a further reason. The living force of all society is *philia*, a term which in Latin can be rendered by *amicitia*, but which in English must be rendered, according to context, by love or friendship. *Philia* is the ultimate substance of all human relations, the bond of feeling, varying in color, intensity, and stability according to the things which are felt to create the community in the concrete case. *Philia* will be incidental, not touching the whole being of man, if it is based on utility or pleasure; it will affect the whole being if it is based on virtue or excellence. On the level of perfect friendship between persons who are not related by family bonds, we would have to characterize a friend as a man who wishes and does what is good for the sake of his friend, who wishes his friend to live and exist for his own sake, and who grieves and rejoices with his friend (*E. N.* 1166a1ff). These characteristics of friendship, however, are derived from the regard which a good man has for himself. For the good man also is in agreement with himself, desires the same things with undivided soul, does his actions for his own sake (that is, for the sake of the noetic self in him), and desires his own life and security, and in particular the safety of his noetic self. "For it is good for the *spoudaios* to be"; and it is good for him to be as he is, and he does not want to possess any goods under the condition of being anyone but himself; he wants to remain what he is in the sense of preserving the identity of his real self which is the *nous* in him (1166a-19–29). Perfect friendship, thus, must be based on love for one's self in the sense just described; self-love in this sense, of the life in harmony with the orienting *nous* in one's soul, is the source of order in human relations in so far as perfect community will be achieved between men who have the order of the *nous* in common. At this juncture of his description, Aristotle touches on the ultimate source of order between men. The specifically human order of society is the order created through the participation of man in the divine *nous;* just order in society will be realized to the degree in which the potentiality of noetic order becomes actualized in the souls of men who live in society. Justice is ultimately founded in *nous* and *philia.* When men live in harmonious existence, in agreement with their true self, and when agreement between them is based on such agreement with themselves, then the relation prevails between them which Aristotle calls *homonoia*—which may be translated as a friendship based on likeness in actualization of the *nous.*[2] *Homonoia* in this sense is the specifically "political friendship" (*politike philia*) (1167b3–4). Political friendship is not an agreement of opinion as it might occur between strangers, or an agreement on scientific propositions; it is an agreement between citizens as to their interests, an agreement on policies and on their execution. One can speak of *homonoia,* for instance, when citizens agree on the electiveness of offices, or on a military alliance, or on the appointment of a ruling officer (1167a22–1167b4). The stability of a polis depends on the enduring sentiment of friendship between good men; for the base men are capable of friendship only on the level of ephemeral utilities and pleasures and hence discord will prevail in a community where the short-range interests of the vulgar are in conflict with each other and with the common interest (1167b5–16).

Aristotle criticizes the Platonic community of women, children, and property in the light of his theory of *philia.* "Friendship is the greatest good of the polis" (*Politics* 1262b7). A polis, in order to be stable, must be organized in such a manner that it becomes a network of diversified relations of friendship. Every human being is a center, radiating relations of friendship in all directions in which community, however ephemeral, is possible with other human beings. When men have nothing which they can put into a community of friendship, the relations of friendship will vanish. When the normal relations between men and women, parents and children, are interrupted through a communal organization of sex relations, then the human qualities which ordinarily are invested in such relations have no range of actualization. The con-

---

[2] The King James Version translates the Christian *homonoia,* the community through participation in Christ, as "likemindedness." In the Latin literature the term is rendered as *concordia.*

creteness of personal relations will disappear and the very substance of community life will evaporate. Such communal organization, Aristotle suggests, should rather be imposed on the lower classes in order to keep them weak and uninterested in their mode of existence than on the upper class, as Plato wishes to do. "For there are two things that make men care for and love each other: that it is your own and that it is your precious possession—and neither can exist in a society thus organized" (1262b23–25).

The same argument is advanced in criticism of a community of property, as suggested by Plato, or of an equalization of property, as suggested by Phaleas of Chalcedon. The love of self in the previously described sense is implanted "by nature"; and from the real self as its center it radiates into the whole area of possession down to property (1263a40–1263b1ff). Aristotle recognizes that the regulation of property is a fundamental problem, and that in the opinion of some thinkers it is even the question on which all revolutions (stasis) turn (1266a37ff). Nevertheless, the evils accompanying the property order cannot be solved ultimately through legislation. Property, as a general rule, should be private, in order to secure for everybody his personal range of action and to enable him to attend to his own business (1263a26ff); legislative measures should not go to the extreme of a futile equalization but rather stop short at limiting the amount of property (1266b27ff). The root of evil is not property itself but the desire of man. Again and again, Aristotle returns to this point. The evils attending the property order are not due to private property "but to the wickedness [mochteria] of man" (1263b23). "The polis properly is a diversified multitude, and it should be made into a unified community through education [paideia]" —and it is strange that the philosopher who wanted to make the polis virtuous through education should have suggested the improvement of his citizens by regulations instead of habituation and philosophy (1263b36ff). "The baseness of man is insatiable. . . . It is the nature of appetite to be unlimited, and most people live for its satisfaction. In such matters the proper beginning is therefore to be sought less in levelling property than in training the more decent natures so that they will not desire more, and in preventing the base ones from getting more —and that can be achieved if they are kept down but not maltreated" (1267b1–9).

The various criticisms are of theoretical importance because they convey a closer insight into the specifically Aristotelian realism with regard to human nature. In laying down standards for the perfect state we are not free to make any assumptions that strike our fancy. "We may assume what we wish, but we should avoid the impossible" (1265a18f and 1325b39f). The nature of the polis is the nature of man in fully developed social existence; and this nature becomes the limiting factor in the speculation on institutional standards. Plato's anthropological principle as the basis of political science is defended by Aristotle against Plato himself. The modern reader should especially be interested in the direction of the Aristotelian attack against certain features of Platonic politics which have a touch of the Utopian. Aristotle recognizes the "impossible" element in Plato's speculation not in his assumptions concerning the nature of man and the proper system of education (where probably the modern reader would look for it), but in the lack of consistent reliance on the educative process and in his short circuit into institutional remedies (which the modern reader would probably consider the realistic approach, for instance, to the abolition of the evils of private property). Moreover, we should note that an excess of institutional regulation and unification of society is not considered an improvement of undeniable evils, but rather an additional evil through the destruction of the full range of human actualization. The nature of man can neither be changed, nor can inherent wickedness be counterbalanced by regulations; political realism must operate through the *paideia* of man; and it must secure social predominance for the *spoudaios*.

2. The Order of the Polis

A polis is perfect when the nature of the polis is fully actualized. If the polis were an organic growth no problem of a perfect polis could arise in a science of action. In this case the contemplator could do no more than describe the existing poleis and note whether the nature is indeed fully actualized, or whether the growth has been stunted or warped for one reason or another. Perfection becomes a problem in action because, as we have seen, the historical intervention of the "author" or the lawgiver is a factor in actualization. As a consequence, perfection must be understood in relation to the range of action of a lawgiver. There is no sense in projects of order beyond anybody's range of action. A lawgiver is limited by the means at his disposition; he must operate with materials given to him by circumstance, that is, by the aggregate of factors which Aristotle calls the *choregia*. The wisest lawgiver cannot achieve perfection when the materials are unsuitable, as for instance, when the people is too large or too small for a perfect polis, when the territory is inadequate, when economic conditions counteract a just order, when the people is of a slavish disposition, and so forth. A theory of the best order must be based on a study of the limiting factors. We can devise standard institutions only if we assume conditions (*hypothesis*) in the realm of materials (*choregia*) that are favorable to perfect actualization; and in assuming such desirable conditions we must beware of assuming the impossible, for, in that case, our nomothetic speculation would lose contact with reality and become futile (1325b33–1326a3). The area of materials is, on principle, beyond the range of nomothetic action. Hence, it becomes all the more important to define this range of action itself as well as to explore its various degrees of narrowing through unfavorable conditions. The lawgiver's nomothetic art will be oriented toward perfect actualization but concretely he must be satisfied with the best he can do. The structure of the range of action is a central problem for the lawgiver and Aristotle has devoted to it Book III of *Politics*.

In the economy of *Politics*, Book III holds the key position. It is the bridge between the introductory exploration of the nature of the polis and the subsequent nomothetic application to concrete cases. The field of action for the lawgiver is the *politeia* or *politeuma*, variously translated as constitution, kind of government, or form of government. Aristotle himself defines the *politeia* as the order (*taxis*) of the householders of a polis (1274b38). The best translation would be "order of the polis," and the varieties would best be named "types of order"; hence we shall use these terms whenever the conventional language of "constitution" or "form of government" could lead to misunderstandings. Such caution in the use of terms is necessary because in Book III Aristotle's concepts undergo certain changes of meaning. The term "polis," for instance, is not used in the same sense as in Books I and II when the "nature of the polis" was the topic. In Book I the polis was a community of which the "parts" could be determined as household and village. In Book III the polis is still a composite thing, but household and village have been replaced by the citizens (*polites*) as its parts. "The polis is a multitude [*plethos*] of citizens." This is the definition which answers the opening question of Book III: "What really is the polis?" And the question must

be asked because Aristotle is now in search of the polis which is the object
of the "statesman's and lawgiver's activity." [3] The lawgiver's polis is
not the philosopher's polis. The lawgiver must know what the nature of
the polis is; but he will actualize this nature, as far as possible, by concen-
trating his efforts on the "order of the polis."

The distinction between nature and order, between a philosopher's
and a lawgiver's polis leads into theoretical difficulties which Aristotle
could not dissolve or, to put it more cautiously, did not dissolve in the
extant work. Moreover, as far as I know, every interpretation of Aristotle
has broken down on this point. In order to avoid a similar breakdown,
the following analysis will be divided into two parts. In the first part
I shall trace Aristotle's theoretical intentions following the text as closely
as possible. In the second part I shall state the nature of the problem
which causes the difficulties and try to show why it cannot be solved
with the means of Aristotelian metaphysics.

The order of the polis, though variable within a certain range, is
not a matter of free choice but closely determined by the external conditions and social forces which come under the title of "materials." From
this variability within limits follow a number of problems with regard
to the range of nomothetic action. Aristotle deals with them in a roughly
systematic sequence, and we shall follow it, disregarding only the re-
sumptions, repetitions, and variants.

From the variability of the order result, first of all, doubts with
regard to the subject of political action. Is a certain action to be considered an action of the polis or merely of the oligarchy or tyranny in
power? The question is of practical importance in as much as democratic
governments, when they suceed to a tyranny or oligarchy, have the habit
of repudiating the debts incurred by their predecessors, with the argument that some governments rest on force and are not established for the
common good. In so far as this argument has the theoretical intention of
identifying the polis with a democratic order and of denying representative character to tyrannies and oligarchies, Aristotle rejects it; for
democracies also rest as often as not on force, and in that case the
actions of a democratic government could be considered no more

---

[3] The new problem will inevitably be obscured if the question, "What really is the polis?"
is rendered—as we find it in one translation—as "What exactly is the essential nature of the
state?" The *nature* of the polis is precisely *not* the topic of Book III.

the actions of the polis than the actions of oligarchies and tyrannies. Whatever the answer to the question of public debts will be, the argument raises the problem of the identity of the polis in principle. Should one say that a polis remains the same while the generations are born and die, as a river remains the same though the water changes continuously? Or should we compare the people of a polis to theatrical personnel that at one time may appear as a comic and then as a tragic chorus, so that with the change of the *politeia* the polis would have changed? Aristotle inclines toward the second alternative. The polis, he reflects, is a community and what the citizens hold in common is their order of the polis; when the form (*eidos*) of the order changes, then we may consider the polis no longer the same, for "a polis is the same chiefly with regard to its *politeia*." If this argument were followed to its conclusion, the polis as a society in history would disappear. Whenever a victorious revolution of oligarchs or democrats in Athens occurs, one would have to speak of the abolition of one polis and the establishment of a new one which only by an arbitrary act is called by the same name. Aristotle lets the question dangle. But he concludes the argument with the sentence: "Whether a polis is bound in justice to fulfill its engagements when it changes its governmental order [*politeia*], is another question" (1276b14f.). In this sentence the polis is again the subject which retains its identity through the changes of the types of order—but now the question of the debts, which under this assumption should be paid, is left dangling. A reconciliation of these various theoretical intentions is impossible.

A second problem arises from the new definition of the polis as a multitude of citizens. Since not all human beings living on the territory of a polis are citizens, the question must be asked: Who may be called a citizen and what is the meaning of the term? (1275a1ff). Proceeding by exclusion Aristotle finds that resident aliens and slaves, persons who have only standing in court through commercial treaties, children who are not yet on the register, old men who are relieved from duty, persons who were deprived of their citizenship, and exiles, should not be included under the term citizen. The citizens should be defined as persons who participate in office, be it judicial or deliberative, mere jury or assembly service. This definition, however, is exposed to difficulties from the same source as the definition of the *politeia*, in that the definition of the citizen would have to change with the different types of order. The definition that has just been advanced would be appropriate to a democracy but less fitting for oligarchies which have no recognized body of citizens (*demos*) meeting in assembly. In such types of order only the persons who participate in judicial and deliberative functions would be citizens. And again the problem of the polis in concrete existence intrudes; for in the concluding sentence of this section Aristotle returns to the assurance that a polis is a multitude of citizens numerous enough for self-sufficiency (1275b20). Does this sentence mean that the persons participating in office in an oligarchy must be numerous enough for this end? Or, would Aristotle deprive a tyranny (in which an insignificant number of persons share in offices) of the name of polis? Or, does it mean that a polis is self-sufficient if it has enough citizens by right of birth even if not all of them are citizens by office?

The questions must remain in suspense for the moment because at this juncture Aristotle introduces a further complicating factor. He raises the question whether the excellence (*arete*) of the good man and the good citizen is the same or not. And in order to answer this question one must have a notion of the excellence of a citizen. The citizens have a common object, that is, the weal (*soteria*) of their community. "And this community is the constitution [*politeia*]." The excellence of the citizen, therefore, will be relative to the constitution, and as there are many forms (*eidos*) of constitutions the excellence of the citizen cannot be the same in all cases. When we speak of a good man, however, we have in mind the one and only goodness. Hence, it is possible to be a good citizen without being a good man (1276b16–36). And this will hold true even for the best form of government. For the polis is composed of dissimilar elements, all of which have to contribute their specific share to the existence of the whole—some in ruling positions, some as subjects —and consequently, while all of them must be good citizens contributing their specific share to the whole, they will occupy varying ranks in the scale of human excellence. This, however, does not mean that the two excellences can never coincide in the same person. The good ruler or statesman, for instance, must also be a wise and mature (*spoudaios*) man. But for the plain citizen wisdom is not necessary and it is quite sufficient if he has the "true opinion" (*doxa alethes*) that will enable him to submit to authority. And then we must consider the "political rule" (*politike arche*) in the specific sense which is rule over equals of one's own race and freemen. In that case the art of rulership can be acquired only by passing through the art of obedience. The good citizen under "political rule" must be equally capable of ruling and obeying, and the good man in the society of freemen and equals will also possess the excellence of the good citizen.

After this digression Aristotle returns to the task of defining the citizen. Is it indeed justified to define the citizen as a person who shares in certain offices, or should not the artisan classes be included in the term? But if we include them we cannot maintain the definition of the good citizen who is capable both of ruling and obeying; and if we exclude them, how should they be classified since they are neither slaves nor aliens? Aristotle decides that not all people who are necessary to the existence of a state can be considered citizens. If the artisans should not be slaves or aliens anyway as they were in ancient times, then we must decide that not all freemen can be considered citizens but only those who are freed from menial work. Those who are engaged in necessary work will be excluded from citizenship "by the best polis." In fact, however, we see artisans admitted to citizenship in many poleis. As a consequence, we must assume several kinds of citizens; and the citizen in the fullest sense will be the man who shares in the honors of the polis.

From this tortuous argument nothing can be concluded with absolute clarity—especially since in a decisive point the manuscript has a lacuna of indeterminate size. Nevertheless, at least a drift of problems can be discerned. Aristotle is concerned with the tension between the one nature of the polis and the many varieties of actualization. From the speculation on this tension emerges the possibility that the form (*eidos*) of order can be brought to coincide maximally with the nature (*physis*) of the polis. We, thus, arrive at the notion of the best polis as the polis whose order (*politeia*) will be an organization of the free and equal men, that is, of the society of mature men as described in *Nicomachean Ethics*. While such maximal coincidence is desirable, the political scientist must recognize that the historical poleis fall far short of such perfection; in fact, Aristotle admits on occasion that none of the 158 constitutions examined by him live up to his standards. Such deficiency, however, is no reason to deny to them the name of polis. The problem of politics is not exhausted by an exploration of the nature of the polis; the metaphysical inquiry must be supplemented by what we may call a sociology of politics. Men, indeed, associate in the polis for the purpose of the good life, and the striving for this end is the nature of the polis; but that does not mean that the striving will be particularly successful. "All men manifestly desire the good life and happiness; but, while some have the power of attaining it, others do not have it because of some factor of fortune or nature; for the good life requires certain means, though fewer for those of a better disposition than for those of a worse one. And others, while having the power, go wrong because they misconceive the end" (1331b39–1332a4). Since "some men can attain excellence, while others have little or none of it, this is clearly the reason that different kinds of poleis arise as well as several varieties of constitutions. For, as different kinds of men seek eudaimonia in different ways, they also will make for themselves different modes of life and different forms of government" (1328a37–1328b2). And such vagaries have taken hold even of the Hellenes who are reputed to be the best governed, "for, the lawgivers who framed their constitutions manifestly did not organize them with a regard to the best end, nor did they institute laws and educational systems with regard to all the excellences, but in a vulgar manner they catered to qualities that seemed useful and made for gain" (1333b5–11).

The polis, thus, is at best a highly diversified society in which the full moral stature will be attained only by a comparatively small group. The best polis would contain an association of such free and equal mature men as its politically dominant group; this association would be the "citizens" in the strict sense of the persons who take turns in deliberative and judicial functions. Even under these most favorable conditions, however, the dominant association of citizens would probably not be homogeneous; differences of excellence would make themselves felt; and the full stature would be achieved perhaps only by one, or a very few at a time, who would qualify as the "statesmen." Below this dominant nucleus extend the ranks of inhabitants of the polis whom Aristotle would like to exclude from citizenship for one reason or another. There is, first, the large stratum of artisans whose hard work and poverty prevents them from developing the excellences of the mature man. And below them are the slaves. Slavery is considered by Aristotle a desirable institution in so far as the persons who are legally slaves are also slaves by nature. "A slave by nature is a man who is capable of being another's (and therefore is another's) because he participates in reason enough to apprehend it, but not enough to possess it" (1324b21ff). The conception of a slave by nature frequently arouses the indignation of egalitarians—

quite without reason, for the conception does not deny the equality of human nature but is an attempt at an empirical differentiation of personality types within that common and equal nature. The slaves by nature who will indulge in mischief when a master does not keep an eye on them are, of course, empirically a rather large sector of every society, our own as well as the Greek. When a member of the British labor government reflected that social improvements increased the number of persons "whose income is higher than their moral stature," he gave as neat a sociological definition of the slave by nature as one could wish.

How can such differentiation of human ranks be reconciled with the idea of human nature equal for all? Aristotle saw the difficulty (*aporia*) especially with regard to the slaves by nature. "Either way there is a difficulty. If they have virtue, how do they differ from freemen? And if they have not, that would be strange, since they are human beings and participate in reason [*logos*]." And similar difficulties could be raised with regard to women and children. The answer to the aporia cannot be sought in the assumption of differences of degree; for the difference of ruling and being ruled is a difference of kind, not of degree. It is evident, therefore, that both slaves and masters must possess virtue, though in a different manner. Aristotle's solution is very similar to Plato's in the *Republic*. The structure of the soul with its ruling and subordinate parts and the ruling function of the soul over the body provide the differentiations of kind. All human beings have, indeed, the same structure of the soul, but differentiated according to the predominance of one or the other of the parts. The slave is not capable of deliberation; the female can deliberate but not with full authority; while the child has the deliberative faculty in undeveloped form. The ruler must possess the dianoetic virtue in completeness, while each of the other types need only have the appropriate share of dianoetic excellence. The same holds true for the ethical excellences. All must partake of them, but not in the same manner. The courage, temperance, and justice of a man is not the same as the corresponding excellences of a woman. It is, therefore, inexpedient to give a general definition of virtue; it would be better to differentiate the virtues terminologically so that the specific variant peculiar to each type of persons is properly distingushed (1259b22 to end of Book I).

Aristotle has not executed his program in any detail worth mentioning. Nevertheless, the principle of his solution is clear. He adopts the Platonic method of describing characters in terms of predominance of one or the other component factors of the soul; but he goes beyond Plato in that he introduces differences of sex and age, of occupation and economic position, of biographical accident (*tyche*), of the civilizational state of society, as well as geographical and racial differences as factors which determine a wide variety of types without breaking the unity of human nature. Within this great variety of human types inhabiting the polis he then distinguishes the association of mature men as the group in which human excellence is maximally actualized. This group is what we might call the virtual representative for the total population of the excellence of life to be actualized by the polis; and their order is the *politeia*, the organizational form of the polis. This conception of government implies that the polis is most perfectly ordered when the ruling association is most strictly confined to men who, indeed, actualize the ethical and dianoetic excellences in their persons (with the qualification that within that group itself degrees of perfection must be allowed). The more the ruling association is diluted by the inclusion of men who are deficient in the excellences, that is, the more the government becomes democratically representative in the modern sense, the less representative it will be in the Aristotelian sense of a rule that represents the excellence of the polis. This Aristotelian idea of government as the representation of the excellence of a polis must be clearly understood if one wants to avoid facile misunderstandings. The vocabulary of Aristotelian politics has survived the ages but it has changed its meaning profoundly. It would be a gross mistake to read our modern democratic constitutionalism (which presupposes the Christian idea of equality) into the Aristotelian constitutionalism of a ruling association which represents the excellence of the community.

An Aristotelian analysis, in the sense of the *Analytica Posteriora*, begins with the pre-analytical observation of problems as they emerge from the materials and tries to penetrate to the essential structure of the respective area of being. In the analysis that we have just traced, the problems on the pre-analytical level induced Aristotle to develop a series of three conceptual distinctions. In the first place, the observation of revolutions, as well as of the corresponding changes of constitutions in a polis, motivated the distinction between nature and order of the polis. Once the order of the constitution was established as a category, it had to be the order of something; and the constitution acquired the function of a "form" in relation to the citizens as its "matter." This second distinction between the constitutional form and the citizens led to the difficulty that a good number of men somehow belong to a polis but cannot be classified as citizens if the citizen be defined as the "matter" that fits into the constitutional "form." That was embarrassing, for the citizens who fitted as matter into the constitutional "form" of the polis were after all the same men who were members of the polis that had a "nature." In order to cope with this problem Aristotle, third, distinguished between the good man and the good citizen. But the result of the analysis conducted by means of these concepts proved not too happy; for Aristotle had to admit that only under exceptional circumstances of constitutional order, such as were not given in any of the historical poleis, could the good man at the same time be the good citizen. If that, however, were admitted without reservations, the theory of the polis as the type of community in which man finds the fulfillment of his nature would break down; the nature of the polis could no longer be linked with the nature of man by the anthropological principle which Aristotle had inherited from Plato; and a perspective would open on the possibility of human existence, in satisfactory modes of actualization of human nature, in societies of a type other than the polis. Aristotle avoided this breakdown of his political science as a science of the order of the polis by admitting, on the one hand, the tension between nature and order of the polis and enjoining, on the other hand, the lawgiver to approach the order to the nature as far as practically possible. The problems arising within the analysis, thus, were not pursued into their theoretical consequences; and the breakdown of the analysis was prevented from becoming manifest by distinguishing between the philosopher's and the lawgiver's polis.

This complex piece of philosophizing must be unravelled from the point of its obvious technical derailment. If we assume with Aristotle that the polis is a thing with a nature or essence at all, the problematic character of his *episteme politike* becomes clear when the inquiry into the nature (*physis*) of the polis in Book I has to be supplemented by an inquiry into its form (*eidos*) in Book III. Since *physis* and *eidos* are synonyms for essence, the polis is a thing with two different essences. There can be no doubt that something is wrong. In order to make the double-headed monster intelligible, I shall explain first the theoretical mechanism of its construction and then the motivations.

The difficulties have their origin in the attempt to apply the ontological categories, which had been developed in *Physics* and *Metaphysics,* without further clarification to the order of human existence in society. The categories of form and matter had been originally constructed so as to fit definite types of entities, *sc.* the organism, the artifact, and the purposive action. In the case of a plant or animal one can indeed describe a phenotypical form which remains the same during the life of the organism while in the process of metabolism matter is absorbed and ejected. In the case of the artifact one can indeed speak of the craftsman's design as the form to be imposed on the matter used. And in the case of purposive action the project can be interpreted as the form which organizes the means as materials for the end. When, however, the categories are applied to the polis, when the constitution becomes its "form" and the citizens its "matter," the difficulties of the Aristotelian argument are inevitable. Should everybody be counted as a citizen who is a permanent resident on the territory of the polis? But then metics and slaves would be citizens, and such language would be in conflict with everyday usage. As a citizen should be counted, therefore, only a man who participates in the governmental process, if not in higher office, at least as a voter in assembly. But that definition runs into the difficulty that not all poleis have the "form" of a democracy; in a tyranny or oligarchy not all free men will have the right to vote in assembly, though they will not lose their status as citizens and sink to the rank of metics or slaves. Aristotle, it is true, admits that the definition of the citizen as a man who participates in the process of government will suit a democracy better than other "forms," but he does not push the analysis further. He wants to retain the constitution as the "form" of the polis; and then the citizens, in their role of "matter," must be defined as persons who have a place and function within the "form." If we, then, trace the argument from the *eidos* back to the *physis* of the polis we run into the oddity of a polis which changes its identity every time the change of the power constellation results in a new "form"; and when we trace it from the citizen forward to man, we find that a man can be a good man without having status as a citizen in the "form" of the polis and that he may be a very bad man precisely when he is a good citizen in terms of the "form." It should be amply clear that the ontological categories, developed on occasion of the enumerated models in *Physics* (II, 3) and *Metaphysics* (I, 9 and XII, 3), are not adequate instruments for the theoretization of order in society. Aristotle's attempt to use them nevertheless is a clear instance of the transformation of philosophical categories into *topoi*, torn out of their context and used in speculation whether they fit the field of problems or not.

Aristotle was aware of the difficulties in which his procedure involved him. As a matter of fact, he has set forth the difficulties with such thoroughness and precision that his exposition is the best guide toward the alternative theoretization that would dissolve them. Since the odd construction certainly does not betray a failing of intellectual powers, the question of its motives imposes itself. What experience of order required the construction as the adequate means of its expression? What gain was so important that he was willing to pay for it the price of the difficulties? These questions will be best approached by first stating the solution to the difficulties which Aristotle did not accept even though his own analysis led to its very brink.

The constiutional order of a society must not be constructed as its essence or form because the institutional cross-cut, at any given time, is not a thing with an ontological status of its own. A society exists in time in as much as it produces a representative that will act for it; and the composition of the representative is liable to change with the changing constellation of forces in the historical course of a society. The constitutional order, *i.e.* the organization of representative social action acceptable for the time being, is a phase of order which may be accorded the rank of a sub-form within the embracing order of society that extends through the duration of its existence. This problem had escaped neither Plato nor Aristotle, as we know, on the level of their empirical observations. Both philosophers knew that the Hellenic poleis displayed a typical sequence of power constellations and corresponding "forms" of constitutions, running the cycle of kingship, aristocracy, popular revolt, tyranny of the Peisistratide type, oligarchy, and democracy of various degrees of radicalism. As far as the practice of political science was concerned, the society in the whole extension of its historical course, with its cycle of constitutional sub-forms, was well established as a unit of inquiry. Moreover, since it was recognized that the cycle of forms applied not only to one particular polis, *e.g.* Athens, but was typical within a range of variations for all Hellenic poleis, even the single polis was already superseded as the ontological unit and had given way to the Hellenic society, organized as a manifold of poleis, as the unit of empirical inquiry. And even the Hellenic world of the poleis in the narrower sense had been superseded as the ultimate unit by the Platonic construction of the course of Greek history which included beyond the Hellenic also the Achaean and Cretan societies. In the practice of science the process was well under way in which the object of inquiry expands from the order of the concrete societies to civilizations, from single civilizations to classes of civilizations which belong to the same type of order, and ultimately to the order of history of a mankind which is no finite unit of observation at all as it extends indefinitely into the future. Whatever appears to be a finite unit of observation in the study of order turns out to be a subunit in the vast process of the history of mankind; and the complicated problems of structure in this process—which are the subject matter of the present study—can obviously not be resolved by declaring one of the sub-units the unit with ontological status and by appointing its structure an essence.

Why did Aristotle, when he theorized, not pursue the problems that were spread out before him on the level of empirical observation? The answer must be that their relevance could not become visible within the Hellenic experience of order. The *episteme politike*, the science of the order of the polis, could expand into a science of order and history only where existence in historical form had been established, *i.e.* in the orbit of Mosaic and Christian revelation. Aristotle's procedure of cutting his own empirical observations short by making the constitution the *eidos* of order is the classic proof of the thesis that the pursuit of science with a maximum of rationality is possible only when the realms of being are completely differentiated.

But why should the study of order be cut short by according the character of *eidos* to the constitution? Could not at least the course of a polis, with its succession of constitutional forms, so well within the range of Aristotle's empirical observation, have been accorded the rank of an ontological unit deserving analysis under the aspect of essence? This further question, concerning the motive of Aristotle's positive decision for the constitution as the *eidos*, must be answered in the light of his construction of the *physis* of the polis. The Aristotelian inquiry into the *physis*, the nature of the polis, is oriented not toward the historical course of the society and its structure but toward the best order of the polis. Aristotle, while admitting that his model of the best polis is tailored to the historical conditions of a society of mature men, of the *spoudaioi*, insists nevertheless that his paradigm articulates the essence of the polis. That proposition is tenable if the two assumptions be granted that (1) the nature of man has achieved its full actualization in the type of the *spoudaios* who cultivates the *bios theoretikos,* and that (2) the full un-folding of human nature is possible only in a society of the polis type. Neither of the two assumptions can be admitted as true after Christ, to be sure—but the relation to the more differentiated Christian anthropol-ogy is of interest at the moment only in that it allows us to circumscribe the Aristotelian analysis of essence as a search for perfection, within the more compact experience of *physis,* of nature, which in Christianity is conducted under the assumption that perfection lies in the beyond. The order of society in history is theoretically irrelevant to Aristotle because he is convinced that perfect order can be realized within his-tory; the order of history itself becomes of absorbing interest only when perfection is recognized as a symbol of eschatological fulfillment beyond history. If however the perfect order is considered realizable in history, the empirical structure of order, though theoretically ir-relevant, acquires pragmatic relevance as the condition under which the perfect order is to be realized. While the philosopher, who is in search of the paradigm of perfection, has no theoretical interest in the historical expanse of nonessential reality (nonessential, if essence is *physis*), the lawgiver needs the thorough, empirical knowledge of this reality as it is the medium in which he wants to build the perfect polis. The inquiry into the essential structure of society and its order had to be cut short with the lawgiver's constitutional *eidos,* because the limit of relevance was set by the philosopher's *physis.* The rise and fall of society, though empirically observed, remains within the fatality of cosmic order; and above this fatality into the realm of essence rise only the theoretic life of the *spoudaios* and the perfect society which ex-presses the order of his soul. Despite the empirical discovery of the his-torical course of Hellenic society, and despite the consciousness of the spiritual epoch marked by Socrates and Plato, history has not yet mean-ing. The philosophers' leap in being has set free the paradigmatic *physis* of man and society, but it has not disengaged, as has the Mosaic and prophetic leap in being, the order of history from the myth of the cosmos.[4]

3. *Types of Order*

There is more than one type of constitutional order (*politeia*). The next task is the determination of the various types and of the differences

[4] For further elaboration of this problem see Chapter 10.

between them (1278b6ff). For the purpose of gaining a suitable principle of differentiation Aristotle gives a new definition of constitutional order. Previously the *politeia* was defined as the order of the householders in a polis; now it is redefined as "the order [*taxis*] of the polis with regard to the various magistracies and especially with regard to the highest ones; for the ruling part [*kyrion*] is everywhere the governing magistracy [*politeuma*] of the polis, and the governing magistracy is the constitution [*politeia*] itself" (1278b9f). In a democracy, for instance, the people (*demos*) are the ruling part, in an oligarchy the few (*oligoi*); and thus the two constitutions can be distinguished. A second principle of differentiation is given through the regard for the common interest (*sympheron*). Constitutions can have regard for the common interest according to strict justice; or they can have regard for the personal interest of the rulers alone. The first type may be called right (or true, *orthos*) constitutions; the second type may be called defective or a perversion (*parekbasis*) of true constitutions. The second type is perverted in so far as it contains an element of despotism, though a polis is supposed to be a community of freemen (1279a17–22). From the combination of these two differentiating principles follows the classification of the types of order in the two series of right and perverted constitutions. The right constitutions are kingship (the true form of monarchy), aristocracy (the true form of a government by the few), and polity (the true form of government by the multitude, the *plethos*).[5] The perverted constitutions are tyranny (in the interest of the monarch), oligarchy (in the interest of the rich), democracy (in the interest of the poor) (1279a26–1279b10).

This classification of the types of order is derived from the classification given by Plato in the *Statesman*. As soon as it is made, Aristotle criticizes it deftly and so effectively that an entirely different classification emerges in the discussion of concrete problems. The point of attack is the uncritical assumption that a government of the few, when it degenerates, is a government of the rich, while a government of the many, when it degenerates, is a government of the poor. Is there indeed such a pre-established harmony between few and rich, and many and

---

[5] The term polity (*politeia*), which otherwise is used generically for all constitutions, is considered by Aristotle the most appropriate for designating the government of the multitude because it is difficult for the multitude of freemen to possess full excellence. The multitude will rather excell in military (*polemike*) virtue. Apparently Aristotle assumed an etymological connection between *politeia* and *polemos* (1279a41–1279b5).

poor? Not necessarily; and in some freakish instance the many actually are the rich and the few the poor. As a rule, however, the rich in fact are few and the poor in fact are the many. This correlation cannot be found by theoretical speculation and logical classification. It is a matter of empirical observation; and the fact of this correlation must be introduced as a constant into the analysis of politics. Aristotle proposes, indeed, something like a primitive formulation of the Pareto curve concerning the distribution of incomes in any society. In practice, therefore, the political struggle is fought among the rich, the poor, and the virtuous who may be either rich or poor. The practical problems of politics arise from the fact that the three types coexist in a polis and that each type raises its specific claim in the name of justice to be the ruling part. The rich claim a ruling position because of their stake in the community; the poor in the name of their freedom; and the virtuous in the name of their excellence. Hence, the discussion of the types of order must proceed in terms of the claims raised by the various social types enumerated.

The anlysis concentrates, first, on the respective claims of the rich and the poor. The claims are raised in the name of justice; but they are partial claims, not exhausting the whole of the idea of justice. Justice can be found, for instance, in equality; and equality is indeed part of justice, but only for equals. And then again, justice may be found in inequality of rights and treatment; and inequality also is part of justice, but only for unequals. When the principles of equality and inequality are taken in the abstract, without regard to the concrete qualities of persons, they will lead to erroneous judgments. Those who are unequal in some respect, as for instance wealth, are inclined to consider themselves unequal from others in every respect. Those who feel themselves equal in some respect, as for instance freedom of birth, are inclined to consider themselves everybody's equal in every respect (1280a17–25). If we should give way to these respective claims we would arrive at the construction of governments as oligarchies or democracies without qualifications. Since, however, "those who are equal in one thing only should not have equality in all things, and those who are unequal with regard to one thing should not have an unequal share in all things, it necessarily follows that constitutions based on these claims are perversions" (1283a26–29).

In political practice the conflict of claims cannot be solved by deciding in favor of one or the other party, nor can it be settled as if it were a conflict of claims arising from a contract in civil law. A polis is not merely a group of persons settling in a territory; nor could one speak of a polis if a number of households would enter into a sort of alliance for defense against evildoers but otherwise remain the same individual units as before. A polis is more than an organization for the prevention of crime and the exchange of goods. It is the community of clans and villages for a happy and honorable life, based on the *philia*, the friendship, between men; and *philia* is rooted in the realization of the true self. The polis exists for the sake of noble actions, and those who contribute most to this end through their political virtue have a greater share in it than those who excel through wealth or those who are no more than their equals through free birth (1280b24–1281a8). The solution to the problem of just order, thus, cannot lie in the harmonization of claims between rich and poor; the justice of the polis derives from *philia* and the actualization of human excellence. The problem of justice can be solved in political practice only if the third social type, the virtuous, is brought into play.

All these reflections still leave the question how a government should be organized in order to secure a maximum of justice. Aristotle does not express himself explicitly on this point in the context of Book III, but his analyses imply that he is falling back on the considerations and solutions given by Plato in the *Laws*. None of the conflicting claims is acceptable as the organizing principle of government. The rich would oppress the poor; and the poor would plunder the rich. Besides, the groups excluded from government would be so many public enemies causing permanent revolutionary instability. The partial claims would result in what Plato called the "no-constitutions." Aristotle goes beyond Plato in also ruling out a government by the virtuous because such a government would only be an even more restricted "oligarchy," dishonoring an even greater number of citizens by excluding them from the honors of office.[6] The solution must be sought in a compromise that will reserve the offices of influence to the rich, well-bred, and responsible citizens, while opening to the mass of the poor freemen an access to government through participation in elections and supervising commissions. This seems to be a somewhat thin answer to the

[6] In this suggestion that the rule of the virtuous is one more "perversion" we may see one of the many subtle attacks on the Platonic *Republic*.

great questions raised, and it becomes even thinner through the reflections on the problem of law which appear in this context. For it would
be best if the magistrate would simply rule according to law. But it
would be the best only if the law were just. In political practice, however, the law must be of the same complexion as the type of order itself. A democracy with oligarchic law is quite as inconceivable as an
oligarchy with democratic law. As long as in practice the order of the
polis will depend on precarious compromises between rich and poor,
the rule of law will not mean much as a guarantee of just order.

The puzzle of these unsatisfactory answers is solved through a few,
very brief remarks on the historical dynamics of the types of order.
The various governmental orders which previously appeared in systematic classification are now transformed into phases of an historical
process. Kingship, as an early form of government, appeared when men
of eminent virtue were few in number and the poleis were small in size.
A man arrived at kingship with consent of his fellow men because he
was distinguished through inventiveness in arts and military matters,
because he gathered them into a community and acquired land for
them, and thus became the founder and natural leader. Such kingships
naturally were rules of the virtuous because only good men could be-
stow such benefits. With prosperity and increase in numbers, then, the
men of excellence became more numerous and were unwilling to submit to kingship; they desired a commonwealth (*koinon*) and set up a
constitution. The aristocratic republic thus was the second form of
government. When the ruling class deteriorated and began to enrich
itself at the expense of the commonwealth, wealth gained honor and
the phase of oligarchy was reached. The concentration of wealth in
fewer hands resulted in tyrannies; and the tyrannies gave way to the
rule of increasing masses of relatively poor freemen. Now that the poleis
have further increased in population, it will no longer be easy to establish any constitution other than a democracy (1286b8–22). The cycle
of political form, thus, is the final answer to the problem of classification. The unsatisfactory deliberation about the good and bad forms
dissolves into the recognition of a civilizational process in which the
cumulative effects of peace, order, prosperity, increase of population,
and concentration of wealth will produce the deterioration of the initial
founding excellence until mass democracy becomes the only historically
possible form. The derivation of this conception from the theory of de-
teriorating form developed by Plato in the *Republic* is obvious.

Surveying the whole course of Aristotle's reflection on types of order, we may say that he attempted the several approaches that were suggested by the *Statesman*, the *Laws* and the *Republic*. None of these approaches seemed quite satisfactory. The second seemed to supersede the first, and the third the second. A unification of the several theoretical intentions into one coherent theory was not attempted and was perhaps impossible.

The unification of the several theoretical intentions was, indeed, not achieved—but one cannot dispose of Aristotelian philosophizing with a flat statement of this kind. In earlier sections of the present chapter we have stressed that the quality of Aristotle's thought must not be sought, and cannot be found, in the perfection of a system, but in the comprehensive inventorying and ordering of problems. Moreover, his philosophizing in general, and especially in ethics and politics, starts from the pre-analytical opinions held about the subject matter in question, assuming that any opinion however erroneous will still contain a part of the truth and that the critical examination of opinions will leave as its sediment the partial truth which they contained. Among these pre-analytical opinions to be examined Aristotle also ranks the opinions of Plato as well as of other thinkers. Thus, in the course of the reflections just analysed the Platonic classification of constitutions in true and perverted forms is rejected as inadequate because the criterion of goodness or badness is sought in the observation or non-observation of the law. "For the laws should be made to suit the constitution, and not the constitution to suit the laws" (1289a13f). While the distinction of true and perverted forms is preserved, the criterion is shifted to the predominance of one or the other of the social types. The subsequent distinction of the three types of rich, poor, and virtuous again remains inconclusive as far as a classification of constitutions is concerned; but it leaves as its valuable result the insight into the fundamental stratification of every society into the classes of the rich and the poor, compelling institutions that will prevent revolutionary explosions. And the final classification of various constitutions as the historical phases of the polis adds a new criterion but does not invalidate the results of the preceding analysis. The process of Aristotelian philosophy has an entelechy. While the result of the train of reflections, its *telos*, is not articulated, it is reached nevertheless. In this case it is the manifold of political form. The varieties of this manifold are determined by the disintegration of the initial founding virtue, by the social stratification into the classes of the rich and the poor, by geographical conditions, historical accidents, and population increases. From the reflections of Book III we emerge into a manifold of political reality that requires empirical investigation and inventorying of details with a degree of differentiation beyond the range of the original classification of six constitutions from which the reflections started. The original six terms, to be sure, can still be used but they must be stretched, in order to fulfill their purpose, by a wealth of subdivisions. This vast, empirical survey of constitutional forms and problems is given in Books IV, V, and VI of *Politics*.

4. The Manifold of Political Reality

The spirit of loving attention to empirical detail which animates the survey of Books IV to VI has found its representative expression not in *Politics* itself but on occasion of a comparable empirical study in zoology. We are referring to a famous page of *De Partibus Animalium*:

"Of things constituted by nature some are ungenerated, imperishable, and eternal, while others are subject to generation and decay. The former are excellent beyond compare and divine, but less accessible to knowledge. The evidence that might throw light on them, and the problems which we long to solve respecting them, is furnished but scantily by sensation; whereas respecting perishable plants and animals we have abundant information, living as we do in their midst, and ample data may be collected concerning all their various kinds, if only we are willing to take sufficient pains. Both departments, however, have their special charm. The scanty conceptions to which we can attain of celestial things give us, from their excellence, more pleasure than all our knowledge of the world in which we live; just as half a glimpse of persons that we love is more delightful than a leisurely view of other things, whatever their number and dimensions. On the other hand, in certitude and in completeness our knowledge of terrestrial things has the advantage. Moreover, their greater nearness and affinity to us balances somewhat the loftier interest of the heavenly things that are the objects of the higher philosophy. Having already treated of the celestial world, as far as our conjectures could reach, we proceed to treat of animals, without omitting, to the best of our ability, any member of the kingdom, however ignoble. For if some have no graces to charm the sense, yet even these, by disclosing to intellectual perception the artistic spirit that designed them, give immense pleasure to all who can trace links of causation, and are inclined to philosophy. Indeed, it would be strange if mimic representations of them were attractive, because they disclose the mimetic skill of the painter or sculptor, and the original realities were not more interesting, to all at any rate who have eyes to discern the reasons that determined their formation. We therefore must not recoil with childish aversion from the examination of the humbler animals. Every realm of nature is marvellous: and as Heraclitus, when the strangers who came to visit him found him warming himself at the furnace in the kitchen and hesitated to go in, is reported to have bidden them not to be afraid to enter, as even in that kitchen divinities were present, so we should venture on the study of every kind of animal without distaste; for each and all will reveal to us something natural and something beautiful. Absence of haphazard and conduciveness of everything to an end are to be found in Nature's works in the highest degree, and the resultant of her generations and combinations is a form of the beautiful." [7]

The inventorization of problems in Books IV–VI is voluminous. We must confine ourselves to an exposition of the principles on which the survey is based. Poleis are not animals, and political science is not a science of natural forms. Political form is still a problem for the craft, the *techne,* of the lawgiver. In the same manner as other crafts, the art of politics must consider its subject, the constitutions, under four aspects: It must (1) explore the constitution which is best by nature as well as by material circumstances; it must (2) consider which constitution is the best under less favorable circumstances actually given; it must (3) consider what the lawgiver can do in the case that an already existing constitution falls short of the relatively best that could have been achieved under the given circumstances; and it must (4) consider an average constitution which is roughly practical for the majority of cases (1288b10–40).

In order to execute this program, Aristotle must, first of all, seriously grapple with the problem of the manifold of forms. A considerably more elaborate apparatus than the classification of six forms will be required, and it will be gained through a resumption of the problem of the "parts" of the polis. This time the polis is likened to an animal. When we deter-

---

[7] Aristotle, *De Partibus Animalium,* trans. by William Ogle, Oxford ed. of *The Works of Aristotle,* 644b21–645a26.

mine the species of animals we must proceed by determining the various organs that are indispensable for an animal. The number of these organs is limited, but each of them may be shaped in many different ways. Hence, we have for each organ a series of varieties; and any member of each series may enter into combination with any member of the other series, thus creating the immense manifold of animal forms. In the same manner we must now proceed with regard to the polis. Each polis consists of a number of necessary elements, and since variations of these elements are possible the combinations of the variations will render an indefinitely large manifold of different poleis. As the necessary elements Aristotle specifies the following:

(1) husbandmen or peasants
(2) artisans
(3) the commercial class—wholesale and retail
(4) day laborers, workers
(5) warriors
(6) the personnel for administration of justice and deliberative assemblies
(7) the wealthy who serve the polis with their property
(8) the men who serve as magistrates and rulers of the polis

This list of parts (*meros, morion*), however, is not put to direct use in the analysis of reality. Aristotle interposes the reflection that several of these functions may appear in the same individual. The warrior may also be a husbandman or an artisan; or he may be a counsellor or a judge; and quite generally most people believe that in addition to their other functions they are quite capable of discharging the duties of a political office. Only two "parts" can never be combined in one individual—for nobody can be rich and poor at the same time. The rich and the poor thus become eminently the "parts" of a polis in that everybody is rich or poor in addition to whatever other function in the community he may have. This distinction of eminent (*malista*) and ordinary parts determines the further procedure of analysis because now again oligarchy and democracy can move into the position of focal constitutional forms while the variations of the ordinary parts allow for the classification of political forms as subvariants of oligarchies and democracies (1290b21–1291b13).

Aristotle concentrates his attention on oligarchies and democracies. Their discussion occupies a major part of Book IV and the whole of Book

VI. Nevertheless, this preoccupation does not make him lose sight of the other forms, *i.e.* of kingship, aristocracy, polity, and tyranny. The survey is exhaustive and clarity about the principle which governs the survey as a whole is important for the understanding of Aristotle's theoretical intention. Moreover, the understanding of the theoretical principle is apt to cast some light on the genesis of Aristotle's thought concerning politics.

The principle becomes clear through one more of the redefinitions of fundamental concepts of which we have already seen so many. When Aristotle programmatically outlines (1289a25ff) the survey that is to follow, he speaks of the "original discourse on constitutions" in which he had outlined the three types of good constitutions and their corresponding perversions; and then he continues: "We have spoken [in the first or original discourse] about aristocracies and kingships—for theorizing about the best constitution is the same as speaking about the forms bearing these names, since each of them implies virtue and equipment with external means." The identification of the best constitution with aristocracy is further sharpened through the explanation that the constitution discussed "in the first discourses" has received its name properly because its citizens are meant to be best (*aristoi*) according to excellence (*arete*) in the strict sense and not simply good according to some other standards; for only "in an aristocracy is the good man and citizen the same" (1293b2ff).

The identification of the perfect polis as the aristocracy discussed in the closing chapters of Book III clarifies the intricate structure of Aristotelian politics in several respects. First of all, the identification entails a revision of the concept of perversion (*parekbasis*). With the strict definition of aristocracy as the best constitution, all other constitutions acquire the character of defection. The "best polis" now becomes, in the scale of the types of order, the "most true" constitution; and the character of defection invades even the category of aristocracy itself. For there are constitutions to which the name of aristocracy cannot be denied and which nevertheless are not the "best constitution," such as the poleis in which the magistrates are chosen "not only because of their wealth but also because of their nobility." [8] They are not best because

---

[8] Politics, 1293b10-12. I have rendered as "nobility" the Greek adverb *aristinden*. Aristotle wishes to distinguish this quality from the excellence which is due to *arete*. *Aristinden* can mean social distinction through nobility of birth, but also distinction through valor or other

the actualization of excellence is not their avowed "public concern";
but they are next to it because in fact they select men with a good reputation for judgment and reliability. An instance of such an aristocracy
where excellence (*arete*) is preferred if coupled with wealth, is Carthage;
and Lacedaemon also may be called an aristocracy because, though tempered by democratic elements, it allows excellence its place (1293b12–
17). As a consequence of such consideration Aristotle arrives at a different
concept of perversion. Kingship, aristocracy, and polity remain the "true"
constitutions as distinguished from the *parekbaseis,* the perversions in the
earlier sense; but with the differentiation of the "best constitution" as the
"most true" (*orthotatos*) constitution, all others "fail" or "fall short"
(*diamarthanein*) of the "most true" and "must be reckoned among perversions [*parekbaseis*]" in the new sense (1293b25ff). The new concept
of perversion corresponds methodologically to the new apparatus of a
more differentiated classification of the forms of government. With the
subdivision of the six main forms into varieties according to the variations in the list of "parts," it also becomes necessary to subdivide the
meaning of "true" and "perverse" so that the gamut of values will correspond to the gamut of forms.

The identification of the best polis with aristocracy, or rather with
one of the subvarieties of aristocracy, furthermore, illuminates the
systematic intentions of Aristotle. The survey of forms in Books IV to VI
is not set off as an empirical survey against speculations on an "ideal"
form in Books III, VII, and VIII. The passages in Book IV just quoted
refer to Book III and incorporate the discussion of monarchy and aristocracy in the earlier book into the comprehensive survey; and one sub-
variety of aristocracy is the best polis itself. Through this inclusion the
perfect polis becomes one of the forms in the manifold studied in Books
IV to VI, on the same systematic level as the deficient forms. In the face
of this explicit declaration by Aristotle himself the thesis of a sharp
break between the speculation on the "ideal" and a study of "reality"
can hardly be maintained. One could argue, to be sure, that the inclusion
of the respective parts of Book III into the survey of Books IV to VI
was an afterthought of the later period, and that the original intention
was an entirely different one. Considering the text, in particular of III,
14 (1284b35–1285b33), however, the argument does not seem convincing. For the chapter in question surveys the types of royalty, dis-

---

merits, except wealth. The distinction through wealth is in this passage specifically given
through the corresponding adverb *ploutinden.*

tinguishing (1) the Lacedaemonian kingship, (2) the barbarian king-ship, closely resembling tyranny, (3) the aesymnetic dictatorship, (4) the heroic kingship of the early Hellenic period, and (5) the patrimonial monarchy (*pambasileia*). Here, in the earliest part of *Politics,* thus, is already fully developed the method of differentiating the primary category of kingship into subvarieties which is explicitly set forth only in Book IV. The late "empirical" method was employed even in the earliest section dealing with the "ideal state." Hence, we can concede that at the time of writing the "first discourse" Aristotle perhaps had not yet planned the later enlargement into a study of the "deficient forms"; but we cannot concede that the method employed in dealing with the "best forms" differed fundamentally from the method which he used in his later study of the "deficient forms." It is fairly certain that the closing chapters of Book III were originally meant as a transition to Books VII and VIII; but when Aristotle reinterpreted them as a transition to Book IV he could do so without doing violence to their contents.

Of the rich content of the survey in Books IV to VI we shall select only a few representative examples.

As an example for the differentiation of primary categories into sub-varieties we may use the case of democracy. Aristotle describes four types of democracy (VI, 4): (1) agricultural, (2) pastoral, (3) urban commercial, and (4) urban popular democracy. The order of the series is an order of value; agricultural is the best, urban popular democracy is the worst type. The criterion of the rank is developed in another context (IV, 4) where democracies are classified according to their realization of justice and equity. Five such types are distinguished: (1) a democracy under laws which provide that the poor should have no more advantages than the rich, that neither should be master, but that both classes should be equal; (2) the type in which the magistrates are elected according to a certain property qualification, but a low one; (3) the democracy in which all citizens not under disqualification share equally in the offices, but in which the law still remains supreme; (4) the kind in which no citizens are disqualified, but still the law is supreme; and (5) the same as four, but with the right of the multitude to supersede the law by their decrees. The two series of types correspond to each other. Aristotle considers that a democracy can be easily and successfully established under the conditions of an agricultural community of free householders. The citizens are too poor to neglect their work and indulge in politics; they

will be satisfied if the more prosperous citizens discharge the public duties, provided that the incumbents of offices do not molest the other citizens; and their desire to share in the government will be satisfied by the
occasional acts of election and control. The urban popular democracy, on
the other hand, with the power of making decrees in the hands of a
multitude, which can easily assemble on the agora and be harangued by
demagogues, is hardly a constitution at all. "For, where the laws do not
rule, there is no constitution."

As a second example we select Aristotle's suggestions concerning an
average constitution that would solve the struggle between the rich and
the poor that was going on in most of the Hellenic poleis of his time. He
introduces his suggestions (IV, 11) as the quest of "the best constitution
and the best way of life for most of the poleis and the great mass of
men." In searching for such a constitution we must "neither assume a
standard of excellence [arete] beyond the level of the common man
[idiotes], nor of an education that requires natural gifts and means,
nor of a constitution equipped according to our desires"; we must assume
a standard that is accessible to most people and most poleis. The previously discussed aristocracies (including the best) fall outside the
range of most poleis, or they approach through the numerical size of their
ruling group to the very type of constitutional government (politeia)
that is now under consideration. For the guiding principle of his suggestions Aristotle has recourse to Nicomachean Ethics. Eudaimonia will be
achieved through a life according to virtue, and virtue is the middle
course (mesotes); the middle course of life is the best, and we are in
search of such a mean that is attainable for men in the mass. Applying
this principle to the polis we find three social strata in every community:
the very rich, the very poor, and those who are in-between, that is, a
middle class in the economic sense. Since it is agreed that the measured
or middle is the best, the middle amount of possessions is best. Such a
middle degree of possessions is most amenable to reason; excessive wealth,
on the other hand, breeds insolence and criminality on the great scale,
while excessive poverty breeds malice and roguery. A polis of only the
rich and the poor is a polis of insolent despots and slavish subjects, the
one despising, the other envying. Companionship and friendship, which
are necessary for the happy existence of a polis, can only grow among
men who are approximately equal; and the middle class is, therefore,
the truly stabilizing element. The men of middle possessions are the safest

because they are neither so poor that they envy the rich, nor so rich that the poor plot for their plunder. Hence a lawgiver will act wisely when he relies strongly on the middle class in framing a constitution. If he frames an oligarchic constitution he will see to it that the laws favor also the middle class for, in that case, the despotic tendencies of the very rich will find a counterweight in the middle group; and he will do the same when framing a democracy, for again the middle class will be a counter-weight to the tendencies of the poor to plunder. Such wisdom, however, will not be of much use to the lawgiver in the cases where there is no middle class, or only a very small one. Only larger cities are apt to have an appreciable middle class; and that fact explains the turbulent course of politics in the smaller poleis and their tendency of degenerating al-ternately into radical oligarchies or democracies. Generally speaking "the middle class is usually small"; and since establishing their own party in power is considered the prize of victory in civil wars by both democrats and oligarchs, the middle form "comes never at all into existence, or very rarely and in a very few places." The best polis that is based on the *mesotes* of wealth seems to share the fate of impracticality with the aris-tocracies. Sadly Aristotle must confess: "Two types of constitution come principally into existence: democracy and oligarchy; for good birth and excellence are found in few men, while wealth and numbers are com-mon. Nowhere are there a hundred men wellborn and good; but rich men we find in many places" (1301b39–1302a3).

It is difficult to select a representative example from Book V on the causes of revolutions and the means of preserving the constitutions. The value of the study lies in the wealth of detail, in the rich casuistry of the turbulent life of the Hellenic poleis. It should be read as a whole. The principles employed in the discussion bring nothing new. "Everywhere inequality causes revolution [*stasis*]. . . . always those who desire equality rise in factional strife" (1301b27ff). The partial justice, dis-cussed in an earlier context, when made the principle of a constitution will cause the resentment of those whose dignity and sense of justice is violated. In a situation that is fraught with explosive tension a series of typical events and motives will furnish the more immediate causes and occasions for revolutionary outbreaks. These typical motives and events are insolence, fear, excessive predominance, contempt shown by the rul-ing class, or contempt engendered by it, disproportionate growth of power in one section of society at the expense of others, election intrigues, carelessness, pettiness, minor concessions that serve as entering wedges for dangerous demands, and dissimilarities of the social groups, as for instance racial differences. A typical application of the principle as well as of the various motivations is to be found in the page on revolutions in democracies: "In democracies the principal cause of revolutions is the insolence of the demagogues. For, either they privately lay information against men of property and thus compel them to combine (for common fear brings together even the greatest enemies), or they stir up the multitude against them in public. And one may see this happening in many instances. In Cos the democracy was overthrown because evil demagogues rose, and the notables combined. At Rhodes the demagogues not only provided pay for the multitude, they also hindered the payment of money owed to the naval captains; and they, because of the suits brought against them, were forced to combine and to overthrow the government of the people. . . . And examination would show that also in other cases revolutions take place very much in this manner" (1304b20ff).

5. *The Best Constitution*

Books VII and VIII of *Politics* contain the speculation on the best constitution (*ariste politeia*). The discourse is incomplete; Book VIII breaks off at what is probably the end of the discussion on musical education. In the extant part, on a few occasions, the reader is referred to a later more detailed exposition of problems which for the moment are touched upon only briefly. Beyond such references we do not know what the missing part would have contained or how long it would have been.

The exploration of the best constitution is not an exercise in wishful thinking; it is a critical study. On the nomothetic level of the study, a people fares best if it has the constitution that is best adapted to its peculiar circumstances; the only criterion of "best" on this level is stability, in the sense that a constitution is suitable if it does not engender dissatisfaction to the point of violent outbreaks. Such empiricism, however, is no basis for a critical, philosophical interpretation of man in political existence. If we want to know what the best constitution is, we must first determine what is "the most eligible life"; for in the philosophical sense that constitution is best which allows the fullest actualization of human nature. Hence, we must first know what human nature is and what actualization is (1323a14–22). In the first three chapters of Book VII, therefore, Aristotle gives a brief exposition of the theory of the goods, of eudaimonia, of the parts of the soul, of the problem of autarky, and of the analogy between perfect human, political, and divine existence. With this complex of problems we are already acquainted.[9]

Neither the best life of man nor of the polis can be actualized under unfavorable external conditions. Hence, the study of the best constitution must, second, determine the materials, the *choregia*, required for perfect actualization. In the choice of these materials the philosopher must use some tact and restraint. Assumptions must be made, for without them the exploration of the best constitution is impossible; but they must not be improbable, for then we would lose contact with reality and the study would be worthless (1235b33ff). Aristotle extends these necessary assumptions to four classes of "materials": (1) size of the population, (2) extent and nature of the territory, (3) site of the polis, and (4) natural character of the population.

With regard to the size of the population, Aristotle requires a number of persons that will be sufficient to realize the autarkous, good life in community, but will not be appreciably larger than the minimum. Beauty and order require measure (*metron*); law is a type of order, and good law is good order; hence, an order of law cannot penetrate a very great multitude—only a nonhuman, divine power can order the universe. Besides, there are certain practical considerations. In the best constitution the officials should be elected and appointed according to merit; if the population is too large, the qualifications of a man are not sufficiently known to his fellow citizens and the filling of offices will be haphazard. Moreover, foreigners and metics would claim citizenship and nobody could find them out.

With regard to extent and nature of the territory similar considerations apply. The territory must be self-sufficient as far as possible, that is, it must contain the agricultural resources and raw materials that are required for the needs of the community. It must be large enough for the inhabitants to live temperately and freely in the enjoyment of leisure. From the military point of view it should be easily defensible. The city itself should be situated in such a manner that, on the one hand, it will serve the protection of the countryside and that, on the other hand, it will be an easily accessible market for the agricultural produce of the territory.

With regard to the site, proximity to the sea has its advantages as

[9] Cf. Ch. 7 and Ch. 8, 1.

well as its disadvantages. Access to the sea is a military asset in various respects; commercially it is also of some importance because it facilitates the import of goods that cannot be produced within the country. Nevertheless, a port development is undesirable because of the influx of strangers, the dissolving effect of foreign customs, and the general looseness of the life of sailors in port. A separate organization of the port area at some distance from the city, preventing as far as possible an intermingling of the people with the sailors, will be the best solution.

With regard to the character of the population, finally, Aristotle develops the theory of regional characters with which we are already acquainted. The character of the Hellenes is the most suitable for the establishment of the best constitution.

The full actualization of human nature as well as the materials are defined as the condition of the construction. Aristotle can now proceed to the organization of the best constitution itself. In opening his reflections on this subject he gives one more redefinition of the relation between the polis and its parts. The polis is a structure or compound (*systasis*). As in other such structures, not all the things that are indispensable for its existence can be called parts of it in a strict sense.[10] A man, for instance, needs instruments and various kinds of property in order to exist; but his property is not a part of the man, it is an instrument for his existence. In the same manner a polis requires property, "but property, though even living beings are included in it, is not part of the polis"; for, "the polis is an association of like people [*koinonia ton homoion*]" striving for the best life, and not an association of just any human beings; and since the perfect actualization of human nature is not possible for everybody, not all human beings can share in the association of equals, and hence cannot be part of the polis. While they cannot be part of the polis they nevertheless are indispensable for its existence. A polis needs farmers who will produce the food, craftsmen, a military class, the wealthy, judges, officials, and priests. The question then arises which of these indispensable functions should be discharged by the members of the association who are the "parts" of the polis. Aristotle decides that in the best polis the citizens (in the sense of "members of the ruling association") must not be farmers, mechanics, or tradesmen because these occu-

[10] The rendering of *systasis* as "organism," or the injection of the adjective "organic" in speaking of the parts, as we find it in several translations, is misleading. The section of Book VII that begins with Chapter 8 does not contain an organic theory of the state in the modern sense; as the text will presently show, Aristotle is developing the very opposite of an organic theory.

pations do not allow for the leisure that is necessary for the development of the excellences. The citizens thus are confined to the occupations of warriors, officials, and priests; and they should participate in all of these functions in the course of their lifetime. The military and governing functions correspond to the two primes of life marked by strength and wisdom; and the priests should be chosen from the old men of the warriors and officials, and on no account from the lower classes, "for it is seemly that the Gods should receive honor from the citizens only." Moreover, the ruling class should have most of the property, for they are the citizens in the strict sense, while the lower classes, "who are not producers of excellence," do not participate in the excellence of the polis. And in as much as the property should be in the hands of the ruling association, the tillers of the soil should be slaves or serfs of an alien race. The formulations are critically pointed against *Republic* 419f. where Plato excludes the warriors from participation in the rule of the polis and even of full happiness; this would be the constitutional arrangement which Aristotle characterizes as an "oligarchy of the virtuous" and, in consequence, as a defective type of order. One cannot make the whole polis happy, Aristotle argues against Plato, without making happy the self-sufficient group of citizens that constitutes the ruling association (*Politics*, 1264b8–25). The best polis, thus, requires a ruling association in which office can be held in turn by all members. The association must include the warrior class, and in view of the size of the class allowance must be made for a certain amplitude in the individual actualization of excellence. Otherwise, however, Aristotle agrees with Plato on the desirability of a caste system and refers to Egypt as a country in which such a system has been maintained since times immemorial.

Since we are living in an age in which public discussion of political matters suffers from ideological confusion, it will not be superfluous to stress that Aristotle's exploration of the best constitution has nothing to do with "fascism." The construction of the best constitution is a theoretical problem of which the solution is determined by axiomatic assumptions. Assuming that it is the function of the constitution to provide an organizational framework for the maximal actualization of human excellence at least for those men who can actualize it at all, what is the best constitution? The resolution of the problem presupposes the existence of a sufficiently large social group that can justly be considered to actualize excellence in the Aristotelian sense. With regard to the existence of such a group Aristotle has expressed his opinions explicitly: Where could one find a hundred men of excellence that would be sufficient to be the ruling association of even one little polis? The answer is: Nowhere in the concrete historical situation. Aristotle agrees with Plato that in the historical situation an "elite," capable of actualizing the best polis, does not exist. By no stretch of imagination can the construction of the best constitution be interpreted as an invitation to a *coup d'état* by a self-appointed elite. Aristotle, as we have seen, even doubted that a middle-class polity, tempering somewhat the radical democracy, was feasible under the circumstances. The age is democratic, and Aristotle is resigned to the prospect that only democratic constitutions can be established with any chance of stability. Such resignation, however, does not imply the abandoning of critical standards; while the urban democracy of his time may be historically and politically inevitable, it still is what it is. Aristotle is a philosopher; he is not an intellectual flunkey for the historically inevitable.

With Book VII, 13 (1331b24) begin the reflections on education. They continue to the end in Book VIII where they break off, as we have said, with musical education. The extant fragment gives no clues concerning the plan of the whole discussion. All that we can extract with safety are a few declarations concerning principles.

The section on education opens with a restatement of the problem of the best polis. At its center is the ruling association of the men of excellence. The existence of such a polis is in part conditioned by the indispensable "materials" over which the lawgiver has no control; in part it is conditioned by an educational process to be institutionalized by laws. The proper framing of these laws presupposes a clear understanding of the aim of education; and since the aim of education in the best polis is the formation of freemen, distinguished by their ethical and dianoetic excellences, Aristotle briefly restates his principles of ethics (1331b24–1332b11). From the restatement emerges as the central problem the division of life into business (*ascholia*) and leisure (*schole*).[11] Business

---

[11] It is practically impossible to render the terms *ascholia* and *schole* adequately in English. In Greek (as in the Latin *otium* and *negotium*) leisure, *schole*, has the positive connotation, while business (*ascholia*) negatively denotes the absence of *schole*. The etymological connection with *schein* (from *echo*) suggests a stopping from activity, a rest, resulting in a "having of oneself" or holding of oneself, as the basic meaning; while *ascholia* would correspondingly suggest a losing of oneself in peripheral activity.

and leisure, war and peace, actions aiming at what is necessary and useful and actions aiming at what is noble—this is the fundamental division. Hence, in the system of Aristotelian preferences war must be conducted for the sake of peace, business must be undertaken for the sake of leisure, and the things necessary and useful for the purpose of things noble. The life in the best polis must be organized in such a manner that the actualization of man in leisure is achieved.

From this principle derive certain problems for education. If education serves the necessary and useful only, or if men are educated for the arts of war but not of peace, like the Lacadaemonians, then the full actualization of human excellence becomes impossible because men will not know what to do with their free time that is supposed to serve leisure. The problem is sharpened through the distinction between leisure and play (*paidia*). Leisure time is not playtime. Play has the purpose of amusement, relaxation, or recreation; play is therefore most suitable for men who are engaged in hard work and need relaxation as a balance. Play may be necessary after work in order to achieve a state of rest as the precondition of leisure, but it is no occupation for leisure itself. Education must, therefore, equip a man with knowledge and train him in intellectual pursuits; for only sciences which serve no further ends and can be pursued for their own sake, as a way of life, are the proper activity for the leisure of a man of excellence. We do not know what other occupation for leisure Aristotle would have admitted, except music of a type that will aid in the formation of character. As far as the text goes, the *bios theoretikos* appears as the way of life in which the nature of man becomes maximally actualized. The education of the best state must habituate and train a man in such a manner that he will be capable of this supreme fulfillment.

6. Conclusion

We have repeatedly stressed that Aristotle was less interested in the construction of a system than in the completeness of his inventory of problems. We shall now, in conclusion, survey the inventory in systematic order.

The Aristotelian speculation on politics starts from the Platonic anthropological principle. Political society is the field for actualization of human nature. If we want to understand the structure of the polis we must understand the nature of man that enters into its formation; and if we have a notion of maximal actualization of human nature we can develop critical standards for judging the effectiveness of a polis for such maximal actualization.

The theoretical principle is deeply embedded in Plato's creation of the myth of the soul. Aristotle's theory of human nature has as its empirical basis the order of the soul revealed through Socrates-Plato. In Plato's *Republic* the new order of the philosopher's soul amalgamated with the Hellenic nomothetic tradition in the creation of the good polis. In Plato's late work the politico-religious founding will dissociated into the consciousness of the new religion and the political reality that was unfit for its adequate absorption. The living presence of the philosopher-king was replaced in the *Laws* by symbolic institutions. In the work of Aristotle the process of dissociation continued. Plato now became the religious founder, marking an epoch in the spiritual history of mankind. Philosophical anthropology developed into an autonomous discipline serving as the basis for a general theory of action. The theory of action itself became a new discipline in the main body of *Nicomachean Ethics;* and the theory of maximal actualization of human nature in the *bios theoretikos* very distinctly pointed in the direction of new spiritual communities beyond the historical polis of the time. The nomothetic science of politics, finally, tended to become an independent craft of devising institutions which, under the given circumstances, would minimize the danger of revolutions. All these centrifugal tendencies, however, were still held together by the notion of the "best polis," that is, by the intellectualized remnant of the Platonic good polis. The Aristotelian best polis was neither a polis ruled by the living presence of the philosopher-king, nor a symbolic play like the polis of the *Laws*. It became something like an intellectual puzzle that must be solved as a matter of tradition. The survival of this remnant showed, if anything, the living force of the Hellenic idea that the life of man could find its fulfillment only in the polis. The theoretical horizon of Aristotle, thus, was seriously limited by the conception of political science as a nomothetic art for the polis and nothing but the polis.

The consequences of this limitation fortunately were less grave than they might have been if Aristotle had been more "systematic." The literary *corpus* of political science was framed by the blocks of the philosophical anthropology at the beginning of *Nicomachean Ethics* and the construction of the best constitution at the end of *Politics*. Between the two framing blocks Aristotle's unsystematic concern about completeness of problems revealed the range of a political science which, if systematically organized, would reach a considerably more impressive stature than the paradigm of the best constitution. We only need recapitulate the most important theoretical complexes:

(1) The foundation of ethics as a science of the mature character.

(2) The constancy of human knowledge through the vicissitudes of history and the importance of the myth as a source of knowledge that has become obscured through pragmatic incrustations.

(3) The cycle of political forms and the understanding of the variety of forms as phases of political order.

(4) The inevitability of social tensions through the coexistence of permanent, empirical, human types, such as (a) the mature and the immature, and (b) the rich and the poor; the tentative ramification of this knowledge into a phenomenology of virtue, differentiated according to the various human types.

(5) The recognition of the historical manifold of political forms; the limitation of the art of the lawgiver; and, more generally, the recognition of the very narrow limits of political action in the given historical situation.

(6) The foundation of justice on *philia*, and of *philia* on the actualization of the true self in community; as a corollary, the foundation of society on the *homonoia* of its members, on their participation in the divine *nous*; and, as a consequence, the function of the ruling association in the order of a society.

This catalogue assembles the topics of a systematic political science, ranging from a philosophical anthropology and an ethics founded on ontology, through a theory of the community substance and its institutionalization, to a philosophy of history and a theory of civilizational crisis. A theory of political dynamics unfolds, ranging from the beneficial authors of the polis to the anarchy of the mob bent on plunder, and from the actualization of dianoetic excellence to the management of urban masses through greed and fear. This range of political science has never been cultivated in continuity; the discontinuous revivals in St. Thomas, Machiavelli, Bodin, Rousseau, or Whiggist constitutionalism extend to no more than parts of this vast body of theory. Only in our own time does the range of Aristotle's political science come into full view again because, under the stress of our own crisis, we are regaining the experiential understanding of the issues involved.

CHAPTER 10

On Types of Character and Skepticism

In his philosophical anthropology Aristotle developed the theory of a human nature common to all, but in his nomothetic science of politics he recognized that the actualization of human nature was the privilege of the few. In his recognition he went so far as to contemplate a differentiation of the theory of excellences according to the variety of human types; the program was outlined but not executed. The problem requires some elaboration beyond the scope of Aristotelian politics in the strict sense.

The problem originates in the situation of the philosopher who is in possession of the Truth. Aristotle knows what the nature of man really is; he knows that eudaimonia consists in the practice of the *bios theoretikos;* and he knows it not only as a proposition in science, but experientially through the habituation of his soul and the practice of his life. This last point is crucial. Prudential science is not a body of knowledge of which the truth is evident to everybody, but requires inclination and habituation for its full understanding. It cannot be transmitted as information, but must be acquired as possession through formation of the soul. The truth of the philosopher is not a recipe for transforming mankind at large, but creates a new type of man among others. The very study of the nature of man reveals it as something which man does not flatly have, but as a potentiality which requires actualization in the process of life. And if such actualization is not too successful, the carrier of human potentiality is still man. The fulfillment of human nature emerges against the background of the mystery of its failure.

The tension between potential and actual man is only one of the sources of Aristotle's concern about the variety of human types that threatens to break the idea of common humanity. A second source becomes apparent in his attitude toward the manifold of political reality.

Measured by the standard of the best polis the contemporary types of order appeared as perversions of various degrees. Politics as a nomothetic science, however, did not have the task of transforming the imperfect forms into the best form. On the contrary, any such attempt was rejected as it would only lead to disturbances and revolutions. The perverse forms were to be accepted as they existed historically; and the lawgiver's art should only minimize their evils in order to preserve and stabilize them. If the Aristotelian premise of the philosopher's polis as a standard be accepted, the sequel in the lawgiver's polis will arouse misgivings. For the nomothetic therapy seems to have no other purpose than to make the perverse form as durable as possible. And we begin to wonder about the wisdom of a study which apparently can do no more than ruffle the ruling groups of all existing poleis by telling them that their order is perverse.

These problems, though not resolved, are at least somewhat illuminated by Aristotle's study of the techniques of political influence, of the *techne rhetorike*.

1. *The* Rhetoric *of Aristotle*

In his *Rhetoric* Aristotle intends to improve the current treatment of the subject matter in two respects. In the first place, he wants to give to deliberative rhetoric, *i.e.* to the statesman's art of persuading his audience to a right course of political action, its proper place by the side of forensic and epideictic rhetoric. In the second place, he wants to raise rhetoric from an art of persuasion through play on emotions to an art of persuasion through reasoning. While neither forensic and epideictic rhetoric nor the play on emotions are neglected in the work, we are specifically interested in the intended improvements as they illuminate Aristotle's attitude toward the practice of politics.

In the practice of persuasion, when the statesman addresses his audience, the occasion of the speech furnishes him with three tools for achieving success: (1) the character (*ethos*) of the speaker, (2) the frame of mind of the audience, and (3) the argument proper. Of the three factors, the character of the speaker easily ranks highest as a means of persuasion, for we trust a man of probity more quickly about things at large, and we put our absolute trust in him when it comes to prudential matters outside exact science. The persuasiveness of the character, however, must be understood not as a reputation preceding the speaker, but as a quality of character which becomes manifest in the competence of the speech itself. And the competence of the speech depends on the mastery of political subject matter, as well as on its adaptation to the character of the audience. Hence, the effective speaker must be able to reason logically, he must understand the varieties of human character (*ethos*) and excellence (*arete*), and he must understand the emotions (*pathos*). Rhetoric, thus, is an offshoot of dialectics and that branch of ethics which properly may be called political (*Rhetoric* 1356a). In brief, we may say, the statesman is supposed to possess a knowledge of Aristotelian dialectics, ethics, and politics which he cannot possess unless his character is formed by the *bios theoretikos.*

The knowledge of the best polis, thus, enters the practice of politics not as a program of reform, but existentially through the statesman whose character has been formed by Aristotelian prudential science. The statesman as one type of character faces the people and its polis as a character of a different type. In the speech the two types are related with each other in so far as the appropriate treatment of the people's character depends on the adequate formation of the statesman's character. The *Rhetoric,* therefore, resumes the topics of *Nicomachean Ethics* and *Politics* but slanted as it were toward the character of the prospective audience. The topic of eudaimonia, for instance, appears as the central theme of deliberative rhetoric. In the *Rhetoric,* however, Aristotle does not disentangle the eudaimonia of the theoretic life from the current ideas about happiness. On the contrary, he leaves the variety of opinion in a state of uncritical factualness. Happiness may be prosperity combined with excellence, or self-sufficient existence, or the secure enjoyment of hedonistic life, and so forth. And "pretty well everybody agrees that happiness is one or more of these things." He then enumerates the "parts" of happiness as good birth, friends, children, wealth, a happy old age, physical advantages, fame, honor, and good luck (I, 5). The only item that is missing in this enumeration is excellence (*arete*). Excellence is not among the aims which a speaker should present to his audience for achievement. In the *Rhetoric* the excellences are transferred to the section on epideictic, or eulogizing, rhetoric, because excellence is a matter for praise and blame rather than for counselling.

While the speaker must not molest the people with a theoretical disquisition on the excellences themselves, his speech should convey the impression of a character that is formed by their possession (1366a23ff). The speaker, while using his theoretical knowledge, must operate with the categories of what we might call the people's morality. In political practice the people is interested in the excellences because of their social usefulness. A virtue is noble (*kalos*) because it is at the same time good and praiseworthy; and it has these qualities because it is a faculty of beneficence (*dynamis euergetike*). Under this aspect, the "parts" of virtue must be arranged in a hierarchy extending from justice, courage, and temperance, through magnificence, liberality, and gentleness, to prudence and wisdom. The rank is determined by "usefulness to others." Justice and courage are most useful to the fellow citizens in war and peace; prudence ranks lowest because it helps only in arriving at right decisions about the relations of various goods and evils to eudaimonia; and wisdom (*sophia*) is not even mentioned in the detailed evaluation (1366a33–1366b22). The speaker must conform to popular opinion in general and he must pay special attention to the variants of opinion in his concrete audience. The accents must be placed differently before Scythians, Lacedaemonians, or Athenians. As a general rule, whatever is esteemed as noble by the audience must be treated as such by the speaker, for in popular opinion what is esteemed and what is noble are practically the same (1367b7–12).

In the choice of his "line of argument" the speaker will be guided by the character of the audience. The study of the varieties of character will, therefore, be a main concern of the statesman. The characters to be studied fall under the two principal heads of individual and collective. As far as individual characters are concerned, Aristotle reflects on audiences composed of young or elderly men, or men in the prime of their life, on audiences of men of good birth, of the rich and the powerful, and inversely on audiences composed of the poor, the unlucky, and the powerless (II, 12–17). Quite as important as the individual characters are the characters of the various types of political order. Briefly reviewing the types (I, 8) Aristotle distinguishes the end (*telos*) of each of them: the freedom of democracy, the wealth of oligarchy, the cultural conservatism and institutionalism of aristocracy, and the self-protection of the tyrant. To each of these types corresponds a moral climate, a character (*ethos*); and the characters of the types of *politeia* must be taken into consideration in the same manner as the characters of individuals (1366a12ff).

The *Rhetoric* brings the peculiar problem of the variety of characters into clearer view. We see Aristotle making a valiant effort at injecting at least a dose of the actualized nature of man into a field of political reality which otherwise would contain only imperfectly actualized potentiality. At least a spark of the best polis will enter reality in as much as his pupils, through their existential presence, will exert a persuasive influence. Like Plato in the *Laws,* he clings to the idea of an attenuated influx of the Truth into politics. The homoeopathic character of the dose, however, makes it all the more apparent that Aristotle was unable to dissolve the tension between the nonexistent best polis and the concrete perversions. The representative of the *bios theoretikos* would be one character-type among others which he would have to respect and confirm in their existence. One might even say that the differentiation of the contemplative type has resulted in the sharper characterization of the non-contemplative types and added to the legitimacy of their existence.

2. *The Failure of Immanentist Metaphysics*

The Aristotelian speculation ends in a serious impasse, both practically and theoretically. Practically, the discovery of the truth seems to serve no other purpose than to forge a new instrument for keeping the rest of mankind in the untruth of their existence. Theoretically, we are faced with an aporia that affects the theory of human nature and its actualization.

The philosopher who is in possession of the Truth should consistently go the way of Plato in the *Republic;* he should issue the call for repentance and submission to the theocratic rule of the incarnate Truth. Aristotle, however, does not issue such a call and, consequently, the imperfections of actualization (though technically called "perversions") tend to become essences in their own right, forming the manifold of reality; they become "characters" and the category of character is even extended from human individuals to the types of constitutions. The dimension of potentiality-actualization, thus, is crossed by a plane on which the grades of imperfection appear as co-ordinated types to be respected and preserved in their essence; the imperfections become actualizations of their specific types. This theoretical conflict could not be reconciled within the "system" because the problem that caused it had not become sufficiently explicit.

The problem underlying the Aristotelian aporia may conveniently be designated the "historicity of Truth." The Truth of the philosopher is discovered in the previously analyzed experiences of Socrates-Plato. The cathartic experience of Thanatos and the enthusiastic experience of Eros open the soul toward transcendental reality; and they become effective in that re-ordering of the soul which Plato symbolized through Dike. Truth is not a body of propositions about a world-immanent object; it is the world-transcendent *summum bonum*, experienced as an orienting force in the soul, about which we can speak only in analogical symbols. Transcendental reality cannot be an object of cognition in the manner of a world-immanent datum because it does not share with man the finiteness and temporality of immanent existence. It is eternal, out-of-time; it is not co-temporal with the experiencing soul. When, through the experiences of the Socratic-Platonic type, eternity enters time, we may say that "Truth" becomes "historical." That means, of course, neither that the flash of eternity into time is the privileged experience of philosophers, nor that now, at a specific date in history, it occurred for the first time. It means that in the critical period under discussion we are advancing, in the Platonic sense, from the symbolizations of the people's myth to the differentiated experiences of the philosophers and to their symbolizations. This advance is part of the historical process in which the older symbolic order of the myth disintegrates in the souls (in the previously described manner) and a new order of the soul in openness to transcendental reality is restored on a more differentiated level. By "historicity of Truth" we mean that transcendental reality, precisely because it is not an object of world-immanent knowledge, has a history of experience and symbolization.

The field of this history is the soul of man. Man, in his knowledge of himself, does not know himself only as a world-immanent existent but also as existing in openness toward transcendental reality; but he knows himself in this openness only historically in the degree of differentiation which his experiences and their symbolization have reached. The self-understanding of man is conditioned and limited by the development of his existence towards transcendence. As a consequence, the nature of man itself as an object of metaphysical inquiry is not altogether a world-immanent object; the formation of the soul through invading transcendence is part of that "nature" that we explore in metaphysics. When the philosopher explores the spiritual order of the soul, he explores a realm of experiences which he can appropriately describe only in the language of symbols expressing the movement of the soul toward transcendental reality and the flooding of the soul by transcendence. At the border of transcendence the language of philosophical anthropology must become the language of religious symbolization.

In the realization of this border problem we touch upon the difficulties of Aristotelian metaphysics. We have studied the religious aspects of the conception of the *bios theoretikos*. In his philosophical anthropology Aristotle, following Plato, penetrated into the region of the *nous* in the religious sense. He arrived at the idea of a "true self" of man and at the idea of *homonoia,* that is, of the parallel formation of the souls of man through *nous,* as the bond of society. Actually, Aristotle penetrated so far into this region that his very terminology could be used by St. Paul in making *homonoia* the central concept in the theory of a Christian community. Nevertheless, there remained in Aristotle the fundamental hesitation which distinguished the Hellenic from the Christian idea of man, that is, the hesitation to recognize the formation of the human soul through grace; there was missing the experience of faith, the *fides caritate formata* in the Thomistic sense. In the case of Aristotle, the most poignant symptom of this hesitation is his insistence that friendship (*philia*) between God and man is impossible. Equality is for him an essential element of friendship; *philia* between unequals is difficult, if not impossible; and it becomes quite impossible if one partner to the friendship is as remote from the other as God through his pre-eminence of qualities is from man (*N. E.* 1158b35ff). This is the Hellenic position, in contrast with the Christian experience of the *amicitia* between God and man. The Aristotelian position does not allow for a *forma supranaturalis,* for the heightening of the immanent nature of man through the supernaturally forming love of God. It is true, the Aristotelian gods also love man (*N.E.* 1179a23ff), but their love does not reach into the soul and form it towards its destiny. The Aristotelian nature of man remains an immanent essence like the form of an organic being; its actualization is a problem within the world. Although the noetic self is the *theiotaton* in man, and although its actualization is conceived as an immortalization, human nature finds its fulfillment immanently. Transcendence does not transform the soul in such a manner that it will find fulfillment in transfiguration through Grace in death.

The metaphysical construction of human nature as an immanent form is technically inadequate because it is supposed to cover structures of the soul that are formed by transcendence. From the conflict between the reality of experiences and metaphysical construction stem the aporias of Aristotelian philosophizing which occupy us at present. The experience of transcendence, on the one hand, is differentiated to the point where the supranatural fulfillment of human potentiality has come into clear view; for the *bios theoretikos* is, within the Hellenic limitations, a sanctification of life leading toward the immortalization of the soul, toward the *beatitudo* in the Christian sense. The metaphysics of immanent form, on the other hand, requires the immanent actualization of human potentiality. From this conflict results the construction of an immanent actualization of the supranatural potentiality of the soul.[1]

We shall meet with a similar theoretical situation at the end of the Middle Ages when, with the disintegration of Christianity and the new wave of immanentism, political thinkers began to evoke the idea of an intramundane realization of perfect human existence. The immanentization of transcendental fulfillment resulted at that time in the development of political "ideals," and ultimately in the political chiliasm of transforming society into a terrestrial paradise by means of organization and violence. The modern, immanentist possessors of Truth do not hesitate to extend its blessedness to everybody whom it does not concern.

A similar movement of political idealism and chiliasm would have lain in the logic of Aristotelian metaphysics. The spiritual sensitiveness and the magnificent realism, both of Plato and Aristotle, however, preserved them from the catastrophic derailment which characterizes modern politics—though in our study of Plato we had occasion to note the danger point of a breakdown into a theocratic tyranny. The conflict between transcendental spiritualism and immanentist metaphysics worked its confusion only at the theoretical stage. The immanentist construction of the best polis, to be sure, compelled Aristotle to classify all empirical constitutions as perversions, but it did not induce him to make war on the perversions in the name of Truth. On the contrary, his careful attention to the manifold of political reality led to the problems that we characterized as a political sociology. It led to the theory of a cycle of political forms, and above all, it led to the problem of the "characters" whose autonomy of historical existence must be respected by the possessor of the Truth.

From the complex of problems just adumbrated we see emerging a genuinely "natural" study of man and of his existence in society and history—"natural" not in a biological sense, but in the sense of those components in the essence of man which determine the structure of intramundane, human existence. "Nature" in this sense, however, is not an independent essence; for the notion of this "nature" is formed on the

---

[1] For the problems of the present section cf. Ch. 9, 2.

experiential occasion which historically brings the supernatural formation of the spiritual soul into view. With the differentiation of the
Socratic-Platonic experiences, immanent nature begins to differentiate
as its correlative. In Aristotle's philosophical anthropology and politics
this correlative differentiation is the all-pervasive problem. It expresses
itself in the differentiation of a *bios theoretikos* which no longer can be
integrated properly into the supposedly all-embracing immanent political
order, and of an immanent political and historical order, to be judged by
the critical standards of the philosopher as a "perversion," but to be left
in its perverted state nevertheless. We see prefigured a differentiation that
later will develop into the temporal and spiritual order of a Christian
society.

3. *The* Characters *of Theophrastus*

The aporias of an immanentist metaphysics remained unsolved not
only in the work of Aristotle but in their time in general. Nevertheless,
the pressure of the problems made itself felt. Even if they did not find
adequate solutions the problems continued to impose themselves, and men
had to grapple with them as best they could. We shall now consider what
may be called the diversions which the problem of immanentism experienced toward the end of the fourth century B.C.

In the society which Aristotle pictures in his work the philosophical
schools could flourish, and the idea and practice of the *bios theoretikos*
could develop. For the rest, however, this society wanted to be left
strictly alone. The Aristotelian works on ethics, politics, and rhetoric
are the monumental evidence for the strength and charm of a society
that will preserve its style of existence at any price, as well as for the
stubbornness that will determine its course toward elimination from history as a power. In the restrained advice of the *Rhetoric,* in particular,
we sense the social atmosphere of men who do not want to be lectured
and demand respect for their "character" as it is, as well as the urbanity,
sometimes desperately strained, of the author who will not impose his
Truth on gentlemen with firm convictions. On the pragmatic level of
history the decisions concerning their political fate were taken out of the
hands of such men through the Macedonian conquest and the rise of
Empire. To be sure, the societies of the poleis, and especially the Attic
society, shorn of their power, continued to exist. But they were now societies in which the "characters" had the field for themselves, societies

that had lost their myth and not gained the spirit, societies of shrewd observation, humor, cultivated sentiments, personal dignity, subtle tact, and a good deal of psychological insight. A peculiar atmosphere for which the Greeks had no word, the atmosphere of what the Romans called *humanitas*, began to spread.[2]

In the new, very humane climate were written the *Characters* of Theophrastus (*c*.370–287), the successor of Aristotle as scholarch of the Lyceum. These clever and entertaining character sketches want to draw typical ways of life, good and bad, as they occur in the Athenian society of the day. They are based, as the Letter Dedicatory says, on the observation of "human nature," and they serve the educational purpose of teaching young men which types of men to avoid and which to cultivate. The human nature observed by Theophrastus (and this holds true even if the *Protheoria* in which the term occurs should be spurious) is no longer the Aristotelian nature of the *politikon zoon;* no problems of potentiality and actualization are raised. It is human nature in its variety of typical characters and behaviors, mean and cowardly, distrustful and pretentious, surly and affable, superstitious, officious, boastful, ambitious, garrulous, roguish, gossiping, arrogant, reckless, boorish, and shameless. It is human nature in its comic, scurrilous, shabby, and pitiable aspects. And it is perhaps no accident that of the projected good and bad characters only the bad ones are preserved—if the good ones were ever written. It is a nature of motivations, a nature without *telos*.

With his *Characters* Theophrastus created a literary model which, in similar social situations, could be followed by others. After the upheavals of the sixteenth century A.D. in our Western civilization we can observe a revival of the Theophrastian art of characterization through the various translations of his work, as well as a further development of the art through the *Caractères* of La Bruyère. In its own time the work of Theophrastus, in spite of its symptomatic importance, appears somewhat pale against the background of the great development of the New Comedy, of which the most distinguished representative was Menander (342–291), the younger friend, and perhaps pupil, of Theophrastus. Through Menander and his rival Philemon this last naturalistic flowering of Attic society was transmitted to the Romans and imitated in the works of Terence and Plautus.

[2] On the development of the *humanitas* in Hellas cf. Snell, *Die Entdeckung des Geistes*, 240ff.

4. *Pyrrho*

The Socratic-Platonic impulse was spent. The murderous tension between Socrates and Athens had given way to a mutual tolerance between citizenry and the schools. Spectacular individuals like Diogenes had even become popular pets. If Athens was declining into a comedy of characters, the philosophers were dangerously close to becoming figures in that comedy themselves.

The cause of this development again must be sought in the immanentism which expressed itself in the Aristotelian metaphysical construction. The experiences of the noetic soul, as we said, point toward the transcendental realissimum which cannot be the object of true propositions in the manner of an immanent object. The symbols in which we express the experiences of the *summum bonum* and of *beatitudo* are the symbols of revelation and, metaphysically, of the *analogia entis*. If we force on this realm of experience the language of immanentist metaphysics, we shall arrive at a metamorphosis of transcendental into immanent fulfillment. The beatitude will become eudaimonia, and the truth of the *summum bonum*, invading the soul and orienting it toward its destiny, will become the truth of a way of life, as a world-immanent human accomplishment of conduct and character leading to happiness. As a consequence of such transformation the problem of happiness will become debatable as an aim to be achieved within human life. Philosophers may agree and disagree on the precise nature of the state of happiness as well as about the means that will produce it. And they will not discuss these questions as a matter of psychological experimentation but with an absolutism of conviction that stems from the transcendental implications of the animating experiences. Between 400 and 300 B.C. developed the Academy and the Lyceum, the schools of the Cynics, the Cyrenaics, the Epicureans, and probably of the Stoics. A multiplicity of possessors of the Truth dispensed their philosophies of conduct; and they used little restraint when they expressed their opinions about one another. A sociological pattern of philosophizing was growing, which had the perennial effect of arousing suspicions about the status of philosophy as a science, and of arousing skepticism with regard to a truth about which as many different propositions can be advanced as there are philosophers in the history of mankind.

Against this background stands the figure of a younger contemporary of Aristotle, the figure of Pyrrho of Elis (365–275). We know nothing about his ideas from a direct source, for neither did he write, nor did he found a school. That is precisely the point of interest. If the philosophers represent the withdrawal from the polis, Pyrrho represents the withdrawal from philosophy. As far as his doctrine becomes tangible with some reliability (through his pupil Timon of Phlius, as reported by Aristocles) he held that, in order to achieve happiness, we must consider first what the things are, second what attitude we shall adopt toward them, and third what the resulting state of mind will be. With regard to the first point, he asserts that the nature of things is indiscernible. Hence, with regard to the second point, we must suspend all judgment and rest without beliefs, opinions, or inclinations. And from this attitude will, third, result silence (*aphasia*) and subsequently ataraxy.[3]

The radical withdrawal from indulgence in any immanentist propositions with regard to the nature of things seems to have been the distinguishing characteristic of Pyrrho's mode of existence rather than a doctrine which under such conditions is impossible. Sextus Empiricus, when he deals with the matter, distinguishes three main types of philosophy: the Dogmatic, the Academic, and the Skeptic. Aristotle, Epicurus, and the Stoics are the representatives of dogmatic philosophy which asserts to have found the truth; Carneades and the later Academics represent the thesis that truth is inapprehensible. Dogmatic philosophy and the skepticism of the new Academy, thus, are opposed to each other. The skepticism of Pyrrho, however, is a third position, neither of dogmatism nor epistemological skepticism, but of an existential suspense of judgment which presupposes a specific mental ability (*dynamis*). The result of such suspense (*epoche*), which neither asserts a truth nor maintains its unknowability, will be a "resting of the mind" (*stasis dianoias*).[4] A further revealing information is tendered by Diogenes Laertius: "Theodosius in his *Skeptic Chapters* denies that Skepticism should be called Pyrrhonism; for if the movement of the mind in either direction is unattainable by us, we shall never know for certain what Pyrrho really intended, and without knowing that, we cannot be called Pyrrhoneans. Besides this (he says), there is the fact that Pyrrho was not the founder of Skepticism; nor had he any positive tenet; but a Pyrrhonean is one

[3] Eusebius, *Praeparatio Evangelica* XIV, 18, 2–3.
[4] Sextus Empiricus, *Pyrrhonean Hypotyposes*, I, 3–4 and 8–10.

who in manners and life resembles Pyrrho." [5] While Pyrrho could be considered a skeptic, there was something in him that made it necessary to distinguish his existential skepticism from the epistemological skepticism of the Academy.

Over the distance of millennia it is difficult to ascertain with precision the experiential core of the Pyrrhonean attitude. Nevertheless, there are some indications in the skeptic literature that will allow us to form at least a probable judgment. In the *Hypotyposes* of Sextus Empiricus there is a chapter on the *telos* of Skepticism. [6] The *telos,* or end, is understood in the Aristotelian sense of the end for which all actions and reasonings are undertaken, while this end itself has no ulterior end. The Skeptics, just as Aristotle, are in search of a science of action, and this science must culminate in the knowledge of the highest, comprehensive end of life. As distinguished from Aristotle, however, the search of the Skeptic has a specific tinge. Since the historical situation with its plurality of philosophical opinions about happiness compels him to search for quietude from the turmoil of opinion, his search for happiness assumes the form of a search for "ataraxy with regard to dogma." For this purpose he will examine opinions and weigh whether they are true or false; in the process he will find himself involved in contradictions; he will at last suspend judgment; and "when thus he suspended judgment there followed, as it were by accident, ataraxy in matters of opinion." The Skeptic, too, hoped to gain quietude through truth; and when the impossibility of decision for a truth compelled suspense (*epoche*) of judgment, then ataraxy followed suspense "like a shadow its body." The happiness of the soul is found when the search for it in terms of immanent goods is given up.

The Sextian account of the movement of the Pyrrhonean soul towards ataraxy seems substantially correct, though it is separated by centuries from the life of Pyrrho. At least, as far as the specific color of the resultant quietude is concerned, it is compatible with certain fragments from a poem of Timon of Phlius, the follower of Pyrrho. On one occasion Timon asks: "How, O Pyrrho, did you ever make your escape from servitude to the empty wisdom [*keneophrosyne*] of sophistic opinions?"; and on another occasion: "Why is it that you alone among men stand forth in the manner [*tropos*] of a God?" And like an answer to such questions sounds the wisdom attributed by Timon to Pyrrho:

[5] Diogenes Laertius, trans. by R. D. Hicks (Loeb Classical Library), IX, 70.
[6] Sextus Empiricus, *Pyrrhonean Hypotyposes,* I, 25–30.

"I shall tell you, indeed, about being as it appears to me. For the right rule of truth do I have in this saying [*mythos*]: That the nature of God and of Good exists in eternity [*aiei*], And from there proceeds for man the most just and equitable [*isotatos*] life." [7]

In this saying Pyrrho seems to have penetrated the problem of immanentism to its core. The object of propositions is the co-temporal world of appearances; God and the Good from which proceeds the equitable order of human life exist in eternity, beyond the reach of immanent propositions. The enigmatic force that let Pyrrho appear as a saintly, semidivine figure to his contemporaries, was the silence of the mystic. Moreover, Diogenes Laertius reports that Pyrrho accompanied Anaxarchus on the latter's travels to India with Alexander, and that there he became acquainted with "gymno-sophists." They impressed him so much that he adopted the philosophy of "agnosticism and suspension of judgment." He also "withdrew from the world and lived in solitude, rarely showing himself even to his relatives"; and he cultivated this habit because he had heard one of the Indians reproach Anaxarchus that "he would never be able to teach others what is good as long as he himself did hang around royal courts." [8] That there exists a chain of influence as simple and direct as Diogenes assumes, may be doubted; but we certainly must take into account the possibility that the mysticism of Pyrrho, as we can sense it in the fragmentary and imperfect accounts, owes something to the campaigns of Alexander and the acquaintance with Hindu mysticism.

Pyrrho was a unique and isolated figure. He neither founded a school nor a religion. And the continuity of his effectiveness seems to have died with his few pupils and close admirers. Nevertheless, the power of his personality asserted itself through the centuries. He was considered the fountainhead of the movement of skepticism into the Roman period, as evidenced by the work of Sextus Empiricus, and skepticism has remained associated with his name into our time.

The mysticism of the *epoche* inevitably had far-reaching consequences in the history of order and ideas. Above all, it discredited the "sage," the *sophos,* who claimed to possess the Truth.[9] In the science of skepticism

---

[7] From Sextus Empiricus, *Adversus Mathematicos,* XI, 20. The two preceding questions are reported by Diogenes Laertius, IX, 65.

[8] Diogenes Laertius, IX, 61 and 63.

[9] See the pointed argument in Sextus Empiricus, *Hypotyposes,* II, 22–47, with its attack on the *sophos,* and with the analysis of nonapprehensibility and inconceivability of "man" and, consequently, of the impossibility of forming the "idea of man."

the discrediting of truth assumed the form of a brilliant and solid analysis of the circumstances of cognition, of the limitations of apprehensive and cognitive faculties, and of the inclinations which cause the variety of "true opinions" held by philosophers on the nature of things. The science of the skeptics was, as it were, an extension of the Theophrastian and Menandrian study of characters in society to the philosophical characters. But it was more than that, in so far as the study of varieties of philosophical dogma and their causes were further extended to embrace the contradictions of legal institutions, moral convictions, customs and mores, myths and legends throughout history in time, and throughout the geographical expanse in space, with its manifold of civilizations that had become better known to Hellenistic thinkers through the conquests of Alexander. The sudden expansion of the civilizational horizon, which swept the polis into a corner of the known world, made itself heavily felt in the reduction of the whole manifold of societies, with their civilizational content, to a field of appearances which could be neither a source nor a vessel of Truth.[10]

As far as the practice of life was concerned, the Skeptic was thrown back to a simple conservatism. "We live in an undogmatic way by following the laws, customs, and natural affections."[11] He accepted the customs and convictions prevalent in the society that surrounded him by the accident of his birth, and he let history be transacted over his head, as it befitted the subject of an Empire.

[10] The vast elaboration of the skeptical position as we find it in the work of Sextus, of course, was not accomplished by Pyrrho. Sextus telescopes the development of centuries into his timeless type of "Pyrrhonism." The great systematic classification of the *tropoi,* for instance, can hardly have been achieved before Aenesidemus, during the first century B.C.

[11] Sextus Empiricus, *Hypotyposes,* I, 231.

Greek Terms

I. Plato

agape, 169

agathon, 96, 112–17, 134, 267; Aeschylus, 204; *to agathon auto*, 112; *tou agathou idea*, 112; *noetos topos*, 113

ageros, 153

aionios, 199

aisthesis, 194

aitia, 55, 200; *anaitios*, 55

akribos, 112

aletheia, 67, 78 f., 80, 105 f., 107, 113, 164, 196, 198, 233; *alethes doxa*, 168; *alethinos logos*, 177, 196, 198

amathia—*megiste amathia*, 243

analogon, 113

angelos, 60

archaios, 190

arche, 177, 200; *ex arches*, 98

arete, 55, 163, 168, 209, 211 f., 222, 260, 266; *aristos phylax*, 81, 84; *see* psyche (Virtues and vices)

ataxia—*see* taxis

athanasia, 222, 239

autarkes, 98; *ouk autarkes*, 98

automatos, 117

basileia, 242

basileus, 155

chora, 201 ff.

daimonion genos, 169

demegoros, 31

demiourgos, 152; *heimarmene, symphytos epithymia*, 152

diagoge, 259

diaphonia, 244

dogma, 81, 233

doxa, 56, 65, 74 f., 78 f., 80, 194, 196, 198; *doxai* of justice, 71–81; *alethes doxa*, 168

dynasteia, 242

eidolon, 117

eidos, 70, 94, 96 f., 102 f., 106, 110, 112, 123

eikon, 113, 195 ff., 199; *eikos mythos*, 196 ff.

ekei, 60

eleutheria, 244

empsychos, 141; *empsychos kosmos*, 239; *empsychos nomos*, 221, 233; *empsychos physis*, 236; *zoon empsychon ennoun*, 196 f.

enthousiasmos, 127

epanodos, 59, 96

epekeina, 113

epideixis, 257

episteme, 65 f., 69, 73, 75, 84, 94 f., 113 ff., 160; *episteme* of justice, 73

epithymia, 76, 125; *symphytos epithymia*, 152

eros, 29; *eros tyrannos*, 127

ethnos, 243

ethos, 236

eudaimonia, 207, 235, 253; *eudaimon*, 146; *eudaimonizein*, 116

eunomia, 266

genesis, 113, 201 f., 223; *geneseos tithene*, 201

heimarmene, 152

homoiosis theo, 146, 157

homonoia, 121, 169

hybris, 168, 207 f.

hypar—onar, 117

hyperesia—*tois nomois, ton theon*, 253

idea, 94, 123, 197

isogonia, 106

kairos, 238

kakia, 64; *kake*, 129

kallipolis, 98

kalon, 96

kata logon, 124; *kata physin*, 94

katabasis, 117; *katabateon*, 117; *kateben*, 52 f., 117

katastasis, 87; *katastasis politeion*, 81

kinesis, 94

koinon, 223; *koinonia*, 36; *koineo*, 118

psyche (Parts of the soul)—*epithymetikon,* 109, 125; *logistikon,* 109, 125 f., 129; *thymoeides,* 100, 109

psyche (Virtues and vices)—*andreia,* 80, 108, 167; *deinotes,* 146; *dikaiosyne,* 59, 64 f., 80, 108 f., 111; *eidolon tes dikaiosynes,* 64; *eumatheia,* 81; *homoiosis theo,* 146; *megaloprepeia,* 81; *oikeia, oikeoprageia,* 65; *phronesis,* 59, 111, 113, 173, 175, 195, 209, 211 f., 244; *sophia,* 80, 108 ff., 111; *sophrosyne,* 80, 108 f., 167—*allotriopragmosyne,* 64; *amathia,* 243; *anandria,* 146; *kakia,* 64; *polymathie,* 64; *polypragmosyne,* 64 f.

schema, 160
schole, 259 f.
soma, 196; *soma-sema,* 41 f.
sophia, 108 ff., 111
sophron, *me sophron,* 254
sophrosyne, 108, 167
soteria, 266 f.
spoude, 234 f.
stasiotes, 247
symphytos epithymia, 152
syngenes, 196
syntheke, 75
systasis, 202, 207

taxis, 196 f., 199; *ataxia,* 196 f., 199
techne—*techne basilike,* 163; *techne metetretike,* 92, 129, 158
theos, 228; *theia politeia,* 267; *theion paradeigma,* 96; *theios kosmos,* 96; *theios nomeus,* 160; *theou moira,* 81; *homoiosis theo,* 146, 157; *hyperesis ton theon,* 239; *phile kai akolouthos theo,* 254
theosebeia, 267
thremma, 143 f., 207
tyche, 238

xynon, 77

zetema, 82 ff., 84 f., 92, 95 f.
zetesis, 84 f., 96
zetetes, 84
Zeus agoraios, 204
zoon empsychon ennoun, 196 f.

II. Aristotle

achreios, 302
agalmata, 309
agapesis, 276

tagathon kai to ariston, 294
aitios, 316
aletheia, 300
arete, 297, 327, 345 f., 348, 360
aristoi, 345
autarkeia, 305, 315
axioma, 318

bios theoretikos, 276, 282, 289, 296 f., 304–14, 317, 336, 355 f., 358, 360, 362, 364 ff.

choregia, 324, 351

demos, 327, 337
doxa alethes, 327
dynamis, 369; *dynamis euergetike,* 361

eidos, 326 ff., 332 f., 335 f.
energeia, 297
episteme, 297; *episteme politike,* 283, 332, 335; *architektonike politike,* 283
ethnos, 295, 312, 317
ethos, 359 f., 361
eu zen, 315 f.
eudaimonia, 296; *teleia eudaimonia,* 305
exis, 298

homonoia, 321, 357, 364
horme, 316
hypothesis, 324

idiotes, 348

kalokagathia, 302
koinon, 340
koinonia, 315; *koinonia ton homoion,* 352
kome, 315
kyrion, 337

logos, 296, 300, 302, 330

mathein, 275
meros, 318, 344; *morion,* 344
mesotes, 297, 300, 348
methexis, 273 f.
metron, 351
mochteria, 322

noesis, 274; *noesis noeseos,* 276, 280
nomothetes, 283
nous, 289, 297, 303, 305 f., 320 f., 357, 364; *bios eudaimonestatos,* 306; *theoretike energeia,* 305; *to kyrion,* 306; *to theiotaton,* 305 f.

Modern Authors

Subjects and Names

Contract Theory, 75 f.

Conversion, 115 f.

Cosmos, 178, 184, 197; creation of, 200; cyclical history, 149; *eikon*, 195 ff.; mode of existence, 199 f.; order of idea, 203; its substance, 198; *zoon empsychon ennoun*, 196 f.

Creation, 199 f., 202

credo ut intelligam, 186

Creed, 263–67

Crete—omphalos of Hellenic world, 229 f.

Crisis—and epoch, 288 f.; and society, 79 f.

Critias, 172

Cycle, 156 f., 287 f.; Aristotle on, 287, 289 ff.; and epoch, 286–88; myth and doctrine, 291 f.; and theory of knowledge, 291 f.; and timelessness, 230; *see* Form of government

Daimon, 55, 85, 116; daimonion, 8, 10

Darkness and Light, 62

Decline (*lysis*), 122; a process in the soul, 125 f.

Definition of Chalcedon, 278

Demiurge, 23, 195 f., 197, 199–202, 204 f., 255; and royal ruler, 204; symbol of Incarnation, 197

Democritus, 182, 277

Demosthenes, 288

Depth and descent, 53–56, 83

Dike, 11 f., 14, 77, 254; *see* Justice

Diogenes Laertius, 6, 369 ff.

Diogenes of Sinope, 368

Dion, 14–18, 220, 224

Dionysiac soul, 62, 70, 92, 115 f.

Dionysius I, 16

Dionysius II, 17, 19 f., 220

Disorder, 36, 63, 69; *eide* of disorder, 63

Dogma—minimum dogma, 263 f., 265, 372

Doxa—pressure of, 80 f.; resistance to, 82

Dream—of passions, 107 f.; of tyranny, 126 f.

dux, 157

Egyptian Myth, 171–80

Enlightenment, 188, 190 f.

Equality—proportional and mechanical, 248 f.; *see* Man

Er the Pamphylian, 54 f.

Eros, 13 f., 14–23; love of demos, 28 f., 38; love of philosophy, 28; metamorphosis of Eros, 128; Eros of Socrates, 28, 31; *Eros tyrannos*, 126 f.; variants of Eros, 28 f.

Eschatology, 157; Iranian eschatology and Platonic dualism, 285

Eudaimonia, 116, 304 ff.; true, 304 f.; types of, 304 f.

Eusebius of Caesarea, 369

Existence—anxiety, 62; augmentation, 91 f., depth, 62; *genesis* and *kosmos*, 200; intramundane, 365; inverted philosophy of, 31–36; nothingness, 149; order of, 89, 95; philosophical, 272 f.; of the Skeptic, 272 f.

Existence (Polarity), 184; asleep and awake, 107; beginning and end, 97, 228–30; darkness and light, 62; faith and reason, 194; fall and rebirth, 213 f.; fulfillment and failure, 358; *genesis* and *kosmos*, 200; good and evil, 127, 148 f., 156, 285 f.; life and death, 62; night and sun, 212; political and theoretical, 310; power and spirit, 225 f.; spiritual and temporal, 117; way up and way down, 52–62; youth and age, 229 f.; *see* Withdrawal and return

Experience—of depth and direction, 83 ff.; logos of, 84; of transcendence, 112 f., 235 ff., 362–65

Faith and reason, 194; myth and knowledge, 194

fides caritate formata, 364

Form as limiting principle, 120

Form of government, 86 f., 158 ff., 219, 324 ff., 336–55; axioms of rulership, 318; best, 350–55; constitution as *eidos*, 331–36; cosmic crystal, 250–53, 257; cycle, 241–46, 317; decline, 122–27; manifold of political forms, 342–50; middle-class polis, 348 f., mixed form, 246–48, 249; necessary elements, 344; ontological status, 334 ff.; paradigms in the household, 318 f.; sequence of declining forms, 123–29; sequence in history, 127 ff., 340; sequence *kata logon*, 124; solstitial form, 248; tale of decline, 124; true and perverted, 337, 341, 345 f.; *see* Polis, Polis (Platonic paradigm)

forma supranaturalis, 364

Friendship—political, 320 f.

Galenus, 94

Generations, 51, 57, 60, 71 f., 83

Gnosis, 193, 278, 307

God, 62, 236 f., 254 f.; beginning and end, 228 f.; dispensation of God, 81; God the Measure, 254, 263; knowability, 307; man in likeness of God, 130 f.; Mover of the Pieces, 236, 250; Player of the Puppets, 231 ff., 259; as the royal ruler, 155; *see* Demiurge, Sons of Zeus (Sons of God)

Gods—visible, 308

Goethe, 188, 192

Golden Age, 153–56, 189, 205